Behind the Veil of Moses

Piecing Together the Mystery
of the Second Coming

by Brian L. Martin

A mind once stretched by a new idea never regains its original dimension.

Oliver Wendell Holmes, Jr.

Acknowledgments

—◊◊◊—

This updated version of *Behind the Veil of Moses* stands on the shoulders of those who helped mold and edit the first version. Without them the original version would not have been worthy of a revised edition. In the years since the first edition was published I have received comments, suggestions, and questions from dozens of individuals who have helped refine and polish that first edition. There are far too many to remember, let alone thank individually. However, there are several individuals without whose time and efforts this revised edition would be of little improvement over the previous.

First and foremost is my wife, Kayla, without whose support this project would have never taken place. Were it only for the amount of time, thought, and energy that she allowed *me* to invest in this project, she would have been at the top of the list. But that wasn't all she gave—she also invested countless hours sitting with me on the couch, reviewing edits, researching grammar and style, etc., all the while never complaining about the stacks of books that migrated from dining room table to coffee table to couch. In addition to all of that, she invested her own time by meticulously going over the manuscript while I was at work. She is truly a helpmeet in everything we do.

Bill Greene, who was also instrumental in the first edition, rose to the occasion again. By his own admission not an avid reader, he nevertheless went over the manuscript several times with a passion for seeing the best possible introduction to Preterism. He labored over individual points until he felt they were communicated clearly and accurately. He also made several significant suggestions about rearranging certain material for readability.

Both Marlene Costa and Mike Beidler have editing experience and possess a superb knowledge of theology and the English language. They provided editing skills that would rival, if not surpass, many professional services available. Many times, as I read their suggested edits, I would find myself thinking, "That's exactly what I wanted it to say," or laughing to myself at how primitive my original version had been.

Whether or not you agree with the material presented here, if you find it presented in a clear, understandable, and structured manner it is due to these individuals. Should you happen upon an occasional typo or grammatical faux pas, it is because I became weary of the editing process and said, "I think it's good enough—let's send it to the printer."

I am also grateful to Garrett and Beverly Brown for their continuing encouragement and support. From many facets the genesis and production of this book can be traced back to them.

Table of Contents

—m—

Preface to the Second Edition

—◊◊◊—

I n the four plus years that have transpired since first publishing *Behind the Veil of Moses* I have had the opportunity to read numerous books on the subject of Preterism—both pro and con—as well as read the Bible through several times. In the course of doing so I have been amazed at how many of my points were corroborated by other Preterist authors and how many additional Scriptures supported the view. This, I am quick to point out, is in no way due to any deep insight or theological knowledge on my part, but rather is a testimony to the veracity (and, dare I say, simplicity?) of the Preterist view, once one begins to allow Scripture to interpret Scripture.

This is not to say that those opposing Preterism have not raised valid questions, or that there are no "sticky issues" within the Preterist view. The numerous denominational and doctrinal positions which abound in the Church are a testimony to this. Likewise, there are differences, and even divisions, within Preterism. When we consider the limitations of man, and "the depth of the riches both of the wisdom and knowledge of God," it is only natural that we will be forever tying up the loose ends and fine-tuning our theological systems.

To the reader who is relatively new to Preterism I would humbly make this request—please resist any temptations of skipping ahead to particular chapters. Rather, read the book through from beginning to end. The book is laid out in a systematic way, with most chapters building upon previous material. Therefore, by skipping ahead the reader may feel that I am building upon assumptions and presuppositions, when in fact the scriptural support for a particular premise was laid out in a previous chapter. Since few of us look up Scripture references as we read, I have printed the full text of the passages under discussion. Thus the reader with a good working knowledge of Scripture will be able to quickly skim these sections, and find that the chapters read quicker than expected. I confess that the book is lengthier than I had hoped, but when one is dealing with a complete paradigm shift a great amount of material needs to be covered. I have been greatly encouraged by the many readers of the first edition who have proclaimed the book to be thorough yet easy to read. I trust that readers of this revised edition will find it the same.

Far from being the "last word" on Preterism, this work is only an introduction. I encourage readers to explore deeper by reading any of the several Preterist works and authors referenced in this work. Additionally, at the time of this writing I am the General Editor of *Fulfilled!* Magazine, and invite readers to sign up for a free subscription online at www. FulfilledMagazine.com, or write us at:

Fulfilled Magazine
1620 Sequoia St.
Napa, CA 94558-2320

In His Service
Brian L. Martin
November, 2008

Preface to the First Edition

——ﾉﾙ—

As I prepare this work for publication, two questions rattle around in my head: *What am I doing?* and *Why am I doing it?* Since I have no formal education in the Bible or Theology, one might easily dismiss this work. On the other hand, as I allude to in the Conclusion, if the layperson is unqualified to "rightly divide the Word of Truth" for herself or himself, then we risk returning to a two-tiered Church—the clergy, made up of professionally trained teachers, and the laity, which must accept their teachings.

The views presented here are not new, having been presented by many other more qualified persons. Yet, as I began my own research into these things some six years ago, several things stood out to me. First, much of what is written seems to be aimed at those in academic theology circles. Secondly, some material, either because of its depth or sheer volume, has been less than appealing to many readers. Lastly, because of the "warm" debates often incited by these views, and the labels often applied to those who hold them, much of what is written in their defense comes across with a certain "attitude." Therefore, this volume is presented as a work by a layperson, for the layperson, as well as, it is hoped, in the spirit of *"come let us reason together . . . ."*

During my 27 years in the Petrochemical industry, I have had a penchant for perusing some of the more technical information available, in order to more fully understand my work environment. This has resulted in a good deal of my career spent writing Operating Procedures and Manuals, and conducting training sessions on the same. This bent has also carried over into my personal Bible study. I enjoy the "deeper" theological works (those that I can understand), and being challenged by alternate, or even opposing views. I have always believed that if I cannot allow my views to be challenged, perhaps it is because I am not very comfortable with, or knowledgeable of, those views. For this reason, when certain groups come knocking at my door, I allow them to challenge my Biblical perspective, if for no other reason than to find out how well I know what I believe.

It was with this mindset that I first began exploring Bible prophecy from this new (to me) angle. Over the years, as I slowly came to accept these views, I wrote various studies as part of my process of "working through" the issues. In addition to these studies, some of the material presented here began as emails, discussing these things with those who do not hold these views. These emails were my attempts to defend my point of view in light of the challenges raised. I never had any thought towards publishing any of my work, and in fact saw no cohesive theme to it. Although all the studies were centered around Bible prophecy, they were merely a collection of independent writings. Then came the theme of "behind the veil of Moses," and they all fell into place. A little editing, and some additional material to fill in the gaps resulted in this current work. While in no way am I claiming, "Thus saith the Lord" in these matters, I do credit the unseen hand of the Holy Spirit in putting this together—it certainly is beyond my abilities.

I once read *if the only bird that sang was the one with the most beautiful voice, then the forest would be silent.* In light of that, though I do not possess one of the more qualified or beautiful "voices," I offer this volume to those in the "forest" of Christianity who may be out of earshot of those other voices.

In His Service
Brian L. Martin
February 2004

Introduction

—ɱ—

By and large, the Christian community is quick to point out how the Jews missed their Messiah—by failing to rightly understand and interpret the Old Testament Scriptures that prophesied His coming. The Jews were looking for an *earthly* King to reestablish Israel as the world's prominent nation, with Jerusalem as His capital. Hindsight, it is said, is 20/20, and looking back it seems obvious to many Christians that numerous Old Testament prophecies were (and are) fulfilled in a spiritual manner by a heavenly kingdom obtained through grace, rather than a physical kingdom obtained through national heritage. As the apostle Paul states:

> *For they are not all Israel who are of Israel, nor are they all children because they are the seed of Abraham; but, "In Isaac your seed shall be called." That is, those who are the children of the flesh, these are not the children of God; but the children of the promise are counted as the seed.* (Rom 9:6-8)

The physical aspect of the kingdom was not to be fulfilled at Christ's first coming, but at His Second Coming—or so we are taught. This physical expectation is why the Jews did not recognize Christ as their Messiah in His first coming. In order to describe this misunderstanding and misinterpretation of the Old Testament passages, Paul used the allegory of the veil that Moses put over his face:

> *Therefore, since we have such hope, we use great boldness of speech—unlike Moses, who put a veil over his face so that the children of Israel could not look steadily at the end of what was passing away. But their minds were blinded. For until this day the same veil remains unlifted in the reading of the Old Testament, because the veil is taken away in Christ. But even to this day, when Moses is read, a veil lies on their heart.* (2 Cor 3:12-15)

The purpose of this volume is to propose and support the premise that Christianity, while having removed the veil far enough to have recognized Christ in His first coming as the Messiah, has failed to completely remove from the Old Covenant the veil that hid the true nature of the New

Covenant. Thus, the Church has not been able to fully discern the nature of the New Covenant, and with it, the Second Coming of Christ.

Paul describes the veil of Moses as symbolic of the veiled typology of the Old Covenant. Though the New Covenant is not entirely spiritual in nature, it is primarily so. Thus the *physical* nature of the Old Covenant was a "veiled" representation, through types and symbols, of the *spiritual* nature of the New Covenant. Even in our day those who read Moses (the Old Covenant) with the veil on still do not see past the physical types to the spiritual substance.

The removing of the veil can be considered a one-time act in reference to conversion—i.e., when one turns to Christ they are completely saved. However, in discerning the reality of the New Covenant the removing of the veil is a process:

> *And we, who with unveiled faces all reflect the Lord's glory, are being **transformed** into his likeness with **ever-increasing** glory, which comes from the Lord, who is the Spirit.* (2 Cor 3:18 NIV; emphasis added)

Paul said that, even to his present day, the Old Covenant veil remained over the Israelites' hearts. They could not see past the "physical" type to its spiritual fulfillment. Just as Moses removed the veil when he turned to speak with God, so the veil of the heart is removed when one turns to Christ. Just as the Old Covenant involved much more than being of Jewish heritage—e.g., the Levitical Law, the Priesthood, the tabernacle and its services—so the New Covenant involves much more than just being "born again." Although we have turned to Christ, thus lifting the veil so that we might recognize Him as our Savior and Messiah, have we allowed the veil to be lifted completely so that we can recognize the spiritual fulfillment of what the Old Covenant typified in the Law, the Priesthood, the tabernacle, etc.? Have we continued the process of being transformed—of pressing on?

That the "unveiling" is a process is demonstrated in the epistle to the Hebrews. The author of Hebrews desired to expound to his readers the New Covenant's spiritual fulfillment, in Christ, of the Old Testament typology found in the priest Melchizedek. Instead, the author felt he must admonish them for having been slack in the "unveiling" process:

> *. . . of whom [Melchizedek] we have much to say, and hard to explain, since you have become dull of hearing. For though by this time you ought to be teachers, you need someone to teach you again the first principles of the oracles of God; and you have come*

to need milk and not solid food. For everyone who partakes only of milk is unskilled in the word of righteousness, for he is a babe. But solid food belongs to those who are of full age, that is, those who by reason of use have their senses exercised to discern both good and evil. (Heb 5:11-14)

Thus we can see that, although the veil is lifted when one comes to Christ, this is only the beginning of the unveiling process. There remain "meatier" things of the Old Covenant typology that are only understood when one has become skilled in the word of righteousness, is spiritually mature, and, by reason of use ("practice" NASB), have their senses exercised ("trained" NASB) to do so.

The following examples are readily recognized as being Old Testament types, or figures, that have a New Testament fulfillment. Thus, we easily see the precedent established of the Old Covenant typifying the New Covenant. What is not so easily seen are the far-reaching truths embodied in these types. As with Melchizedek in Hebrews, *"there is much to say, and hard to explain,"* since we are perhaps a little more dull of hearing than we care to admit. If, at first, some of the implications seem "hard to swallow," perhaps it is because (at least in the case of this writer) we have *come to need milk,* and are unskilled in *solid food.* While we claim no special anointing or revelation in discerning between the "milk and meat," we offer this volume as "food for thought," and hope that it provides the reader with "something to chew on."

Adam

Nevertheless death reigned from Adam to Moses, even over those who had not sinned according to the likeness of the transgression of Adam, who is a type of Him who was to come. (Rom 5:14)

And so it is written, "The first man Adam became a living being." The last Adam became a life-giving spirit. (1 Cor 15:45)

Abraham, Ishmael, and Isaac

For it is written that Abraham had two sons: the one by a bondwoman, the other by a freewoman. But he who was of the bondwoman was born according to the flesh, and he of the freewoman through promise, which things are symbolic. For these are the two covenants . . . . (Gal 4:22-24)

The priesthood and sacrifices

And having been perfected, He [Jesus] became the author of eternal salvation to all who obey Him, called by God as High Priest "according to the order of Melchizedek . . . ." (Heb 5:9-10)

. . . you also, as living stones, are being built up a spiritual house, a holy priesthood, to offer up spiritual sacrifices acceptable to God through Jesus Christ. (1 Pet 2:5)

Therefore by Him let us continually offer the sacrifice of praise to God, that is, the fruit of our lips, giving thanks to His name. (Heb 13:15)

Jerusalem

. . . for this Hagar is Mount Sinai in Arabia, and corresponds to Jerusalem which now is, and is in bondage with her children—but the Jerusalem above is free, which is the mother of us all. (Gal 4:25-26)

But you have come to Mount Zion and to the city of the living God, the heavenly Jerusalem . . . . (Heb 12:22)

Israel

But it is not that the word of God has taken no effect. For they are not all Israel who are of Israel, nor are they all children because they are the seed of Abraham; but, "In Isaac your seed shall be called." That is, those who are the children of the flesh, these are not the children of God; but the children of the promise are counted as the seed. (Rom 9:6-8)

For in Christ Jesus neither circumcision nor uncircumcision avails anything, but a new creation. And as many as walk according to this rule, peace and mercy be upon them, and upon the Israel of God. (Gal 6:15-16)

The Kingdom—Christ's Kingdom is spiritual, not of this world

Now when He was asked by the Pharisees when the kingdom of God would come, He answered them and said, "The kingdom of God does not come with observation; nor will they say, 'See here!' or 'See there!' For indeed, the kingdom of God is within you." (Luke 17:20-21)

Jesus answered, "My kingdom is not of this world. If My kingdom were of this world, My servants would fight, so that I should not be delivered to the Jews; but now My kingdom is not from here." (John 18:36)

Therefore, since we are receiving a kingdom which cannot be shaken, let us have grace, by which we may serve God acceptably with reverence and godly fear. (Heb 12:28)

Just this cursory glance reveals that much of the physical nature of the Old Testament covenant and kingdom was a type, a foreshadow, of the New Covenant. But have we truly ascertained the depth to which the Old Covenant typified the New? As Christians, we often are amazed at how a Jew can "overlook" more than 300 messianic prophecies that Jesus fulfilled during His first coming, and how He was the consummate anti-type (fulfillment) of the types seen in all of the temple sacrifices and offerings. *How*, we ask ourselves, *can someone ignore such obvious texts and find alternate meanings and interpretations? How can one, for example, look for another interpretation for Isaiah 53 when the crucifixion so obviously fulfills it?*

And yet, ironically, much of Christianity has done the very same thing. By having a preconceived concept of the New Covenant and Christ's Second Coming (as the Jews did with His first coming), we have "overlooked" obvious texts and found alternate meanings and interpretations. Dispensationalists like Jack Van Impe, Tim LaHaye, John MacArthur, and others have gone to great lengths to explain why, when Jesus said *"this generation will by no means pass away till all these things are fulfilled,"* He did not mean *His* generation. And why terms such as *near, at hand*, and *quickly*, were not in reference to the original audience of the New Testament generation, but to our present-day generation. But is this truly what the Bible is teaching? It is time to pull the veil back a little further.

Because we are provided with the inspired commentary of the New Testament authors on many of these Old Testament passages, we have a distinct advantage over the first-century Jews in the area of rightly interpreting Old Testament prophecies. While not every Old Testament prophecy is interpreted for us by a New Testament author, there are enough examples to lay a foundation, establish a precedent, and provide us with a springboard for interpreting most, if not all, of the rest. For example, in Galatians 3, Paul, by inspiration of the Holy Spirit, interprets the *seed* of Abraham as being Christ, rather than all of Abraham's physical offspring:

Now to Abraham and his Seed were the promises made. He does not say, "And to seeds," as of many, but as of one, "And to your Seed," who is Christ. And this I say, that the law, which was four hundred and thirty years later, cannot annul the covenant that was confirmed before by God in Christ, that it should make the promise of no effect. For if the inheritance is of the law, it is no longer of promise; but God gave it to Abraham by promise. (Gal 3:16-18)

Thus, the promises given to Abraham and his seed are realized in Christ, not in national Israel. That this has far-reaching implications cannot be overstated. Many, while looking for physical and material fulfillments of these promises in the nation of Israel, have overlooked the fact that they are fulfilled *spiritually* in Christ. This is neither a personal opinion nor a "private interpretation of Scripture"—this is *Scripture interpreting Scripture!* One has to wonder, apart from Paul's divinely inspired commentary, how many of us would have reached this same conclusion regarding Abraham's Seed? As we shall see, Paul refers to this as "removing the veil of Moses."

Consider Hosea's statement: *When Israel was a child, I loved him, And out of Egypt I called My son* (Hos 11:1). Would we not naturally understand that to be a recounting of the deliverance of Israel from bondage in Egypt? And yet Matthew, inspired by the Holy Spirit, states that Hosea was not merely recounting Israel's deliverance, but was, in fact, prophesying that Jesus would be called out of Egypt (Matt 2:15).

Many such examples exist where the inspired New Testament authors provide interpretations of Old Testament passages that are much different than what their contemporary Jews held—including their teachers of the Law. While New Testament saints were allowed to look behind the veil of Moses, those who did not turn to Christ were unable to discern what was behind the veil.

But the natural man does not receive the things of the Spirit of God, for they are foolishness to him; nor can he know them, because they are spiritually discerned. (1 Cor 2:14)

Unfortunately, much of the Church today has also failed to fully appreciate the New Testament authors' discernment—especially in regard to the Second Coming of Christ. We would even go so far as to say that when the New Testament authors comment on Old Testament passages, they do not provide *an* interpretation but *the* interpretation. Guided by these New Testament authors, let us look behind the veil of Moses.

Part I:

Behind the Veil

All of us need to be constantly asking ourselves what it is which we want to believe to be true, and whether our desires so to believe are stronger than our desires to know the truth, however uncongenial to us that truth may be.

Antony Flew (renowned former atheist)

If You Are Willing to Receive It

—ᴍ—

"For all the prophets and the law prophesied until John. And if you are willing to receive it, he is Elijah who is to come. He who has ears to hear, let him hear!" (Matt 11:13-15)

Prior to embarking on a comparison of the two covenants, we can gain valuable insight from an example of Jesus pulling the veil back for the disciples. In Matthew 17, we read an account of Jesus being transfigured on the Mount. We note two things from that event: (1) the disciples saw the prophets Elijah and Moses, and (2) they heard the voice of God proclaiming that Jesus was His beloved Son. (We are not told how the disciples recognized these Old Testament figures, but we must trust the inspired text.) Being eyewitnesses of Jesus' ministry, and now hearing a voice from heaven, the disciples were beginning to realize that Jesus was the Messiah. As they considered this fact, they questioned Jesus about the coming of Elijah, who was supposed to come before the Messiah and *"prepare a way before Him."* The person that the disciples had just seen during the transfiguration was not ministering publicly as Jesus was. Thus the disciples' question:

"Why then do the scribes say that Elijah must come first?" (Matt 17:10b)

What was Christ's reply? Elijah had come!

Jesus answered and said to them, "Indeed, Elijah is coming first and will restore all things. But I say to you that Elijah has come already, and they did not know him but did to him whatever they wished. Likewise the Son of Man is also about to suffer at their hands." Then the disciples understood that He spoke to them of John the Baptist. (Matt 17:11-13)

Clearly, the disciples had understood the prophecies well enough to know that Elijah was to come first, yet they had missed the fulfillment of those prophecies before their very eyes. Because they were still looking

21

upon the veil, they did not understand that the Elijah of the Old Covenant was a *type* that saw its fulfillment in John the Baptist. They understood properly the timing of the fulfillment (Elijah before Messiah), but not the nature of the fulfillment (not literally Elijah, but, as we shall see, one in the *spirit and power* of Elijah). Let us look at the specific prophecies:

The voice of one crying in the wilderness:
"Prepare the way of the LORD*;*
Make straight in the desert
A highway for our God.
Every valley shall be exalted
And every mountain and hill brought low;
The crooked places shall be made straight
And the rough places smooth;
The glory of the LORD *shall be revealed,*
And all flesh shall see it together;
For the mouth of the LORD *has spoken."* (Isa 40:3-5)

"Behold, I send My messenger,
And he will prepare the way before Me.
And the Lord, whom you seek,
Will suddenly come to His temple,
Even the Messenger of the covenant,
In whom you delight. Behold, He is coming,"
Says the LORD *of hosts . . .*
"Behold, I will send you Elijah the prophet
Before the coming of the great and dreadful day of the LORD,
And he will turn
The hearts of the fathers to the children,
And the hearts of the children to their fathers,
Lest I come and strike the earth with a curse." (Mal 3:1; 4:5-6)

And now, let us look at the New Testament fulfillments as seen in John the Baptist:

*But the angel said to him, "Do not be afraid, Zacharias, for your prayer is heard; and your wife Elizabeth will bear you a son, and you shall call his name John. And you will have joy and gladness, and many will rejoice at his birth. For he will be great in the sight of the Lord, and shall drink neither wine nor strong drink. He will also be filled with the Holy Spirit, even from his mother's womb. And he will turn many of the children of Israel to the Lord their God. He will also go before Him in **the spirit and power of Elijah**,*

*'to turn the hearts of the fathers to the children,' and the disobe-
dient to the wisdom of the just, to make ready a people prepared
for the Lord."* (Luke 1:13-17)

*In those days John the Baptist came preaching in the wilderness
of Judea, and saying, "Repent, for the kingdom of heaven is at
hand!" For this is he who was spoken of by the prophet Isaiah,
saying: "The voice of one crying in the wilderness: 'Prepare the
way of the* LORD*; Make His paths straight.'"* (Matt 3:1-3)

*As they departed, Jesus began to say to the multitudes concerning
John: "What did you go out into the wilderness to see? A reed
shaken by the wind? But what did you go out to see? A man
clothed in soft garments? Indeed, those who wear soft clothing
are in kings' houses. But what did you go out to see? A prophet?
Yes, I say to you, and more than a prophet. For **this is he of whom
it is written**: 'Behold, I send My messenger before Your face, Who
will prepare Your way before You.'"* (Matt 11:7-10)

*"For all the prophets and the law prophesied until John. And if
you are willing to receive it, **he is Elijah who is to come.** He who
has ears to hear, let him hear!"* (Matt 11:13-15)

*And you, child, will be called the prophet of the Highest;
For you will go before the face of the Lord to prepare His ways
. . . .* (Luke 1:76)

*Now this is the testimony of John, when the Jews sent priests and
Levites from Jerusalem to ask him, "Who are you?" He confessed,
and did not deny, but confessed, "I am not the Christ." And they
asked him, "What then? Are you Elijah?" He said, "I am not."
"Are you the Prophet?" And he answered, "No." Then they said
to him, "Who are you, that we may give an answer to those who
sent us? What do you say about yourself?" He said: "I am 'The
voice of one crying in the wilderness: "Make straight the way of
the* LORD*,"' as the prophet Isaiah said."* (John 1:19-23)
(emphasis added)

Undeniably, Jesus taught that John the Baptist was the "Elijah" who
was prophesied to come and prepare a way for the Lord. Yet the way in
which He states it seems to imply that He understood the fulfillment was
not entirely obvious to those around Him. Even John acknowledged that
he was not Elijah, yet he knew that he was *the voice of one crying in the
wilderness.*" Notice again Jesus' words in Matthew 11 (emphasis added):

23

*14 And **if you are willing to receive it,** he is Elijah who is to come.*
*15 **He who has ears to hear, let him hear!***

IF you are willing to receive it! This almost suggests that Christ thought some of them might have a difficult time believing the fact that a prophecy that they had waited centuries to see fulfilled had just been fulfilled before their eyes. Christ knew, as the disciples' question implies, that they were taking the prophecy much too literally and looking for the physical Old Testament Elijah. Is it far-fetched to conclude that many of us have made the same mistake regarding other prophecies? Just as the Jews misinterpreted the "second coming" of Elijah and the first coming of the Messiah because of the veil of Moses, the Church is, unfortunately, viewing many of the prophecies regarding the Second Coming of Christ through the same veil.

Before we pursue that thought, let us take a closer look at the prophecies of Elijah and their fulfillments by John the Baptist. The following chart lists the details of the ministry of "Elijah," and whether or not they were "literally" fulfilled:

Prophecy	*Fulfilled Literally?*
The voice of one crying in the wilderness . . .	Yes, John lived and preached in the wilderness
Every valley shall be exalted And every mountain and hill brought low . . .	**No**, there is no record of geographical changes
The crooked places shall be made straight And the rough places smooth . . .	**No**, same as above
The glory of the LORD shall be revealed, And all flesh shall see it together . . .	**No**, not <u>all</u> flesh together

Prophecy	*Fulfilled Literally?*
Behold, I send My messenger, And he will prepare the way before Me . . .	Yes, John preached repentance, for the kingdom was at hand—all the while claiming that One was coming after him Who was greater, and that he bore witness of Him (John 1:27, 29, 32ff, 36; 3:30)
Behold, I will send you Elijah the prophet Before the coming of the great and dreadful day of the LORD.	**No,** not Elijah himself but one in the spirit and power of Elijah
And he will turn The hearts of the fathers to the children, And the hearts of the children to their fathers, Lest I come and strike the earth [land – NASB/NIV] with a curse.	Although individual Jews repented in response to John's preaching, Israel as a nation did not repent, hence its destruction in AD 70. Was the entire earth struck with a curse? When we realize that both Hebrew and Greek words translated "earth" can also be translated "land" (as do the NASB and NIV) we can see in the destruction of Jerusalem a fulfillment of this portion

Over half of the details concerning the coming of Elijah were not fulfilled in what we would consider to be a literal sense! Keep in mind that not being fulfilled literally (in a physical, material sense) is not synonymous with not being fulfilled at all. Philip Mauro elaborates:

> . . . in Scripture the contrast is not between the *spiritual* and the *literal*, but between the *spiritual* and *natural*; for a passage of Scripture may refer, when taken "literally," either to "that which is *natural*" or to "that which is *spiritual*." In other words, the literal interpretation may call for a thing which exists in the realm of nature, or for the counterpart of that thing which exists in the realm of spiritual realities . . . . (*The Hope of Israel: What Is It?*, p. 14; emphasis in original)

R. C. Sproul writes:

To interpret something literally is to pay attention to the *litera* or to the letters and words which are being used. To interpret the Bible literally is to interpret it as *literature*. That is, the natural meaning of a passage is to be interpreted according to the normal rules of grammar, speech, syntax and context. (*Knowing Scripture*, p. 48; emphasis in original)

Thus, we see that in the strictest sense to interpret something literally does not mean that it is physically realized. However, many within Christendom equate a "literal" interpretation with a "physical, earthly" interpretation—with some even priding themselves on taking the Bible "literally":

"A literal fulfillment involves something that actually happened in history. . . . A non-literal fulfillment would have been something that did not actually take place in time-space history." (*Pre-Trib Perspectives*, Dr. Thomas Ice—Vol. VIII, Number 24, June 2005)

Because of this common equating of literal with physical, we will maintain that usage, providing clarification when necessary.

The New Testament specifically teaches that John the Baptist was the fulfillment of Old Testament prophecies in Isaiah and Malachi about the coming messenger, Elijah. Because he was not the literal (physical) Elijah, we must look for some other type of fulfillment. Call it what you will— *spiritual*, *typical*, or *symbolic*—there is a fulfillment to be found. Although John the Baptist was not Elijah resurrected (or returned to earth), he was a prophet *in the spirit of Elijah*, proclaiming the way of the Lord.

For those who were willing to receive it, Jesus was illustrating a paradigm shift in the nature of fulfilled prophecy. Certain fulfillments were seen in the spiritual realm, not necessarily in the physical. This necessitates viewing through the "eyes of the heart" instead of using our natural vision; this is because *the natural man does not receive the things of the Spirit of God, for they are foolishness to him; nor can he know them, because they are spiritually discerned*" (1 Cor 2:14). We will develop this theme and its ramifications in the ensuing chapters.

The literal valleys and mountains, and the crooked and rough places of Judea, did not change as a result of John's preaching. Instead, these geographic transformations may represent the difficulty of coming to God through the encumbrances of the Mosaic Law and the priesthood. Consider how Acts 13:10 is translated in the NASB95 (NASB Updated Version):

> *But Saul, who was also known as Paul, filled with the Holy Spirit, fixed his gaze on him [Elymas the sorcerer], and said, "You who are full of all deceit and fraud, you son of the devil, you enemy of all righteousness, will you not cease to* **make crooked the straight ways of the Lord?** *(Acts 13:9-10 NASB95 cf. Heb 12:12-13; emphasis added)*

The following Old Testament passages also equate "crooked paths" with separation from God:

> *The way of peace they have not known,*
> *And there is no justice in their ways;*
> *They have made themselves crooked paths;*
> *Whoever takes that way shall not know peace.* (Isa 59:8)

> *He has blocked my ways with hewn stone;*
> *He has made my paths crooked.* (Lam 3:9)

Just as the tearing in two of the temple's curtain during Christ's crucifixion symbolized new access to the presence of God, the valleys and mountains, the crooked and rough pathways of the law have been replaced by Christ, the one Mediator between God and man. Compared to the Law, the gospel is truly a smooth and level journey. Note Jesus' response to the disciples one more time:

> *Jesus answered and said to them, "Indeed, Elijah is coming first and will restore all things. But I say to you that Elijah has come already, and they did not know him but did to him whatever they wished. Likewise the Son of Man is also about to suffer at their hands." Then the disciples understood that He spoke to them of John the Baptist.* (Matt 17:11-13)

Elijah had already come, and *the scribes did not know him*. Likewise, they did not know Christ at His first coming. Unless we make every effort to allow the New Testament to remove the veil from the Old Testament prophecies concerning the nature of Christ's kingdom and the New Covenant, we are in danger of misinterpreting details concerning the Second Coming. The interpretation of the Second Coming held by most Christians today sounds strangely like the "veiled" interpretation the Jews had of His first coming. But we are getting ahead of ourselves!

If we can comprehend obvious spiritual prophetic fulfillment in one place in the Bible, perhaps it is to be found in other places as well. In fact, should we not expect it? No one would argue that the *spirit* (i.e., the intent, the objective, the substance) of the prophecy concerning Elijah was fulfilled. To do so would be calling Christ either mistaken or a liar. Of course, this begs the question, *"If Christ had not mentioned that John the Baptist was 'the Elijah to come,' would the Christian community still be looking for him, as the Jews are today?"* Strangely enough, by identifying Elijah as one of the two witnesses in Revelation, many are.

2 Corinthians 3:6 states that the letter of the law kills, but the Spirit gives life. The Pharisees were living examples of this. They took the law, the spirit of which served as a path to Christ, and made a dead religion out of it. Are we in danger of doing the same thing with prophecy? Are we so intent on literalizing every last detail, and then looking for the fulfillment in our morning paper, that we are in danger of missing the spirit of the prophecy altogether, just as the disciples almost did with John the Baptist?

"How can we know anything, then," you might ask, *"if everything is spiritual?"* Before you throw your hands up in despair, consider a few points. First, the premise is not that *everything* is spiritual, but that not everything is *literal*—or more precisely, natural/physical. Secondly, consider Christ's response to the disciples' question about Elijah. He did not rebuke them for being ignorant, or say "ye of little faith." He affirmed their basic understanding of the prophecy: *"Indeed, Elijah is coming first and will restore all things."* He then went on to clarify their understanding. Is there not a lesson to be learned here? When unsure about the interpretation and fulfillment of prophecy, to whom should we look for truth? Should it not be Jesus, as opposed to the latest prophecy pundit? And how else do we seek out Christ's truth than by studying the Bible? Whenever the New Testament provides inspired interpretations to explain the Old Testament passages, those interpretations should be our guide. Certainly, there are many honest and educated Bible scholars, teachers, and commentators who offer valuable insight. Nevertheless, we must remember that each is writing from their own theological perspective, which is bound to influence their work.

The question that we must ask ourselves is, *"When the inspired commentary of the New Testament does not fit with the popular and even time-honored interpretations we hold dear, **are we willing to receive it?**"*

The Veil of Moses

—ᴡᴡ—

Not that we are sufficient of ourselves to think of anything as being from ourselves, but our sufficiency is from God, who also made us sufficient as ministers of the new covenant, not of the letter but of the Spirit; for the letter kills, but the Spirit gives life. But if the ministry of death, written and engraved on stones, was glorious, so that the children of Israel could not look steadily at the face of Moses because of the glory of his countenance, which glory was passing away, how will the ministry of the Spirit not be more glorious? For if the ministry of condemnation had glory, the ministry of righteousness exceeds much more in glory. For even what was made glorious had no glory in this respect, because of the glory that excels. For if what is passing away was glorious, what remains is much more glorious. Therefore, since we have such hope, we use great boldness of speech—unlike Moses, who put a veil over his face so that the children of Israel could not look steadily at the end of what was passing away. But their minds were blinded. For until this day the same veil remains unlifted in the reading of the Old Testament, because the veil is taken away in Christ. But even to this day, when Moses is read, a veil lies on their heart. Nevertheless when one turns to the Lord, the veil is taken away. Now the Lord is the Spirit; and where the Spirit of the Lord is, there is liberty. But we all, with unveiled face, beholding as in a mirror the glory of the Lord, are being transformed into the same image from glory to glory, just as by the Spirit of the Lord. (2 Cor 3:5-18)

In the above passage, the apostle Paul contrasts the Old and New Covenants. Although the Old Covenant was glorious, it was a glory that was passing away. It was the letter that killed, having been a ministry of death and condemnation. The letter was also a physical covenant, written on stones and lived out in the priesthood and the Levitical law.

In contrast, the New Covenant is of the Spirit, and lived out in the Spirit. *"Where the Spirit of the Lord is,"* Paul writes in verses 17-18, *"there is liberty. But we all, with unveiled face, beholding as in a mirror the glory of the Lord, are being transformed into the same image from glory to glory, just as by the Spirit of the Lord."* This transforming process takes place as the inner man conforms to the Spirit of God, not by the outer man conforming to external laws as he did with the Old Covenant:

> *And do not be conformed to this world, but be transformed by the renewing of your mind, that you may prove what is that good and acceptable and perfect will of God.* (Rom 12:2)

> *I have been crucified with Christ; it is no longer I who live, but Christ lives in me; and the life which I now live in the flesh I live by faith in the Son of God, who loved me and gave Himself for me.* (Gal 2:20)

Paul uses the veil of Moses, which dimmed the passing glory of the countenance of his face, as an allegory of the Old Covenant, with its passing glory, veiling the surpassing glory of the New Covenant. While the Old Covenant spoke in types and shadows, the New Covenant was proclaimed with *great boldness* (King James Version = "plainness," Young's Literal Translation = "freedom") *of speech*. Whereas Moses covered his face with a veil, so that the Israelites might not look steadily at what was passing away, Paul states that the gospel is proclaimed boldly, for the veil is removed in Christ. Several commentators make note of this fact, e.g., Matthew Henry; Barnes; Adam Clarke; Jamieson, Fausset and Brown; and Wycliffe. We provide two quotations here as examples:

> The gospel is a more clear dispensation than the law; the things of God are revealed in the New Testament, not in types and shadows. (*Matthew Henry's Commentary on the Whole Bible*, commentary on 2 Cor 3:12-18)

> The obscurity which rested on the prophecies and types of the former dispensation is withdrawn; and as the face of Moses could have been distinctly seen if the veil on his face had been removed, so it is in regard to the true meaning of the Old Testament by the coming of the Messiah. What was obscure is now made clear; and the prophecies are so completely fulfilled in him, that his coming has removed the covering, and shed a clear light over them all. Many of the prophecies, for example, until the Messiah actually appeared, appeared obscure, and almost contradictory. Those which spoke of him, for illustration, as man and as God; as suffering, and yet reigning; as dying, and yet as ever-living; as a mighty Prince, a conqueror, and a king, and yet as a man of

sorrows; as humble, and yet glorious: all seemed difficult to be reconciled until they were seen to harmonize in Jesus of Nazareth. Then they were plain, and the veil was taken away. Christ is seen to answer all the previous descriptions of him in the Old Testament; and his coming casts a clear light on all which was before obscure. (*Barnes' Notes*, commentary on 2 Cor 3:14)

Many of the Jews' concepts of Old Testament teachings were incorrect because they failed to realize that the Old Covenant was merely a shadow of the New Covenant. The New Testament confirms that the material things of the Old Covenant were *copies*, *shadows*, and *symbols* of the spiritual substance found in the New Covenant:

> *So let no one judge you in food or in drink, or regarding a festival or a new moon or sabbaths,* **which are a shadow of things to come, but the substance is of Christ.** (Col 2:16-17)

> *For if He were on earth, He would not be a priest, since there are priests who offer the gifts according to the law; who serve* **the copy and shadow of the heavenly things**, *as Moses was divinely instructed when he was about to make the tabernacle. For He said,* **"See that you make all things according to the pattern shown you on the mountain."** (Heb 8:4-5)

> *. . . the Holy Spirit indicating this, that the way into the Holiest of All was not yet made manifest while the first tabernacle was still standing.* **It was symbolic** *for the present time in which both gifts and sacrifices are offered which cannot make him who performed the service perfect in regard to the conscience . . . .* (Heb 9:8-9)

> *Therefore it was necessary that* **the copies** *[the temple and its furnishings]* **of the things in the heavens** *should be purified with these [the blood of animals], but the heavenly things themselves with better sacrifices than these. For Christ has not entered the holy places made with hands,* **which are copies of the true**, *but into heaven itself, now to appear in the presence of God for us.* (Heb 9:23-24)

> *For the law,* **having a shadow of the good things to come, and not the very image of the things**, *can never with these same sacrifices, which they offer continually year by year, make those who approach perfect.* (Heb 10:1)
> (emphases added)

Wycliffe made the observation that our opening passage in 2 Corinthians is Paul's *inspired interpretation* of the Old Testament! While most would give assent to this fact, many have failed to apprehend its ramifications. The same Spirit that inspired Moses as he penned the accounts found in the Pentateuch also inspired Paul to interpret and expound upon portions of that text. As 2 Timothy 3:16 says, "*All Scripture is inspired by God . . .*" (NASB). Although some argue that the Scripture referred to here is only the Old Testament, Peter does, in fact, equate the writings of Paul with the Old Testament Scriptures:

> *. . . as also our beloved brother Paul, according to the wisdom given to him, has written to you, as also in all his epistles, speaking in them of these things, in which are some things hard to understand, which untaught and unstable people twist to their own destruction, as they do also **the rest of the Scriptures**. (2 Pet 3:15-16; emphasis added)*

If we believe that Peter was inspired as he wrote this, then we have confirmation that when Paul comments on the Old Testament, it serves as a Spirit-inspired commentary. Furthermore, if we accept that our present New Testament was written and compiled under the inspiration of the Holy Spirit, then we have in our possession an inspired commentary on many Old Testament passages. Granted, it is not a verse-by-verse commentary, but concerning those passages that it does interpret, we would do well to put every volume written by man back on the shelf, and seek to discover the answer to the question, *"WHAT DOES THE SCRIPTURE SAY?"* For every commentary written by man—no matter his education, insight, inspiration or communication skills—is the product of a fallible being. The New Testament, however, was authored by the Holy Spirit, whose ministry is to lead people into the Truth:

> *. . . knowing this first, that no prophecy of Scripture is of any private interpretation, for prophecy never came by the will of man, but holy men of God spoke as they were moved by the Holy Spirit. (2 Pet 1:20-21)*

> *However, when He, the Spirit of truth, has come, He will guide you into all truth; for He will not speak on His own authority, but whatever He hears He will speak; and He will tell you things to come. (John 16:13)*

Unfortunately, instead of interpreting the Old Testament through the lens of the New Testament, we tend to do just the opposite. Because the

Old Testament is older than the New Testament, and is positioned first in our Bibles, we have a mental picture of it as the foundation upon which the New Testament is built. Thus, we try to harmonize our interpretation of the New Testament with our understanding of the Old Testament. While it is true that all sixty-six books of the Bible are inspired, and that the Bible is truly "one book," we have failed to grasp completely the interrelation of those books, particularly between the two testaments. We tend to view the Bible as sixty-six volumes, which we attempt to interpret with the use of extrabiblical and human-inspired lexicons, commentaries, dictionaries, etc. What we have failed to recognize is that the last twenty-seven books are, in many instances, a *divinely inspired* Lexicon, Commentary, Dictionary, etc., for the first thirty-nine books. Again, not a verse-by-verse commentary, but sufficient commentary to establish interpretative principles which enable us to read uninspired commentaries judiciously, regardless of their popularity or appeal. This is not to say that the Holy Spirit has not inspired preachers, teachers, and authors throughout the history of the Church; this is a different level of inspiration. We believe that the canon of Scripture falls under the type of inspiration described in 2 Peter 1:21 ("*. . . for prophecy never came by the will of man, but holy men of God spoke as they were moved by the Holy Spirit*"), while all other inspiration falls under 1 Corinthians 14:32 ("*The spirits of prophets are subject to the control of prophets*," NIV). In those areas that the New Testament interprets the Old Testament, it should be the first, last, and final word. Instead of (re)interpreting the New Testament to fit our *a priori* (preconceived) interpretation of the Old Testament, all Old Testament interpretations should align themselves with those passages which are divinely interpreted for us by the New Testament. Once the New Testament authors establish a precedent for interpreting particular Old Testament texts, we must accept nothing less than scriptural support to deviate from that precedent. As Max R. King states in *The Spirit of Prophecy* (1983, second printing), "it is never wise to allow our concept of a Biblical subject to place us in opposition to inspiration" (p. 115).

Milton S. Terry writes in his *Biblical Hermeneutics* (hermeneutics is the study of the methodological principles of interpretation):

> It is of the first importance to observe that, from a Christian point of view, the Old Testament cannot be fully apprehended without the help of the New. The mystery of Christ, which in other generations was not made known unto men, was revealed unto the apostles and prophets of the New Testament (Eph 3:5), and that

revelation sheds a flood of light upon numerous portions of the Hebrew Scriptures. (p. 18)

We believe that Terry's point, that *the Old Testament cannot be fully apprehended without the help of the New,* cannot be overemphasized. The Old Testament contained mysteries that were not fully revealed apart from the Gospel. There were truths in the Old Testament that were shrouded in darkness, awaiting the "flood of light" of revelation that the New Testament apostles and prophets shed upon them. This important point is confirmed by the following passages:

> *Then He turned to His disciples and said privately, "Blessed are the eyes which see the things you see; for I tell you that many prophets and kings have desired to see what you see, and have not seen it, and to hear what you hear, and have not heard it."* (Luke 10:23-24)

> *. . . according to the revelation of the mystery kept secret since the world began but now made manifest . . . .* (Rom 16:25-26)

> *. . . and to make all see what is the fellowship of the mystery, which from the beginning of the ages has been hidden in God who created all things through Jesus Christ; to the intent that now the manifold wisdom of God might be made known by the church to the principalities and powers in the heavenly places . . . .* (Eph 3:9-10)

> *. . . how that by revelation He made known to me the mystery (as I have briefly written already, by which, when you read, you may understand my knowledge in the mystery of Christ), which in other ages was not made known to the sons of men, as it has now been revealed by the Spirit to His holy apostles and prophets . . . .* (Eph 3:3-5)

> *. . . which God, who cannot lie, promised before time began, but has in due time manifested . . . .* (Titus 1:2-3)

Paul states that the mystery of Christ was not revealed prior to the gospel age. Therefore, to formulate any doctrine apart from the fuller revelation of the New Testament apostles is attempting to build a house before the foundation is finished. This is because the revelation given to the New Testament apostles was not merely *building upon* the foundation laid by the Old Testament prophets—it was an *integral part* of that foundation:

Now, therefore, you are no longer strangers and foreigners, but fellow citizens with the saints and members of the household of God, having been built on the foundation of the apostles and prophets, Jesus Christ Himself being the chief cornerstone . . . . (Eph 2:19-20)

Beloved, I now write to you this second epistle (in both of which I stir up your pure minds by way of reminder), that you may be mindful of the words which were spoken before by the holy prophets, and of the commandment of us, the apostles of the Lord and Savior . . . . (2 Pet 3:1-2)

But you, beloved, remember the words which were spoken before by the apostles of our Lord Jesus Christ . . . . (Jude 17)

Now the wall of the city had twelve foundations, and on them were the names of the twelve apostles of the Lamb. (Rev 21:14)

This revelation to the apostles and prophets is the removing of the veil of Moses. What was previously a mystery, veiled in types and shadows, was revealed by the Holy Spirit. The Holy Spirit's arrival at Pentecost and His subsequent ministry in the early church was (and is) pivotal to understanding the truths of God:

*"I still have many things to say to you, but you cannot bear them now. However, when He, the Spirit of truth, has come, **He will guide you into all truth**; for He will not speak on His own authority, but whatever He hears He will speak; and **He will tell you things to come**."* (John 16:12-13; emphases added)

Not only was the Holy Spirit to guide the disciples into all truth; specifically, He was to guide them into knowledge of the "things to come." We shall develop those "things to come" in later chapters.

Removing the Veil Through the Enlightening Ministry of the Holy Spirit

At the end of the first chapter of Acts, just prior to Pentecost, the apostles cast lots to find Judas' replacement to be numbered among the twelve. After Pentecost, however, the apostles never used lots again. It is the Spirit that directs their lives, using a vision to send Peter to the Gentiles, forbidding Paul to minister in Asia, setting apart Paul and Barnabas for the gospel, etc. Similarly, they now understood the Scriptures—*the veil of Moses had been removed!* Prior to Pentecost, the apostles, during their discipleship under Jesus, were fairly ignorant as to the meaning of Scripture. Any understanding of the Scriptures they had, apart from their traditional background, was limited to either direct teaching or special revelation:

> *Simon Peter answered and said, "You are the Christ, the Son of the living God." Jesus answered and said to him, "Blessed are you, Simon Bar-Jonah, for **flesh and blood has not revealed this to you, but My Father who is in heaven**."* (Matt 16:16-17)

> *Then He said to them, "These are the words which I spoke to you while I was still with you, that all things must be fulfilled which were written in the Law of Moses and the Prophets and the Psalms concerning Me." **And He opened their understanding, that they might comprehend the Scriptures.*** (Luke 24:44-45)

> *Then Peter answered and said to Him, "**Explain this parable to us.***" (Matt 15:15; cf. Mark 4:13)

> *"**Do you not yet understand**, or remember the five loaves of the five thousand and how many baskets you took up? Nor the seven loaves of the four thousand and how many large baskets you took up? How is it you do not understand that I did not speak to you concerning bread—but to beware of the leaven of the Pharisees and Sadducees?"* (Matt 16:9-11)

> *And He said to them, "**Do you not understand this parable?** How then will you understand all the parables?"* Mark 4:13

> *For He taught His disciples and said to them, "The Son of Man is being betrayed into the hands of men, and they will kill Him. And after He is killed, He will rise the third day." **But they did not understand this saying**, and were afraid to ask Him.* (Mark 9:31-32)

> ***They did not understand*** *that He spoke to them of the Father.* (John 8:27)

> ***His disciples did not understand these things at first***; *but when Jesus was glorified, then they remembered that these things were written about Him and that they had done these things to Him.* (John 12:16)
> (emphases added)

We note that, in Luke 24:45, Jesus "opened their minds to understand the Scriptures." The context, however, suggests that the Scriptures were those pertaining to Christ's death and resurrection. Thus the disciples still needed the Spirit to teach them the *things to come*.

In stark contrast to their lack of discernment during Christ's ministry, after Pentecost the apostles understood the Scriptures. For example, Peter begins by immediately expounding on Joel's prophecy, and Philip is able to explain Isaiah 53 to the Eunuch:

> *But Peter, standing up with the eleven, raised his voice and said to them, "Men of Judea and all who dwell in Jerusalem, let this be known to you, and heed my words. For these are not drunk, as you suppose, since it is only the third hour of the day. But this is what was spoken by the prophet Joel:*
>
> *'And it shall come to pass in the last days, says God,*
>
> *That I will pour out of My Spirit on all flesh;*
> *Your sons and your daughters shall prophesy,*
> *Your young men shall see visions,*
> *Your old men shall dream dreams.'"* (Acts 2:14-17)
>
> *So Philip ran to him, and heard him reading the prophet Isaiah, and said, "Do you understand what you are reading?" And he said, "How can I, unless someone guides me?" And he asked Philip to come up and sit with him . . . . Then Philip opened his mouth, and beginning at this Scripture, preached Jesus to him.* (Acts 8:30-31, 35)

This newfound insight into the Scriptures is too easily glossed over. We cannot overemphasize its importance, for it is the very crux to understanding biblical truths. Prior to Pentecost, the New Testament saints could only apprehend what was behind the veil of Moses either by special revelation from God, or by specific teaching from Jesus. After Pentecost, however, when the Holy Spirit was poured out upon all believers, they understood the Scriptures, and the mysteries of God were revealed to the apostles. Thus, the veil is removed in Christ when those who turn to Him receive His Spirit, Who in turn gives spiritual discernment:

> *For until this day the same veil remains unlifted in the reading of the Old Testament, because the veil is taken away in Christ. But even to this day, when Moses is read, a veil lies on their heart. Nevertheless when one turns to the Lord, the veil is taken away.* (2 Cor 3:14-16)

These things we also speak, not in words which man's wisdom teaches but which the Holy Spirit teaches, comparing spiritual things with spiritual. But the natural man does not receive the things of the Spirit of God, for they are foolishness to him; nor can he know them, because they are spiritually discerned. But he who is spiritual judges all things, yet he himself is rightly judged by no one. For "who has known the mind of the LORD that he may instruct Him?" But we have the mind of Christ. (1 Cor 2:13-16)

Just as the page between Malachi and Matthew separates the Old and New Testaments—just as the death and resurrection of Christ separate the Old and New Covenants—*so the day of Pentecost separates the veiled understanding of Scripture from the unveiled understanding of Scripture.* Before Pentecost, Peter needed a revelation from the Father to recognize Jesus as the Messiah. After Pentecost, the Holy Spirit reveals this to us through the written Word:

. . . but these are written that you may believe that Jesus is the Christ, the Son of God, and that believing you may have life in His name. (John 20:31)

Prior to Pentecost, the disciples asked in ignorance, "explain to us," because their understanding was based upon the incomplete teaching of the Scribes and Pharisees. After Pentecost, *the disciples* were explaining the Scriptures to others with confidence, and the Scribes and Pharisees marveled, knowing that the disciples were uneducated and untrained. What was hidden to the "wise" of the Mosaic age had been revealed to the "babes" of the messianic age! Thus, the wise of the passing age had become foolish, because through their wisdom they did not know God:

Now when they saw the boldness of Peter and John, and perceived that they were uneducated and untrained men, they marveled. (Acts 4:13)

At that time Jesus answered and said, "I thank You, Father, Lord of heaven and earth, that You have hidden these things from the wise and prudent and have revealed them to babes." (Matt 11:25)

For Jews request a sign, and Greeks seek after wisdom; but we preach Christ crucified, to the Jews a stumbling block and to the Greeks foolishness, but to those who are called, both Jews and Greeks, Christ the power of God and the wisdom of God. Because the foolishness of God is wiser than men, and the weakness of God is stronger than men. (1 Cor 1:22-25)

Even the Old Testament prophets did not completely understand their own prophecies, because they were hidden (at least in part) until the days of the New Testament apostles:

> *. . . and when the power of the holy people has been completely shattered, all these things shall be finished. Although I heard, **I did not understand**. Then I said, "My lord, what shall be the end of these things?" And he said, "Go your way, Daniel, for the words are closed up and sealed till the time of the end. Many shall be purified, made white, and refined, but the wicked shall do wickedly; and none of the wicked shall understand, but the wise shall understand."* (Dan 12:7-10)

> *Of this salvation **the prophets have inquired and searched carefully**, who prophesied of the grace that would come to you, **searching what, or what manner of time**, the Spirit of Christ who was in them was indicating when He testified beforehand the sufferings of Christ and the glories that would follow. To them it was revealed that, not to themselves, but to us they were ministering the things which now have been reported to you through those who have preached the gospel to you by the Holy Spirit sent from heaven—**things which angels desire to look into**.* (1 Pet 1:10-12)

> *. . . which **in other ages was not made known** to the sons of men, as it **has now been revealed by the Spirit** to His holy apostles and prophets . . . .* (Eph 3:5)
> (emphases added)

After Pentecost, the Holy Spirit not only revealed the mysteries of God to the New Testament apostles and prophets, but He taught all believers:

> *But you have an anointing from the Holy One, and you know all things. I have not written to you because you do not know the truth, but because you know it, and that no lie is of the truth. . . . But the anointing which you have received from Him abides in you, and you do not need that anyone teach you; but as the same anointing teaches you concerning all things, and is true, and is not a lie, and just as it has taught you, you will abide in Him.* (1 John 2:20-21, 27)

Since the Gospels were written after Pentecost, the authors were able to say with hindsight, "this was done that the words of the prophet might be fulfilled." At the time, the disciples did not necessarily recognize that

39

prophecy was being fulfilled before their eyes (except in a very limited way). After Pentecost, however, they *did* recognize that they had been eyewitnesses to fulfilled prophecy, and recorded it in the Gospels. But notice who informed the people of all of this fulfilled prophecy in the Gospels: a tax collector, an understudy of a fisherman, a (possibly Gentile) doctor, and a fisherman. It was not the religious leaders. It was not the scribes. It was neither the Sadducees nor the Pharisees:

> *And the disciples came and said to Him, "Why do You speak to them in parables?" He answered and said to them, "Because it has been given to you to know the mysteries of the kingdom of heaven, but to them it has not been given."* (Matt 13:10-11)

The closing words of Malachi are followed by what are known as the "four hundred years of silence." During that period, there is no account of any inspired words from God. That silence was broken by the ministry of John the Baptist. Contrary to tradition, however, his message dismissed the importance of Jewish heritage in attaining the kingdom of God:

> *In those days John the Baptist came preaching in the wilderness of Judea, and saying, "Repent, for the kingdom of heaven is at hand! . . . Therefore bear fruits worthy of repentance, and do not think to say to yourselves, 'We have Abraham as our father.' For I say to you that God is able to raise up children to Abraham from these stones."* (Matt 3:1-2, 8-9)

Not only did John understand that the true children of Abraham were not the physical Jews, he also knew that he was the fulfillment of the Messiah's forerunner:

> *Then they said to him, "Who are you, that we may give an answer to those who sent us? What do you say about yourself?"*
> *He said: "I am*
> *'The voice of one crying in the wilderness:*
> *"Make straight the way of the LORD,"'*
> *as the prophet Isaiah said."* (John 1:22-23)

John was able to look behind the veil of Moses, understand the fulfillment of prophecy, and discern the nature of the kingdom of God—this in stark contrast to the disciples, who did *not* understand that John was the Elijah to come. As we shall see in coming chapters, neither did they understand the nature of the kingdom of God. Why was John able to "see" behind the veil of Moses while the disciples could not? Because unlike the disciples, who had to wait until Pentecost, he was filled with the Holy Spirit from conception:

> *For he will be great in the sight of the Lord, and shall drink neither wine nor strong drink. He will also be filled with the Holy Spirit, even from his mother's womb.* (Luke 1:15)

Jesus continued in this vein of proclaiming a prophetic fulfillment that was contrary to current tradition. After His baptism by John, which marked the beginning of His public ministry, He was led by the Spirit into the wilderness to be tempted by Satan. Returning from the wilderness in the power of the Spirit, He proclaimed in the synagogue that the words of the prophet Isaiah were fulfilled in Him. His subsequent commentary filled those in the synagogue with such rage that they tried to kill Him!

> *Then Jesus returned in the power of the Spirit to Galilee, and news of Him went out through all the surrounding region. . . . And He was handed the book of the prophet Isaiah. And when He had opened the book, He found the place where it was written:*
>
> *"The Spirit of the LORD is upon Me,*
> *Because He has anointed Me*
> *To preach the gospel to the poor;*
> *He has sent Me to heal the brokenhearted,*
> *To proclaim liberty to the captives*
> *And recovery of sight to the blind,*
> *To set at liberty those who are oppressed;*
> *To proclaim the acceptable year of the LORD."*
>
> *Then He closed the book, and gave it back to the attendant and sat down. And the eyes of all who were in the synagogue were fixed on Him. And He began to say to them, "Today this Scripture is fulfilled in your hearing." . . . So all those in the synagogue, when they heard these things, were filled with wrath, and rose up and thrust Him out of the city; and they led Him to the brow of the hill on which their city was built, that they might throw Him down over the cliff.* (Luke 4:14, 17-21, 28-29)

Certainly, no one would argue against the fact that both John the Baptist and Jesus were fulfilling Old Testament prophecy; however, they were fulfilling prophecy in a manner which did not conform to the teaching of the religious leaders of their day. The religious leaders of the day did not even recognize that Jesus was the Messiah; they knew all of the passages concerning Him, but interpreted them wrongly. While they understood that the Messiah was to be born in Bethlehem, they did not recognize the Child Who was born there. As we saw in the previous chapter, the disciples likewise did not recognize John the Baptist as Elijah. Neither the disciples nor the religious leaders could see behind the veil. This is why we must not build our theology upon those "experts" of the law, but rather upon *the inspired revelation of the New Testament authors.* After Pentecost, the mysteries of God, which were hidden in previous ages, were revealed to them; but, as we shall see, what was revealed to them contrasted sharply to what they had been brought up to believe. God was doing a new thing:

> *"Do not remember the former things,*
> *Nor consider the things of old.*
> *Behold, I will do **a new thing**,*
> *Now it shall spring forth;*
> *Shall you not know it?*
> *I will even make a **road in the wilderness***
> *And rivers in the desert."* (Isa 43:18-19)

Upon receiving the Holy Spirit, the New Testament apostles continued what began with the teaching of John the Baptist and Jesus—clarification of Old Testament prophecies. The above passage is reminiscent of John the Baptist's ministry, which we have already seen was associated with the Gospel's arrival:

> *The voice of one crying in the wilderness:*
> *"Prepare the way of the LORD;*
> *Make straight in the desert*
> ***A highway for our God.***
> *Every valley shall be exalted*
> *And every mountain and hill brought low;*
> *The crooked places shall be made straight*
> *And the rough places smooth;*
> *The glory of the LORD shall be revealed,*
> *And all flesh shall see it together;*
> *For the mouth of the LORD has spoken."* (Isa 40:3-5)

Surely the *road in the wilderness* of Isaiah 43 identifies with *Make straight in the desert a highway for our God* in Isaiah 40. Thus the *new thing* that God was doing occurred simultaneously with the ministry of John the Baptist, who was the voice crying in the wilderness. By inspiration of the Holy Spirit, the New Testament authors were interpreting Old Testament prophecies rightly. Therefore, rather than letting the theological elite interpret the Old Testament for us, we must allow the inspired authors of the New Testament to interpret the Old Testament. In this way, we truly allow Scripture to interpret Scripture instead of letting man interpret Scripture. To construct a theology based solely upon the Old Testament (or to force our understanding of the New Testament to fit traditional Old Testament theology) is to formulate doctrine before all of the facts are considered. Those missing facts were revealed to the apostles and prophets of the New Testament. As we shall see in the coming chapters, it was because the Jews based their theology solely upon the Old Testament that they were in such opposition to the Christian message, just as they were in opposition to Jesus. The Church, which possessed the full revelation, could now formulate doctrine correctly and reveal that which had previously been a mystery. Those Jews who accepted the full revelation removed the veil of Moses and became sons and daughters of God (John 1:12). Those who stubbornly refused that revelation continued on in their inadequately founded doctrine, the veil of Moses remaining over their hearts.

Because it was to the apostles and prophets of the New Testament that the mysteries of God were revealed, we feel that it is with them that the search for a proper understanding of Bible prophecy must begin and end. As we have noted previously, the Holy Spirit taught them the "things to come":

> *However, when He, the Spirit of truth, has come, He will guide you into all truth; for He will not speak on His own authority, but whatever He hears He will speak; and **He will tell you things to come**.* (John 16:12-13; emphasis added)

Again, this is not to say that we cannot benefit from the education and gifting of others within the Body of Christ. However, we must come to all extrabiblical interpretations with the same attitude as the Bereans:

> *Now the Bereans were of more noble character than the Thessalonians, for they received the message with great eagerness and examined the Scriptures every day to see if what Paul said was true.* (Acts 17:11 NIV)

Do the interpretations in the commentaries on our shelves regarding Old Testament prophecy (and, by implication, our understanding of it) agree with the interpretations presented by the New Testament authors? As Paul wrote in his epistle to the Corinthians, the Jews still had a "veil" over their hearts when the words of Moses were read. Although the Jews were experts in the law, their expertise, their studies, and their interpretative methods failed to penetrate the veil and discern the glorious truth hidden behind it. If we are to discern the truth represented by the types and shadows of the Old Covenant, our starting place should be with those whose veils were removed by Christ—the inspired authors of the New Testament.

As mentioned previously, the precedent of the New Testament authors' understanding of Old Testament prophecy is established for us in the Gospels, which were written after Pentecost. Although they often did not understand prophecy as it unfolded before their eyes, they did understand it later when they wrote their Gospels (and epistles). Thus, we often read in the Gospels phrases such as "that it might be fulfilled what was spoken by the prophet . . . ."

> *Then was fulfilled what was spoken by Jeremiah the prophet, saying:*
>
> *"A voice was heard in Ramah,*
> *Lamentation, weeping, and great mourning,*
> *Rachel weeping for her children,*
> *Refusing to be comforted,*
> *Because they are no more."* (Matt 2:17-18)
>
> *So the Scripture was fulfilled which says, "And He was numbered with the transgressors."* (Mark 15:28)

Perhaps it was because most of the Jews did not recognize the fact of these fulfilled prophecies that the Gospel authors took pains to establish a record of these fulfillments. In essence, what they were saying was, "this is what lies behind the veil." Even though the Gospel authors were writing after-the-fact, they still felt it necessary to explain the fulfillments of these Old Testament prophecies. Why? Because those fulfillments did not necessarily meet the expectations of their contemporaries. The Gospel authors provided an inspired commentary on those Old Testament passages that did not agree with the traditional interpretations of their day. What we have failed to fully grasp is that these actions continued beyond the events recorded in the Gospels, into the book of Acts and the Epistles. As we shall see, the interpretations that the New Testament authors provide are often markedly different than the prevailing teachings—even those of our day. We must remember, however, that those interpretations were also markedly different from the prevailing teachings of their contemporaries, leading to the persecution of Jesus and the early Christians by the Jews. In choosing between markedly different interpretations of Old Testament passages, and in establishing doctrine, mustn't we choose the inspired authors of the New Testament over and against any theologian or prophecy expert, past or present?

In order to establish a *biblical* interpretation of the New Covenant, as well as the time of the return of that covenant's Mediator (Heb 8:6; 9:15; 12:24), we should first complete the foundation upon which that interpretation is built by adding the inspired interpretation of the New Testament authors. Anything that does not conform to that foundation must surely be questioned. In the preceding chapter we asked, "*Are we willing to receive it?*" In this chapter we ask, "*Are we willing to lay aside the tradition of man in favor of the inspiration of the New Testament authors?*" Many of the Jews, to whom the very oracles of God were entrusted (Rom 3:2), answered no to both questions. Thus Paul lamented, "*even to this day, when Moses is read, a veil lies on their heart.*"

The Two Covenants and the Two Sons of Abraham

—ᗰ—

Tell me, you who desire to be under the law, do you not hear the law? For it is written that Abraham had two sons: the one by a bondwoman, the other by a freewoman. But he who was of the bondwoman was born according to the flesh, and he of the free-woman through promise, which things are symbolic. For these are the two covenants: the one from Mount Sinai which gives birth to bondage, which is Hagar—for this Hagar is Mount Sinai in Arabia, and corresponds to Jerusalem which now is, and is in bondage with her children—but the Jerusalem above is free, which is the mother of us all. . . . Now we, brethren, as Isaac was, are children of promise. But, as he who was born according to the flesh then persecuted him who was born according to the Spirit, even so it is now. Nevertheless what does the Scripture say? "Cast out the bondwoman and her son, for the son of the bondwoman shall not be heir with the son of the free woman. So then, brethren, we are not children of the bondwoman but of the free. (Gal 4:21-26, 28-31)

In his letter to the Galatians, Paul was addressing Christians who were being influenced by Judaizers—Jews who taught that Gentile believers had to follow the law of Moses in order to be accepted by God. They could not see past the veil. They did not realize that the law of Moses was given under a covenant that was passing away, while the gospel of grace is the everlasting covenant of surpassing glory. They were trying to get Christians, who were walking in the covenant of the substance, to conform to the covenant of the shadow:

O foolish Galatians! Who has bewitched you that you should not obey the truth, before whose eyes Jesus Christ was clearly portrayed among you as crucified? This only I want to learn from you: Did you receive the Spirit by the works of the law, or by the hearing of faith? Are you so foolish? Having begun in the Spirit, are you now being made perfect by the flesh? (Gal 3:1-3)

Although it is true that the early Jewish Christians continued observing the law, Paul provides a reasonable explanation for their choice:

Though I am free and belong to no man, I make myself a slave to everyone, to win as many as possible. To the Jews I became like a Jew, to win the Jews. To those under the law I became like one under the law (though I myself am not under the law), so as to win those under the law. To those not having the law I became like one not having the law (though I am not free from God's law but am under Christ's law), so as to win those not having the law. To the weak I became weak, to win the weak. I have become all things to all men so that by all possible means I might save some. I do all this for the sake of the gospel, that I may share in its blessings. (1 Cor 9:19-23 NIV)

Even though Paul chose to observe the law, he was not under it, that is, he was not bound by it. The early Jewish believers' observance of the law was not a matter of salvation, but one of evangelism. This is borne out by the letter issued by the Jerusalem council concerning Gentile believers:

The apostles, the elders, and the brethren,

To the brethren who are of the Gentiles in Antioch, Syria, and Cilicia:

Greetings.

Since we have heard that some who went out from us have troubled you with words, unsettling your souls, saying, "You must be circumcised and keep the law"—to whom we gave no such commandment—it seemed good to us, being assembled with one accord, to send chosen men to you with our beloved Barnabas and Paul, men who have risked their lives for the name of our Lord Jesus Christ. We have therefore sent Judas and Silas, who will also report the same things by word of mouth. For it seemed good to the Holy Spirit, and to us, to lay upon you no greater burden than these necessary things: that you abstain from things offered to idols, from blood, from things strangled, and from sexual immorality. If you keep yourselves from these, you will do well.

Farewell. (Acts 15:23-29)

So we see that observance of the law, the Old Covenant, was not necessary for salvation. In fact, Peter, when addressing the council earlier, stated, *"but we [Jewish believers] believe that through the grace of the*

Lord Jesus Christ we shall be saved in the same manner as they [Gentile believers]," that is, through grace (Acts 15:11).

In Galatians 4, Paul reasoned from the law to demonstrate the futility of trusting in it: *"Tell me, you who desire to be under the law, do you not hear the law?"* (v. 21). Paul then explains how Abraham's two sons, Ishmael and Isaac, and their respective mothers, represent the two covenants. Paul writes that these things are *symbolic* (NASB95 = "allegorical," NIV = "figurative," NLT = "illustrative"). *Can't you see behind the veil?* Paul is asking. *Don't you realize that the covenant you refuse to let go of is passing away?* In 2 Corinthians 3, Paul stated that the Old Covenant was one of death and condemnation, and was passing away. He confirms this concept in his letter to the Galatians:

> *But, as he who was born according to the flesh then persecuted him who was born according to the Spirit, even so it is now. Nevertheless what does the Scripture say? "Cast out the bondwoman and her son, for the son of the bondwoman shall not be heir with the son of the freewoman." So then, brethren, we are not children of the bondwoman but of the free.* (Gal 4:29-31)

The Old Covenant would not share in the inheritance of the New. Just as Hagar and Ishmael were cast out, so the Old Covenant was passing away:

> *In that He says, "A new covenant," He has made the first obsolete. Now what is becoming obsolete and growing old is ready to vanish away.* (Heb 8:13)

The danger for the Galatians was that they desired to align themselves with a covenant that would soon be done away with. Although the Old Covenant, with its physical temple, laws, and rituals, may have seemed to have more "substance" than the gospel of grace, just the opposite is true:

> *. . . for the kingdom of God is not eating and drinking, but righteousness and peace and joy in the Holy Spirit.* (Rom 14:17)

> *Therefore, if you died with Christ from the basic principles of the world, why, as though living in the world, do you subject yourselves to regulations— "Do not touch, do not taste, do not handle," which all concern things which perish with the using—according to the commandments and doctrines of men? These things indeed have an appearance of wisdom in self-imposed religion, false humility, and neglect of the body, but are of no value against the indulgence of the flesh.* (Col 2:20-23)

49

The danger for Christians today is not that of being enticed to observe the law, but of *neglecting to fully comprehend the truths about the New Covenant which Paul and others revealed.*

There are two items in this present passage that demand our further attention, for they are foundational truths upon which much of New Testament prophecy rests. This is especially true when we consider that Paul's allegory is a divinely inspired commentary by which the Holy Spirit pulls back the veil from the Old Testament types to reveal the substance. These two are: (1) the nature of the New Covenant, and (2) the end of the Old Covenant, which was ready to vanish away in the first century. *These truths are like hinges, anchored to the framework of the Old Testament, upon which the door of New Testament prophecy swings.*

The Nature of the New Covenant

The Old Covenant, which was represented by Hagar and Ishmael, includes Mount Sinai in Arabia, where the Law was received, and the Jerusalem of Paul's day. It was material and physical. The New Covenant, on the other hand, consists of spiritual counterparts:

> . . . *but the Jerusalem above is free, which is the mother of us all.* (Gal 4:26)

> *For you have not come to the mountain that may be touched and that burned with fire [Mount Sinai], and to blackness and darkness and tempest . . . . But you have come to Mount Zion and to the city of the living God, the heavenly Jerusalem . . . .* (Heb 12:18, 22)

While the Israelites received the Old Covenant at Mount Sinai, written on stone with Jerusalem as its eventual focal point, Christians receive the New Covenant at Mount Zion, written on their hearts with their citizenship in the heavenly Jerusalem:

> *For this is the covenant that I will make with the house of Israel after those days, says the LORD: I will put My laws in their mind and write them on their hearts; and I will be their God, and they shall be My people.* (Heb 8:10)

> *For our citizenship is in heaven . . . .* (Phil 3:20)

The Old Covenant was the letter of the law, which led to death. The New Covenant, in contrast, centers on the Spirit of the law, which brings life:

. . . who also made us sufficient as ministers of the new covenant, not of the letter but of the Spirit; for the letter kills, but the Spirit gives life. (2 Cor 3:6)

The Old Covenant was earthly and material, whereas the New Covenant is heavenly and spiritual. Ishmael and Isaac illustrate this difference between the two covenants. Ishmael was born of the flesh, while Isaac was the son of promise, born after Abraham and Sarah became unable physically to bear children. The birth of Ishmael was natural; the flesh of Abraham and Hagar could never produce the son of promise. Isaac's origin, on the other hand, was supernatural, born of the power of God. Similarly, the Old Covenant could not produce righteousness through the law:

Therefore, if perfection were through the Levitical priesthood (for under it the people received the law), what further need was there that another priest should rise according to the order of Melchizedek, and not be called according to the order of Aaron? . . . for the law made nothing perfect; on the other hand, there is the bringing in of a better hope, through which we draw near to God. (Heb 7:11, 19)

For if that first covenant had been faultless, then no place would have been sought for a second. (Heb 8:7)

For the law, having a shadow of the good things to come, and not the very image of the things, can never with these same sacrifices, which they offer continually year by year, make those who approach perfect. (Heb 10:1)

The New Covenant, on the other hand, has the power of God to cleanse us from sin and make us righteous:

But now the righteousness of God apart from the law is revealed, being witnessed by the Law and the Prophets, even the righteousness of God, through faith in Jesus Christ, to all and on all who believe. (Rom 3:21-22)

For what the law could not do in that it was weak through the flesh, God did by sending His own Son in the likeness of sinful flesh, on account of sin: He condemned sin in the flesh, that the righteous requirement of the law might be fulfilled in us who do not walk according to the flesh but according to the Spirit. (Rom 8:3-4)

This dichotomy of the material vs. spiritual natures of the covenants is reinforced in God's promise to Abraham regarding his offspring:

> *. . . blessing I will bless you, and multiplying I will multiply your descendants as the stars of the heaven and as the sand which is on the seashore; and your descendants shall possess the gate of their enemies. In your seed all the nations of the earth shall be blessed, because you have obeyed my voice.* (Gen 22:17-18)

Here we see two classes of descendants, represented by the sand on the seashore and the stars of the heaven. Once again, we observe earthly and heavenly figures—material and spiritual. Matthew Henry sees the "heavenly" descendants as the Church, and Christ as the "seed" in which all nations shall be blessed:

> And so here is a promise,
>
> (1) Of the great blessing of the Spirit: In blessing, I will bless thee, namely, with that best of blessings the Gift of the Holy Ghost; the promise of the Spirit was that blessing of Abraham which was to come upon the Gentiles through Jesus Christ, Gal 3:14.
>
> (2) Of the increase of the church that believers, his spiritual seed, should be numerous as the stars of heaven.
>
> (3) Of spiritual victories: Thy seed shall possess the gate of his enemies. Believers, by their faith, overcome the world, and triumph over all the powers of darkness, and are more than conquerors. Probably Zacharias refers to this part of the oath (Luke 1:74), that we, being delivered out of the hand of our enemies, might serve him without fear. But the crown of all is the last promise.
>
> (4) Of the incarnation of Christ: In thy seed, one particular person that shall descend from thee (for he speaks not of many, but of one, as the apostle observes, Gal 3:16), shall all the nations of the earth be blessed, or shall bless themselves, as the phrase is (Isa 65:16). In him all may be happy if they will, and all that belong to him shall be so, and shall think themselves so. Christ is the great blessing of the world. Abraham was ready to give up his son for a sacrifice to the honor of God, and, on that occasion, God promised to give his Son a sacrifice for the salvation of man.
> (*Matthew Henry's Commentary on the Whole Bible*—Gen 22:15-19)

This foundational truth about the spiritual nature of the New Covenant cannot be overemphasized. It is upon this foundation that we will establish, in the following chapters, what the New Testament teaches about components of this covenant (e.g., the kingdom, the temple, the priesthood, Israel, etc.). Granted, the application of this truth can be taken too far, but usually just the opposite is true because we have failed to appreciate this concept fully. Again, we must ask ourselves, *Are we willing to receive it?* And if we are not, does that lessen the truth in the slightest? If the disciples had not been willing to receive John the Baptist as Elijah, would that have made him any less of a fulfillment of those Old Testament prophecies? If we balk at the idea of the New Covenant being primarily spiritual in nature, does that change the covenant in the least? We need look no further than the first-century Jews to answer that question. They balked at this idea—and died looking for the Messiah, who had been walking among them.

The End of the Old Covenant

Just as establishing the spiritual nature of the New Covenant is foundational, the end of the Old Covenant is also foundational in establishing the timing of the New Testament prophecies associated with its end. Therefore, if we can determine when the Old Covenant ended, we will have established when the prophecies associated with it took place. (Those prophecies will be the subject of Part II.) Returning to the allegory of Ishmael and Isaac, Paul makes another application to the two covenants and, more specifically, to the adherents of those two covenants:

> *Now we, brethren, as Isaac was, are children of promise. But, as he who was born according to the flesh then persecuted him who was born according to the Spirit, even so it is now. Nevertheless what does the Scripture say? "Cast out the bondwoman and her son, for the son of the bondwoman shall not be heir with the son of the freewoman." So then, brethren, we are not children of the bondwoman but of the free.* (Gal 4:28-31)

Paul wrote that just as Ishmael persecuted Isaac, so it was in his day—the children of the Old Covenant law persecuted the children of the New Covenant promise:

> *And Sarah saw the son of Hagar the Egyptian, whom she had borne to Abraham, scoffing. Therefore she said to Abraham, "Cast out this bondwoman and her son; for the son of this bondwoman shall not be heir with my son, namely with Isaac."* (Gen 21:9-10)

Under the inspiration of the Holy Spirit, Paul interprets the scoffing of Ishmael as persecution. Were the Christians of Paul's day (followers of the New Covenant) being persecuted by the Jews (followers of the Old Covenant)? Absolutely!

> *At that time [after Stephen's stoning by the Jews] a great persecution arose against the church which was at Jerusalem; and they were all scattered throughout the regions of Judea and Samaria, except the apostles. And devout men carried Stephen to his burial, and made great lamentation over him. As for Saul [a Jew], he made havoc of the church, entering every house, and dragging off men and women, committing them to prison.* (Acts 8:1-3)

> *. . . and when they [the Jewish council] had called for the apostles and beaten them, they commanded that they should not speak in the name of Jesus, and let them go.* (Acts 5:40)

> *Then Saul, still breathing threats and murder against the disciples of the Lord, went to the high priest and asked letters from him to the synagogues of Damascus, so that if he found any who were of the Way, whether men or women, he might bring them bound to Jerusalem.* (Acts 9:1-2)

> *Now about that time Herod the king stretched out his hand to harass some from the church. Then he killed James the brother of John with the sword. And because he saw that **it pleased the Jews**, he proceeded further to seize Peter also. . . . Now behold, an angel of the Lord stood by him, and a light shone in the prison; and he struck Peter on the side and raised him up, saying, "Arise quickly!" And his chains fell off his hands . . . . And when Peter had come to himself, he said, "Now I know for certain that the Lord has sent His angel, and has delivered me from the hand of Herod and from all **the expectation of the Jewish people**."* (Acts 12:1-3, 7, 11; cf. Acts 9:23; 13:45, 50; 14:19; 17:5, 13) (emphasis added)

So we see that Ishmael's persecution of Isaac was a foreshadowing, finding its substance in the Jews' persecution of the Church. Just as Ishmael and Isaac coexisted for a time, so the two covenants coexisted for a time — but only for a time. Ishmael was not destined to share in the inheritance with Isaac; therefore, he and Hagar were cast out. In the same manner, the Old Covenant, with its types and shadows, had no enduring place amongst the substance of the New Covenant. Though they coexisted during the days of the New Testament, the end of the Old Covenant was imminent:

For if what is passing away was glorious, what remains is much more glorious. (2 Cor 3:11)

In that He says, "A new covenant," He has made the first obsolete. Now what is becoming obsolete and growing old is ready to vanish away. (Heb 8:13)

These verses show us that the Old Covenant was still in existence during the days of the New Testament, but that it was growing old and ready to vanish away. Although the New Covenant had already been inaugurated, and the Old declared obsolete, the Old Covenant had not yet passed away. Ishmael was still dwelling with Isaac. Both the 2 Corinthians and Hebrews passages quoted above were written after Pentecost. Therefore we know that nothing in Christ's earthly ministry, nor the outpouring of the Holy Spirit, can be equated with the Old Covenant vanishing and Ishmael being cast out. The author of Hebrews helps us ascertain when that would occur:

The Holy Spirit was showing by this that the way into the Most Holy Place had not yet been disclosed as long as the first tabernacle was still standing. This is an illustration for the present time, indicating that the gifts and sacrifices being offered were not able to clear the conscience of the worshiper. (Heb 9:8-9 NIV)

The way into the spiritual Holy of Holies of the New Covenant could not be revealed until its physical type was removed. Just as David did not sit upon the throne of Israel until Saul (the former king) was removed, so the righteous could not enter into the heavenly throne room of God until the temple (the former dwelling place of God; Matt 23:21) was removed from existence. With the temple being the very icon of the Old Covenant, the Holy Spirit indicated that when it was removed, the Old Covenant was done away with, and those in the New Covenant would be sole heirs of God's promise. Having already established that the Old Covenant consisted of the material things (the temple, the priesthood, etc.), all we have to do is determine the time when these things "passed away." History establishes indisputably that time for us: The destruction of Jerusalem and the temple by Titus and the Roman army occurred in late AD 70. The Jewish historian Josephus informs us as to the totality of that destruction:

And where is now that great city, the metropolis of the Jewish nation, which was fortified by so many walls round about, which

55

had so many fortresses and large towers to defend it, which could hardly contain the instruments prepared for the war, and which had so many ten thousands of men to fight for it? Where is this city that was believed to have God himself inhabiting therein? It is now demolished to the very foundations, and hath nothing but that monument of it preserved, I mean the camp of those that hath destroyed it, which still dwells upon its ruins . . . . (*Wars*, 7.8)

. . . but for all the rest of the wall, it was so thoroughly laid even with the ground by those that dug it up to the foundation, that there was left nothing to make those that came thither believe it had ever been inhabited. This was the end which Jerusalem came to by the madness of those that were for innovations; a city otherwise of great magnificence, and of mighty fame among all mankind. (*Wars*, 6.1)

Hagar—who "*corresponds to Jerusalem which now is*" (that is, the physical city of Paul's time)—and Ishmael had been cast out. Physical Jerusalem was destroyed and the Old Covenant had passed away. Only the *Jerusalem above* remained.

Against the greater backdrop of the epistle of Galatians, we can see the persecution, at least in part, by the Judaizers. They wanted to pull Gentile believers back under the Law—back behind the veil of Moses. Because they did not comprehend the spiritual fulfillment of prophecy, they were still clinging to the physical type, and teaching others to do the same. Hence Paul's question to the Galatians: ". . . having begun in the Spirit, are you now being made perfect by the flesh?" Having entered His kingdom via grace and faith, are you now going to be perfected by returning to the works of the Law, which was only a type and shadow to begin with? In the next several chapters we will explore some of the spiritual fulfillments in the New Covenant of the physical types that were done away with when the Old passed away.

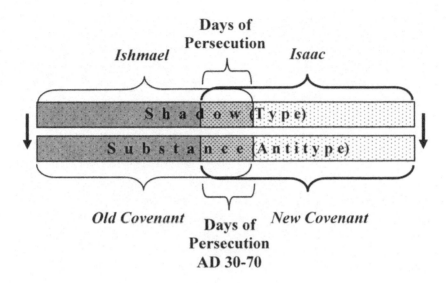

The New Covenant and the Kingdom

—〰—

As we noted earlier, the reason that the Jews missed Jesus as their Messiah is because they had misinterpreted Old Testament prophecies concerning His ministry. One of the primary areas of their misunderstanding was the nature of the kingdom of God. They were looking for a restoration of the kingdom as it was under David—a literal, physical kingdom, with the Messiah reigning on the throne of David in Jerusalem (as many prophecy experts are teaching today). A brief look at some Old Testament prophecies reveals how one could arrive at that understanding:

"Sing and rejoice, O daughter of Zion! For behold, I am coming and I will dwell in your midst," says the LORD. "Many nations shall be joined to the LORD in that day, and they shall become My people. And I will dwell in your midst. Then you will know that the LORD of hosts has sent Me to you. And the LORD will take possession of Judah as His inheritance in the Holy Land, and will again choose Jerusalem. Be silent, all flesh, before the LORD, for He is aroused from His holy habitation!" (Zech 2:10-13)

Thus says the LORD:
"I will return to Zion,
And dwell in the midst of Jerusalem.
Jerusalem shall be called the City of Truth,
The Mountain of the LORD of hosts,
The Holy Mountain." (Zech 8:3)

Now it shall come to pass in the latter days
That the mountain of the LORD's house
Shall be established on the top of the mountains,
And shall be exalted above the hills;
And all nations shall flow to it.
Many people shall come and say,
"Come, and let us go up to the mountain of the LORD,
To the house of the God of Jacob;
He will teach us His ways,
And we shall walk in His paths."
For out of Zion shall go forth the law,

And the word of the LORD from Jerusalem. (Isa 2:2-3)

At that time Jerusalem shall be called The Throne of the LORD, and all the nations shall be gathered to it, to the name of the LORD, to Jerusalem. No more shall they follow the dictates of their evil hearts. (Jer 3:17)

Christianity has been divided over the interpretation of these, and similar, passages. Are they to be understood as an earthly kingdom, with Jesus reigning bodily in physical Jerusalem? Or do they have instead a spiritual fulfillment, experienced through the reign of Christ in His church? Using the New Testament as a commentary on the subject, John F. Walvoord finds support for an earthly kingdom:

> The history of interpretation in the New Testament likewise gives credence to the fulfillment of the promise of the messianic kingdom. As brought out in connection with the Davidic covenant, Mary was assured that her child, Jesus, would sit on the throne of David and reign over the house of Jacob forever (Luke 1:32-33). Obviously, Mary shared the faith of other Jews that when the Messiah came he would set up his kingdom on earth. Gabriel's reaffirmation is evidence that this was God's interpretation of the Old Testament prophecies.
>
> Jesus himself affirmed that the disciples would sit on thrones judging the twelve tribes of Israel in the future kingdom (Luke 22:29-30). When the disciples asked Jesus about the time of the restoration of the kingdom of Israel in Acts 1:6, he told them that God had not revealed the time (v. 7), but he did not say that they were in error. (*Major Bible Prophecies* by John F. Walvoord, p. 118. © 1991 by John F. Walvoord. Used by permission of The Zondervan Corporation)

But do these New Testament passages *demand* a physical interpretation of the kingdom? Concerning the disciples sitting on thrones, Paul stated that believers were already sitting in the heavenly places in Christ Jesus (Eph 2:6), who is seated at the right hand of the Father (Eph 1:20; Col 3:1). Does this not at least open the door for spiritual thrones and, therefore, spiritual reigning and judgment?

Gabriel's reaffirmation to Mary is merely an echo of God's prophecies in the Old Testament. It does not interpret them at all. And while Jesus did not correct the disciples for asking about an earthly kingdom, neither did He affirm their position. The most we can discern from this passage is that the disciples (and Mary), being Jews, were still holding to the expectations that they had been taught from their youth—not whether those expectations were correct or incorrect:

> *Therefore, when they had come together, they asked Him, saying, "Lord, will You at this time restore the kingdom to Israel?" And He said to them, "It is not for you to know times or seasons which the Father has put in His own authority." (Acts 1:6-7)*

Why did the disciples ask this question? Because from their youth they were taught that Israel would one day be restored as the preeminent nation on earth. The Messiah would reign in Jerusalem, and all nations would come there to worship Him. But we must keep in mind that the same religious leaders who were teaching about a restored national Israel as the kingdom of God missed their Messiah. In answering the disciples' question, Christ neither rebukes them for asking amiss, nor does He confirm the correctness of their query.

We really cannot determine from Christ's answer whether the nature of the kingdom is to be physical or spiritual. Although He spoke to them of things pertaining to the kingdom for forty days after His resurrection (Acts 1:3), we have no record of those things. Based upon what the disciples had been taught and their present understanding, it was only natural for them to ask about a physical, restored Israel as the kingdom of God. But as we look past Acts 1:6 and beyond the day of Pentecost, we notice a significant change in their level of understanding. As we established in the chapter "The Veil of Moses," the disciples were fairly ignorant of the Scripture prior to Pentecost. After Pentecost, however, when they received the Holy Spirit, Who led the disciples into all truth, their teaching about the kingdom is quite noteworthy. It is closely tied with the teaching of the gospel:

> *But when they believed Philip as he preached the things **concerning the kingdom of God** and **the name of Jesus Christ**, both men and women were baptized. Then Simon himself also believed; and when he was baptized he continued with Philip, and was amazed, seeing the miracles and signs which were done. Now when the apostles who were at Jerusalem heard that Samaria had received **the word of God**, they sent Peter and John to them . . . . (Acts 8:12-14)*

> *And when they had **preached the gospel** to that city and made many disciples, they returned to Lystra, Iconium, and Antioch,*

strengthening the souls of the disciples, exhorting them to continue in the faith, and saying, "We must through many tribulations enter **the kingdom of God.**" (Acts 14:21-22)

But none of these things move me; nor do I count my life dear to myself, so that I may finish my race with joy, and the ministry which I received from the Lord Jesus, to testify to **the gospel of the grace of God.** *And indeed, now I know that you all, among whom I have gone preaching* **the kingdom of God**, *will see my face no more.* (Acts 20:24-25)
(emphases added)

Just as Jesus had before him, Paul also experienced rejection by the Jews for his teaching about the kingdom:

And he went into the synagogue and spoke boldly for three months, reasoning and persuading concerning **the things of the kingdom of God.** *But when some were hardened and did not believe, but spoke evil of the Way before the multitude, he departed from them and withdrew the disciples . . . .* (Acts 19:8-9)

So when they had appointed him a day, many came to him at his lodging, to whom he explained and solemnly testified **of the kingdom of God**, *persuading them concerning Jesus from both the Law of Moses and the Prophets, from morning till evening. And some were persuaded by the things which were spoken, and some disbelieved.* (Acts 28:23-24)
(emphases added)

Certainly the Jews would not have struggled with a teaching that affirmed their belief in a physical kingdom. Could it be that one of the *"mysteries of the kingdom of heaven,"* and one of the truths and *"things to come"* into which the Spirit guided the disciples, was the nature of the kingdom of God? If anyone understood the Jewish interpretation of the kingdom, it would have been Paul:

Then he said: "I am indeed a Jew, born in Tarsus of Cilicia, but brought up in this city at the feet of Gamaliel, taught according to the strictness of our fathers' law, and was zealous toward God as you all are today. I persecuted this Way to the death . . . ." (Acts 22:2-4)

For you have heard of my former conduct in Judaism, how I perse-cuted the church of God beyond measure and tried to destroy it.

And I advanced in Judaism beyond many of my contemporaries in my own nation, being more exceedingly zealous for the traditions of my fathers. (Gal 1:13-14)

Because of the different interpretations applied by Christianity and Judaism to the Old Testament, Paul persecuted the Christian Church *beyond measure.* Yet after his conversion to Christianity, it was *Paul's* teaching with which the Jews took issue. Note, however, how Paul connects his new understanding of doctrine back to the Old Testament:

And now I stand and am judged for the hope of the promise made by God to our fathers. (Acts 26:6)

*And it came to pass after three days that Paul called the leaders of the Jews together. So when they had come together, he said to them: "Men and brethren, though **I have done nothing against our people or the customs of our fathers**, yet I was delivered as a prisoner from Jerusalem into the hands of the Romans . . . ." **[Paul] explained and solemnly testified of the kingdom of God, persuading them concerning Jesus from both the Law of Moses and the Prophets**, from morning till evening.* (Acts 28:17, 23; emphasis added)

In the above passages, Paul still claims that his hope is in the promise to the fathers. He also states that he had done nothing against the customs of the fathers and based his teaching upon both the law of Moses and the Prophets. Yet something had obviously changed in his understanding of the Law and the Prophets for him to now be in disfavor with the Jews. Mauro elucidates this thought:

What then *is* the true and biblical "Hope of Israel"? To obtain a full answer to this question it is necessary that we search the Scriptures from beginning to end. But in order merely that we may have in mind a general idea of the answer while we pursue our study, it will suffice to refer to a few incidents in Paul's ministry, as recorded in the last chapters of Acts.

The subject is very prominent there, and indeed it was because of Paul's views and his preaching in regard thereto that he was furiously persecuted by the Jews, and was finally sent in chains to Rome. For we have his own testimony to "the chief of the Jews" at Rome, to whom, when he had called them together, he said: "For this cause therefore have I called for you, to see you and to speak with you; because that, for *the hope of Israel* I am bound with this chain" (Acts 28:17-20).

Inasmuch as what Paul had been preaching, both to the Jews and also to the Gentiles, was the gospel of Jesus Christ, and nothing else, it follows that the true "hope of Israel" is an essential part of that gospel; and therefore it is a matter regarding which we cannot afford to be mistaken.

The above quoted statement of Paul to the Jewish leaders at the imperial city is very illuminating. It shows, to begin with, that, whatever it was he had been preaching as "the hope of Israel," it was something *so contrary to the current Jewish notion thereof* that it caused the people to clamour for his death (Acts 22:22), and led to his being formally accused before the Roman Governor as "a pestilent fellow, and a mover of sedition among all the Jews throughout the world" (Acts 24:5). Had he been preaching what the Jews themselves believed to be, and what their rabbis had given them as, the true interpretation of the prophecies (namely, that God's promise to Israel was a kingdom of earthly character which should have dominion over all the world), they would have heard him with intense satisfaction. But what Paul and all the apostles preached was, that what God had promised afore by His prophets in the Holy Scriptures was a kingdom over which Jesus Christ of the seed of David should reign *in resurrection*, a kingdom which flesh and blood *cannot inherit*, a kingdom which does *not* clash with the duly constituted governments of this world, and one into which the Gentiles are called *upon terms of perfect equality* with Jews (Acts 13:23, 34; Acts 17:2,3,7; Rom 1:1-4; 14:17; 1 Cor 15:50; 1 Pet 1:12; cf. Luke 24:26).

Thus the teaching of Christ and His apostles in respect to the vitally important subject of the Kingdom of God, the hope of Israel, came into violent collision with that of the leaders of Israel; and because of this *He* was crucified and *they* were persecuted. (*The Hope of Israel: What Is It?*, pp. 10-12; emphasis in original)

Without doubt, the fact that Gentiles were coheirs of the kingdom was one of the mysteries of the kingdom (Eph 3:6). But how do we resolve that with a physical kingdom? Are believing Gentiles somehow considered physical "Jews"? How will Gentiles participate in a physical kingdom revolving around national Jews? Will the Church and the nation of Israel coexist? After "*He who has made both one, and has broken down the middle wall of separation . . . so as to create in Himself one new man from the two . . . that He might reconcile them both to God in one body through the cross"* (Eph 2:14-16), is He going to divide them into two separate entities again? Or will the Church be contained *within* the physical kingdom of Israel? If that is the case, and there is neither Jew nor Greek, then can we really call that kingdom *physical* or *national* Israel? Even that scenario seems to have "spiritual" connotations.

If one searches for the word "kingdom" from Acts to Revelation, it seems that there is only one passage that definitely speaks of a physical kingdom—Acts 1:6. After Pentecost, we do not see the kingdom spoken of in a physical context. Admittedly, not all usages are definitely spiritual either, but most seem to be. For example:

- *The kingdom is not eating and drinking* (Rom 14:17)
- *Flesh and blood cannot inherit the kingdom* (1 Cor 15:50)
- Delivered *from the power of darkness into the kingdom of His Son* (Col 1:13)
- Paul is preserved *for His <u>Heavenly</u> kingdom* (2 Tim 4:18)
- The *kingdom which cannot be shaken*, not made [in the physical realm] (Heb 12:27-28)

The bulk of the remaining "kingdom" passages refer to walking worthy of the kingdom and those deeds of the flesh that will prevent access to the kingdom. These passages clearly speak more to the spiritual walk of Christians on this earth, as opposed to existence in a future age. One is hard-pressed to find a single post-Pentecost passage that speaks of a physical kingdom. On the other hand, there are several that indicate that the kingdom possesses a spiritual nature, several that link it with the preaching of the gospel, and several that show that the Jews did not accept Paul's teaching about the kingdom (thus putting Paul's teaching at odds with their interpretation). The remaining passages, as we have noted, seem to lean toward our walk in the Spirit. When added together, we think that the scales tip heavily in favor of a spiritual kingdom.

Just as the Spirit directed the ministries of the disciples after Pentecost and ceased any need for the disciples to cast lots, is it too far-fetched to believe that the Spirit had also corrected the erroneous teaching of the Jewish leaders of the day regarding a physical kingdom? The Spirit had led them into "all truth" and taught them of the "things to come." Why would Jesus, Paul, and others even need to teach about the kingdom unless the current teaching of the Jewish leaders was either inadequate or inaccurate? Do we not observe, subsequent to Pentecost, the Spirit pulling back the veil, and, through the apostles, revealing the substance of the kingdom of the New Covenant?

In light of the many passages that indicate a nonphysical nature of God's kingdom, how do we resolve those passages that speak seemingly of physical things, such as sitting on thrones, ruling and reigning, or receiving authority over cities? How does anyone describe a realm—a dimension—that exists outside of our known physical universe? How can nonphysical things be described to beings that only know and understand physical things? Look at the problem Nicodemus had trying to understand the spiritual concept of salvation, of being "born again." He was a teacher of Israel, but he did not understand the things of heaven (John 3:10-12). To Nicodemus those mysteries had not been revealed. He still believed in a physical, earthly kingdom. Is it possible that we are doing the same with Old Testament prophecies? Consider this passage from Daniel:

"You, O king, were watching; and behold, a great image! This great image, whose splendor was excellent, stood before you; and its form was awesome. This image's head was of fine gold, its chest and arms of silver, its belly and thighs of bronze, its legs of iron, its feet partly of iron and partly of clay. You watched while a stone was cut out without hands, which struck the image on its feet of iron and clay, and broke them in pieces. Then the iron, the clay, the bronze, the silver, and the gold were crushed together, and became like chaff from the summer threshing floors; the wind carried them away so that no trace of them was found. And the stone that struck the image became a great mountain and filled the whole earth.

"This is the dream. Now we will tell the interpretation of it before the king. You, O king, are a king of kings. For the God of heaven has given you a kingdom, power, strength, and glory; and wherever the children of men dwell, or the beasts of the field and the birds of the heaven, He has given them into your hand, and has made you ruler over them all—you are this head of gold. But after you shall arise another kingdom inferior to yours; then another, a third kingdom of bronze, which shall rule over all the earth. And the fourth kingdom shall be as strong as iron, inasmuch as iron breaks in pieces and shatters everything; and like iron that crushes, that kingdom will break in pieces and crush all the others. Whereas you saw the feet and toes, partly of potter's clay and partly of iron, the kingdom shall be divided; yet the strength of

the iron shall be in it, just as you saw the iron mixed with ceramic clay. And as the toes of the feet were partly of iron and partly of clay, so the kingdom shall be partly strong and partly fragile. As you saw iron mixed with ceramic clay, they will mingle with the seed of men; but they will not adhere to one another, just as iron does not mix with clay. And in the days of these kings the God of heaven will set up a kingdom which shall never be destroyed; and the kingdom shall not be left to other people; it shall break in pieces and consume all these kingdoms, and it shall stand forever. Inasmuch as you saw that the stone was cut out of the mountain without hands, and that it broke in pieces the iron, the bronze, the clay, the silver, and the gold—the great God has made known to the king what will come to pass after this. The dream is certain, and its interpretation is sure." (Dan 2:31-45)

Most commentators recognize these successive kingdoms as Babylon, Medo-Persia, Greece and Rome. The final kingdom, which is established by God, is often assumed by many of these same commentators to be yet future; but if this is the case, why does the vision only acknowledge four empires, and then remain silent about all succeeding empires for the next 2,000 years and into the indefinite future? What about the British Empire or the global influence of the United States? Why such a gap? And where is any mention of a "revived" Roman Empire? Dispensationalism is somehow able to discern a gap in this passage between the legs of iron, which represent the old Roman Empire, and the feet, which supposedly represent this unnamed revived Roman Empire. Although nothing in this particular text lends itself to this interpretation, if it is indeed the correct interpretation one would expect the inspired authors of the New Testament to reveal this mystery. But we read nothing regarding either a gap or a revived Roman Empire in the New Testament. On the other hand, if the stone represents the Church as a spiritual kingdom (cut without hands—corresponding to Mount Zion of Hebrews 12:18ff), then it *was* established in the days of the Roman Empire, and there are no gaps. Thus the image represents earthly history from Daniel's day until the establishment of the Church. The fact that the final kingdom is made of stone, whereas the previous ones were made of various metals, also indicates a different nature for this kingdom. Interestingly, the New Testament authors pick up the theme of the Church being built of stone:

> . . . *you also, as **living stones**, are being built up a spiritual house, a holy priesthood, to offer up spiritual sacrifices acceptable to God through Jesus Christ.* (1 Pet 2:5)

*Now, therefore, you are no longer strangers and foreigners, but fellow citizens with the saints and members of the household of God, having been built on the foundation of the apostles and prophets, Jesus Christ Himself being the chief **cornerstone** . . . .* (Eph 2:19-20)
(emphases added)

After giving the parable of the wicked vinedressers, Christ alludes to Himself as the chief cornerstone:

Jesus said to them, "Have you never read in the Scriptures:
'The stone which the builders rejected
*Has become **the chief cornerstone**.*
This was the LORD's doing,
And it is marvelous in our eyes'?

Therefore I say to you, the kingdom of God will be taken from you and given to a nation bearing the fruits of it. And whoever falls on this stone will be broken; but on whomever it falls, it will grind him to powder." (Matt 21:42-44)

Note also that the kingdom is taken from the Jews and given to a nation bearing the fruits of it. National Israel had failed to represent God's plan of redemption to the world and bear the fruit of repentance among the nations. Thus the kingdom was taken from them and given to the Church, which would turn the whole world upside down with the gospel, making converts from every tongue, tribe, and nation. Those who fall upon Christ in repentance are broken by the conviction of their sinful natures. In contrast, those who refuse to acknowledge their need of Christ are crushed by the judgment of God and He becomes a rock of offense to them:

He will be as a sanctuary,
But a stone of stumbling and a rock of offense
To both the houses of Israel,
As a trap and a snare to the inhabitants of Jerusalem. (Isa 8:14)

Both the nations in Nebuchadnezzar's dream and the unrepentant individuals of Christ's parable of the wicked vinedressers were crushed into fine particles:

Then the iron, the clay, the bronze, the silver, and the gold were crushed together, and became like chaff from the summer threshing floors; the wind carried them away so that no trace of them was found. (Dan 2:35)

*And whoever falls on this stone will be broken; but on whomever
it falls, it will grind him to powder.* (Matt 21:44)

In both instances, the wicked are turned to dust that can be blown away;
the righteous, however, possess a firm foundation:

How often is the lamp of the wicked put out?
How often does their destruction come upon them,
The sorrows God distributes in His anger?
They are like straw before the wind,
And like chaff that a storm carries away. (Job 21:17-18)

You have also given me the necks of my enemies,
So that I destroyed those who hated me.
They cried out, but there was none to save;
Even to the LORD, but He did not answer them.
Then I beat them as fine as the dust before the wind;
I cast them out like dirt in the streets. (Ps 18:40-42; cf.
Prov 10:25, 30)

One of the reasons that Christ was a stone of stumbling and a rock
of offense was because He was proclaiming a spiritual kingdom: *My
kingdom is not of this world* (John 18:36); *the kingdom of God is within
you* (Luke 17:20-21). Clearly, the Jews missed their Messiah because they
were looking for a physical kingdom. The disciples, too, were looking
for a physical kingdom prior to Pentecost. After Pentecost, when they
received the Holy Spirit, Who led them "into all truth" and taught them of
the "things to come," their understanding of the nature of the kingdom was
enlightened, and they no longer taught of a physical kingdom. Rather, they
applied spiritual interpretations to Old Testament prophecies, used them to
describe the Church, and associated the kingdom with the gospel. The veil
had been removed.

In ca. AD 30, Jesus instructed the disciples, *"It is not for you to know
times or seasons which the Father has put in His own authority"* (Acts
1:7). After approximately 20 years of instruction by the Holy Spirit, Paul
wrote, *"concerning the **times and the seasons**, brethren, you have no need
that I should write to you. For you yourselves know perfectly that the day
of the Lord so comes as a thief in the night."* (1 Thess 5:1-2; emphases
added—the words *times* and *seasons* in both passages are the same in the
Greek.)

Was Paul saying that no man could know the times and the seasons?
No, what he says is, *"concerning the times and the seasons, brethren, you*

have no need that I should write to you." Is he then contradicting Jesus' statement in Acts that the disciples were not permitted to know the "times and seasons." Again, no. What Paul says is that the Thessalonians did not need to be *instructed* about the times and the seasons. Why? "*For you yourselves,*" Paul states, "*know perfectly . . . .*" Paul's words did not intimate that it was pointless to instruct them about something which no man could know. Rather, the implication is that the Thessalonians *already knew* and knew perfectly! Furthermore, Paul's statement implies that *had* there been a need for instruction, he could have supplied it (*no need that I should write you*). We feel that the implication is that Paul knew about the times and the seasons. If one man could know about them, then certainly others could.

Some may argue that what the disciples "*knew perfectly*" was that the day of the Lord would come "*as a thief in the night*;" that is, it would be unannounced and secretive. Therefore, the day of the Lord could not be known and there was no reason for Paul to waste his time on the subject. However, we must be careful to not equate "times and seasons" with "day of the Lord." Timing can be either general or specific. We agree that no one knows the *specific* timing of the day of the Lord, as Jesus Himself taught, "*but of that day and hour no one knows*" (Matt 24:36). However, Jesus also taught His disciples regarding events that would indicate the *general* timing of His return—"*when these things begin to happen, look up . . . because your redemption draws near*" (Luke 21:28)—thus indicating that the general timing could, and should, be known.

When we recall that one of the ministries of the Holy Spirit was to teach the disciples of the *things to come* (John 16:13), we feel that it is safe to assume that after some twenty years of that very teaching, the disciples would know perfectly that which could be known: the general timing, or "times and seasons," of God's redemptive plan. In our opinion, the scenario that better fits the two passages of Acts 1:7 and 1 Thessalonians 5 is that the Spirit had been removing the veil in the years following Pentecost. They now *understood* the times and the seasons, that the kingdom of God was spiritual in nature, that it was bound up in the day of the Lord, and that it was coming within their lifetimes. We believe that one of the mysteries of the kingdom/Church was not that the Church Age was a parenthetical age between "this age" and "the age to come." Rather, the Church Age *is* the "age to come" and the Gospel is the New Covenant.

That the kingdom of God was transferred from the physical realm of the Old Covenant to the spiritual realm of the New Covenant is attested by the "veiled" typology of Saul and David. In these two kings of Israel, we see a parallel to the allegory of Ishmael and Isaac. Where Ishmael and Isaac typified the two covenants, Saul and David typify the two kingdoms. In 1 Samuel 15, Saul was commanded to utterly destroy the Amalekites (v. 3); yet Saul and the people spared King Agag and the best of the livestock (v. 9). Because of Saul's disobedience, the kingdom of Israel was taken from him:

> *Because you have rejected the word of the L*ORD*,* **He also has rejected you from being king.** *(1 Sam 15:23)*

> *But Samuel said to Saul, "I will not return with you; for you have rejected the word of the L*ORD*, and* **the L**ORD **has rejected you from being king over Israel."** *As Samuel turned to go, Saul seized the edge of his robe, and it tore. So Samuel said to him, "***The L***ORD **has torn the kingdom of Israel from you today and has given it to your neighbor, who is better than you.** *Also the Glory of Israel will not lie or change His mind; for He is not a man that He should change His mind." (1Sam 15: 26-29 NASB95)*
> (emphases added)

This foreshadows the fact that the kingdom of God, which had been entrusted to national Israel, was also taken from them and given to someone "better":

> *"Hear another parable: There was a certain landowner who planted a vineyard and set a hedge around it, dug a winepress in it and built a tower. And he leased it to vinedressers and went into a far country. Now when vintage-time drew near, he sent his servants to the vinedressers, that they might receive its fruit. And the vinedressers took his servants, beat one, killed one, and stoned another. Again he sent other servants, more than the first, and they did likewise to them. Then last of all he sent his son to them, saying, 'They will respect my son.' But when the vinedressers saw the son, they said among themselves, 'This is the heir. Come, let us kill him and seize his inheritance.' So they took him and cast him out of the vineyard and killed him. Therefore, when the owner of the vineyard comes, what will he do to those vinedressers?" They said to Him, "He will destroy those wicked men miserably, and lease his vineyard to other vinedressers who will render to him the fruits in their seasons." Jesus said to them, "Have you never read in the Scriptures:*

'The stone which the builders rejected
Has become the chief cornerstone.
This was the LORD's doing,
And it is marvelous in our eyes'?

Therefore I say to you, the kingdom of God will be taken from ***you and given to a nation bearing the fruits of it.*** *And whoever* *falls on this stone will be broken; but on whomever it falls, it will* *grind him to powder." Now when the chief priests and Pharisees* *heard His parables, they perceived that He was speaking of them.* *But when they sought to lay hands on Him, they feared the multi-* *tudes, because they took Him for a prophet.* (Matt 21:33-46; emphasis added)

The religious leaders of the Jews realized that Christ had spoken this parable against them. The kingdom was to be taken from them. In fact, in Mark's account (12:1-12 NIV), they were so offended they wanted to arrest Jesus. But to whom was the kingdom to be given? Those children of Abraham represented by Isaac, the son of the promise—the Church:

Not everyone who says to Me, "Lord, Lord" will enter the kingdom *of heaven, but he who does the will of My Father who is in heaven* *will enter.* (Matt 7:21 NASB95)

He answered and said to them, "Because it has been given to you *to know the mysteries of the kingdom of heaven, but to them it has* *not been given."* (Matt 13:11)

The kingdom is not made up of any nationality, but of believers of all nations:

. . . and do not think to say to yourselves, "We have Abraham as *our father." For I say to you that God is able to raise up children* *to Abraham from these stones.* (Matt 3:9)

But it is not as though the word of God has failed. For they are *not all Israel who are descended from Israel . . . .* (Rom 9:6 NASB95)

There is neither Jew nor Greek, there is neither slave nor free, *there is neither male nor female; for you are all one in Christ* *Jesus.* (Gal 3:28)

That the kingdom was taken from national Israel and given to the church, *never to return to Israel,* is borne out by the typology of Saul. The kingdom of Israel was taken from Saul; it never returned to his lineage.

These typologies speak against the doctrine that the Church is merely a parenthetical gap in the administration of God's kingdom, and that it is only a matter of time before a physical kingdom is returned to Israel:

> *"Also **the Glory of Israel will not lie or change His mind; for He is not a man that He should change His mind.**"* (1 Sam 15:29 NASB95; emphasis added)

David, the newly anointed king, became the type of Christ, the man after God's own heart. Thus, the Messiah is called the "Son of David," not the "Son of Saul." After Saul disobeyed God, Samuel anointed David as king of Israel. Yet David did not ascend to the throne until after the death of Saul. In the interim, David respected Saul as God's anointed, even though David was persecuted by him.

We again see a picture of the New Covenant gospel coexisting with the Old Covenant law (Gal 4). The Jewish believers continued in their respect and observance of the law, even though the Jews persecuted them. Just as David waited on God to remove Saul from the throne, so the New Covenant waited for God to end the Old Covenant officially that the New might succeed it:

> *When He said, "A new covenant," He has made the first obsolete.* ***But whatever is becoming obsolete and growing old is ready to disappear.*** *(Heb 8:13 NASB95)*

> *The Holy Spirit is signifying this, that the way into the holy place has not yet been disclosed **while the outer tabernacle is still standing, which is a symbol for the present time**. (Heb 9:8-9 NASB95)*
> (emphases added)

Although the first covenant was obsolete, it had not yet disappeared. While the tabernacle (temple), which symbolized the Old Covenant, was still standing, the fullness of the New Covenant had not yet been disclosed. Once the temple was destroyed in AD 70, the Old Covenant ended forever, confirming the New Covenant as God's final phase of redemptive history.

During the Old Covenant when Israel asked for a king, God said that they had rejected Him from being King over them:

> *The LORD said to Samuel, "Listen to the voice of the people in regard to all that they say to you, for they have not rejected you, but they have rejected Me from being king over them." (1 Sam 8:7 NASB95)*

From the time that Israel rejected God as their King, until David ascended to the throne (even though he had been anointed much earlier), about forty years had elapsed:

> *"And afterward they asked for a king; so God gave them Saul the son of Kish, a man of the tribe of Benjamin, for forty years."* (Acts 13:21)

From the time that Israel rejected their Messiah (ca. AD 30), until the time that the Old Covenant was eradicated (AD 70), about forty years had elapsed. David, who is a type of Christ in the New Covenant, ascended the throne of the physical kingdom at 30 years of age. Likewise, Jesus, the fulfillment of that type, was about 30 years of age when He began preaching that the spiritual kingdom of God was at hand.

> *David was thirty years old when he began to reign, and he reigned forty years.* (2 Sam 5:4)

> *When He began His ministry, Jesus Himself was about thirty years of age* . . . . (Luke 3:23 NASB95)

Scripture declares that when Saul died, *"all his house died together"* (1 Chr 10:6). Consider the strength of the analogy of Scripture and the fact that Jesus prophesied the "death" of Jerusalem by saying, *"your house is left to you desolate"* (Matt 23:38).

Thus, in the transference of the physical kingdom from Saul to David, we see a foreshadowing of the spiritual kingdom transferred from national Israel to the spiritual Church. And just as we never see the physical kingdom returned from David's lineage back to the lineage of Saul, so we should not expect a spiritual kingdom to return to physical Israel. The kingdom of God is not physical, as Jesus Himself said: *My kingdom is not of this world . . . My kingdom is not of this realm* (John 18:36 NASB95); *The kingdom of God is not coming with signs to be observed* . . . (Luke 17:20 NASB95).

The kingdom was torn from the physical realm and delivered into the spiritual realm, never to return, as typified by the kingdom being torn from Saul. This is in stark contrast to what many teach today, saying that Jesus must return and establish a physical kingdom on the earth and sit physically on David's throne in Jerusalem.

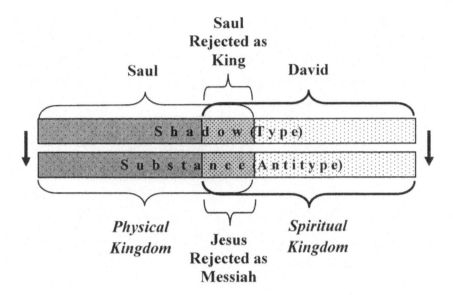

The New Covenant and the Temple

—ᴍ—

If there was a focal point to the Old Covenant, it was Jerusalem's temple. The temple was the centerpiece of the Levitical Law; therefore, all Jewish males were to appear before it three times a year (Deut 16:16). Within the temple, inside the Holy of Holies, the presence of God dwelt above the mercy seat of the Ark of the Covenant (Lev 16:2; Num 7:89). Even Christ's disciples were enamored by the structure:

> Then as He went out of the temple, one of His disciples said to Him, "Teacher, see what manner of stones and what buildings are here!" (Mark 13:1; cf. Matt 24:1)

Considering the temple's central role in the Old Covenant, it is reasonable to expect an equally central New Covenant counterpart. What could be more central to the gospel than the saints, the lambs of God—those who place their faith in the New Covenant? Consider the following passages:

> Do you not know that **you are the temple of God** and that the Spirit of God dwells in you? If anyone defiles the temple of God, God will destroy him. For the temple of God is holy, **which temple you are**. (1 Cor 3:16-17)

> Or do you not know that **your body is the temple of the Holy Spirit** who is in you, whom you have from God, and you are not your own? (1 Cor 6:19)

> And what agreement has the temple of God with idols? For **you are the temple of the living God**. (2 Cor 6:16; see also Eph 2:19-22; 1 Tim 3:15; 1 Pet 2:4-5)
> (emphases added)

In light of these passages, can there be any doubt that we, the saints of Christ, are the temple of the New Covenant? (We note that in a certain respect Christ is also the temple—John 2:19; Col 2:9; Rev 21:22.) Although none of the above passages quote from the Old Testament, it is not difficult to make the connection to Zechariah 6:

77

Take the silver and gold, make an elaborate crown, and set it on the head of Joshua the son of Jehozadak, the high priest. Then speak to him, saying, "Thus says the LORD of hosts, saying:

'Behold, the Man whose name is the BRANCH!
From His place He shall branch out,
And He shall build the temple of the LORD;
Yes, He shall build the temple of the LORD.
He shall bear the glory,
And shall sit and rule on His throne;
So He shall be a priest on His throne,
And the counsel of peace shall be between them both . . . .'"
(Zech 6:11-13)

This man, whose name is the BRANCH, is Jesus Christ:

There shall come forth a Rod from the stem of Jesse,
And a Branch shall grow out of his roots.
The Spirit of the LORD shall rest upon Him,
The Spirit of wisdom and understanding,
The Spirit of counsel and might,
The Spirit of knowledge and of the fear of the LORD.
(Isa 11:1-2; see also Isa 4:2; 53:2; Jer 23:5; 33:15; Zech 3:8.)

Interestingly, "Branch" is a messianic term:

. . . of the Messiah, a branch out of the root of the stem of Jesse (Isa 11:1), the "beautiful branch" (4:2), a "righteous branch" (Jer 23:5), "the Branch" (Zech 3:8; 6:12).
(*Easton's Bible Dictionary*—Branch)

As we read earlier in the New Testament, the temple that Christ built, and is continuing to build, is His Church. Jesus declared that He would build His Church (*. . . on this rock I will build My church, and the gates of Hades shall not prevail against it.* Matt 16:18), but the only reference that He ever made to constructing a temple was that of raising the temple of His body from the grave:

Jesus answered and said to them, "Destroy this temple, and in three days I will raise it up." Then the Jews said, "It has taken forty-six years to build this temple, and will You raise it up in three days?" But He was speaking of the temple of His body. (John 2:19-21)

Therefore, even though the New Testament does not quote Zechariah 6:12 in stating that the Church is the fulfillment of that prophecy, Scripture leaves us no other option. The prophecy states that the BRANCH, whom we believe to be Jesus, would build His temple. Jesus never spoke of building a physical temple (although He prophesied its destruction), but He did speak of building His Church. The New Testament authors confirm that the Church, and the individuals that comprise it, are indeed the temple and the house of God. Consider also the fact that the New Testament authors *never* mention the building of a future physical temple by Christ. Therefore, to interpret Zechariah 6:12 as a physical temple would be forcing that passage to stand against the teaching of the New Testament, when there is an obvious and fitting spiritual fulfillment available.

Once we acknowledge the spiritual nature of the temple in Zechariah 6:12, we have established a precedent that may be applied to other Old Testament prophetic passages about the temple. In fact, given that this precedent is clearly established by Scripture, must we not require the same level of scriptural support to force us to interpret other prophetic temple passages as referring to a *physical* temple? Having already demonstrated that neither Jesus nor the New Testament authors ever referred to the establishment of a future physical temple—rather, they equated the temple of God with the Church—where are we going to find the scriptural support for a future physical temple?

In his exhaustive volume *The Coming Last Days Temple*, popular Dispensationalist Dr. J. Randall Price argues against the spiritual temple position in several ways. One is by showing that, although Jesus cleansed the temple and foretold its destruction, He still revered it as "His Father's House." This, Price believes, demonstrates that Christ saw no inherent need to do away with the physical temple, but merely the corrupt system that ministered in it, thus leaving the door open for a future physical temple. However, the author of Hebrews claimed that the entire temple system was merely a copy and shadow of the heavenly system (Heb 8:5) and was obsolete and ready to vanish away (Heb 8:13).

Price also tries to demonstrate that Paul's doctrine did not preclude a future physical temple by showing that Paul too did not denigrate it, claiming that Paul's allegory of the Church as the temple referred only to the spiritual aspect of the physical temple. He develops four reasons why Paul might have used the temple metaphor for the Church, of which only the headings are given here:

- Paul's education in Jerusalem as a Pharisee
- Paul's journey to Jerusalem to learn from the apostles
- Paul's view of the church as sharing the same theological distinctives as the Jerusalem temple
- Paul's metaphorical use was consistent with the hermeneutics of first-century Judaism (Ibid., pp. 288-290)

We prefer another reason why Paul used the temple as a metaphor for the Church—he was inspired by the Holy Spirit to do so. We do not deny that Paul revered the temple, and even remained a practicing Jew subsequent to his conversion to Christianity. As we shall argue, the Church, as the spiritual temple of God, was anointed on Pentecost, even though it coexisted with the physical temple for forty years until God removed the physical temple during the destruction of Jerusalem in AD 70. This fits perfectly with the typology of David, who was anointed king, but still regarded Saul as "the Lord's anointed" until the day that God removed him from office. Though Paul revered the temple while it was standing, we cannot deny that he taught that the Old Covenant—of which their present-day Jerusalem and the temple were part and parcel—was a ministry of death, and was passing away.

Although it is not within the scope of this study to explore the various future temple scenarios, we acknowledge that many prophecy teachers see two future temples: one, called the "Tribulation Temple" which will be desecrated and destroyed by a future Antichrist, and another called the "Millennial Temple," which will be built by the Messiah. Having demonstrated that the New Testament authors provide inspired interpretations of Old Testament prophecies, we note that the New Testament does not provide so much as a hint—much less a direct prophecy—regarding *one* future temple, let alone two. However, since many associate Ezekiel's temple vision with a Millennial temple, we will examine that text briefly.

The Millennial Temple

Chapters 40-46 of Ezekiel describe Ezekiel's vision of God's future temple—future, that is, to Ezekiel, who saw this vision during Israel's captivity after Solomon's temple had been destroyed. Ezekiel watched while a man, whose appearance was like bronze, took painstaking measurements of the temple, its courtyards, gates, and structures. The sacrifices and feasts are also described in detail, very reminiscent of Moses' description of the tabernacle and its services in the book of Exodus. Does Ezekiel's temple belong to a yet future millennial period, as Price and others believe? There is certainly no New Testament support for a future physical temple, although some have equated it with the temple mentioned in Revelation. It is the belief of many, and of this author, that the temple mentioned in Revelation is one and the same with the temple that was destroyed in AD 70. (This theme will be explored further in Part II.) Putting the Revelation passages aside for the moment, we are left with no New Testament support for a future physical temple. Just as Jesus prophesied the destruction of the temple of His day, but never prophesied of a future rebuilt temple, neither do any of the New Testament authors mention a future physical temple. Hank Hanegraaff provides a significant quote from Colin Chapman's *Whose Holy City?*:

> The fall of Jerusalem is to be an act of divine judgment, compared in a shocking way to the judgment on Babylon described by Isaiah. What seems to be most significant, therefore, is that whereas the Old Testament prophets predicted judgment, exile *and* a return to the land, Jesus predicts destruction and exile, *but says nothing about a return to the land.* Instead of predicting the restoration of Israel, he speaks about the coming of the kingdom of God through the coming of the Son of Man. (*The Apocalypse* Code, p. 194; emphasis in original)

So we must ask ourselves, are the Ezekiel passages compelling enough that we *must* understand them to be of a future physical temple that is for some reason outside the scope of the New Testament? On the other hand, perhaps we should be asking ourselves if the Ezekiel passages could find a fulfillment in the past, or in the spiritual temple of God, the Church!

In *The Hope of Israel: What Is It?*, Philip Mauro dealt quite extensively with this very topic. We offer several quotes from chapter XII of that work, in which he discusses the "millennial" temple of Ezekiel's latter chapters (note that Mauro wrote prior to 1948, before Israel was reestablished as a nation; hence his reference to *if* Israel occupies the land of Canaan again):

IS IT THE PLAN OF A TEMPLE FOR THE MILLENNIUM?

> One solution of the problem we are studying (a solution much favored in certain quarters) is that Ezekiel's vision relates to Millennial times; that Israel will then be reconstituted as a nation on earth, and as such will reoccupy the land of Palestine; and

that then the temple shown to Ezekiel will be erected on Mt. Moriah, and the system of worship described in these chapters will be instituted and carried on. This view is characteristic of that peculiar system of interpreting the Scriptures [dispensationalism] which we are examining in the present volume; for, according to the principles thereof, all difficulties in the prophetic Word, and all problems of like nature are solved by the simple expedient of postponing their fulfillment to the Millennial age. Thus the Millennium becomes the convenient and promiscuous dumping place of all portions of Scripture which offer any difficulty; and the unhappy consequence is that many prophecies which were fulfilled at the first coming of Christ, or are being fulfilled in this age of the gospel, and many Scriptures, such as the Sermon on the Mount, which apply directly to the saints of this dispensation, are wrenched out of their proper place, and are relegated to a distant future, much to the loss of the people of God and to the dislocation of the Scriptures as a whole.

The "postponement" system doubtless owes the popularity it enjoys to the circumstance that its method is both safe and easy. It is *safe* because, when a fulfillment of prophecy is relegated to the Millennium, it cannot be conclusively refuted until the time comes. All date-setting schemes owe their measure of popularity to the same fact. It is *easy* because it relieves the Bible student of the trouble of searching for the meaning and application of difficult passages.

But, coming to the special case in hand, which is illustrative of many others, we are bold to say, and undertake herein to show, that there are insurmountable objections to the view that Ezekiel's temple is for Millennial times.

To begin with, there is no proof that, even if Israel does indeed occupy the land of Canaan again as an earthly nation, they will restore the ancient system of temple-worship, either according to the plan shown to and described by Ezekiel, or according to any other plan. On the contrary, we maintain that the Scriptures plainly forbid that supposition. For it was by God's own hand that the ancient system of worship was abolished and obliterated; and the obliteration thereof was for reasons so closely connected with the redeeming work of the Lord Jesus Christ, that to reestablish it again would be to do dishonor to that work and its results. (*The Hope of Israel: What Is It?*, pp. 114-116—emphasis in original)

Although Mauro raises several issues with relegating Ezekiel's temple to the millennium, perhaps the most potent is that of the last sentence, which bears repeating:

> For it was by God's own hand that the ancient system of worship was abolished and obliterated; and the obliteration thereof was for reasons so closely connected with the redeeming work of the Lord Jesus Christ, that to reestablish it again would be to do dishonor to that work and its results.

Truly, one has to ask what purpose or place a revived system of types and shadows would have in the presence of the spiritual fulfillment of those types? Especially when the fulfillment is the Lamb of God Himself! While the Jews may not care about dishonoring Christ, clearly Christians should have no desire to see the Mosaic Law reestablished, unless they see it as necessary for the fulfillment of Bible prophecy. We hope to demonstrate that a revival of the Mosaic Law is *not* necessary for the fulfillment of Bible prophecy.

Mauro establishes that Ezekiel's temple is to be identified only with the Old Covenantal system of sacrifice:

> At present we wish only to point out that the most conspicuous features of the temple shown in this vision are the various appointments for *the slaughter of animals*, and for offering the same upon the altar, sprinkling their blood, etc. Thus we find a description of the tables, eight in number, for slaying the burnt offerings and other sacrifices, and upon which "they laid the instruments wherewith they slew the burnt offering and the sacrifice" (40:38-43). Therefore, in the clear light of the Epistle to the Hebrews and of all Scripture pertaining to the Sacrifice of Christ, it is impossible to place this temple in any dispensation subsequent to Calvary. (Ibid., p. 117; emphasis in original)

Mauro even answers those who see these revived types existing in some sort of "memorial" manner:

> But an attempt has been made to avoid this objection and to make possible the locating of Ezekiel's temple in the Millennium, by saying that the sacrifice of animals in that era will be only for a "reminder" or a "memorial" of the former days. But this is a

very weak effort of the imagination. For what warrant have we for supposing that God would require any memorial of those sacrifices in which, even in the time when they were needed, He had no pleasure? And how preposterous is the idea that He would require the slaughter of innumerable creatures merely to revive the memory of those other defective sacrifices which could never take away sins! Surely they who advance this idea have forgotten the Scripture, which they all apply to the Millennium, and which says, "They shall not hurt nor destroy in all My holy mountain" (Isa 11:9).

But the passage itself completely refutes this idea; for it plainly declares that the sacrifices there specified were not at all for a remembrance or a memorial, but were for the very different purposes of *sin* offerings, *trespass* offerings, *peace* offerings, etc.; also for *cleansing* the house, *making reconciliation* both for the princes of Israel and for the people, and the like. *All the five offerings of the Levitical system are mentioned by name* (40:39, 42:13, 43:27; 45:17; 46:20); and provision is made for sprinkling the blood of the sin offering upon the corners of the altar, upon the posts of the house and court in order to cleanse them (43:20; 45:18,19). In a word the sacrifices are the *Levitical sacrifices*, and they are expressly declared to be for the identical purposes thereof. Hence it is impossible to locate this temple, as an actual structure (apart from the spiritual signification thereof), in any other era than that of the law. (Ibid., pp. 117-118; emphasis in original)

We would add to Mauro's argument the fact that Christ has already instituted the memorial for His sacrifice, known as the Lord's Supper. Here the bread and the wine, not animal sacrifices, memorialize His body and blood, broken and shed for those who partake in the New Covenant (Luke 22:19-20).

We note that some Dispensationalists, in order to stay true to their "literal" interpretation of the Bible, acknowledge that these "millennial" sacrifices are for the purpose of atonement. Thomas Ice writes:

The sacrifices of the millennial Temple will not be a return to the Mosaic Law, since that Law has forever been fulfilled and discontinued through Christ (Rom 6:14-15; 7:1-6; 1 Cor 9:20-21; 2 Cor 3:7-11; Gal 4:1-7; 5:18; Eph 2-3; Heb 7:12; 8:6-7, 13; 10:1-14). Instead it will be a new Law, containing a mixture of Mosaic type new laws under the jurisdiction of the New Covenant (Heb 7:12).

The millennial system will have Jesus the Messiah physically present instead of the Shechinah glory presence in conjunction with the ark of the covenant; a new Law instead of the Mosaic Law; a new priestly order from the sons of Zadok (Ezek 40:46; 43:19; 48:11) instead of the Levites; a new Temple measuring one mile square (Ezek 40:48-41:26) instead of the much smaller Solomonic model.

. . . Critics of future millennial sacrifices seem to assume that all sacrifices, past and future, always depict Christ's final sacrifice for sin. They do not! There were various purposes for sacrifice in the Bible. An overwhelming majority of sacrifices under the Mosaic system were for purification of the priests and objects used in various rites. This is why atonement can be said in the past to be effective, yet still need Christ's future sacrifice, because many of the sacrifices did atone ceremonially, cleansing participants and objects in Temple ritual. Just as we never finish the task of washing cloths [*sic*], ceremonial cleansing was an ongoing need. The same is clearly the case in Ezekiel. In Ezekiel 43:20 and 26, the atonement is specifically directed at cleansing the altar in order to make it ritually fit for sacrifice. . . . Dr. Jerry Hullinger has worked through all of the related issues involved in an interpretation of the millennial sacrifices and tells us the following:

> . . . a solution that maintains dispensational distinctives, deals honestly with the text of Ezekiel, and in no way demeans the work Christ did on the cross. This study suggests that animal sacrifices during the millennium will serve primarily to remove ceremonial uncleanness and prevent defilement from polluting the temple envisioned by Ezekiel. This will be necessary because the glorious presence of Yahweh will once again be dwelling on earth in the midst of a sinful and unclean people.

> Because of God's promise to dwell on earth during the millennium (as stated in the New Covenant), it is necessary that He protect His presence through sacrifice . . . (*Literal Sacrifices in the Millennium*: http://www.pre-trib. org/article-view.php?id=39)

To actually believe that the Creator of the Universe needs to have His presence protected through the means of some animal's blood stretches credulity beyond limit. Is not Jesus "fully God"? Did He not spend some 33 years on this earth with no need to have His presence protected by animal sacrifices? On the contrary, rather than needing His presence protected, He guaranteed our presence before the Father with His own blood!

While acknowledging that there may be further spiritual significance to Ezekiel's temple, Mauro makes a strong case for the physical nature of its existence within the era of the law. Knowing that the era of the law, the Old Covenant, ended in AD 70, can we find Ezekiel's temple within that era? We quote again from Mauro:

> First we would point out that, in the sixth year of Jehoiachin's captivity, that is to say, *while Solomon's temple was yet standing*, Ezekiel had a wonderful vision in which he saw the glory of the Lord departing from the house (8:1; 10:18). The vision of the *new* temple was 19 years later; for Ezekiel is careful to record that it was "the fourteenth year *after* that the city was smitten" (40:1,2). . . .

> What then was the immediate purpose of this vision? We think this question admits of a simple answer in the light of the passage itself and that of other Scriptures.

> Ezekiel prophesied during the captivity. That captivity was to be of seventy years duration, as predicted by Jeremiah. At its end the captives were to return and *re-build the city and the temple*. This new temple was to serve as the sanctuary of God until Christ should come. God's plan had always been to give to His people the exact pattern of the sanctuary they were to build for His Name. To Moses He had shown the pattern of the tabernacle, giving him at the same time the strictest injunctions to make every detail in exact accordance with that pattern. Likewise to David God had revealed the pattern of the temple which was to be built at Jerusalem, with all its appointments, vessels of service, etc. "All this," says David, "the Lord made me understand in writing by His hand upon me, even all the works of this pattern" (1 Chr 28:11-19).

> And now again a house was about to be built for the Name of the Lord in Jerusalem. Therefore, having in mind His invariable method in such case, we should expect to find at this period a revelation from heaven of the pattern to be followed in the building of that house. And just here we *do* find the revelation from God of the completed pattern and appointments of a temple, with directions to the prophet to show the same to the house of Israel.

Furthermore we find that even as Moses was admonished to make all things like unto the pattern shown him "in the mount," so Ezekiel was taken to "a very high mountain" where this pattern was shown him; and he was bidden to set his heart upon all that should be shown him, and to declare all he should see to the house of Israel (40:3,4; 44:5). . . .

So far as we are aware there is no evidence now available as to the plan of the temple built in the days of Ezra. Herod the Great had so transformed it in the days of Christ, though without interrupting the regular services and sacrifices, as to destroy all trace of the original design. That question, however, which we cannot now answer, does not affect the question of the purpose for which the pattern was revealed to Ezekiel.

(*The Hope of Israel*, pp. 117, 118-120, 121; emphasis in original)

Granted, Mauro's premise does not agree with some of the current "popular" interpretations, but in light of the fact that neither Jesus nor the New Testament authors teach of a future physical temple, perhaps we should reexamine the "popular" interpretations. It only makes sense that if God revealed specific plans to Moses about the tabernacle, and to David about the first temple, that He would do the same regarding the second temple, especially when we consider that this pattern was incorporated into the New Covenant's spiritual temple, the Church. One of the titles of the Church is the "bride" of Christ, which is synonymous with the New Jerusalem in the book of Revelation. Just as the specific details of the tabernacle and the temple of the Old Covenant were revealed from heaven, so the details of the spiritual temple, the bride of Christ and the New Jerusalem, are revealed from heaven:

*Then I, John, saw the holy city, New Jerusalem, coming down out of heaven from God, **prepared as a bride adorned for her husband** . . . .* (Rev 21:2)

*Then one of the seven angels who had the seven bowls filled with the seven last plagues came to me and talked with me, saying, "Come, **I will show you the bride**, the Lamb's wife." And he carried me away in the Spirit to **a great and high mountain, and showed me the great city, the holy Jerusalem**, descending out of heaven from God, having the glory of God. Her light was like a most precious stone, like a jasper stone, clear as crystal. Also she had a great and high wall with twelve gates, and twelve angels at the gates, and names written on them, which are the names of* *the twelve tribes of the children of Israel: three gates on the east, three gates on the north, three gates on the south, and three gates on the west.*

Now the wall of the city had twelve foundations, and on them were the names of the twelve apostles of the Lamb. And he who talked with me had a gold reed to measure the city, its gates, and its wall. The city is laid out as a square; its length is as great as its breadth. And he measured the city with the reed: twelve thousand furlongs. Its length, breadth, and height are equal. Then he measured its wall: one hundred and forty-four cubits, according to the measure of a man, that is, of an angel. The construction of its wall was of jasper; and the city was pure gold, like clear glass. The foundations of the wall of the city were adorned with all kinds of precious stones: the first foundation was jasper, the second sapphire, the third chalcedony, the fourth emerald, the fifth sardonyx, the sixth sardius, the seventh chrysolite, the eighth beryl, the ninth topaz, the tenth chrysoprase, the eleventh jacinth, and the twelfth amethyst. The twelve gates were twelve pearls: each individual gate was of one pearl. And the street of the city was pure gold, like transparent glass. (Rev 21:9-21)
(emphases added)

Admittedly, there appears to be some confusion in the typology at first glance, because in the very next verse John states, *"but I saw no temple in it, for the Lord God Almighty and the Lamb are its temple."* Who is the temple—the Church, or God? We must remember that types and shadows are limited in their ability to represent the true article. We have already established that the New Testament authors equated the Church with the spiritual fulfillment of the temple in the New Covenant. Just as God's presence dwelt among the Israelites in the temple, so the presence of His Holy Spirit now dwells within us. When John, in the peculiar apocalyptic language of the Jews, expands the typology of the Church from being a temple, to being the heavenly Jerusalem, it is only fitting that God would be the temple within that city, for that is where His presence dwelt in the physical type. The fact that there is no temple in John's vision only confirms that the Old Covenant was to pass away. There was no longer to be a mediatory system between God and man, *"for there is one Mediator between God and men, the Man Christ Jesus"* (1 Tim 2:5).

For the purpose of our study, the point of this Revelation passage is the description of the detail and design of the heavenly Jerusalem. As previously stated, this heavenly Jerusalem is also the Bride of Christ, the Church and the spiritual temple of the New Covenant. Thus we see the pattern of giving detailed information of the design of both the tabernacle and the temple to Moses and David, culminating in the description of the heavenly Jerusalem given to John. Therefore, if the design given to Ezekiel was *not* for the rebuilding of Solomon's temple (which had been destroyed), then that pattern is broken. Note also that, just as with Moses and Ezekiel, John was taken up on a mountain to receive the description of the temple (Bride of Christ).

Perhaps none of the above points compel us to remove Ezekiel's temple from some future millennium. Taken as a whole, however, we believe that we are compelled at least to demand *explicit* scriptural statements that require that Ezekiel's temple be put into a future age, especially when none of the New Testament authors mention it. And we see no such references to either a future temple(s) or a future age other than that of the gospel. (We will consider the millennium in a later chapter.)

Mauro mentioned that although the actual structure of the temple belonged to the era of the law, it might still have "spiritual signification." We should expect nothing less, seeing that our study to this point has been centered upon those very "spiritual significations."

The Day of Pentecost—In the Upper Room?

A premise that is gaining acceptance among Christian scholars is that the disciples were not in the upper room when the Holy Spirit fell upon them at Pentecost, but rather in the temple. There are several reasons for believing this to be the case. All that the Scriptures tell us is that the eleven apostles were staying in "the upper room":

> *And when they had entered, they went up into the upper room where they were staying: Peter, James, John, and Andrew; Philip and Thomas; Bartholomew and Matthew; James the son of Alphaeus and Simon the Zealot; and Judas the son of James.* (Acts 1:13)

It is doubtful that, even if their room could have accommodated one hundred-twenty people, that is where they would have been on the day of Pentecost. As Mauro observes, there was, in fact, but *one place* in the city of Jerusalem where devout Jews, of whatever sect, would have congregated on that morning—in the temple. Just prior to His ascension, Jesus told His disciples to wait in Jerusalem for the promise of the Father. Luke records in his Gospel that after watching their Lord ascend, the disciples returned to Jerusalem and were in the temple continually:

> *And they worshipped Him, and returned to Jerusalem with great joy, and were continually in the Temple, praising and blessing God.* (Luke 24:52-53)

In Acts, Luke informs us that the disciples were continuing, up to the day of Pentecost, in one accord and in one place. Since he has already informed us that they were in the temple continually, this must be their place of gathering in Acts as well, since they could not be in two different places *continually*:

> *These all continued with one accord in prayer and supplication, with the women and Mary the mother of Jesus, and with His brothers.* (Acts 1:14)

> *When the Day of Pentecost had fully come, they were all with one accord in one place.* (Acts 2:1)

Even if the upper room could have accommodated one hundred-twenty people, it surely could not have held three thousand. Thus we see the early Church continuing daily in the temple, just as the disciples had been doing since Christ's ascension (Acts 2:46). Can there be any doubt that the place where the disciples were gathered, all in one accord, was not the upper room, but within the temple complex? It must be remembered that the temple complex was quite large, with many side chambers for just such gatherings. Thus, the spiritual temple, the Church, was birthed within the physical temple complex. Mauro states that *the material House of God served as the womb for the spiritual House.* This is in perfect harmony with our study. God's presence, which dwelt in the Old Covenant temple, was now descending upon His New Covenant temple; not only was the physical temple a type of the spiritual one, it was its birthplace!

Thus we see that, for a while, the two *coexisted*—the physical temple with the spiritual temple. Just as Ishmael and Isaac coexisted for a short time, so did the Old Covenant and the New, Israel after the flesh and the Israel of God, and the physical temple and the spiritual temple. We will return to this thought, but we must conclude the spiritual application of Ezekiel's temple.

In Ezekiel 47, Ezekiel is shown a vision of water flowing from under the threshold of the temple. As the waters of healing flow from the temple, they get deeper:

And it shall be that every living thing that moves, wherever the rivers go, will live. There will be a very great multitude of fish, because these waters go there; for they will be healed, and everything will live wherever the river goes. (Ezek 47:9)

These waters bear a striking resemblance to the waters proceeding from the throne of God in Revelation:

And he showed me a pure river of water of life, clear as crystal, proceeding from the throne of God and of the Lamb. In the middle of its street, and on either side of the river, was the tree of life, which bore twelve fruits, each tree yielding its fruit every month. The leaves of the tree were for the healing of the nations. (Rev 22:1-2)

Zechariah speaks of "living waters" flowing from Jerusalem (Zech 14:8), and Joel of a fountain flowing from the house of the LORD (Joel 3:18). Since we have no grounds for a physical temple after AD 70, and since these prophecies were not seen as being fulfilled in the earlier physical temple, can we not assign them to the spiritual temple? This is, we feel, the significance of the Holy Spirit falling upon the disciples at the temple, as Mauro observes:

As with respect to Zechariah's prophecy concerning the "living waters" (Zech 14:8), . . . so with respect to this vision of Ezekiel, we confidently submit that the fulfillment thereof is in *the living waters of the gospel*; which began, on the day of Pentecost, to flow out from the Temple at Jerusalem. Our Lord uses the expression "rivers of living water," in John 7:38; and the meaning of the expression is given in the next verse: "But this spake He *of the Spirit*, which they that believe on Him should receive." This explanation controls the passage we are considering. (Ibid., p. 122; emphasis in original)

That these living waters of healing are the gospel message in the power of the Holy Spirit seems to be attested by the following:

Therefore with joy you will draw water
From the wells of salvation. (Isa 12:3)

Jesus answered and said to her, "If you knew the gift of God, and who it is who says to you, 'Give Me a drink,' you would have asked Him, and He would have given you living water." The woman said to Him, "Sir, You have nothing to draw with, and the well is deep.

91

Where then do You get that living water? Are You greater than our father Jacob, who gave us the well, and drank from it himself, as well as his sons and his livestock?" Jesus answered and said to her, "Whoever drinks of this water will thirst again, but whoever drinks of the water that I shall give him will never thirst. But the water that I shall give him will become in him a fountain of water springing up into everlasting life." (John 4:10-14)

On the last day, that great day of the feast, Jesus stood and cried out, saying, "If anyone thirsts, let him come to Me and drink. He who believes in Me, as the Scripture has said, out of his heart will flow rivers of living water." But this He spoke concerning the Spirit, whom those believing in Him would receive; for the Holy Spirit was not yet given, because Jesus was not yet glorified. (John 7:37-39)

And the Spirit and the bride say, "Come!" And let him who hears say, "Come!" And let him who thirsts come. Whoever desires, let him take the water of life freely. (Rev 22:17)

We feel that the Church, as the custodian of the gospel, is the temple to which many peoples will come for instruction from the Lord. Zion, the mountain of the Lord, is the heavenly Jerusalem, the mountain that cannot be touched:

*In the last days
the mountain of the LORD's temple will be established
as chief among the mountains;
it will be raised above the hills,
and all nations will stream to it.*

Many peoples will come *and say,*

*"Come, let us go up to the mountain of the LORD,
to the house of the God of Jacob.*
He will teach us his ways,
*so that we may walk in his paths."
The law will go out from Zion,
the word of the LORD from Jerusalem.* (Isa 2:2-3 NIV)

*For you have not come to **the mountain that may be touched** and that burned with fire, and to blackness and darkness and tempest, and the sound of a trumpet and the voice of words, so that those who heard it begged that the word should not be spoken to them*

*anymore. . . . **But you have come to Mount Zion** and to the city of the living God, **the heavenly Jerusalem**, to an innumerable company of angels, to the general assembly and church of the firstborn who are registered in heaven, to God the Judge of all, to the spirits of just men made perfect, to Jesus the Mediator of the new covenant, and to the blood of sprinkling that speaks better things than that of Abel.* (Heb 12:18-24)
(emphases added)

Whereas the nation of Israel used to be God's representatives on earth, those in the Church are now His ambassadors of the New Covenant gospel, reconciling unbelievers to God:

*So Jesus said to them again, "Peace to you! As the Father has sent Me, **I also send you.**"* (John 20:21)

***Now then, we are ambassadors for Christ**, as though God were pleading through us. . . .* (2 Cor 5: 20)

Truly, all nations are coming to that "temple." Thus, we see the Church as not only the fulfillment of the typological Old Covenant temple, but also the fulfillment of prophetic passages regarding the temple. As we mentioned at the outset of our study, it was the Jews' misinterpretation of these and similar passages that caused them to miss their fulfillment.

We now return to the subject of the coexistence of the physical temple and the spiritual temple. As we established previously, the Old Covenant was passing away (2 Cor 3:11; Heb 8:13). The New Covenant, on the other hand, is to be everlasting:

*Now may the God of peace who brought up our Lord Jesus from the dead, that great Shepherd of the sheep, through the blood of the **everlasting** covenant . . . .* (Heb 13:20; emphasis added)

Accordingly, we should expect to see an end to the physical temple, while the spiritual temple remains eternal:

And Jesus answered and said to him, "Do you see these great buildings? Not one stone shall be left upon another, that shall not be thrown down." (Mark 13: 2)

And I also say to you that you are Peter, and on this rock I will build My church, and the gates of Hades shall not prevail against it. (Matt 16:18)

Jesus not only predicted the destruction of the physical temple, but also the prevailing of the spiritual temple—His Church. As previously mentioned, the physical temple was destroyed in AD 70. Josephus says that from the time of David, who made preparations to build the temple, until its destruction by Titus, was 1,179 years. The spiritual temple has lasted nearly 2,000 years and is still growing.

Lastly, as we have with the transition of the two covenants and the two kingdoms, we look for a typological illustration of the two temples. We do not see one as easily recognizable as that of Ishmael and Isaac, nor of Saul's robe's being torn, but we do believe that we are not left wanting, and that we need not twist the Scripture to make it fit. We will let the reader be the judge.

We have already seen that the Old Covenant was a "ministry of death," for it was of the letter of the law that killed (2 Cor 3:6-7). The New Covenant gospel, being of the life-giving Spirit, was also known as the "gospel of peace":

*And how shall they preach unless they are sent? As it is written: "How beautiful are the feet of those who preach the **gospel of peace**, Who bring glad tidings of good things!"* (Rom 10:15)

*. . . and having shod your feet with the preparation of the **gospel of peace** . . . .* (Eph 6:15)

*The word which God sent to the children of Israel, **preaching peace through Jesus Christ** . . . .* (Acts 10:36)

*Grace to you and **peace** from God our Father and the Lord Jesus Christ.* (Rom 1:7)

*For to be carnally minded is death, but **to be spiritually minded is life and peace** . . . .* (Rom 8:6)
(emphases added)

Although David received instructions from the Lord (1 Chr 28:11-19) and made preparations to build the temple, he was not allowed to do so because he had shed blood:

Then King David rose to his feet and said, "Hear me, my brethren and my people: I had it in my heart to build a house of rest for the ark of the covenant of the LORD, and for the footstool of our God, and had made preparations to build it. But God said to me, 'You shall not build a house for My name, because you have been a man of war and have shed blood.'" (1 Chr 28:2-3)

Thus, David's son Solomon was to be the one to build the temple:

> *Now He said to me, "It is your son Solomon who shall build My house and My courts; for I have chosen him to be My son, and I will be his Father." (1 Chr 28:6)*

Incidentally, Solomon's name means "peaceful":

> Old Testament: 8010 Shelomoh (shel-o-mo'); from Old Testament: 7965; peaceful; Shelomah, David's successor:
> KJV — Solomon.
> (*Strong's Numbers and Concordance with Expanded Greek-Hebrew Dictionary*)

So we see David associated with death in the shedding of blood, just as the Old Covenant was a "ministry of death." Because he was a man of blood, David was not allowed to build the temple; likewise, the Old Covenant could not "build" the Church because it was a "ministry of death." David, however, was allowed to prepare for the building of the temple, and that very same temple and its Old Covenant economy prepared for the Church and the New Covenant by foreshadowing them. And just as the physical temple was built by Solomon (Peaceful), so the New Covenant was the gospel of peace, and the spiritual temple was built and indwelt by the Prince of Peace:

> *For unto us a Child is born,*
> *Unto us a Son is given;*
> *And the government will be upon His shoulder.*
> *And His name will be called*
> *Wonderful, Counselor, Mighty God,*
> *Everlasting Father, **Prince of Peace**. (Isa 9:6; emphasis added)*

This is in stark contrast to those in Christianity who wait with bated breath for the Jews to rebuild their temple and reestablish animal sacrifices, and even support that purpose financially.

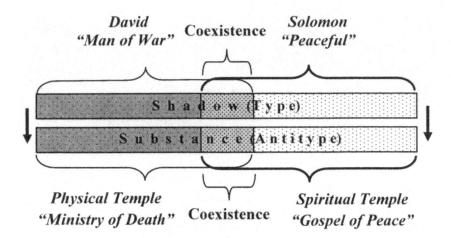

The New Covenant and the Priesthood

—ɯ—

Therefore, holy brethren, partakers of the heavenly calling, consider the Apostle and High Priest of our confession, Christ Jesus . . . . (Heb 3:1)

The epistle to the Hebrews, perhaps more than any other New Testament book, describes the transition of the covenants and the supremacy of the New over the Old. One of the areas upon which the author focuses is the changing of the law and the priesthood—a change necessitated by the Old Covenant law's shortcomings:

Therefore, if perfection were through the Levitical priesthood (for under it the people received the law), what further need was there that another priest should rise according to the order of Melchizedek, and not be called according to the order of Aaron? For the priesthood being changed, of necessity there is also a change of the law. For He of whom these things are spoken belongs to another tribe, from which no man has officiated at the altar. For it is evident that our Lord arose from Judah, of which tribe Moses spoke nothing concerning priesthood. (Heb 7:11-14)

Although Christ fulfills the type seen in the Old Covenant high priest, His Priesthood is even more encompassing, reaching back to the pre-Old Covenant days of Abraham and fulfilling the type seen in Melchizedek, the priest of Salem. As mentioned in the "Introduction," this connection was missed by the Jews because of the "veil of Moses," according to Paul (2 Cor 3:14), or their "dullness of hearing" (Heb 5:11).

Let us explore Christ's fulfillment of the Levitical priesthood first, after which we will return to the typology of Melchizedek. First, both the high priest and Christ were appointed by God:

For every high priest taken from among men is appointed for men in things pertaining to God, that he may offer both gifts and sacrifices for sins. He can have compassion on those who are ignorant and going astray, since he himself is also subject to weakness. Because of this he is required as for the people, so also for himself, to offer sacrifices for sins. And no man takes this honor to himself, but he who is called by God, just as Aaron was. So also Christ did not glorify Himself to become High Priest, but it was He who said to Him:

"You are My Son,
Today I have begotten You."

As He also says in another place:

"You are a priest forever
According to the order of Melchizedek . . . ." (Heb 5:1-6)

Under the Old Testament law, the priests began their ministry in the temple (or tabernacle) at age thirty:

Then the LORD spoke to Moses and Aaron, saying: "Take a census of the sons of Kohath from among the children of Levi, by their families, by their fathers' house, from thirty years old and above, even to fifty years old, all who enter the service to do the work in the tabernacle of meeting." (Num 4:1-3; see also Num 4:23, 30, 35, 39, 43, 47; 1 Chr 23:3)

Now Jesus Himself began His ministry at about thirty years of age . . . . (Luke 3:23)

As our spiritual High Priest, Jesus serves in the true tabernacle (temple), the heavenly one—not the physical type of that tabernacle:

Now this is the main point of the things we are saying: We have such a High Priest, who is seated at the right hand of the throne of the Majesty in the heavens, a Minister of the sanctuary and of the true tabernacle which the Lord erected, and not man. For every high priest is appointed to offer both gifts and sacrifices. Therefore it is necessary that this one also have something to offer. For if He were on earth, He would not be a priest, since there are priests who offer the gifts according to the law; who serve the copy and shadow of the heavenly things, as Moses was divinely instructed when he was about to make the tabernacle. For He said, "See that you make all things according to the pattern shown you on the mountain." But now He has obtained a more excellent ministry, inasmuch as He is also Mediator of a better covenant, which was established on better promises. (Heb 8:1-6)

We have already read that the Levitical priesthood could make no one perfect (Heb 7:11), but Christ is the Mediator of a better covenant, which is established on better promises:

For if that first covenant had been faultless, then no place would have been sought for a second. (Heb 8:7)

Having reiterated the imperfection and shadowy nature of the Old Covenant, the author of Hebrews then goes on to describe the better covenant by quoting Jeremiah. Once again the Holy Spirit is taking us behind the veil of Moses by giving us a divinely inspired interpretation of an Old Testament passage:

*Because finding fault with them, He says: "Behold, the days are coming, says the L*ORD*, when I will make a new covenant with the house of Israel and with the house of Judah—not according to the covenant that I made with their fathers in the day when I took them by the hand to lead them out of the land of Egypt; because they did not continue in My covenant, and I disregarded them, says the L*ORD*. For this is the covenant that I will make with the house of Israel after those days, says the L*ORD*: I will put My laws in their mind and write them on their hearts; and I will be their God, and they shall be My people. None of them shall teach his neighbor, and none his brother, saying, 'Know the L*ORD*,' for all shall know Me, from the least of them to the greatest of them. For I will be merciful to their unrighteousness, and their sins and their lawless deeds I will remember no more."* (Heb 8:8-12; cf. Jer 31:31-34)

There can be no doubt that the Old Covenant to which the author of Hebrews has been referring is the Mosaic covenant of Judaism. Neither can there be any doubt that the new and better covenant is the gospel of Christ, which is written on our hearts by the Holy Spirit (Heb 8:10), as we have seen previously:

But you have an anointing from the Holy One, and you know all things. I have not written to you because you do not know the truth, but because you know it, and that no lie is of the truth. . . . But the anointing which you have received from Him abides in you, and you do not need that anyone teach you; but as the same anointing teaches you concerning all things, and is true, and is not a lie, and just as it has taught you, you will abide in Him. (1 John 2:20-21, 27)

Nevertheless, the passage from Jeremiah is typical of Old Testament passages that are often used to support a physical reign in the New Covenant, perhaps in a millennial period. Yet the New Testament saints were already living in the New Covenant. Of course, the Old Covenant had not passed away yet, but it was in the process of doing so:

> *In that He says, "A new covenant," He has made the first obsolete. Now what is becoming obsolete and growing old is ready to vanish away.* (Heb 8:13)

But the New Covenant did not have to wait for the Old Covenant to pass away before it could be inaugurated. In the chapter "The Two Covenants and the Two Sons of Abraham," we saw how the two covenants coexisted for a time, as illustrated by Ishmael and Isaac. Thus, while the Old Covenant was becoming obsolete, the New Testament saints were already experiencing the New Covenant. If that was the case, and the Holy Spirit's inspiration equated Jeremiah 31:31-34 with the gospel, how can we say that it refers to a yet future era? To do so would be saying that the New Covenant is merely a type of an even "newer" and "better" Covenant! That this is not the case is borne out in the typology of Melchizedek and Christ's fulfillment of it:

> *For this Melchizedek, king of Salem, priest of the Most High God, who met Abraham returning from the slaughter of the kings and blessed him, to whom also Abraham gave a tenth part of all, first being translated "king of righteousness," and then also king of Salem, meaning "king of peace," without father, without mother, without genealogy, having neither beginning of days nor end of life, but made like the Son of God, remains a priest continually.* (Heb 7:1-3)

Who better fits the titles "king of righteousness" and "king of peace" than Christ? The mention that he was *"without father, mother, or genealogy, having neither beginning of days nor end of life,"* we believe, alludes to Melchizedek's brief appearance on the stage of God's history. His interaction with Abraham involves only three verses in Genesis 14. Obviously, Melchizedek existed prior to and after his meeting with Abraham, but none of this is recorded for us. Thus, the Holy Spirit inspired the author of Hebrews to interpret this as his *"having neither beginning of days, nor end of life."*

Likewise, Christ only stepped onto the physical stage of God's history for a brief time, though He existed for eternity before His incarnation and will exist for eternity after it. Because of His eternal nature, Christ, like Melchizedek, remains a priest continually. Aside from Genesis 14 and the book of Hebrews, the only other mention of Melchizedek is in the Psalms:

> *The* LORD *said to my Lord,*
> *"Sit at My right hand,*
> *Till I make Your enemies Your footstool."*
>
> *The* LORD *has sworn*
> *And will not relent,*
> *"You are a priest forever*
> *According to the order of Melchizedek."* (Ps 110:1, 4)

That the Jews considered this passage from Psalm 110 to be messianic is demonstrated by Jesus' using verse 1 to turn the tables on them as they tried to trip Him up in His understanding of the Old Testament:

> *And He said to them, "How can they say that the Christ is the Son of David? Now David himself said in the Book of Psalms:*
>
> *'The* LORD *said to my Lord,*
> *"Sit at My right hand,*
> *Till I make Your enemies Your footstool."'*
> *Therefore David calls Him 'Lord'; how is He then his Son?"*
> (Luke 20:41-44)

Jesus was asking, "how can the Christ (the Messiah) be both David's Son and his Lord?" He was using a messianic passage to confound them. The context of Psalm 110 shows that the Messiah was still the subject when God swore, *"You are a priest forever according to the order of Melchizedek."* Even though the Jews understood that the Messiah would be a priest according to the order of Melchizedek, the veil of Moses prevented them from making the connection between that passage and Jesus, or the fact that the priesthood would change. The author of Hebrews pulls the veil back for us, revealing Jesus to be the priest according to the order of Melchizedek.

The point to take note of is the fact that the Messiah will be a priest *forever*. Just as the author of Hebrews says that Melchizedek remains a priest continually, so David prophesies that the Messiah would be a priest forever, according to the order of Melchizedek. The author of Hebrews drives this point home by quoting the phrase *a priest forever* four times (5:6; 6:20; 7:17, 21). The author also stresses that this eternal priesthood is according to the order of Melchizedek (5:6, 10; 6:20; 7:1, 10, 11, 15, 17, 21), to which he assigns a transcendent, or spiritual, nature:

. . . without father, without mother, without genealogy, having neither beginning of days nor end of life, but made like the Son of God, remains a priest continually. (Heb 7:3)

This eternal Priesthood of Christ is in agreement with "*of the increase of His government and peace there will be no end* (Isa 9:7)" and "*the everlasting covenant* (Heb 13:20)." There is no end to the New Covenant gospel of Christ or any future changes to be made to the New Covenant: "*But He, because He continues forever, has an unchangeable priesthood*" (Heb 7:24).

The Old Covenant was temporary, but the gospel of the New Covenant is *everlasting* and *unchangeable*. This is a key to understanding the theme of "the last days," which is woven throughout the New Testament. The reference cannot be to the last days of the Christian era, for the Christian era is the everlasting and unchangeable age of the gospel. Because the early Church was declared to already be in the last days (Acts 2:16-17; Heb 1:2), we must understand those days to be the last days of the era of Judaism, of the Old Covenant, for we know that it was coming to an end:

For if what is passing away [the Old Covenant] was glorious, what remains [the New Covenant] is much more glorious. (2 Cor 3:11)

In that He says, "A new covenant," He has made the first obsolete. Now what is becoming obsolete and growing old is ready to vanish away. (Heb 8:13)

The subject of the last days will be further developed in Part II. We have one last thought to consider in this chapter. In the Old Covenant, there was one high priest, with many subordinate priests to minister in the tabernacle (or temple). In the New Covenant, Jesus is the High Priest. Who are the subordinate priests?

*. . . you also, as living stones, are being built up a spiritual house, **a holy priesthood**, to offer up spiritual sacrifices acceptable to God through Jesus Christ.* (1 Pet 2:5)

*But you are a chosen generation, **a royal priesthood** . . . .* (1 Pet 2:9)

*To Him who loved us and washed us from our sins in His own blood, and **has made us** kings and **priests** to His God and Father, to Him be glory and dominion forever and ever. Amen.* (Rev 1:5-6)
(emphases added)

We are a holy priesthood, with Jesus as our High Priest. We are offering up spiritual sacrifices acceptable to God through Jesus Christ:

I beseech you therefore, brethren, by the mercies of God, that you present your bodies a living sacrifice, holy, acceptable to God, which is your reasonable service. (Rom 12:1)

Therefore by Him let us continually offer the sacrifice of praise to God, that is, the fruit of our lips, giving thanks to His name. But do not forget to do good and to share, for with such sacrifices God is well pleased. (Heb 13:15-16)

Nowhere in the New Testament do we read of a priesthood from the sons of Zadok (Ezek 40:46) or of a rebuilt temple.

The New Covenant and Israel

—ɯ—

But it is not that the word of God has taken no effect. For they are not all Israel who are of Israel, nor are they all children because they are the seed of Abraham; but, "In Isaac your seed shall be called." That is, those who are the children of the flesh, these are not the children of God; but the children of the promise are counted as the seed. (Rom 9:6-8)

In the above passage, Paul once again differentiates between Abraham's fleshly and spiritual children, as he did in Galatians 4. Whereas in the Galatians passage, the two sons of Abraham were used to illustrate the two covenants, here in Romans Paul is describing the two Israels—natural Israel and spiritual Israel. The fact that the physical offspring of Abraham were not automatically heirs of the New Covenant is introduced back in the Gospels:

Therefore bear fruits worthy of repentance, and do not begin to say to yourselves, "We have Abraham as our father." For I say to you that God is able to raise up children to Abraham from these stones. (Luke 3:8: cf. Gal 3:29 which states that if you are Christ's, then you are Abraham's seed—not that if you are Abraham's seed, *then* you are in Christ.)

"I know that you are Abraham's descendants, but you seek to kill Me, because My word has no place in you. I speak what I have seen with My Father, and you do what you have seen with your father." They answered and said to Him, "Abraham is our father." Jesus said to them, "If you were Abraham's children, you would do the works of Abraham. But now you seek to kill Me, a Man who has told you the truth which I heard from God. Abraham did not do this. You do the deeds of your father . . . . You are of your father the devil, and the desires of your father you want to do." (John 8:37-41, 44)

Jesus acknowledged that although the Jews were Abraham's physical descendants, they were not necessarily Abraham's "spiritual" children. If they were, they would do the works of Abraham. Instead, they were doing the deeds of their "spiritual" father, the devil. Paul develops this theme in the allegory of Ishmael and Isaac. We have already looked at the fleshly and spiritual seed of Abraham representing the Old (fleshly) Covenant and the New (spiritual) Covenant in Galatians. In Romans, Paul applies the allegory to two Israels—fleshly Israel and spiritual Israel. It is only fitting that fleshly Israel would foreshadow the spiritual Israel of the New Covenant, and that fleshly (or national) Jews would have spiritual counterparts:

> *For he is not a Jew who is one outwardly, nor is circumcision that which is outward in the flesh; but he is a Jew who is one inwardly; and circumcision is that of the heart, in the Spirit, not in the letter; whose praise is not from men but from God.* (Rom 2:28-29)

> *For in Christ Jesus neither circumcision nor uncircumcision avails anything, but a new creation. And as many as walk according to this rule, peace and mercy be upon them, and upon the Israel of God.* (Gal 6:15-16)

Again, there were hints in the Old Testament of spiritual applications to these physical types, but they were behind the veil of Moses. God was never looking for a physical nation of people, identified by the circumcision of the flesh, but for a spiritual people identified by the circumcision of the heart:

> *But if they confess their iniquity and the iniquity of their fathers, with their unfaithfulness in which they were unfaithful to Me, and that they also have walked contrary to Me, and that I also have walked contrary to them and have brought them into the land of their enemies; if their uncircumcised hearts are humbled, and they accept their guilt—then I will remember My covenant with Jacob, and My covenant with Isaac and My covenant with Abraham I will remember . . . .* (Lev 26:40-42)

> *And the LORD your God will circumcise your heart and the heart of your descendants, to love the LORD your God with all your heart and with all your soul, that you may live.* (Deut 30:6)

> *Circumcise yourselves to the LORD,*
> *And take away the foreskins of your hearts,*
> *You men of Judah and inhabitants of Jerusalem,*
> *Lest My fury come forth like fire,*
> *And burn so that no one can quench it,*
> *Because of the evil of your doings.* (Jer 4:4)

For all these nations are uncircumcised, and all the house of Israel
are uncircumcised in the heart. (Jer 9:26)

Clearly, God is not looking for a people that follow a set of rules ritualistically (as represented by physical circumcision), but for those whose hearts are toward Him (as represented by circumcision of the heart). As we shall see in the next chapter, Paul connects the gathering of scattered Israel, in the passage from Deuteronomy 30 above, with the salvation message of the gospel. In Romans 2, as we have read, he states that circumcision, in the New Covenant, is of the heart. So we see that even in the initiation of the Old Covenant by the sign of physical circumcision, the seed of the New Covenant, with its circumcision of the heart, was planted.

We established previously that the New Testament often provides a divinely inspired commentary and interpretation of the Old Testament. In light of that, consider how the New Testament apostles interpret the following Old Testament passages, which many believe refer to the restored nation of Israel:

"On that day I will raise up
The tabernacle of David, which has fallen down,
And repair its damages;
I will raise up its ruins,
And rebuild it as in the days of old;
That they may possess the remnant of Edom,
And all the Gentiles who are called by My name,"
Says the LORD who does this thing. (Amos 9:11-12)

In Acts 15, during the Jerusalem council, James applies this passage to the Church and the Gentile believers being added to Jewish believers:

And after they had become silent, James answered, saying, "Men
and brethren, listen to me: Simon has declared how God at the first
visited the Gentiles to take out of them a people for His name. And
with this the words of the prophets agree, just as it is written:

'After this I will return

And will rebuild the tabernacle of David, which has fallen down;
I will rebuild its ruins,
And I will set it up;
So that the rest of mankind may seek the LORD,
Even all the Gentiles who are called by My name,
Says the LORD who does all these things.'" (Acts 15:13-17)

Clearly, James did not equate the rebuilding of David's tabernacle with the tent the Israelites had carried through the desert, or with the subsequent temple, as a strictly "literal" interpretation would demand. Rather, James understood Barnabas and Paul's description of Gentiles coming to faith in Christ as a fulfillment of this Old Testament passage. This is a prime example of why we insist that we must allow the inspired New Testament authors to interpret the Old Testament, rather than carrying Old Testament prophecies forward into an *a priori* schema.

Likewise, note how Paul assigns the following passage from Isaiah to the Jews, who would "*be ever hearing but never understanding.*" Therefore, salvation was sent to the Gentiles. Obviously, individual Jews did accept Christ, so we take this to mean that, as a nation, the Jews were no longer the custodians of the gospel. Custodianship was "torn" from them and given to the Church (which included Gentiles), who would bear fruit:

And He said, "Go, and tell this people:
'Keep on hearing, but do not understand;
Keep on seeing, but do not perceive.'
Make the heart of this people dull,
And their ears heavy,
And shut their eyes;
Lest they see with their eyes,
And hear with their ears,
And understand with their heart,
And return and be healed." (Isa 6:9-10)

So when they had appointed him [Paul] a day, many came to him at his lodging, to whom he explained and solemnly testified of the kingdom of God, persuading them concerning Jesus from both the Law of Moses and the Prophets, from morning till evening. And some were persuaded by the things which were spoken, and some disbelieved. So when they did not agree among themselves, they departed after Paul had said one word: "The Holy Spirit spoke rightly through Isaiah the prophet to our fathers, saying,

'Go to this people and say:
"Hearing you will hear, and shall not understand;
And seeing you will see, and not perceive;
For the hearts of this people have grown dull.
Their ears are hard of hearing,
And their eyes they have closed,
Lest they should see with their eyes and hear with their ears,

Lest they should understand with their hearts and turn,
So that I should heal them.'"

"Therefore let it be known to you that the salvation of God has been sent to the Gentiles, and they will hear it!" And when he had said these words, the Jews departed and had a great dispute among themselves. (Acts 28:23-29)

The following passages are applied by Paul to the Church, consisting of both Jews and Gentiles:

Yet the number of the children of Israel
Shall be as the sand of the sea,
Which cannot be measured or numbered.
And it shall come to pass
In the place where it was said to them,
"You are not My people,"
There it shall be said to them,
"You are sons of the living God." (Hos 1:10)

. . . that He might make known the riches of His glory on the vessels of mercy, which He had prepared beforehand for glory, **even us whom He called, not of the Jews only, but also of the Gentiles?** *As He says also in Hosea:*

"I will call them My people, who were not My people,
And her beloved, who was not beloved.
And it shall come to pass in the place where it was said to them,
'You are not My people,'
There they shall be called sons of the living God." (Rom 9:23-26) (emphases added)

According to Paul, although the Jews were God's people under the Old Covenant, the Church, which includes Gentiles, is now His people under the New Covenant:

I will walk among you and be your God, and you shall be My people. (Lev 26:12)

For you [Christian saints] are the temple of the living God. As God has said:
"I will dwell in them
And walk among them.
I will be their God,
And they shall be My people." (2 Cor 6:16)

As we noted earlier in Galatians 4, Paul wrote that we (the Church) are children of the promise, belonging not to an earthly Jerusalem but the Jerusalem that is above. Just as Paul sees the Church and the Gospel as the fulfillments of Old Testament prophecy, Peter also describes the Church using terms with which God formerly described Israel:

> *But **you are a chosen generation, a royal priesthood, a holy nation, His own special people** . . . who were once not a people but are **now the people of God** . . . . (1 Pet 2:9, 10)*

> *Now therefore, if you will indeed obey My voice and keep My covenant, then you shall be a **special treasure** to Me above all people; for all the earth is Mine. And you shall be to Me a **kingdom of priests** and a **holy nation**. (Exod 19:5-6)*

> *For you are **a holy people** to the LORD your God; the LORD your God has chosen you to be a people for Himself, **a special treasure** above all the peoples on the face of the earth. (Deut 7:6)*

> *Also today the LORD has proclaimed you to be **His special people**, just as He promised you, that you should keep all His commandments, and that He will set you high above all nations which He has made, in praise, in name, and in honor, and that you may be a **holy people** to the LORD your God, just as He has spoken." (Deut 26:18-19)*

> (emphases added)

Indeed, as Hanegraaff notes, "the precise terminology used to describe the children of Israel in the Old Testament is ascribed to the church in the New Testament" (*The Apocalypse Code*, p. 49).

Does this mean, then, that the Church has replaced Israel? Absolutely not; rather, the Church is the *spiritual fulfillment* of the *physical type*, just as Christ did not come to abolish the law but to fulfill it (Matt 5:17). Just as Christ and the Church, as elements of the next stage of God's redemptive plan, did not abolish or annul the previous stage, so the law did not annul the previous promise to Abraham and his Seed:

> *Now to Abraham and his Seed were the promises made. He does not say, "And to seeds," as of many, but as of one, "And to your Seed," who is Christ. And this I say, that the law, which was four hundred and thirty years later, cannot annul the covenant that was confirmed before by God in Christ, that it should make the promise of no effect. For if the inheritance is of the law, it is no longer of*

*promise; but God gave it to Abraham by promise. . . . Is the law
then against the promises of God? Certainly not! For if there had
been a law given which could have given life, truly righteousness would have been by the law. But the Scripture has confined
all under sin, that the promise by faith in Jesus Christ might be
given to those who believe. But before faith came, we were kept
under guard by the law, kept for the faith which would afterward
be revealed. Therefore the law was our tutor to bring us to Christ,
that we might be justified by faith. But after faith has come, we are
no longer under a tutor.* (Gal 3:16-18, 21-25)

In effect, the law was a "placeholder" between the promise given to
Abraham and his Seed, and the fulfillment of that promise in Christ and the
gospel. It kept the people *under guard* until the faith of the New Covenant
arrived. Although God's plan of redemption has progressively unfolded,
He has always had an elect remnant—spiritual Israel. Paul uses Abraham's
salvation to demonstrate this:

*Does this blessedness then come upon the circumcised only, or
upon the uncircumcised also? For we say that faith was accounted
to Abraham for righteousness. How then was it accounted? While
he was circumcised, or uncircumcised? Not while circumcised,
but while uncircumcised. And he received the sign of circumcision, a seal of the righteousness of the faith which he had while
still uncircumcised, that he might be the father of all those who
believe, though they are uncircumcised, that righteousness might
be imputed to them also, and the father of circumcision to those
who not only are of the circumcision, but who also walk in the
steps of the faith which our father Abraham had while still uncircumcised.* (Rom 4:9-12)

Note that Abraham was one of God's elect *before* he was circumcised.
In fact, circumcision was given to him as a sign of his righteous position
before God. In this way, he was not just the father of the physical Jews but
also *"the father of all those who believe"*—the spiritual Jews. Thus we see
that God had a people (e.g., Enoch, Noah, Abraham, etc.) unto Himself
prior to the establishment of national Israel and the law. Israel and the law
were just the next stage of God's plan of redemption, designed to lead His
people to Christ, the consummation of His plan:

*Therefore the law was our tutor to bring us to Christ, that we
might be justified by faith.* (Gal 3:24)

God's redemptive plan progressed in the Old Testament, from the sign of circumcision given to Abraham to the Law given to national Israel through Moses. In the same manner, His plan progressed in the New Testament, from the Law and national Israel to the New Covenant and the Church. Just as the law was glorious, but the New Covenant is more glorious (2 Cor 3:7-11), so national Israel was glorious, but the Church (spiritual Israel) is more glorious. Unfortunately, many of His people of the Old Covenant failed to make the transition into the next stage of the plan of redemption. They still could not see behind the veil of Moses. Throughout the ages, those who did walk according to God's plan, in whatever particular stage they were living, were His elect.

Many call this particular view of the Church and Israel "Replacement Theology" because they claim those who teach it are replacing Israel with the Church. Dispensationalism, which sees two separate plans for Israel and the Church in the New Covenant, especially decries "Replacement Theology." However, a more accurate term would be "Fulfillment Theology," for Christ did not come to destroy the Law but to fulfill it. The New Covenant only replaced the Old Covenant in the sense that the Old Covenant had fulfilled its purpose. Since its types and shadows pointed toward Christ and the New Covenant, Christ's inauguration of the New Covenant made the Old obsolete. Likewise, physical Israel, as part of that Old Covenant system of types and shadows, fulfilled its purpose of foreshadowing the Church, passing away along with the Law. Neither the Law nor Israel was arbitrarily destroyed (abolished), leaving the New Covenant to be started "from scratch." Rather, Paul declared that he taught *no other things than those which the prophets and Moses said would come*. Thus Paul's gospel was the fulfillment, not the replacement, of what the Law taught.

While most might acknowledge and even receive the points thus far discussed about spiritual Israel, there remains a sticking point. What about Paul's statement in Romans 11:26 that "*all Israel will be saved?*" We will address this issue in a subsequent chapter after we have completed laying the foundation upon which our eschatology is built.

The New Covenant and Canaan

—⚏—

Is the physical land of Israel promised to the Jews forever? A cursory look at Scripture seems to affirm that it is:

And the LORD said to Abram, after Lot had separated from him: "Lift your eyes now and look from the place where you are— northward, southward, eastward, and westward; for all the land which you see I give to you and your descendants forever." (Gen 13:14-15)

Also I give to you and your descendants after you the land in which you are a stranger, all the land of Canaan, as an everlasting possession; and I will be their God. (Gen 17:8)

He remembers His covenant forever,
The word which He commanded, for a thousand generations,
The covenant which He made with Abraham,
And His oath to Isaac,
And confirmed it to Jacob for a statute,
To Israel as an everlasting covenant,
Saying, "To you I will give the land of Canaan
As the allotment of your inheritance . . . ." (Ps 105:8-11)

It certainly appears that the land of Canaan was promised to Abraham's seed forever. But in the previous chapter we saw that Abraham's children of the promise were not physical Jews, but spiritual Jews:

That is, those who are the children of the flesh, these are not the children of God; but the children of the promise are counted as the seed. (Rom 9:8)

For it is written that Abraham had two sons: the one by a bond-woman, the other by a freewoman. But he who was of the bond-woman was born according to the flesh, and he of the freewoman through promise. . . . Now we, brethren, as Isaac was, are children of promise. (Gal 4:22-23, 28)

Scripture affirms for us that the spiritual seed of Abraham, the Church, are the heirs of the promise. This is because we are joint heirs with Christ, Who is the "Seed" of Abraham in Whom the promises are fulfilled:

> *The Spirit Himself bears witness with our spirit that we are children of God, and if children, then heirs—heirs of God and joint heirs with Christ, if indeed we suffer with Him, that we may also be glorified together.* (Rom 8:16-17)

> *Now to Abraham and his Seed were the promises made. He does not say, "And to seeds," as of many, but as of one, "And to your Seed," who is Christ . . . . And if you are Christ's, then you are Abraham's seed, and heirs according to the promise.* (Gal 3:16, 29)

In spite of this clear teaching of Scripture, many in the Church (especially among Dispensationalism) believe that God *promised* the land to the Jews forever. This may be due in part to the belief that all *physical* Israel will be saved; naturally, a physical nation would require a physical land. To be sure, the land was promised to Abraham's descendants. However, Paul states clearly that the fulfillments of the promises to Abraham were realized by his spiritual seed of the New Covenant, typified by Isaac.

But this presents us with a problem: how does a physical land fit with the spiritual heirs of a spiritual kingdom? Is the Church to eventually be headquartered in the land of Israel? If so, then we are faced with the problem of having an element of the Old Covenant continuing on in the New Covenant. On the other hand, if the pattern that has worked so well to this point is valid, there should be a spiritual antitype to the physical land of Israel. Can we find one?

Canaan was the "Promised Land" toward which the generation of Moses journeyed:

> *"Also I give to you and your descendants after you the land in which you are a stranger, all the land of Canaan, as an everlasting possession; and I will be their God."* (Gen 17:8)

> *So I have come down to deliver them out of the hand of the Egyptians, and to bring them up from that land to a good and large land, to a land flowing with milk and honey, to the place of the Canaanites and the Hittites and the Amorites and the Perizzites and the Hivites and the Jebusites.* (Exod 3:8)

Is there a corresponding "Promised Land" to which the Church is looking forward? Yes! As the Father gives the Old Covenant promise, so the Son gives the New Covenant promise:

In My Father's house are many mansions; if it were not so, I would have told you. I go to prepare a place for you. And if I go and prepare a place for you, I will come again and receive you to Myself; that where I am, there you may be also. (John 14:2-3)

So we see that both Canaan and heaven are "Promised Lands." They are also both places of bounty:

Then they came to the Valley of Eshcol, and there cut down a branch with one cluster of grapes; they carried it between two of them on a pole. They also brought some of the pomegranates and figs . . . . Then they told him, and said: "We went to the land where you sent us. It truly flows with milk and honey, and this is its fruit." (Num 13:23, 27)

And he showed me a pure river of water of life, clear as crystal, proceeding from the throne of God and of the Lamb. In the middle of its street, and on either side of the river, was the tree of life, which bore twelve fruits, each tree yielding its fruit every month. The leaves of the tree were for the healing of the nations. (Rev 22:1-2)

The bulk of Hebrews chapters 3 and 4 speaks to the parallels of the Israelites entering Canaan, and Christians entering their "final rest," or heaven. Consider this portion from Hebrews 4:

Therefore, since a promise remains of entering His rest, let us fear lest any of you seem to have come short of it. For indeed the gospel was preached to us as well as to them; but the word which they heard did not profit them, not being mixed with faith in those who heard it. For we who have believed do enter that rest . . . . For if Joshua had given them rest, then He would not afterward have spoken of another day. There remains therefore a rest for the people of God. (Heb 4:1-3, 8-9)

Here again the author of Hebrews is pulling back the veil and revealing to us that the physical "promised land of rest" was just a type of the true place of rest for God's people. Just as Canaan was the final rest for physical Israel, so heaven is the final rest for spiritual Israel. That the physical land was only a type, and not the final rest, is borne out by the following:

By faith Abraham obeyed when he was called to go out to the place which he would receive as an inheritance. And he went out, not knowing where he was going. By faith he dwelt in the land of promise as in a foreign country, dwelling in tents with Isaac and Jacob, the heirs with him of the same promise; for he waited for the city which has foundations, whose builder and maker is God. . . . These [the early Patriarchs] all died in faith, not having received the promises, but having seen them afar off were assured of them, embraced them and confessed that they were strangers and pilgrims on the earth. For those who say such things declare plainly that they seek a homeland. And truly if they had called to mind that country from which they had come out, they would have had opportunity to return. But now they desire a better, that is, a heavenly country. Therefore God is not ashamed to be called their God, for He has prepared a city for them. (Heb 11:8-10, 13-16)

Here the Scripture states explicitly that Abraham "*dwelt in the land of promise as in a foreign country.*" Why? Because even though it was the "Promised Land," it was not the final resting place. While in the "Promised Land," Abraham was waiting for the city, in that heavenly country, whose builder and maker was God. So we see the earthly "Promised Land" as a type of the heavenly "Promised Land."

This theme is reiterated in the life of David. When David desired to build a house for the Lord, God replied through Nathan the prophet that David's son, not David himself, would build the house. But first, God makes an interesting statement to David:

Now therefore, thus shall you say to My servant David, "Thus says the LORD of hosts: 'I took you from the sheepfold, from following the sheep, to be ruler over My people, over Israel. And I have been with you wherever you have gone, and have cut off all your enemies from before you, and have made you a great name, like the name of the great men who are on the earth. Moreover I will appoint a place for My people Israel, and will plant them, that they may dwell in a place of their own and move no more . . . .'" (2 Sam 7:8-10; cf. 1 Chr 17:9)

While David was dwelling in Jerusalem, the capital of Israel (Canaan), God told him that He would appoint a place for His people Israel, and would plant them that they may dwell in a place of their own. Notice the future tense in what God said—I *will* appoint, I *will* plant. Yet Israel had been in the land of Canaan for approximately 400 years! Not only that, but at the time that God spoke this, they were at what was perhaps the kingdom's zenith, as evidenced just a few verses earlier:

> *Now it came to pass when the king was dwelling in his house, and the Lord had given him rest from all his enemies all around, that the king said to Nathan the prophet, "See now, I dwell in a house of cedar, but the ark of God dwells inside tent curtains."* (2 Sam 7:1-2)

How much more "planted" could the Israelites have been, than having rest from all of their enemies? Why then, at the peak of the Davidic kingdom, would God speak of *yet* appointing a place for Israel, and *yet* planting them? Because, just as the earthly kingdom was merely a temporary foreshadow of the spiritual kingdom, so the land in which it was planted was a mere foreshadow of the spiritual dwelling place of the citizens of that heavenly kingdom.

Does this mean that all of the promises regarding Israel and the land are to only be taken in a spiritual sense, and that physical Israel and physical Canaan were never in view? Absolutely not! The land was promised to them, and they did enter it. This is the assurance to the believer that just as God brought physical Israel into physical Canaan, so will He bring spiritual Israel into spiritual Canaan.

The apparent problem of the "forever" language disappears when we investigate further and find that Israel's occupation of the land was *conditional* and dependent upon their obedience to God's commands. And just as He promised that He would bless them in the land, He also promised to destroy them *from* the land if they became disobedient:

> *Now, **O Israel, listen** to the statutes and the judgments which I teach you to observe, **that you may live**, and go in **and possess the land** which the Lord God of your fathers is giving you.* (Deut 4:1; cf. Deut 8:1; 11:8-9)

> *You shall not go after other gods, the gods of the peoples who are all around you (for the Lord your God is a jealous God among you), lest the anger of the Lord your God be aroused against you and **destroy you from the face of the earth**.* (Deut 6:14-15)

> *And it shall be, that just as the Lord rejoiced over you to do you good and multiply you, so the **Lord will rejoice over you to destroy you** and bring you to nothing; and **you shall be plucked from off***

the land which you go to possess. (Deut 28:63; cf. Deut 8:19-20; 11:16-17)
(emphases added)

The fact that the promise of the physical land was conditional is indisputable. Time and space prevent us from detailing the numerous acts by which the Israelites failed to meet those conditions. If the reader is not familiar with them, then it should be sufficient to know that God Himself foretold that Israel would break His covenant:

> And the LORD said to Moses: "Behold, you will rest with your fathers; and this people will rise and play the harlot with the gods of the foreigners of the land, where they go to be among them, and they will forsake Me and break My covenant which I have made with them. Then My anger shall be aroused against them in that day, and I will forsake them, and I will hide My face from them, and they shall be devoured. And many evils and troubles shall befall them, so that they will say in that day, 'Have not these evils come upon us because our God is not among us?' And I will surely hide My face in that day because of all the evil which they have done, in that they have turned to other gods." (Deut 31:16-18)

Added to this conditional element are the testimonies of Joshua and Solomon, specifically, that the promises to Abraham and his physical seed *were* fulfilled:

> So the LORD gave to Israel all the land of which He had sworn to give to their fathers, and they took possession of it and dwelt in it. The LORD gave them rest all around, according to all that He had sworn to their fathers. And not a man of all their enemies stood against them; the LORD delivered all their enemies into their hand. Not a word failed of any good thing which the LORD had spoken to the house of Israel. All came to pass. (Josh 21:43-45)

> Then he [Solomon] stood and blessed all the assembly of Israel with a loud voice, saying: "Blessed be the LORD, who has given rest to His people Israel, according to all that He promised. There has not failed one word of all His good promise, which He promised through His servant Moses." (1 Kgs 8:55-56)

Furthermore, Joshua attests to the fact that the promises were fulfilled by sending two-and-a-half tribes back home to the east of the Jordan:

Then Moses said to them [the Reubenites, the Gadites, and half the tribe of Manasseh]: "If you do this thing, if you arm yourselves before the LORD for the war, and all your armed men cross over the Jordan before the LORD until He has driven out His enemies from before Him, and the land is subdued before the LORD, then afterward you may return and be blameless before the LORD and before Israel; and this land shall be your possession before the LORD." (Num 32:20-23)

Then Joshua called the Reubenites, the Gadites, and half the tribe of Manasseh, and said to them: "You have kept all that Moses the servant of the LORD commanded you, and have obeyed my voice in all that I commanded you. You have not left your brethren these many days, up to this day, but have kept the charge of the commandment of the LORD your God. And now the LORD your God has given rest to your brethren, as He promised them; now therefore, return and go to your tents and to the land of your possession, which Moses the servant of the LORD gave you on the other side of the Jordan." (Josh 22:1-4)

So we see that the promises to physical Israel *were* fulfilled. Any further fulfillment, as Paul asserts, is spiritual in nature, and belongs to the "children of the promise"—spiritual Israel. That there was to be a future spiritual fulfillment is established by the fact that, although the above passage declares Joshua had given them rest, the author of Hebrews states:

For if Joshua had given them rest, then He would not afterward have spoken of another day. There remains therefore a rest for the people of God. (Heb 4:8-9)

Hanegraaff concurs:

[Stephen] Sizer astutely sums up the problem by saying that the essence of the matter is not whether one interprets the Bible literally or spiritually, but whether one understands the Bible in terms of old covenant types (shadows) or new covenant realities. "The failure to recognize this principle is the basic hermeneutical error which Christian Zionists make and from which flow the other distinctive doctrines that characterize the movement." Nowhere is this more clearly seen than in Zionist misinterpretations regarding the promise God made to Abraham with respect to the land. . . . The writer of Hebrews makes clear that the rest the descendants of Abraham experienced when they entered the land is but a type of the rest we experience when we enter an eternal relationship with the Lord. The land provided temporal rest for the *physical* descendants of Abraham, but the Lord provides eternal rest for the *spiritual* descendents of Abraham. (*The Apocalypse Code*, pp. 174-175, 182; emphasis in original)

Thus, we believe that the physical promises were fulfilled in the Old Testament era, and that any subsequent fulfillments were spiritual in nature. But what of Deuteronomy 30 and similar passages, which speak of a future gathering of Israel after they have been scattered because of their disobedience?

> *"Now it shall come to pass, when all these things come upon you, the blessing and the curse which I have set before you, and you call them to mind among all the nations where the LORD your God drives you, and you return to the LORD your God and obey His voice, according to all that I command you today, you and your children, with all your heart and with all your soul, that the LORD your God will bring you back from captivity, and have compassion on you, and gather you again from all the nations where the LORD your God has scattered you. If any of you are driven out to the farthest parts under heaven, from there the LORD your God will gather you, and from there He will bring you. Then the LORD your God will bring you to the land which your fathers possessed, and you shall possess it. He will prosper you and multiply you more than your fathers."* (Deut 30:1-5)

Many see the fulfillment of this passage in the reestablished nation of Israel and its recent repopulation. It cannot be denied that, since 1948, Jews have been immigrating to Israel from the nations where they had been scattered. But is this *the* fulfillment of Deuteronomy 30? We believe that a closer look at the text rules out that possibility categorically. The reason that the Jews were scattered was because they turned away from God. Moses clearly laid out their options in chapters 27-29. The blessings and curses of God hinged upon the actions of the Israelites after they took possession of the land. No less than five times does the phrase "if you . . ." occur in chapter 28. Thus, the blessings and curses are an "if/then" proposition. If the Israelites were obedient God would bless them; if they were disobedient God would curse them.

The Old Testament and the gospels are replete with examples of Israel fulfilling the "if" stipulation of the curse clause. Certainly, if Israel had *not* fulfilled the "if" stipulation by breaking His covenant, God would have been unjust in bringing the curses upon Israel. As it was, God was required to fulfill the "then" portion of the curse clause and *pluck them from the land* (Deut 28:63). Returning to the promise of restoration in chapter 30, we see that it is also an "if/then" proposition:

> *Now it shall come to pass, when all these things come upon you* *... **and you return to the LORD your God and obey His voice**, according to all that I command you today, you and your children, **with all your heart and with all your soul**, that the LORD your God will bring you back from captivity, and have compassion on you, and gather you again from all the nations where the LORD your God has scattered you. . . . For the LORD will again rejoice over you for good as He rejoiced over your fathers, **if you obey the voice of the LORD your God, to keep His commandments and His statutes** which are written in this Book of the Law, and **if you turn to the LORD your God with all your heart and with all your soul**.* (Deut 30:1-3, 9-10; emphases added)

Clearly, the gathering of Israel described above is conditional upon their return to God in obedience, with all their heart and soul. So the question must be asked, *Have they done that?* Lest we think that a return to Old Testament ritualistic religion would suffice for present-day Israel, remember Christ's words about coming to God:

> *... I am the way, the truth, and the life. No one comes to the Father **except through Me**.* (John 14:6; emphasis added; cf. Acts 4:12)

The Old Covenant has passed away and we are now under the New Covenant in the Gospel age. Therefore, a resurrection of the Old Covenant would *not* constitute a return to God. The only way to return to God is through Christ. Not only must the Jews return to God through Christ, but unless they do so, as Peter quotes from Moses, they will be cut off from God:

> *For Moses truly said to the fathers, "The LORD your God will raise up for you a Prophet like me from your brethren. Him you shall hear in all things, whatever He says to you. And it shall be that every soul who will not hear that Prophet shall be utterly destroyed from among the people."* (Acts 3:22-23)

Not only is present-day Israel not Christian, it is not even practicing Judaism on a national scale. According to J. Randall Price in *The Coming Last Days Temple*, "modern-day Israel is largely a secular state" and "largely non-religious" (p. 25). Consider his following observation:

Despite a secular society comprising about 85% of the population and a secular government in control of the state, the religious parties represented in the Israeli Knesset (Parliament) have managed to **force** conformity to Jewish law since the founding of the state. (p. 27; emphasis added)

Clearly, the Jews have not returned to God with all their heart and soul—not by any stretch of the imagination. Previously we stated that if Israel had *not* fulfilled the "if" portion of the curse, God would have been unjust in bringing the curses upon them. Likewise, would He not be unjust to *gather them* when they have not fulfilled the "if" portion of this promise? Therefore, present-day Israel cannot be seen as a fulfillment of Deuteronomy 30.

Dispensationalism recognizes this issue of modern Israel being established apart from a return to God. To address this problem, they posit two "regatherings" of Israel, as Thomas Ice describes:

There are dozens of biblical passages that predict an end-time regathering of Israel back to her land. However, it is a common mistake to lump all of these passages into one fulfillment time frame, especially in relation to the modern state of Israel. Modern Israel is prophetically significant and is fulfilling Bible prophecy. But readers of God's Word need to be careful to distinguish which verses are being fulfilled in our day and which references await future fulfillment. In short there will be two end-time regatherings: One before the tribulation and one after the tribulation.

Hebrew Christian scholar Dr. Arnold Fruchtenbaum—a graduate of Dallas Seminary—explains the biblical basis for the current state of Israel as follows:

The re-establishment of the Jewish state in 1948 has not only thrown a wrench in amillennial thinking, but it has also thrown a chink in much of premillennial thinking. Amazingly, some premillennialists have concluded that the present state of Israel has nothing to do with the fulfillment of prophecy. For some reason the present state somehow does not fit their scheme of things, and so the present state becomes merely an accident of history. On what grounds is the present state of Israel so dismissed? The issue that bothers so many premillennialists is the fact that not only have the Jews returned in unbelief with regard to the person of Jesus, but the majority of the ones who have returned are not even Orthodox Jews. In fact the majority are atheists or agnostics. Certainly, then, Israel does not fit in with all those biblical passages dealing with the return. For it is a regenerated nation that the Bible speaks of, and the present state of Israel hardly fits that picture. So on these grounds, the present state is dismissed as not being a fulfillment of prophecy.

However, the real problem is the failure to see that the prophets spoke of two international returns. First, there was to be a regathering in unbelief in preparation for judgment, namely the judgment of the tribulation. This was to be followed by a second world-wide regathering in faith in preparation for blessing, namely the blessings of the messianic age. Once it is recognized that the Bible speaks of two such regatherings, it is easy to see how the present state of Israel fits into prophecy. (*Is Modern Israel Fulfilling Prophecy?* at www.pre-trib.org)

Because, as we have demonstrated above, Deuteronomy 30 requires Israel to turn to God before He gathers them, Ice assigns that passage to the second "regathering in faith." The Scriptures he cites for a "regathering in unbelief" are: Ezekiel 20:33-38; 22:17-22; 36:22-24; 37:1-14; 38-39; Isaiah 11:11-12; and Zephaniah 2:1-2. Ice demonstrates that these passages speak of God gathering Israel for "the day of the LORD" and times of "wrath," which Ice associates with a yet-future Tribulation. However, he omits conveniently any mention of the destruction of Jerusalem in AD 70. Jesus warned His disciples that when they saw *"Jerusalem surrounded by armies, then know that its desolation is near. . . . For these are the days of vengeance [God's punishing wrath], that all things which are written may be fulfilled"* (Luke 21:20, 22). As our study progresses we will show that the destruction of Jerusalem was indeed the Tribulation of which the Scriptures speak. That destruction was the "day of the LORD" and the time of "wrath" that fulfilled the passages Ice lists above. On a side note, one wonders if modern Israelis and even most Dispensationalists realize that (according to Dispensationalism) the millions of dollars donated by Evangelicals to support Israel are for the purpose of gathering them for the slaughter of the Tribulation!

For those who believe that the curses of Deuteronomy 28, which were ultimately fulfilled in AD 70 at the destruction of Jerusalem, brought an end to the nation of Israel and God's dealing with them, what is to be done with chapter 30? We believe that the answer lies in the fact that Paul, under the inspiration of the Holy Spirit, applies the context of this passage to the gospel:

> *For this commandment [about the blessing and the curse] which I command you today is not too mysterious for you, nor is it far off. It is not in heaven, that you should say, "Who will ascend into heaven for us and bring it to us, that we may hear it and do it?" Nor is it beyond the sea, that you should say, "Who will go over the sea for us and bring it to us, that we may hear it and do it?" But the word is very near you, in your mouth and in your heart, that you may do it.* (Deut 30:11-14)

> *But the righteousness of faith speaks in this way "'Do not say in your heart, 'Who will ascend into heaven?' (that is, to bring Christ down from above) or, 'Who will descend into the abyss?'" (that is, to bring Christ up from the dead). But what does it say? "The word is near you, in your mouth and in your heart" (that is, the word of faith which we preach): that if you confess with your mouth the Lord Jesus and believe in your heart that God has raised Him from the dead, you will be saved. For with the heart one believes unto righteousness, and with the mouth confession is made unto salvation. For the Scripture says, "Whoever believes on Him will not be put to shame." For there is no distinction between Jew and Greek, for the same Lord over all is rich to all who call upon Him. For "whoever calls on the name of the LORD shall be saved."* (Rom 10:6-13)

Paul equates the promise of restoration not with *physical* Jews and the land of Israel, but with *spiritual* Jews and the gospel. (We note that some see the fulfillment of Deuteronomy 30 in the return of the exiles from the Babylonian captivity. We do not deny that this may be the case. However, in light of Paul's inspired application of this passage to the gospel, we feel that the return of the Babylonian exiles would be a "type" of the spiritual gathering of which Paul is speaking.) In God's sight there is no distinction between Jew and Greek. This agrees with the author of Hebrews' application of Jeremiah's New Covenant to the gospel (Jer 31; Heb 8). Once again the veil of Moses is being removed. Those Jews who did not accept what was behind the veil continued to insist upon a physical kingdom in the land of Israel. The connection between Deuteronomy 30 and the gospel is further strengthened by God's promise to those whom He gathers:

And the LORD your God will circumcise your heart and the heart of your descendants, to love the LORD your God with all your heart and with all your soul, that you may live. (Deut 30:6)

For circumcision is indeed profitable if you keep the law; but if you are a breaker of the law, your circumcision has become uncircumcision. Therefore, if an uncircumcised man keeps the righteous requirements of the law, will not his uncircumcision be counted as circumcision? And will not the physically uncircumcised, if he fulfills the law, judge you who, even with your written code and circumcision, are a transgressor of the law? For he is not a Jew who is one outwardly, nor is circumcision that which is outward in the flesh; but he is a Jew who is one inwardly; and circumcision is that of the heart, in the Spirit, not in the letter; whose praise is not from men but from God. (Rom 2:25-29)

As we studied earlier, circumcision of the heart identifies the "children of promise," the gospel saints of the New Covenant. That the message of the cross is the means by which the scattered people of God are gathered is seen in the following passage:

*And one of them, Caiaphas, being high priest that year, said to them, "You know nothing at all, nor do you consider that it is expedient for us that one man should die for the people, and not that the whole nation should perish." Now this he did not say on his own authority; but being high priest that year he prophesied that Jesus would die for the nation, and not for that nation only, but also that He would **gather together in one the children of God who were scattered abroad**.* (John 11:49-52; emphasis added)

While Deuteronomy 30 certainly contains physical terms (land, livestock, etc.), we cannot deny Paul's inspired application of it to the gospel. Consider also that Jesus speaks of his followers possessing a hundred times more mothers, brothers, fathers, sisters, etc. in the kingdom (Matt 19:28-29).

In the passage above we see the gospel as the means by which God's children are gathered. The misconception of applying eternal promises to physical Israel occupying physical Canaan is corrected by the following points:

- The promises regarding physical Israel occupying the physical land were conditional

- Scripture affirms that all the promises concerning physical occupation were fulfilled
- Any remaining fulfillments are of a spiritual nature, promised to the spiritual seed of Abraham, not the physical seed
- The divine commentary of the New Testament equates God's gathering of scattered Israel with the spread of the gospel

Having cleared the hurdle of the "forever" promises about the land, we are once again in perfect harmony with the pattern of the previous chapters. The physical land of Israel is a type of heaven—both of them being "Promised Lands." Again, the physical element of the Old Covenant foreshadows the spiritual fulfillment of the New Covenant. As we shall see in the chapter "The Veiled Generation," there was a transition generation in both cases, lasting a period of forty years.

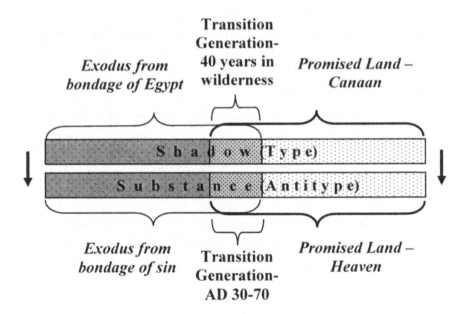

Summary to Part I

—m—

And Moses indeed was faithful in all His house as a servant, for a testimony of those things which would be spoken afterward . . . . (Heb 3:5)

A s we have demonstrated in the preceding chapters, the entire Mosaic economy—the Covenant, the kingdom, the temple, the priesthood, the Israelites and the land—was only a foreshadow of things which would be realized in the New Covenant. And though the spiritual fulfillment was veiled in that old administration, there were allusions of a future, better administration; for example, "a priest forever according to the order of Melchizedek" and Abraham's dwelling as a stranger while in the Promised Land. Perhaps "allusions" is putting it too mildly, for the New Testament says that the old administration "witnessed" to the righteousness of the gospel:

But now the righteousness of God apart from the law is revealed, being witnessed by the Law and the Prophets . . . . (Rom 3:21)

Unfortunately, the Jews missed that "witness of the Law" and the testimony proclaiming there was something behind the veil of Moses, and most of them fell short of discerning the New Covenant. Instead of looking for, and understanding, the substance of the New Covenant, they were holding on tenaciously to the shadow of the Old Covenant. More important than missing the witness of the Law, they rejected the inspired teaching of the New Testament apostles. These inspired apostles understood the substance behind the veil, although even they had failed to discern the witness of the Law prior to Pentecost. For example, they did not realize that John the Baptist fulfilled the prophecies of Elijah (until Jesus' explanation), and they asked Jesus repeatedly about a physical kingdom. After Pentecost, however, this changed dramatically when they received the Holy Spirit, Who led them into all truth and taught them of the things to come. Their new understanding of Old Testament prophecy was contrary to public opinion, and this became *the* major point of contention between Judaism and Christianity:

Then some rose up and bore false witness against Him, saying, "We heard Him say, 'I will destroy this temple made with hands,

and within three days I will build another made without hands.'"
(Mark 14:57)

Then they secretly induced men to say, "We have heard him [Stephen] **speak blasphemous words against Moses and God."** *And they stirred up the people, the elders, and the scribes; and they came upon him, seized him, and brought him to the council. They also set up false witnesses who said, "This man does not cease to* **speak blasphemous words against this holy place and the law**; *for we have heard him say that this Jesus of Nazareth will destroy this place and* **change the customs which Moses delivered to us."** (Acts 6:11-14)

When Gallio was proconsul of Achaia, the Jews with one accord rose up against Paul and brought him to the judgment seat, saying, "This fellow persuades men to worship God **contrary to the law."** (Acts 18:12-13)

And when they [the elders in Jerusalem] heard it [God's work among the Gentiles], they glorified the Lord. And they said to him [Paul], "You see, brother, how many myriads of Jews there are who have believed, and they are all zealous for the law; but they have been informed about you **that you teach all the Jews who are among the Gentiles to forsake Moses**, *saying that they ought not to circumcise their children* **nor to walk according to the customs**. (Acts 21:20-21)

This is the man [Paul] **who teaches all men everywhere against the people, the law, and this place**; *and furthermore he also brought Greeks into the temple and has defiled this holy place."* (Acts 21:28)
(emphases added)

Because the Jews lacked an understanding of the physical-to-spiritual transition, and the necessity for the physical type to be done away with, the teachings of Christ and the apostles were perceived as attempts to change the Law of Moses. The Jews did not realize that Christ, as the Messiah, came to *fulfill* the law so that the type could be done away with, and that He might be established as Mediator of a New Covenant:

Do not think that I came to destroy the Law or the Prophets. I did not come to destroy but to fulfill. (Matt 5:17)

But now He has obtained a more excellent ministry, inasmuch as He is also Mediator of a better covenant, which was established on better promises. (Heb 8:6)

Though the experts in the Law devoted their lives to understanding it, still they failed to see that Christ was its fulfillment, in spite of His clear attempts to enlighten them:

For if you believed Moses, you would believe Me; for he wrote about Me. But if you do not believe his writings, how will you believe My words?" (John 5:46-47)

You search the Scriptures, for in them you think you have eternal life; and these are they which testify of Me. But you are not willing to come to Me that you may have life. (John 5:39-40)

This propensity for clinging to the type is illustrated by the fact that the Old Testament-era Israelites continued to worship the bronze serpent up until the days of King Hezekiah:

He removed the high places and broke the sacred pillars, cut down the wooden image and broke in pieces the bronze serpent that Moses had made; for until those days the children of Israel burned incense to it, and called it Nehushtan. (2 Kgs 18:4)

Although the bronze serpent had played a specific role in Israel's history, that role had long since ended, yet the Israelites could not "let go" of that tangible reference to God's previous work. The only way to get the Israelites to cease their obsession with it was to destroy it. Just as the bronze serpent had to be destroyed, so the Old Covenant system, which had served its purpose, had to be removed to prevent the Israelites from clinging to what was only types and shadows. Have we, like the Israelites before us, been clinging to some of the obsolete types of the Old Covenant? Is it possible that we too have been guilty of failing to remove the veil fully? To be sure, we have removed it far enough to perceive and accept the New Covenant. But have we truly understood the overwhelming spiritual nature of the New Covenant? In this book's introduction, we said that while the New Covenant is not entirely spiritual in nature, it is primarily so. Certainly, physical people living on this physical Earth since Pentecost have been born again into the spiritual kingdom. But while we may have acknowledged certain spiritual aspects of the New Covenant, how many of us have coalesced those aspects into a comprehensive whole to reveal the extent to which the New Covenant is spiritual in nature? Hopefully, Part I of this work has done just that. Once again, we must ask ourselves, are we willing to receive it? Are we willing to lay aside man-made tradition in favor of the inspired commentary of the New Testament authors?

Having established this foundation, in Part II we will attempt to build upon it by removing the veil from the Second Coming of Christ. In order to do this, we must look using the same lens of Paul and the New Testament saints:

> *. . . we do not look at the things which are seen, but at the things which are not seen. For the things which are seen are temporary, but the things which are not seen are eternal.* (2 Cor 4:18)

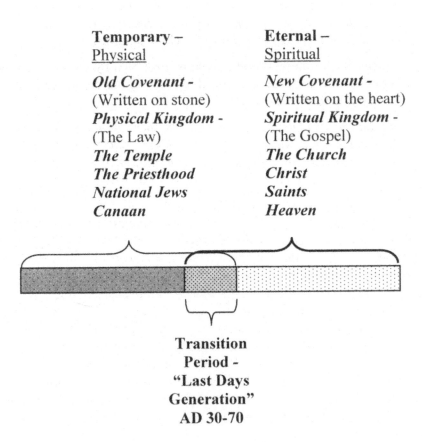

Temporary –
Physical

Old Covenant -
(Written on stone)
Physical Kingdom -
(The Law)
The Temple
The Priesthood
National Jews
Canaan

Eternal –
Spiritual

New Covenant -
(Written on the heart)
Spiritual Kingdom -
(The Gospel)
The Church
Christ
Saints
Heaven

**Transition
Period -
"Last Days
Generation"
AD 30-70**

Part II:

Unveiling the Second Coming

Is it faith to understand nothing, and merely submit your convictions implicitly to the Church?

John Calvin

Putting On the Veil?

—ɯ—

Having spent dozens of pages and numerous passages of Scripture to establish the spiritual nature of the New Covenant, we are presented with an interesting dilemma: Does not the popular understanding of the Second Coming of Christ—in which Jesus vanquishes the physical armies of the Earth, sets up a physical throne in physical Jerusalem, and reigns over a physical kingdom—sound suspiciously like the expectations the Jews had for Jesus' first coming? Hence the question of this chapter's title, "Putting On the Veil?" Is it possible that, just as the Jews allowed the veil of Moses to shroud elements of Christ's first coming, the Church has allowed that same veil to shroud elements of His Second Coming? Could it be that, while discerning the speck in the Jews' eyes regarding Christ's first coming, our own vision is obscured by a speck (if not a plank) in regard to His Second Coming?

Would not a return to the physical realm be tantamount to putting back on the veil of Moses and resurrecting the physical types, putting them over and against their spiritual fulfillments? Quoting Goppelt, Hanegraaff writes: "The type is not essentially a miniature version of the antitype, but is a prefiguration in a different stage of redemptive history that indicates the outline or essential features ... of the future reality and *that loses its own significance when that reality appears*" (p. 173, *The Apocalypse Code*; emphasis added). Don K. Preston elaborates:

> The millennial insistence that national Israel must be restored in earthly splendor misses God's ultimate purpose for Israel. She was not the goal, Israel was the foreshadowing image, the precursor, of what God was preparing. He used Israel to prepare the way for the "better things," fully intending that when those better things arrived, the Old Covenant form would be cast aside. Having fulfilled her purpose, God's exclusive Theocratic relationship with her would end. Berkhof wrote of Old Covenant Israel, "The theocratic nation itself was merely a type, a shadow of the spiritual realities of a better day, and, therefore, destined to vanish as soon as the antitype made its appearance. *The restoration of the*

ancient theocracy in the future would simply mean the recurrence of the type." (Like Father, Like Son, p. 129; emphasis added)

We have already demonstrated that the Old Covenant was obsolete and requiring change:

For if what is passing away was glorious, what remains is much more glorious. (2 Cor 3:11)

In that He says, "A new covenant," He has made the first obsolete. Now what is becoming obsolete and growing old is ready to vanish away. (Heb 8:13)

Therefore, if perfection were through the Levitical priesthood (for under it the people received the law), what further need was there that another priest should rise according to the order of Melchizedek, and not be called according to the order of Aaron? For the priesthood being changed, of necessity there is also a change of the law. (Heb 7:11-12)

There is no intimation that the "passing away" was to be merely temporary, nor that any elements of the Old Covenant were to play some future role in the New Covenant. Rather, we see that the Old Covenant had fulfilled its purpose; hence, it was obsolete and no longer needed. As Paul stated, the law was not against the promise (the Old Covenant was not against the New); it was designed to reveal our sin and prepare us for redemption through faith in Christ. Once that faith—God's redemptive plan—was revealed fully, the law had served its purpose:

Is the law then against the promises of God? Certainly not! For if there had been a law given which could have given life, truly righteousness would have been by the law. But the Scripture has confined all under sin that the promise by faith in Jesus Christ might be given to those who believe. But before faith came, we were kept under guard by the law, kept for the faith which would afterward be revealed. Therefore the law was our tutor to bring us to Christ, that we might be justified by faith. But after faith has come, we are no longer under a tutor. (Gal 3:21-25)

On the other hand, there is no indication of an end to the New Covenant; rather, it is declared to be everlasting:

And it is yet far more evident if, in the likeness of Melchizedek, there arises another priest who has come, not according to the law of a fleshly commandment, but according to the power of an endless life. For He testifies:

> *"You are a priest forever*
> *According to the order of Melchizedek."*

But He, because He continues forever, has an unchangeable priesthood. (Heb 7:15-17, 24)

Now may the God of peace who brought up our Lord Jesus from the dead, that great Shepherd of the sheep, through the blood of the everlasting covenant . . . . (Heb 13:20)

Christ's priesthood is unchangeable, and His blood was shed to provide for an everlasting covenant. So by what scriptural support and hermeneutic do we reapply elements of the obsolete Old Covenant to the New Covenant? Although not every Old Testament prophecy dealing with Israel, the land, the kingdom, the temple, etc., is interpreted for us by the New Testament authors, clearly those which are interpreted for us set the precedent for spiritual applications. That being the case, should we not demand undeniable compulsion from Scripture to *break* that precedent in other passages?

We find no such compulsion in the New Testament. After Pentecost, there is no mention of a future physical kingdom. After describing the Church as the temple of God, there is no mention of a future physical temple. After stating that true Israel is made up of spiritual Jews circumcised of the heart, Paul never says that being a true Israelite will ever be dependent upon a bloodline and physical circumcision.

This is borne out by Old Testament typology as well. After being cast out, Ishmael is never reintroduced into God's redemptive history. After the kingdom is torn from Saul, it never returns to his family line. The fact that Paul only used Hagar, Sarah, and their sons to represent covenant ages indicates that there is no age to follow the New Covenant age, which is everlasting. Abraham had more sons by his second wife (Keturah; Gen 25:1-2), thus, if there was another age, covenant, or phase in God's redemptive plan, Paul had the perfect opportunity to incorporate that into his analogy. He could have used three different sons, borne by three different mothers, to represent three different ages, covenants, or phases in God's redemptive plan. But he did not. Inspired by the Holy Spirit, Paul only used two (Gal 4:20ff). The New Covenant was the next and *final* phase in God's progressive plan of redemption.

Clearly then, we can find no support in Scripture which allows us, after having removed the veil and recognizing Christ in His first coming, to pull that very same veil over His Second Coming. Some may argue, however, that the Jews' error was not that of wholesale misinterpretation, but that they merely applied their interpretation to the *wrong* coming of the Messiah. They were looking for the Lion of Judah and a reigning King, while Jesus came first as the Lamb of God and a suffering servant. It would not be until His Second Coming that Jesus takes on his role as the Lion of Judah and reigning King. Thus the Jews were not *misinterpreting* as much as they were *misapplying* the Old Testament passages. The Church, they say, has correctly applied to His Second Coming what the Jews expected in His first coming.

This sounds plausible at first glance, but it is merely a hollow attempt to sustain a structure that cannot be supported by Scripture. As we have demonstrated amply by Scripture, the purpose of the Old Covenant was to foreshadow and lay a foundation for the New Covenant. Once fulfilled by Christ, the Old Covenant's purpose was achieved, becoming obsolete and eventually passing away. In contrast, the New Covenant is everlasting and unchangeable, thus closing the door on the possibility of some type of return to portions of the Old Covenant system. Added to this is the fact that the New Covenant is a *better* covenant (Heb 7:22; 8:6); to reintroduce elements of the Old Covenant would only dilute or corrupt it. Preston writes, "Now, if Christ's *current* New Covenant is a *better covenant*, and is built on *better promises*, then any discussion of the restoration of the nation of Israel and her cultus, no matter how modified the form of restoration, is to suggest the restoration of what was inherently inferior" (*Like Father, Like Son*, p. 138; emphasis in original). Surely, we will not deny that Christ can be the Lion of Judah Who reigns as King over His *spiritual* kingdom, the Church?

Sadly, the New Testament Jews looked for a restoration of the Davidic kingdom, just as many in the Church do today. Yet, having this type of worldly kingdom like other nations was, in fact, a sign of Israel's rejection of God:

> But the thing displeased Samuel when they said, "Give us a king to judge us." So Samuel prayed to the LORD. And the LORD said to Samuel, "Heed the voice of the people in all that they say to you; for they have not rejected you, but they have rejected Me, that I should not reign over them." (1 Sam 8:6-7)

God was so displeased with this matter that He thundered from Heaven:

136

"Now therefore, stand and see this great thing which the LORD will do before your eyes: Is today not the wheat harvest? I will call to the LORD, and He will send thunder and rain, that you may perceive and see that your wickedness is great, which you have done in the sight of the LORD, in asking a king for yourselves." So Samuel called to the LORD, and the LORD sent thunder and rain that day; and all the people greatly feared the LORD and Samuel. And all the people said to Samuel, "Pray for your servants to the LORD your God, that we may not die; for we have added to all our sins the evil of asking a king for ourselves." (1 Sam 12:16-19)

Are we to believe, then, that a physical kingdom with a king on a physical throne is what God ultimately had in mind, and that the Israelites were chastised only for wanting it too soon? Was not God reigning over Israel in a nonphysical manner prior to Israel's request for a king? Is not Christ reigning presently over His Church (spiritual Israel) in a nonphysical manner? Do the Scriptures really teach that Jesus will reign physically from Jerusalem, or are we, like the Old Testament Jews before us, wanting His kingdom to be *like all the nations*? Instead of trying to pull the veil of Moses over the Second Coming, is it not time that we remove it? Though easier said than done, we need to erase from the blackboard of our minds the traditions of man. Then, on a clean slate, we can write down only what is taught in Scripture.

In the following chapters we will attempt to do just that. Building upon our foundation of the New Covenant and its spiritual nature, we will explore the three main eschatological texts: the book of Revelation, Jesus' Olivet discourse in Matthew 24 (and its parallels in Mark 14 and Luke 21), and Daniel's Seventy Weeks. Although these will not be expository studies, we will attempt to view these texts in a different framework—one that fits the scriptural foundation laid in Part I.

The Dating of Revelation

—⟋m⟍—

In the chapter "The New Covenant and the Temple," we mentioned that the only reference in the New Testament to what could be interpreted as a future *physical* temple was to be found in the book of Revelation. In Revelation 11, John is instructed to measure the temple; the court, however, was not to be measured, for it was to be trampled by the Gentiles, thus indicating that the temple was not the heavenly one. Because the widely held date for the writing of Revelation is ca. AD 96, a quarter-century after the temple of Jesus' day was destroyed in AD 70, many interpret this temple of which Revelation speaks as being a future one.

We also noted that there are those who believe that the physical temple referred to in Revelation is the same one that was destroyed in AD 70. This is based upon certain evidence that Revelation was actually written in ca. AD 60-65, *before* the temple was destroyed; thus, it is the temple of Jesus' day which Revelation has in view. Accordingly, in this viewpoint, there is no reference to a future physical temple. Prior to addressing the dating issue, we wish to briefly introduce the major interpretative views of Revelation.

Revelation: The Four Major Views

A little known fact, at least in some Christian circles, is that there are four primary views, or interpretive positions, for the book of Revelation. Naturally, there are many subdivisions within each of the four; even the lines between the four are not always black and white, but sometimes gray. The following information is gleaned mostly from Steve Gregg's *Revelation: Four Views*. The various millennial views, often confused with the various interpretive views of Revelation as a whole, are defined as well.

Historicist:

Sees the Book of Revelation as a prewritten record of the course of history, describing events to occur between the era in which the book was written up until the end of the world. Thus, fulfillment has been unfolding for nearly two thousand years and is considered to be in progress at present.

Preterist:

Sees the fulfillment of Revelation's prophecies as already having occurred in what is now the ancient past, not long after the author's own time. Thus, the fulfillment was in the future from the point of view of the inspired author, but it is now to be relegated to the past from our vantage point in history. Some Preterists believe that the final chapters of Revelation look forward to the Second Coming of Christ. Others think that everything in the book reached its culmination in the past.

Futurist:

Postulates that the majority of the prophecies of the Book of Revelation have not yet been fulfilled and await future fulfillment. Futurist interpreters usually apply everything after chapter four to a relatively brief period before the return of Christ.

Idealist (Spiritualist, Symbolic):

Does not attempt to find concretely historical fulfillments of the visions, but takes Revelation to be a great drama depicting transcendent spiritual realities, such as the spiritual conflict between Christ and Satan, between the saints and the antichristian world powers, and depicting the final victory of Christ and the heavenly vindication of His saints. Fulfillment is seen either as entirely spiritual or as recurrent, finding representative expression in historical events throughout the age. Thus, the prophecy is rendered applicable to Christians in any age.

The Millennium

The Millennium, described in Revelation 20, is the 1,000-year-long reign of Christ and the concurrent binding of Satan. There are three major views, or interpretations, of the Millennium. Though often confused with the four eschatological viewpoints described above, they are, in fact, different hermeneutical approaches to a particular facet of eschatology. Each of the three views of the Millennium has its adherents in each of the four eschatological views, though some of the views offer themselves to each other more readily than others.

Premillennialism (Chiliasm, derived from the Greek word for "thousand"):

The belief that the Second Coming of Christ will precede the millennial kingdom. Taking a mostly literal (physical) approach, premillenarians expect the kingdom to endure for a period of one thousand years, during which Christ will reign with His saints here on earth prior to the establishment of the eternal new heavens and new earth. The millennial reign will be characterized by international peace and justice resulting from the universally-enforced rule of Christ over the saved and unsaved alike. At the end of time, Satan's brief period of freedom will put humanity to one final test just before the final judgment.

There are two principal varieties of premillennialism: historic premillennialism and dispensational premillennialism (or simply dispensationalism). The latter differs from the former in its emphasis on the continuing centrality of national Israel in God's eschatological program and in anticipating a Rapture of Christians to heaven before the beginning of the Tribulation.

Premillennialism has been accused by its critics of promoting a pessimistic outlook for the temporal future (although, if this is indeed what Scripture teaches, premillennialists can hardly be faulted for such pessimism). This view is most likely to be held by those adopting a Futurist approach to Revelation.

Postmillennialism:

Teaches that Christ returns after the millennial period. According to this view, the millennial kingdom will be established through the evangelistic mission of the Church. This enterprise will be so successful that most (if not all) people will become Christians, resulting in a thousand years of peace on earth before Christ's Second Coming. Postmillennialists are often (but not always) inclined toward the Preterist approach to Revelation, since their optimistic view of the future works better if the disasters described in Revelation are seen as belonging to a time long past, rather than to the end of history.

Amillennialism:

Understands the thousand years of Revelation 20 to symbolize an indefinitely long period of time, which happens to correspond to the entire span of time from the first coming of Christ until his Second Coming. Most aspects of chapter 20 (like most aspects of the rest of Revelation) are believed to be symbolic: the binding of Satan happened spiritually at the Cross; the reign of the saints is the present age; the loosing of Satan is a final period of deception that comes upon the world at the end of the age; the fire from heaven that devours the wicked is the Second Coming of Christ. Although Amillennialists may be found among all of the various approaches to Revelation, they rarely adhere to the Futurist interpretation.

It should be remembered that the various eschatological approaches to Revelation are not linked inseparably to any particular millennial position, so that one's eschatology does not necessarily dictate which approach to the millennium is to be preferred.

It is our opinion that of the four major views defined above, the one that fits best upon the scriptural foundation laid in Part I is that of Preterism. This view holds to the early date for the writing of Revelation, interpreting it as a prophecy of the impending destruction of Jerusalem. The last days spoken of in the New Testament were the last days of the Old Covenant, and Revelation is a prophecy, couched in apocalyptic language, of its passing. Like Ishmael and Isaac, the Old and New Covenants had coexisted for a time (ca. AD 30-70). In AD 70, Ishmael was "cast out" and the Old Covenant passed away. Not coincidently, the time span of that coexistence was roughly 40 years, the length of a biblical generation. In the remainder of Part II we will attempt to establish these views and their ramifications scripturally. Though the reader may be surprised, or even shocked, by some of the interpretations put forth, we trust that the fair treatment of, and respect for, the Holy Scriptures thus far has earned the author further consideration.

As one can see from the definitions above of the four major interpretive views, only Preterism depends upon an early date for the writing of

Revelation, and it is to that we now turn our attention. We begin with a quote from King's *The Spirit of Prophecy*:

> Since our prophetical structure is consummated in the fall of Judaism, it is essential that the pre-destruction of Jerusalem placement of Revelation be authenticated. Generally, the date of Revelation is assigned to two periods of Roman history; namely, during the reign of Nero in the early or mid 60's and in the latter part of Domitian's reign, about AD 96. Since a claim for either date cannot be substantiated by history, and scholars are about equally divided on the two dates, we shall consider the internal evidence that overwhelmingly favors the early Neronian date.

The Things Shown Must Shortly Come To Pass

John's introductory statement that the things shown in the Revelation message must shortly come to pass (Rev 1:1), furnishes us with *inspired* testimony that it is not a book of prophecy that stretches over centuries and millenniums, but rather it contained a succession of immediate events. This is further supported in verse three. "Blessed is he that readeth, and they that hear the words of this prophecy, and keep those things which are written therein: for the time is at hand." There is no principle of exegesis that can eliminate from prophecy of Scripture a plain statement of time such as *shortly* and *at hand*. These time statements were implanted to impress upon the recipients of that message the urgent need for hearing, reading, understanding, and keeping the things that were written therein. Also, they must serve as a guide for future generations in a proper placement of the Revelation message, lest the true meaning of God's word and eternal purpose becomes lost in a Babel of confusion. If a time statement resident in a Scripture cannot be trusted, neither can any other portion of that Scripture.

A further emphasis upon the immediacy of those events is made in the last chapter of the book. In verse six the angel affirmed that "These sayings are faithful and true: and the Lord God of the holy prophets sent his angel to shew unto his servants the things which must shortly be done." Then in verse ten John was instructed to "Seal not the sayings of the prophecy of this book: for the time is at hand." Thus, the message of Revelation is securely trapped at both ends by time statements that hold its contents a prisoner of first century historical events. All that remains is the identity of those events, which should be quite discernible from the background of prophecy that bears upon the end-time.

The Identity of Revelation With The Book of Daniel

Revelation, just as the book of Daniel, is an end-time message, except Daniel's book is a *prophecy* of the end-times, whereas Revelation is a *revealing* of that end-time, being written at the time of the end. Daniel's prophecy was sealed until the time of the end (Dan 12:9), but John was forbidden to seal his book because it was a revelation of what had been sealed in Daniel's prophecy, and the time for those things was at hand (Rev 22:10). Now what did Daniel prophesy? He foretold of the destruction of Jerusalem and the temple (Dan 9:26, 27). He predicted the coming of the Ancient of days (Christ) and the saint's possessing the kingdom (Dan 7:21, 22). He saw in connection with the coming of Christ, the judgment and the defeat of the beast (Dan 7:9-11), followed by Christ's receiving an eternal kingdom of world wide dominion (Dan 7:13, 14). (*The Spirit of Prophecy*, pp. 256-257; emphasis in original)

If we could put ourselves in the place of Revelation's original readers, whether they lived in AD 65 or AD 96, when we read terms such as "at hand" and "shortly come to pass," would we understand them to mean two thousand years in the distant future? Regardless of when one believes Revelation to have been written, there is an undeniable message that the events depicted were to transpire within the lifetime of the original readers. Some argue that the word translated "shortly" and the word translated "quickly" in Revelation 22:6, 12, 20 ("*behold I am coming quickly*") are from the same root word in the Greek. Therefore, they argue that although the events of Revelation were not *soon* to take place, they would occur *speedily* when they did come to pass. How does that argument hold up in the following verse, which translates "shortly" from the same root word in the Greek?

> *. . . knowing that shortly I must put off my tent, just as our Lord Jesus Christ showed me.* (2 Pet 1:14)

Both John and Peter had Jesus reveal something to them that would "shortly" take place. Are we to assume that what Jesus revealed to Peter was not that he was *about* to die, but that when he did die it would be quickly? Just as a plain reading of 2 Peter 1:14 leads us to believe that Peter was about to die, so a plain reading of Revelation leads us to believe that the events it foretold were about to take place. J. Stuart Russell states this truth both powerfully and eloquently:

> Yet if the book were meant to unveil the secrets of distant times, must it not of necessity have been unintelligible to its first readers — and not only unintelligible, but even irrelevant and useless. If it spake, as some would have us believe, of Huns and Goths and Saracens, of mediæval emperors and popes, of the Protestant Reformation and the French Revolution, what possible interest or meaning could it have for the Christian churches of Ephesus, and Smyrna, and Philadelphia, and Laodicea? Especially when we consider the actual circumstances of those early Christians — many of them enduring cruel sufferings and grievous persecutions, and all of them eagerly looking for an approaching hour of deliverance which was now close at hand — what purpose could it have answered to send them a document which they were urged to read and ponder, which was yet mainly occupied with historical events so distant as to be beyond the range of their sympathies, and so obscure that even at this day the shrewdest critics are hardly agreed on any one point? Is it conceivable that an apostle would mock the suffering and persecuted Christians of his time with dark parables about distant ages? If this book were really intended to minister faith and comfort to the very persons to whom it was sent, it must unquestionably deal with matters in which they were practically and personally interested. And does not this very obvious consideration suggest the true key to the Apocalypse? *Must it not of necessity refer to matters of contemporary history?* The only tenable, the only reasonable, hypothesis is that it was intended to be understood by its original readers; but this is as much as to say that it must be occupied with the events and transactions of their own day, and these comprised within a comparatively brief space of time.

LIMITATION OF TIME IN THE APOCALYPSE.

This is not a mere conjecture, it is certified by the express statements of the book. If there be one thing which more than any other is explicitly and repeatedly affirmed in the Apocalypse it is the *nearness* of the events which it predicts. This is stated, and reiterated again and again, in the beginning, the middle, and the end. We are warned that 'the time is *at hand*;' 'These things must *shortly* come to pass,' 'Behold, I come *quickly*;' 'Surely I come *quickly.'* Yet, in the face of these express and oft-repeated declarations, most interpreters have felt at liberty to ignore the limitations of time altogether, and to roam at will over ages and centuries, regarding the book as a syllabus of church history, an almanac of politico-ecclesiastical events for all Christiandom [*sic*] to the end of time. This has been a fatal and inexcusable blunder. To neglect the obvious and clear definition of the time so constantly thrust on the attention of the reader by the book itself is to stumble on the very threshold. Accordingly this inattention has vitiated by far the greatest number of apocalyptic interpretations. It may truly be said that the key has all the while hung by the door, plainly visible to every one who had eyes to see; yet men have tried to pick the lock, or force the door, or climb up some other way, rather than avail themselves of so simple and ready a way of admission as to use the key made and provided for them. (*The Parousia*, pp. 366-367; emphasis in original)

Hanegraaff adds, "If Revelation is principally a book that describes what is about to take place in the twenty-first century, it would have been largely irrelevant to first-century Christians" (*The Apocalypse Code*, p. 159).

Russell asks a pointed question: if the book unveils the secrets of the distant future (that is, distant to the original readers), must it not, then, have been unintelligible, indeed even irrelevant and useless to them? We trust that the reader understands that Russell is not denying the "living and powerful" characteristic of the Word (Heb 4:12), nor the timeless profitability of all Scripture (2 Tim 3:16). Rather, unlike Daniel's prophecy, which was declared *not* to be for Daniel's generation, Revelation gives every indication that it *was* for the generation of its *original* readers:

> *But you, Daniel, shut up the words, and **seal the book until the time of the end**; many shall run to and fro, and knowledge shall increase.* (Dan 12:4)

> *And he said to me, "**Do not seal the words of the prophecy of this book, for the time is at hand.** He who is unjust, let him be unjust still; he who is filthy, let him be filthy still; he who is righteous, let him be righteous still; he who is holy, let him be holy still."* (Rev 22:10-11)
> (emphases added)

Gabriel told Daniel to seal up the prophecy until the time of the end. The end of what? As we shall see in the coming chapter "Revelation, AD

70, and the End of the World," the end that Bible prophecy has in view is the end of the *age*, not the end of the world. John, on the other hand, was told to *not* seal up the prophecy because the time was at hand. In fact, it was so close that there was seemingly not even enough time for people to change their ways. Returning to the quote from King, why were the original readers exhorted to hear, read, understand, and keep the things that were written in Revelation if they referred to events of the distant future? Even if one holds to the later date (AD 96) for the writing of Revelation, should we not look for events and fulfillments within the time frame of that generation?

If we are willing to receive (remember the Elijah/John the Baptist connection?) that the events of Revelation were to transpire within the lifetime of the original readers, then we must look to history to see what major events happened *shortly* after ca. AD 65 as well as AD 96. While there may have been some upheaval in the Roman Empire shortly after AD 96, surely those events are eclipsed by the destruction of Jerusalem in AD 70, which occurred "shortly" after ca. AD 65. It should also be noted that the siege of Jerusalem, which led to its eventual destruction, commenced in ca. AD 66-67. When we consider that the Bible is God's unfolding plan of redemption and *His*tory, not world history, can there be a better fit for the catastrophic prophecies of Revelation than that of the judgment upon the apostate Jews who said of their Messiah, *"crucify Him, crucify Him"*? This was none other than the "casting out of Ishmael" and the "passing away of the Old Covenant." Certainly any upheaval in the Roman Empire would pale in comparison to the destruction of Jerusalem, when viewed from the perspective of God's redemptive plan.

Undoubtedly, the reader that is unfamiliar with Preterism is asking a host of questions. "What about one third of the grass being destroyed, one third of the waters turning to blood, the plagues, the mark of the Beast, the return of Christ," etc., etc.? It is hoped that the subsequent chapters will sufficiently address these issues. Our primary purpose here is to establish the time frame of the events of Revelation, after which we will turn our attention to the substance of those events.

The facts that Revelation, Daniel, and Jesus' Olivet discourse are all related to the end times, and that both Daniel and the Olivet discourse (at least to a degree) foresee the destruction of Jerusalem and the temple, only solidifies our position that Revelation is also a *revealing* of that destruction. Alfred Edersheim, in his book *The Temple: Its Ministry and Services*, agrees that the internal evidence points to a date prior to the destruction of Jerusalem for the writing of Revelation. He notes (pp. 95-96) that only the reader who has studied rabbinical accounts of the temple services can discern the references to minute details of those services found in both Revelation and the Gospel of John. Based upon these references, he concludes that not only was John probably, at some point in time, a participant in those services, but that both of his accounts were written before those services had ceased.

While King opts to rely solely on the internal evidence for dating Revelation, which is very convincing in itself, we can perhaps strengthen our position with some external evidence as well. We commend to the reader the excellent volume by Dr. Kenneth L. Gentry, Jr., *Before Jerusalem Fell*. In this book, we feel that Gentry not only casts serious doubts on the late date authorship, but thoroughly establishes the early date. He not only expounds upon the internal evidence, which we have already briefly explored, but he also examines the external evidence exhaustively. The chief external evidence for a late date of Revelation's writing is the testimony of the early church fathers. Gentry demonstrates that the testimony of these fathers is built upon a single observation from Irenaeus, one of the earliest fathers. Gentry states:

> Undoubtedly, Irenaeus' observation is the strongest weapon in the late date arsenal . . . . Irenaeus is an "obstacle" who cannot be overlooked by the early date school. (*Before Jerusalem Fell*, p. 46; revised edition, American Vision Press)

The "observation" of Irenaeus is the following quote:

> We will not, however, incur the risk of pronouncing positively as to the name of Antichrist; for if it were necessary that his name should be distinctly revealed in this present time, it would have been announced by him who beheld the apocalyptic vision. For that was seen no very long time since, but almost in our day, towards the end of Domitian's reign.

Gentry points out from the Greek that what "was seen no very long time since" is not necessarily the apocalypse but John. He goes on to illuminate the ambiguity of Irenaeus' text and offers alternative translations which lend themselves to an early date interpretation. He also examines Irenaeus' credibility as a historian, noting that Irenaeus claimed Jesus lived to be almost fifty years of age. We quote a few paragraphs from Gentry's "A Summation of the Early Date Argument," located at the book's closing:

In attempting to demonstrate the proper dating of this most influential book of our sacred canon, our investigation carefully considered both the external and internal witness of Revelation. Although much weight has long been credited the external evidence, especially that associated with Irenaeus, we noted that such a procedure is in danger of quieting the voice of God in deference to the voice of man. That is, when engaged from the perspective of an unflinching commitment to Scripture as the Word of God, it should be the procedure of Biblical Introduction to allow the most weight to the Scripture's *self-testimony* regarding its own historical composition. In deference to common practice, however, and in light of the nature of the present work as largely concerned with a rebuttal to the current late date position, we began with an inquiry into the external considerations of tradition.

In the portion of this study dealing with the external evidence, we gave extensive consideration to the statement of Irenaeus regarding Revelation's date. There we noted that the commonly received interpretation of Irenaeus is not without ambiguity. The all-important question in the matter is: Did Irenaeus mean to say that *Revelation* was seen by John in Domitian's reign? Or did he mean that *John*, who saw the Revelation, was seen in Domitian's reign? By the very nature of the case, verbal inflection alone is incapable of resolving the matter. More helpful are the contextual indicators available that suggest Irenaeus meant the latter of the two options.

Even if this re-interpretive approach to Irenaeus fails, however, we pointed out that Irenaeus was subject to error—even on matters he claims to have heard from first-hand sources (such as when he asserted that Jesus lived to be almost fifty years old). It is time for biblical scholars and Church historians to consider afresh Irenaeus's statement regarding Revelation. Especially is this the case since so much weight is granted to his witness, despite its ambiguity. (Ibid., p. 334; emphasis in original)

We agree with Gentry that, in putting so much weight on the external evidence for the date of Revelation, we are "in danger of quieting the voice of God in deference to the voice of man." We concur with the apostle John, "*If we receive the witness of men, the witness of God is greater*" (1 John 5:9). That being said, we feel that Gentry thoroughly nullifies the external evidence for a late date, while fortifying the internal evidence for an early date.

Predating Gentry's work is John A. T. Robinson's *Redating the New Testament*, first published in 1976. Robinson sees the lack of any mention of the destruction of Jerusalem not only as evidence for an early date of Revelation, but the entire New Testament as well:

> One of the oddest facts about the New Testament is that what on any showing would appear to be the single most datable and climactic event of the period—the fall of Jerusalem in AD 70, and with it the collapse of institutional Judaism based on the temple—is never once mentioned as a past fact. (*Redating the New Testament*, p. 13; Wipf and Stock Publishers, October 2000)

Concerning the book of Revelation specifically, Robinson quotes Hort as saying, "If external tradition alone could decide, there would be a clear preponderance for Domitian," and immediately follows it with:

> Yet, despite this, Hort, together with Lightfoot and Westcott, none of whom can be accused of setting light to ancient tradition, still rejected a Domitianic date in favour of one between the death of Nero in 68 and the fall of Jerusalem in 70. It is indeed a little known fact that this was what Hort calls "the general tendency of criticism" for most of the nineteenth century, and Peake cites the remarkable consensus of "both advanced and conservative scholars" who backed it. (Ibid., p. 225)

Indeed, Gentry provides an eight-page list of scholars who held an early date authorship for Revelation. This list contains, among others: Adam Clarke, Frederic W. Farrar, Philip Schaff, Henry B. Swete, Milton S. Terry, Alfred Edersheim, Joseph B. Lightfoot, Sir Isaac Newton, Augustus Strong, Moses Stuart, and Cornelius Vanderwaal. Kurt Simmons provides a pertinent quote from Robert Young:

> Robert Young, author of *Young's Analytical Concordance*, wrote a commentary on Revelation, published in 1885, wherein he makes the following statement: "It was written in Patmos about AD 68, whither John had been banished by Domitius Nero, as stated in the title of the Syriac version of the book; and with this concurs the express statement of Irenaeus in AD 175, who say it happened in the reign of Domitia*nou* – i.e, Domitius (Nero). Sulpicius, Orosius, *etc.*, stupidly mistaking Domitia*nou* for Domitian*ikos*, supposed Irenaeus to refer to Domitian, AD 95, and most succeeding writers

have fallen into the same blunder. The internal testimony is wholly in favor of the early date." (*The Consummation of the Ages*, p. 16; emphasis in original)

Simmons makes another observation which casts further doubt on a late date:

Irenaeus states concerning the number of the Beast, "Now since this is so, and since this number is found in all the good and ancient copies, and since those who have seen John face to face testify, and reason teaches us that the number of the beast appears according to the numeration of the Greeks by the letters in it . . ." Irenaeus' statement immediately raises the question of how, if Irenaeus indeed referred to the Apocalypse as having been seen "almost in our own generation," can copies of John's vision be termed "ancient?" (Ibid., p. 17)

Robinson makes another pertinent observation in his comparison between a supposed late date for Revelation and "contemporary" writings:

The central vision of II Esdras 3-14 dates itself (and there is no good reason to doubt it) in the year 100, "in the thirtieth year after the fall of Jerusalem" (3.1), and the contrast with the perspective of Revelation could hardly be greater. In this book, as in I and II Baruch, the Epistle of Barnabas and the Sibylline Oracles, there are unmistakable allusions to the destruction of Jerusalem. In Revelation there are none at all — in fact just the opposite. And whereas in II Esdras the tally of kings to date is twelve, and in the Epistle of Barnabas ten, in Revelation the sixth is still reigning. Yet we are asked to believe by those who hold to a Domitianic date that Revelation and II Esdras are virtually contemporary. (*Redating the New Testament*, p. 247)

Hanegraaff provides a very thought-provoking corollary from contemporary history:

. . . just as it is unreasonable to suppose that someone writing a history of the World Trade Center in the aftermath of September 11, 2001, would fail to mention the destruction of the twin towers, so too it stretches credulity to suggest that Revelation was written in the aftermath of the devastation of Jerusalem and the Jewish temple and yet makes no mention of this apocalypse. (*The Apocalypse Code*, p. 157)

Returning to the directive given to John to measure the temple, we note that Russell observes that measuring is often a term associated with judgment. Though at times, as in Ezekiel's passage, measuring may refer to construction, the context of Revelation, as judgment upon the apostate nation of Israel, fixes this measuring as being for destruction. That measuring is an indication of judgment is not unheard of in the Scriptures, as the following verses indicate:

*Also **I will make justice the measuring line**,*
*And **righteousness the plummet** . . . .* (Isa 28:17)

Thus He showed me: Behold, the Lord stood on a wall made with a plumb line, with a plumb line in His hand. And the LORD said to me, "Amos, what do you see?"
And I said, "A plumb line."
Then the Lord said:
*"**Behold, I am setting a plumb line***
***In the midst of My people Israel**;*
I will not pass by them anymore.
The high places of Isaac shall be desolate,
And the sanctuaries of Israel shall be laid waste.
I will rise with the sword against the house of Jeroboam." (Amos 7:7-9)

But the pelican and the porcupine shall possess it,
Also the owl and the raven shall dwell in it.
And He shall stretch out over it
***The line** of confusion and the stones of emptiness.* (Isa 34:11)

The LORD has purposed to destroy
The wall of the daughter of Zion.
***He has stretched out a line**;*
He has not withdrawn His hand from destroying;
Therefore He has caused the rampart and wall to lament;
They languished together. (Lam 2:8)
(emphases added)

Robinson concurs, stating:

But to interpret the command to "measure" the temple as a promise of preservation is to ignore the Old Testament background of the imagery. Often indeed the measuring-line and plummet are symbols rather of judgment and destruction. (Ibid., p. 241)

As we noted in our chapter "The Two Covenants and the Two Sons of Abraham," Ishmael and Hagar represent the Old Covenant and physical Jerusalem. Ishmael was cast out and the Old Covenant done away with in AD 70 at the destruction of Jerusalem. When we view the book of Revelation from this framework, especially in light of the above passages, we can easily see it as a grand vision of Christ's prophecy:

Now as He drew near, He saw the city and wept over it, saying, "If you had known, even you, especially in this your day, the things that make for your peace! But now they are hidden from your eyes. For days will come upon you when your enemies will build an embankment around you, surround you and close you in on every side, and level you, and your children within you, to the ground; and they will not leave in you one stone upon another, because you did not know the time of your visitation." (Luke 19:41-44)

In the forthcoming chapters we will see just how precisely this prophecy was fulfilled during the fall of Jerusalem. While we have only addressed briefly the dating of Revelation, we hope that we have been thorough enough to impress upon the reader the probability that Revelation was written prior to the destruction of Jerusalem. As we continue our study, we feel it will be seen that, with an early date, Revelation fits naturally into place in the eschatological puzzle, whereas a late date is forcing it into a place where it does not belong.

This Generation

—⚍—

As we noted in the end of "Part I" and illustrated in the accompanying diagram, the time during which the two covenants coexisted was forty years—a biblical generation. If we can accept that Revelation (as well as Daniel and Jesus) foretold the destruction of Jerusalem in AD 70, it is amazing how the various pieces of the puzzle that say "all these things shall come upon this generation" fall into place. We say "fall" into place because this is what they naturally do rather than being "forced" into place in some other historical era.

> *For as the lightning that flashes out of one part under heaven shines to the other part under heaven, so also the Son of Man will be in His day. But first He must suffer many things and be rejected by this generation.* (Luke 17:24-25)

Is there any doubt as to which generation is the one at whose hands Christ "suffered many things and was rejected?" Obviously, it was Christ's current generation. In fact, no one claims that it is today's generation or a future generation. By what right, then, do we interpret the following passages as any generation but Christ's current generation?

> *Then Jesus went out and departed from the temple, and His disciples came up to show Him the buildings of the temple. And Jesus said to them, "Do you not see all these things? Assuredly, I say to you, not one stone shall be left here upon another, that shall not be thrown down." Now as He sat on the Mount of Olives, the disciples came to Him privately, saying, "Tell us, when will these things be? And what will be the sign of Your coming, and of the end of the age?"*
> *". . . know that it is near—at the doors! Assuredly, I say to **you, this generation** will by no means pass away till all these things take place."* (Matt 24:1-3, 33-34)

> *For whoever is ashamed of Me and My words in **this adulterous and sinful generation**, of him the Son of Man also will be ashamed when He comes in the glory of His Father with the holy angels.* (Mark 8:38)

*Therefore the wisdom of God also said, "I will send them prophets and apostles, and some of them they will kill and persecute," that the blood of all the prophets which was shed from the foundation of the world may be required of **this generation**, from the blood of Abel to the blood of Zechariah who perished between the altar and the temple. Yes, I say to you, it shall be required of **this generation**.* (Luke 11:49-51)
(emphases added)

Certainly Christ's current generation is still in view in these passages. This is demonstrated by the disciples' question about the end of the age. The age they were expecting to end was not the Church age of the New Covenant, for as we have seen, it is everlasting and unchangeable. Besides, if we hold that the Church age began at Pentecost, then the Church age had not yet begun! Even if we view the death and resurrection of Christ as the beginning of the New Covenant, the New Covenant age still would not have been inaugurated at the time the disciples posed their question. Surely, they were not expecting the end of "the age to come," but rather the end of their present age—that of the Law and the Old Covenant. As we shall see, the fact that that age ended in AD 70 fits perfectly with the time frame of "this generation" not passing away till all things were fulfilled.

To make the generation *to* which Christ and the New Testament authors spoke different from the generation *of* which they spoke is to force a puzzle piece into a place where it was not designed to fit. As an example of forcing a piece into the puzzle, we return to John the Baptist. Recall that John, in the spirit of Elijah, was sent to Israel before the great and dreadful Day of the Lord:

"Behold, I will send you Elijah the prophet
Before the coming of the great and dreadful day of the LORD.
And he will turn
The hearts of the fathers to the children,
And the hearts of the children to their fathers,
Lest I come and strike the earth [land] with a curse."
(Mal 4:5-6)

If we force the generation upon which *all these things* were to come to pass to be a yet-future generation, then either John the Baptist showed up nearly 2,000 years too early or the great Day of the Lord is nearly 2,000 years late. On the other hand, if we realize that the word "earth" can also be translated "land" (as do the NASB and NIV), and understand the curse to find its fulfillment in the destruction of Jerusalem, then the "puzzle piece" of Jesus' and John's generation fits quite naturally.

We cannot overemphasize a proper understanding of the term *this generation*, for it is a main point of Futurist eschatology that the Second Coming is yet to occur. We need to make several points here. First, if you look up these passages in a red-letter edition Bible, you will find that they are all spoken by Jesus. Second, the Greek word γενεα (*genea*) is translated as *generation* in all of these passages. Third, the word γενεα is used 43 times in the New Testament and not once is it ever translated as *race*, as some attempt to do with it in Matthew 24:34. The KJV translates γενεα twice as *time* or *times*, and twice as *ages*. In three of those instances, the translators of the NKJV chose to render γενεα as *generation* or *generations*. The exception is Ephesians 3:5. Here it is in context:

> *For this reason I, Paul, the prisoner of Christ Jesus for you Gentiles—if indeed you have heard of the dispensation of the grace of God which was given to me for you, how that by revelation He made known to me the mystery (as I have briefly written already, by which, when you read, you may understand my knowledge in the mystery of Christ), which in other **ages** was not made known to the sons of men, as it has now been revealed by the Spirit to His holy apostles and prophets . . . .* (Eph 3:1-5; emphasis added)

We would ask the reader, which word could replace **ages** and not change the meaning of the passage: *races* or *generations*? How then can we read the passages above and think that they refer to any generation other than the one to which Christ was speaking? Which generation rejected Christ and caused Him to suffer many things? Which generation saw Christ buried three days and three nights in the heart of the earth? The generation to which He was speaking! Why then would the other passages not also refer to that same generation? How can we say that judgment is not decreed upon the generation *to* whom Christ was speaking?

"Oh, but it was decreed," some will say, "and it is reserved for the last days, when all will be judged. The text does not say that those people will 'rise up in judgment' in *that* generation, but that 'in the judgment—which is still future—they will rise up,' and *then* condemn it" (Matt 12:41-42). Or, some may say, that generation *was* judged in AD 70. But that was just the judgment of *that* generation, not the final judgment at the Second Coming. There is still the Great Tribulation and the Great White Throne judgment yet to occur. What, then, do we do with Luke 21:32 (cf. Matt 24:34), which states, "*Assuredly, I say to you, this generation will by no means pass away till all things take place*"? What are "all things"? "All things" include the Great Tribulation and the Great White Throne judgment. (Note that the tribulation of Matthew 24 and the judgment of Matthew 25 are one continuous discourse, which we believe is synonymous with the tribulation and judgment depicted in the Book of Revelation.) What does "assuredly" mean? What does Jesus mean when He says "assuredly"? How could it be any more emphatic? Earlier in this same passage, Jesus said:

> *"But when you see Jerusalem surrounded by armies, then know that its desolation is near. Then let those who are in Judea flee to the mountains, let those who are in the midst of her depart, and let not those who are in the country enter her. For these are the days of vengeance, that **all things which are written may be fulfilled**."*
> (Luke 21:20-22; emphasis added)

Here, Jesus emphatically states that "all things which are written"—that is, all Old Testament prophecies—would be fulfilled during the days of vengeance, namely, the destruction of Jerusalem. The key to properly placing the time frame of "this generation" is *audience relevance*. Of course, the assigning of the Great Tribulation to that first-century generation begs the question: Are we to relegate "the sign of [Christ's] coming" to the disciples' generation as well? Again, audience relevance is the key.

Audience Relevance

While the Bible is written *for* all people, it was not written *to* all people. The book of 1 Corinthians was written to a specific first-century church, with specific first-century challenges and concerns. While Paul's letter contains timeless truths, it also features time-specific events. For example:

> *Now concerning the collection for the saints, as I have given orders to the churches of Galatia, so you must do also: On the first day of the week let each one of you lay something aside, storing up as he may prosper, that there be no collections when I come. And when I come, whomever you approve by your letters I will send to bear your gift to Jerusalem. But if it is fitting that I go also, they will go with me.* (1 Cor 16:1-4)

The timeless truth is that it is prudent to lay aside money ahead of time for various needs within the Church. The time-specific event is that Paul was going to send someone with the gift to Jerusalem. Too often when we read pronouns such as *we, you, us*, etc., we read ourselves into the text. Consider the following:

> *Be anxious for nothing, but in everything by prayer and supplica-*
> *tion, with thanksgiving, let **your** requests be made known to God;*
> *and the peace of God, which surpasses all understanding, will*
> *guard **your** hearts and minds through Christ Jesus.* (Phil 4:6-7;
> emphasis added)

Do we not include ourselves in the *your* of this passage? Was Philippians written to you or me? The *your* here is the Philippian saints, not us. Does this mean that the truth communicated applies to only them? Absolutely not! This illustration is meant to show how easily we read ourselves into the text subconsciously. Consider the following:

> *Then **we** went ahead to the ship and sailed to Assos, there intending*
> *to take Paul on board; for so he had given orders, intending*
> *himself to go on foot. And when he met **us** at Assos, **we** took him*
> *on board and came to Mitylene. **We** sailed from there, and the next*
> *day came opposite Chios. The following day **we** arrived at Samos*
> *and stayed at Trogyllium. The next day **we** came to Miletus.* (Acts
> 20:13-15; emphasis added)

Here is an example of a text we *don't* read ourselves into. Why? Because it is *event*-specific. It is not teaching a spiritual truth. But are not the *end of the age*, and the *Second Coming of Christ* event-specific items? Should we not, then, use the same hermeneutic of audience relevance in dealing with *those* events? Consider the following passages concerning those events (the **pronouns** are in a bold font, and the event is underlined; remember that the audience is the first-century Church):

> *For the Son of Man will come in the glory of His Father with*
> *His angels, and then He will reward each according to his works.*
> *Truly I say to **you**, there are some of those who are standing here*
> *who shall not taste death until **they** see the Son of Man coming*
> *in His kingdom.* (Matt 16:27-28; compare this to Simeon (Luke
> 2), to whom it was revealed that he would not see death before
> he had seen the Lord's Christ. Did Simeon see the Christ before
> his death? If so, why would some of those standing there not see
> Christ coming in His kingdom?)

> *Then Jesus went out and departed from the temple, and His disci-*
> *ples came up to show Him the buildings of the temple. And Jesus*
> *said to **them**, "Do **you** not see all these things? Assuredly, I say*

to **you**, <u>not one stone shall be left here upon another, that shall not be thrown down</u>." *Now as He sat on the Mount of Olives, the disciples came to Him privately, saying, "Tell **us**, <u>when will these things be? And what will be the sign of Your coming, and of the end of the age?</u>" . . . when **you** see <u>all these things</u>, recognize that He is near, right at the door. Truly I say to **you, this generation** <u>will not pass away until all these things take place</u>."* (Matt 24:1-3, 33b-34 NASB95)

*And if I go and prepare a place for **you**, <u>I will come again</u>, and receive **you** to Myself; that where I am, there **you** may be also.* (John 14:3)

*But this I admit to you, that according to the Way which they call a sect I do serve the God of our fathers, believing everything that is in accordance with the Law, and that is written in the Prophets; having a hope in God, which **these men** cherish themselves, that <u>there shall certainly be [Gk. implies "about to be"] a resurrection of both the righteous and the wicked</u>.* (Acts 24:14-15 NASB95)

*And this do, knowing the time, that it is already the hour for **you** to awaken from sleep; for now salvation is nearer to **us** than when **we** believed. The night is almost gone, and <u>the day is at hand</u>. Let **us** therefore lay aside the deeds of darkness and put on the armor of light.* (Rom 13:11-12 NASB)

*. . . so that **you** are not lacking in any gift, awaiting eagerly <u>the revelation of our Lord Jesus Christ</u> . . . .* (1 Cor 1:7 NASB)

*But this I say, **brethren**, <u>the time has been shortened</u>, so that from now on **those** who have wives should be as though **they** had none; and **those** who weep, as though **they** did not weep; and **those** who rejoice, as though **they** did not rejoice; and **those** who buy, as though **they** did not possess; and **those** who use the world, as though **they** did not make full use of it; for <u>the form of this world is passing away</u>.* (1 Cor 7:29-31 NASB)

*Now these things happened to them as an example, and they were written for **our** instruction, <u>upon whom the ends of the ages have come</u>.* (1 Cor 10:11 NASB)

*Behold, I tell you a mystery; **we** shall not all sleep, but **we** shall all be changed, in a moment, in the twinkling of an eye, <u>at the last</u>*

*trumpet; for the trumpet will sound, and the dead will be raised imperishable, and **we** shall be changed.* (1 Cor 15:51-52 NASB)

*Let **your** forbearing spirit be known to all men. The Lord is near.* (Phil 4:5 NASB)

*For **they** themselves report about us what kind of a reception **we** had with **you**, and how **you** turned to God from idols to serve a living and true God, and to wait for His Son from heaven, whom He raised from the dead, that is Jesus, who delivers **us** from the wrath to come.* (1 Thess 1:9-10 NASB)

*For who is **our** hope or joy or crown of exultation? Is it not even **you**, in the presence of our Lord Jesus at His coming?* (1 Thess 2:19 NASB)

*For if **we** believe that Jesus died and rose again, even so God will bring with Him those who have fallen asleep in Jesus. For this **we** say to **you** by the word of the Lord, that **we** who are alive, and remain until the coming of the Lord, shall not precede those who have fallen asleep. For the Lord Himself will descend from heaven with a shout, with the voice of the archangel, and with the trumpet of God; and the dead in Christ shall rise first. Then **we** who are alive and remain shall be caught up together with them in the clouds to meet the Lord in the air, and thus **we** shall always be with the Lord. Therefore comfort one another with these words.* (1 Thess 4:14-18 NASB)

*Now may the God of peace Himself sanctify **you** entirely; and may **your** spirit and soul and body be preserved complete, without blame at the coming of our Lord Jesus Christ.* (1 Thess 5:23 NASB)

*This is a plain indication of God's righteous judgment so that **you** may be considered worthy of the kingdom of God, for which indeed **you** are suffering. For after all it is only just for God to repay with affliction those who afflict **you**, and to give relief to **you** who are afflicted and to **us** as well when the Lord Jesus shall be revealed from heaven with His mighty angels in flaming fire, dealing out retribution to those who do not know God and to those who do not obey the gospel of our Lord Jesus. And **these** will pay the penalty of eternal destruction, away from the presence of the Lord and from the glory of His power, when He comes to be glorified in His saints on that day, and to be marveled at among all who* *have believed—for our testimony to you was believed.* (2 Thess 1:5-10 NASB)

Now we request you, brethren, with regard to the <u>coming of our Lord Jesus Christ</u>, and our gathering together to Him, that you may not be quickly shaken from your composure or be disturbed either by a spirit or a message or a letter as if from us, to the effect that the day of the Lord has come. (2 Thess 2:1-2 NASB; the implication here is that there was such an expectation of the Day of the Lord that some thought that it had already come—thus supporting the argument that they understood Jesus' return to be a spiritual coming, not a physical one, as we shall develop in a later chapter)

I charge you in the presence of God, who gives life to all things, and of Christ Jesus, who testified the good confession before Pontius Pilate, that you keep the commandment without stain or reproach until <u>the appearing of our Lord Jesus Christ.</u> (1 Tim 6:13-14 NASB)

For the grace of God has appeared, bringing salvation to all men, instructing us to deny ungodliness and worldly desires and to live sensibly, righteously and godly in the present age, looking for the blessed hope and <u>the appearing of the glory of our great God and Savior, Christ Jesus.</u> (Titus 2:11-13 NASB)

. . . and let us consider how to stimulate one another to love and good deeds, not forsaking our own assembling together, as is the habit of some, but encouraging one another; and all the more, as you see <u>the day drawing near</u>. (Heb 10:24-25 NASB)

For you have need of endurance, so that when you have done the will of God, you may receive what was promised. For yet in a very little while, <u>He Who is coming will come</u>, and will not delay. (Heb 10:36-37 NASB)

You too be patient; strengthen your hearts, for <u>the coming of the Lord is at hand</u>. (Jas 5:8 NASB)

Know this first of all [first-century saints], that in the last days mockers will come with their mocking, following after their own lusts, and saying, "Where is <u>the promise of His coming</u>? For ever since the fathers fell asleep, all continues just as it was from the beginning of creation." (2 Pet 3:3-4 NASB)

*Children, <u>it is the last hour</u>; and just as **you** heard that antichrist is coming, even now many antichrists have arisen; from this **we** know that <u>it is the last hour</u>.* (1 John 2:18 NASB)

*And now, little children, abide in Him, so that <u>when He appears</u>, **we** may have confidence and not shrink away from Him in shame at <u>His coming</u>.* (1 John 2:28 NASB)

*<u>I am coming quickly</u>; hold fast what **you** have, in order that no one take **your** crown.* (Rev 3:11 NASB)

In spite of all of these passages (and many more—see the Appendix for 101 verses), many still doubt that Jesus and the inspired New Testament authors taught the New Testament saints that the return of Christ would occur in their generation. But is this not what a plain and straightforward reading of these passages implies? If we read the New Testament from that perspective, we begin to see passages that we did not equate formerly with the imminence of His return as being exactly that; for example:

Therefore do not go on passing judgment before the time, but wait until the Lord comes who will both bring to light the things hidden in the darkness and disclose the motives of men's hearts; and then each man's praise will come to him from God. (1 Cor 4:5 NASB)

What we might have considered as a general directive to the church throughout the ages, we now see as a directive to a particular church in a particular age. This particular church was instructed to wait until the Lord comes, which Paul seems to imply *they* would see. (Why wait for something that you will never experience in your lifetime?) Also, in the context of a time-specific event, when we read the pronouns *we* or *you*, etc., we should take them as meaning specific people, not necessarily an ethereal collection of saints. Thus, when you include all passages containing phrases such as "*at hand*," "*near*," "*passing away*," "*soon*," "*wait until*," "*look for*," etc., the list becomes quite substantial.

When one starts reading the New Testament from the perspective of the first-century church and an imminent Second Coming, the list grows even longer. The aforementioned verses are merely the most apparent! Furthermore, we have yet to find *a single verse in the whole New Testament* that even hints at a far-distant, future Second Coming. And in light of all of these *soon, at hand, near* and *shortly* time indicators, consider that Jeremiah considered seventy years to be a long time!

> *And this whole land shall be a desolation and an astonishment,*
> *and these nations shall serve the king of Babylon **seventy years**.*
> (Jer 25:11)

> *For he [Jeremiah] has sent to us in Babylon, saying, "**This captivity***
> ***is long**; build houses and dwell in them, and plant gardens and eat*
> *their fruit."* (Jer 29:28; emphasis added)

Perhaps the closest New Testament passage that might be construed as indicating a long time is 2 Peter 3:8, in which Peter, defending the Lord's apparent delay, quotes the words of Moses from Psalm 90, saying, " . . . *with the Lord one day is as a thousand years, and a thousand years as one day.*" But this passage simply illustrates how God views time. With us, a day is still a day. Moreover, in many instances it is conveniently overlooked that this passage is a "two-way street." There is just as much precedent to interpret time statements in the opposite "direction," for example, when Jesus said that He would die and rise again on the third day; using 2 Peter 3:8, we could interpret Jesus' words as meaning that He would rise 3,000 years later! Add to this the fact that Peter tells his readers just four verses later that *they* are to be looking for the coming Day of the Lord. To this we add an observation from late-19th century theologian Milton S. Terry:

> The language in question is a poetical citation from Psalm 90:4, and is adduced to show that the lapse of time does not invalidate the promises of God. Whatever he has pledged will come to pass, however men may think or talk about his tardiness. Days and years and ages do not affect him. From everlasting to everlasting he is God (Ps 90:2). But this is very different from saying that when the everlasting God promises something *shortly*, and declares that it is *close at hand*, he may mean that it is a thousand years in the future. Whatever he has promised indefinitely he may take a thousand years or more to [fulfill], but what he affirms to be at the door let no man declare to be far away. (*Biblical Hermeneutics*, p. 496)

Also of note is the fact that none of the Old Testament prophets use Psalm 90:4 to "explain away" any of the Old Testament time statements. It has been argued that because God exists outside of time, and therefore views time differently than we do, we should not expect to understand these timing passages from a human perspective. But if God communicates to us on His level of understanding, rather than ours, how is it that we can understand *anything* in God's Word? For example, God states that

164

"*as the heavens are higher than the earth, So are His ways higher than our ways, And His thoughts than our thoughts*" (Isa 55:9). That being so, how can we ever "*rightly divide the Word of truth*" unless God has communicated that Word to us, not on His level, but on ours? We feel that the following passage demonstrates that God communicates time statements in Scripture from mankind's perspective, not His:

> *And the word of the Lord came to me, saying, "Son of man, what is this proverb that you people have about the land of Israel, which says, 'The days are prolonged, and every vision fails'? Tell them therefore, 'Thus says the Lord God: "I will lay this proverb to rest, and they shall no more use it as a proverb in Israel." But say to them, "The days are at hand, and the fulfillment of every vision. For no more shall there be any false vision or flattering divination within the house of Israel. For I am the Lord. I speak, and the word which I speak will come to pass; it will no more be postponed; for in your days, O rebellious house, I will say the word and perform it," says the Lord God.'" Again the word of the Lord came to me, saying, "Son of man, look, the house of Israel is saying, 'The vision that he sees is for many days from now, and he prophesies of times far off.' Therefore say to them, 'Thus says the Lord God: "None of My words will be postponed any more, but the word which I speak will be done," says the Lord God.'"* (Ezek 12:21-28)

Is this not an example of God clarifying that His prophetic time statements are given within the context of man's understanding of time and not His? Consider Sproul's words:

> The only way that God can ever speak to us is in human language, because if he spoke to us in divine language we wouldn't understand a word of it. He has to condescend to speak to us in our terms. (*Alike but Very Different*, Renewing Your Mind With R. C. Sproul; 10-7-08 podcast)

Some attempt to counter the "imminency" passages with the following so-called "delay" passages:

> *Therefore you also be ready, for the Son of Man is coming at an hour you do not expect. Who then is a faithful and wise servant, whom his master made ruler over his household, to give them food in due season? Blessed is that servant whom his master, when he comes, will find so doing. Assuredly, I say to you that he will make*

*him ruler over all his goods. But if that evil servant says in his heart, **"My master is delaying his coming,"** and begins to beat his fellow servants, and to eat and drink with the drunkards, the master of that servant will come on a day when he is not looking for him and at an hour that he is not aware of, and will cut him in two and appoint him his portion with the hypocrites. There shall be weeping and gnashing of teeth.* (Matt 24:44-51)

*Then the kingdom of heaven shall be likened to ten virgins who took their lamps and went out to meet the bridegroom. Now five of them were wise, and five were foolish. Those who were foolish took their lamps and took no oil with them, but the wise took oil in their vessels with their lamps. But while **the bridegroom was delayed**, they all slumbered and slept. And at midnight a cry was heard: "Behold, the bridegroom is coming; go out to meet him!" Then all those virgins arose and trimmed their lamps. And the foolish said to the wise, "Give us some of your oil, for our lamps are going out." But the wise answered, saying, "No, lest there should not be enough for us and you; but go rather to those who sell, and buy for yourselves." And while they went to buy, the bridegroom came, and those who were ready went in with him to the wedding; and the door was shut. Afterward the other virgins came also, saying, "Lord, Lord, open to us!" But he answered and said, "Assuredly, I say to you, I do not know you." Watch therefore, for you know neither the day nor the hour in which the Son of Man is coming.* (Matt 25:1-13)

*For the kingdom of heaven is like a man traveling to a far country, who called his own servants and delivered his goods to them. And to one he gave five talents, to another two, and to another one, to each according to his own ability; and immediately he went on a journey. Then he who had received the five talents went and traded with them, and made another five talents. And likewise he who had received two gained two more also. But he who had received one went and dug in the ground, and hid his lord's money. **After a long time the lord of those servants came** and settled accounts with them.* (Matt 25:14-19)
(emphases added)

That these passages speak of a delay we do not deny; but the delay is not one of millennia, or even centuries. In each parable, the expected arrival—though delayed—happens *within the lifetime* of those awaiting it:

*. . . the master of that servant **will come** on a day when **he** is not looking for him . . .*

*And while **they** went to buy, **the bridegroom came** . . .*

*After a long time the **lord of those servants came** and settled accounts with **them**.*

The point of the parables was to teach the listeners to expect the return of the Son of Man, not within a few months or even years, but certainly within the lifetime of some of those listening. This agrees with what the New Testament authors taught, as well as Jesus Himself:

For the Son of Man will come in the glory of His Father with His angels, and then He will reward each according to his works. Assuredly, I say to you, there are some standing here who shall not taste death till they see the Son of Man coming in His kingdom. (Matt 16:27-28)

Consider Russell's commentary on the above passage:

This remarkable declaration is of the greatest importance in this discussion, and may be regarded as the key to the right interpretation of the New Testament doctrine of the Parousia [Thayer's Lexicon defines *Parousia* as follows: 1. presence: 2. the presence of one coming, hence, the coming, arrival, advent parousia. In the New Testament especially of the advent, i.e., the future, visible, return from heaven of Jesus, the Messiah, to raise the dead, hold the last judgment, and set up formally and gloriously the kingdom of God]. Though it cannot be said that there are any special difficulties in the language, it has greatly perplexed the commentators, who are much divided in their explanations. It is surely unnecessary to ask what is the *coming of the Son of man* here predicted. To suppose that it refers merely to the glorious manifestation of Jesus on the mount of transfiguration, though an hypothesis which has great names to support it, is so palpably inadequate as an interpretation that it scarcely requires refutation. The same remark will apply to the comments of Dr. Lange, who supposes it to have been partially fulfilled by the resurrection of Christ. . . . How could the resurrection of Christ be called His coming in the glory of His Father, with the holy angels, in His kingdom, and to judgment? Or how can we suppose that Christ, speaking of an event which was to take place in about twelve months, would say, 'Verily I say unto you, There be some standing here which shall not taste of death till they see' it? The very form of the expression shows that the event spoken of could not be within the space of a few months, or even a few years: it is a mode of speech which suggests that not *all* present will live to see the event spoken of; that not *many* will do so; but that *some* will. It is exactly such a way of speaking as would suit an interval of thirty or forty years, when the majority of the persons then present would have passed away, but some would survive and witness the event referred to. (*The Parousia*, pp. 29-31)

Rather than countering the imminency passages, we feel that these "delay" passages actually strengthen the case for "this generation." To be sure, there are verses exhorting the readers to wait, to be patient, to endure, etc., but they are encouraged to do so because the time is short! Hang in there just a while longer, "*For yet a little while, And He who is coming will come and will not tarry*" (Heb 10:37). How encouraging, or ethical, would it be to "tease" the New Testament believers with something that was really two thousand years (or more) away? How could the Thessalonians comfort one another by looking for the return of Christ (1 Thess 4:18), if it would not happen for at least two millennia? Any comfort they, and subsequent generations, received would have been hollow and based upon a misplaced hope.

Also of note is the fact that Jesus explicitly warned His disciples about false prophets who would claim that His return was near, while James claims that very thing:

And He said: "Take heed that you not be deceived. For many will come in My name, saying, 'I am He,' and, 'The time has drawn near.' (Luke 21:8)

You too be patient; strengthen your hearts, for the coming of the Lord is near. (Jas 5:8 NASB95)

The conclusion is obvious: either James was one of the false prophets Christ had warned about, or, by the time James wrote the time had indeed drawn near.

Having established that there is an impressive amount of text indicating that the return of Christ was imminent *two thousand years ago*, there are a limited number of possible explanations for the apparent discrepancy:

1. Christ and the New Testament authors were mistaken in their understanding of the timing of the Second Coming.

2. Christ and the New Testament authors understood the timing, but deliberately misled their generation for any of a number of reasons, which are secondary to the point at hand.

3. In light of our understanding of (the nature of) *how* Christ will return (based upon our understanding of Scripture), we must be misunderstanding these verses concerning *when* He will return. In other words, our understanding of the *nature* of His return dictates that we must reinterpret the verses concerning the *timing* of His return. (This is the *Futurist* position, also the dominant position of the church today.)

4. In light of our understanding of *when* Christ will return (based upon the above Scriptures), we must be misunderstanding the verses that describe *how* He will return. In other words, our understanding of the *timing* of His return dictates that we must reinterpret the verses concerning the *nature* of His return. (This is the *Preterist* position.)

One would think that those who believe that Christ was the Son of God incarnate, that the Bible is the inspired Word of God, and that the authors wrote as they were "inspired by the Holy Spirit" would immediately dismiss the first two possibilities. However, this is not the case. For example, renowned Christian apologist C. S. Lewis admits that the first-century Church expected Christ to return within their generation. The reason for that expectation was because Christ Himself instilled that expectation within them with the words "this generation shall not pass till all these things be done." Because "all these things" did not come to pass, at least according to Lewis, he states, "It is certainly the most embarrassing verse in the Bible" because Christ was wrong (*The Essential C. S. Lewis*, p. 385).

John MacArthur offers several reasons for the New Testament teaching of an imminent Second Coming, one of which is:

"... that He desired to keep His people on the very tiptoe of expectation, continually looking for Him. (*The Second Coming*, p. 206)

While MacArthur does not use the terms "misled" or "deceived," that concept certainly seems inherent in his statement. Yet earlier MacArthur states, "God is not in the business of giving false hope. He knows what we are waiting for" (ibid., p. 48). Perhaps we misunderstand the concept of false hope, but if we are still waiting today for what the early Church was expecting, did they not have a false hope? To those who would say that God intended a sense of imminency purposefully so that the Church would always be looking for the return of Christ, we would ask: Why is there no such sense of imminency in the Old Testament? Why were none of the Old Testament prophets declaring that *the kingdom of God was at hand*? There was not even a sense of imminency in regard to Christ's *first* coming in the Old Testament (not to mention His Second Coming!) until the final years of Daniel's seventy weeks were fulfilled in the New Testament era. If, as this view would have us believe, God wants His people to be ever looking for His kingdom's arrival in their lifetimes, *why did He not instill this expectation in His Old Testament saints?* As for the possibility of Christ and the apostles being wrong about His return, if they could be wrong about the time of the Second Coming, what else might they have been wrong about? In light of Christ's deity and the inerrancy of Scripture, we are very uncomfortable with these (and similar) positions, agreeing rather with Paul, who wrote, "*let God be true and everyman a liar*" (Rom 3:4).

Because the majority of prophecy teachers and pundits adhere to a yet-future Second Coming, the majority of Christians have been raised upon the premise that it is the *timing* issue that must be clarified; viz., that even though the New Testament *sounds* like it is teaching that Christ would return in that generation, that is not what it is really saying. To deal with the apparently imminent Second Coming, several devices have been employed. Christ's discourse in Matthew chapter 24 has been divided into sections, with some verses relating to what the disciples would see, and other verses relating to what a future, unnamed generation will see. Some believe that the various New Testament authors perceived distant events as mountain peaks in the distance, not recognizing the existence of the spacious valleys (of time) that separate the peaks. Then there is the fact that "a day with the Lord is as a thousand years," so that while two thousand years have passed for us, only two days have passed for God, so that the Second Coming is still "soon" from His perspective. And the list goes on. Some explanations might find a foothold; others require a stretch of more than the imagination. For example, Dr. J. Randall Price handles the Olivet discourse as follows:

> The Olivet Discourse, as interpreted by the schools of Historicism and Preterism, is exclusively a warning of judgment that was fulfilled with the Temple's destruction by the Romans in AD 70 . . . . In Preterism, the basis for this interpretation rests upon understanding the phrase "this generation" as always having reference to the first-century generation to whom Jesus spoke. Futurism, by

contrast, accepts some uses of "this generation" as having reference to the people of Jesus' day, but only because the immediate context demands this application. (*The Coming Last Days Temple*, pp. 277-279)

Here Price admits that the context demands, at least in part, that the generation *of* whom Jesus spoke was also the generation *to* which He was speaking. Yet, Price intimates that Futurists allow this application with reluctance, and only because the immediate context *demands* it. However, if the context did not demand this application, by what "scriptural" precedent would Futurists apply it to a future generation? In contrast, Preterists believe that when a specific generation asks Jesus specific questions, and He answers by saying *YOU* watch for these things, we should not apply it to any other generation unless the context demands that we do so. Price continues:

Other uses, however, determined by their contexts, may refer to generations of different time periods. For example, the use of "this generation" in Matthew 23:36 is applied as an indictment (in context) to the generation of the scribes and Pharisees (Matt 23:29) whose actions against Jesus demonstrate their affinity with previous persecutors of the prophets (verses 30-35). Jesus then pronounces judgment with the words "all these things shall come upon this generation." The phrase "these things" must also be interpreted in its context. In this case, the next verse (verse 36) describes "these things" as the future experience of Temple desolation. It is important to observe here that when Jesus' statement was made, "this generation" indicated a *future* generation. It was future from the perspective of the sins "this generation" (in context) would yet commit (complicity in the crucifixion) and the judgment they would receive (the Roman destruction in AD 70—see Luke 21:20-24).

Jesus' use of a future sense of "this generation" in a *near* future judgment context sets a precedence for its interpretation in a context of *far* future (eschatological) judgment. (Ibid., p. 279; emphasis in original)

This is nothing more than a prime example of linguistic gymnastics. Because all the sins for which that generation was to be judged had not yet been committed by them, Price applies a future perspective to the generation to whom Jesus was speaking. He then uses this "foot in the door" in the form of a so-called "*near* future judgment context" to set a precedent for so-called "*far* future judgment." But what can be more plain and clear than the fact that future events were prophesied to the *current* generation? The only futuristic perspective that exists is not one belonging to a future *generation* but rather a prospect of future *events* for that *current* generation. Prophecy, by its very nature, has a futuristic context; but if we are to believe that future *events* in prophecy give us the license to "raise the anchor" of the time-stamp of a given prophecy, then we are adrift, subject to the whim of every wind and wave of prophetic interpretation. Recall King's contention that "if a time statement resident in a Scripture cannot be trusted, neither can any other portion of that Scripture" (*The Spirit of Prophecy*, p. 256). Terry echoes these thoughts:

> The same [that uncertainty and confusion are introduced into biblical interpretation] may be said about explicit designations of time. When a writer says that an event will shortly and speedily come to pass, or is about to take place, it is contrary to all propriety to declare that his statements allow us to believe the event is in the far future. It is a reprehensible abuse of language to say that the words *immediately*, or *near at hand*, mean *ages hence*, or *after a long time* . . . for it is manifest that if there could be such ambiguity and uncertainty in respect to *time*, there might be no less ambiguity and uncertainty in respect to every thing else . . . . (*Biblical Hermeneutics*, pp. 495-496; emphasis in original)

Price then attempts to illustrate this far-future precedent with Moses' farewell speech to the Israelites:

> Even though in context Jesus may refer to the future "this genera- tion" as "you," this is a conventional usage of language with respect to reference and thus it does not have to apply to a present audience. Such usage may also be found in the Old Testament. For example, Moses speaks in a way similar to Jesus when he says, "So it shall be when *all of these things* have come upon *you*" (Deuteronomy 30:1a, (emphasis added)). Even though he is speaking to the present generation ("you"), **it is evident from the context that his words speak about a future generation that will live thousands of years later and into the eschatological period.** (*The Coming Last Days Temple*, p. 280; bold emphasis added)

We would agree with Price that the "you" to which Moses referred in Deuteronomy chapter 30 is a distant future generation. As we have seen previously, this passage from Deuteronomy chapter 30 is an if/then, conditional prophecy. *If* and *when* the Israelites conduct themselves in a particular manner, *then* God will respond in a particular manner. The time-stamp in this prophecy is open-ended: "So it shall be *when* all of these things have come upon you . . . ." In fact, we believe that Moses puts the time-stamp on this whole prophecy of blessings and curses in the next chapter:

> *"For I know that after my death you will become utterly corrupt, and turn aside from the way which I have commanded you. And evil will befall you in the latter days, because you will do evil in the sight of the LORD, to provoke Him to anger through the work of your hands."* (Deut 31:29)

We see this as referring to the ultimate corruption and evil of the latter days of the Old Covenant. In Moses' speech, the "when" of the events would be determined by the Israelites themselves. Moses was not telling them *when* the events would happen, but what the results would be when their predicted behavior occurred. Price claims above that "it is evident from the context that his [Moses'] words spoke about a future generation that would live thousands of years later and into the eschatological period." However, we find no evidence in the *context* for thousands of years—it is only ascertained by hindsight! Certainly Moses' statement, "When you beget children and grandchildren and have grown old in the land" (Deut 4:25) indicates the passage of time, and the term "latter days" (31:29) establishes the eschatological period. But while this context *allows* for thousands of years, it is not evidence thereof. Yet *where is this evidence for the Matthew chapter 24 generation?* Nothing in Matthew chapter 24 speaks of grandchildren, growing old in the land, or anything remotely similar. Jesus took great care to stress when the judgment of which He was speaking would occur—in *this* (His) generation. These facts mitigate against the "you" of Matthew 24 being an "editorial" or "collective" you. Price rightly discerns that Moses was addressing a generation that would live into the eschatological period. We believe that Jesus was living in that period, and that a simple and plain reading of the texts, in both cases, provides the most logical and harmonious interpretation. Furthermore, when one considers that Peter (1 Pet 4:17), John (1 John 2:18), and the author of Hebrews (Heb 1:2) claimed that *they* were living in the last days (Moses' "latter days"), the New Testament era is affixed as the eschatological period of which both Moses and Jesus spoke.

The reason many believe that the Second Coming is yet future is because they have not removed the veil of Moses, as was demonstrated earlier in this book. Like the Jews of the first century, they have wrongly interpreted passages that describe the Day of the Lord and the elements of the New Covenant. Having laid a sound scriptural foundation of the spiritual nature of the New Covenant in Part I, we can safely say that option 3 above—that the imminency passages do not refer to the New Testament generation—is not viable. Option 3 assumes that the New Covenant and Christ's return each possess a primarily physical aspect, an assumption that, for all intents and purposes, puts the veil of Moses back on.

But what about the other possibility? What if the imminent return passages are understood at face value, requiring a *re*interpretation of our understanding of the *nature* of Christ's return? Those who adhere to Futurism must be willing to accept that the *timing* of Christ's return has been misunderstood (because it sounds like the New Testament generation expected Him). Therefore, Futurists reinterpret the New Testament's time statements so that they comply with their interpretation of the *nature* of His return. This being the case, perhaps we should at least entertain the premise that we may have misunderstood the *nature* of His return and reinterpret the *nature* verses so that they comply with the *timing* of His return. What gives one scenario precedent over the other, except our own prejudices? (It should be noted, however, that Preterists do not just simply latch onto the "time" statements and then force the nature verses to fit their *a priori* dogma. Rather, Preterists claim to allow Scripture to interpret Scripture, providing them with scriptural precedent for their nonphysical interpretation of those verses discussing the *nature* of Christ's return.)

When we say "reinterpret the *nature* verses," what we mean is that we must remove the veil of Moses to *rightly* interpret them. For example, it was the *nature* of the Messiah's first coming that the Jews misinterpreted, *not* the timing. The same was true of the disciples' understanding of Elijah's "second coming." Indeed, some Jews even thought that Jesus was Elijah (Matt 16:14), because they knew that Elijah must come before the Christ did. To be sure, Elijah's return was not unexpected either, for Daniel's prophecy of the seventy weeks led many first-century Jews to expect the arrival of the Messiah within their own generation. Mauro stated, "Thus, when our Lord said, 'The *time is* fulfilled' (Mark 1:15), He doubtless had reference to the time revealed to Daniel, the time when Christ was to be made manifest to Israel" (*The Seventy Weeks and the Great Tribulation*, p. 72). Because of the expected messianic deliverance from Roman rule, we see Simeon waiting for the Messiah (Luke 2:25ff), others being deceived by false Messiahs, and an increasing frequency in popular uprisings (Mark 15:7; Acts 5:36). Sadly, Paul observed that, during his day, whenever Moses was read, the Jews still had a veil on, which caused them to miss their Messiah in Christ's first coming. Although He came at the *time* in which they expected Him they missed Him because He did not come in the manner (i.e., *nature*) in which they expected Him. Likewise, we believe the Church has committed a similar error for almost two millennia and must remove the veil of their traditional expectations regarding the Second Coming and *"search the Scriptures to find out whether these things are so"* (Acts 17:11).

If we allow the Bible's time statements to speak for themselves, then the pieces of the puzzle fit perfectly. It is a historical fact that the New Testament saints were expecting the end of the age and Christ's return within their own generation. Yet, just as David waited after being anointed king for God Himself to remove Saul from the throne, so the Church, after being "anointed" at Pentecost, waited for God to remove the vestiges of the earthly kingdom and reveal the spiritual kingdom as "His anointed." That wait was the space of one generation, the "last days" generation, in which the New Testament authors believed themselves to be:

> *But Peter, taking his stand with the eleven, raised his voice and declared to them: "Men of Judea and all you who live in Jerusalem, let this be known to you and give heed to my words. For these men are not drunk, as you suppose, for it is only the third hour of the day; but **this is what was spoken of** through the prophet Joel:*
>
> *'AND IT SHALL BE **IN THE LAST DAYS** . . . .'"* (Acts 2:14-17 NASB)

> *God, after He spoke long ago to the fathers in the prophets in many portions and in many ways, **in these last days** has spoken to us in His Son.* (Heb 1:1-2 NASB)

> *Little children, **it is the last hour**; and as you have heard that the Antichrist is coming, even now many antichrists have come, by which we know that **it is the last hour**.* (1 John 2:18)
> (emphases added)

Added to all the evidence that "this generation" was the generation of the New Testament is the fact that the New Testament authors, by the inspiration of the Holy Spirit, were able to see beyond the veil of Moses and understand that *all* of the Old Testament prophets foresaw the New Testament generation:

> *Yes, and all the prophets, from Samuel and those who follow, as many as have spoken, have also foretold **these days**.* (Acts 3:24)

For everything that was written in the past was written to teach us, so that through endurance and the encouragement of the Scriptures we might have hope. (Rom 15:4 NIV)

And all these [heroes of the faith], having obtained a good testimony through faith, did not receive the promise, God having provided something better for us, that they should not be made perfect apart from us ["us" being the author and readers of Hebrews, not you and me]. (Heb 11:39-40)

Of this salvation the prophets have inquired and searched carefully, who prophesied of the grace that would come to you, searching what, or what manner of time, the Spirit of Christ who was in them was indicating when He testified beforehand the sufferings of Christ and the glories that would follow. To them it was revealed that, not to themselves, but to us they were ministering the things which now have been reported to you through those who have preached the gospel to you by the Holy Spirit sent from heaven—things which angels desire to look into. (1 Pet 1:10-12; emphases added)

Do not the above passages indicate that the New Testament generation was the focal point of Old Testament prophecy, and that all things were summed up within *that* generation? Jesus also taught that the Old Testament prophets pointed toward His generation:

For all the prophets and the law prophesied until John. (Matt 11:13)

. . . for assuredly, I say to you that many prophets and righteous men desired to see what you see, and did not see it, and to hear what you hear, and did not hear it. (Matt 13:17)

But when you see Jerusalem surrounded by armies, then know that its desolation is near . . . . For these are the days of vengeance, that all things which are written may be fulfilled. (Luke 21:20, 22)
(emphases added)

The last passage is from Luke's account of the Olivet discourse. In Matthew's and Mark's accounts of that discourse (Matt 24:15; Mark 13:14), Jesus referred to Daniel's prophecy of the abomination of desolation. Could Jesus have also had Daniel in mind when He spoke the words recorded in Luke's version of the discourse?

Then I, Daniel, looked; and there stood two others, one on this riverbank and the other on that riverbank. And one said to the man clothed in linen, who was above the waters of the river, "How long shall the fulfillment of these wonders be?" Then I heard the man clothed in linen, who was above the waters of the river, when he held up his right hand and his left hand to heaven, and swore by Him who lives forever, that it shall be for a time, times, and half a time; and **when the power of the holy people has been completely shattered, all these things shall be finished.** *(Dan 12:5-7; emphasis added)*

In both instances, *all things* are finished (fulfilled) when Jerusalem is surrounded by armies and destroyed, shattering the power of the holy people. Like Daniel, the disciples also asked for clarification on when the prophetic revelation of the temple's destruction would occur. The difference between the two is that, while Daniel was told that the words were sealed up till the end time, Jesus told His disciples that *they* would see Jerusalem surrounded by armies; that *their* generation would see all these things fulfilled:

Although I heard, I did not understand. Then I said, "My lord, what shall be the end of these things?" And he said, "Go your way, Daniel, for the words are closed up and sealed till the time of the end." (Dan 12:8-9)

But when **you** *see Jerusalem surrounded by armies . . . . (Luke 21:20)*

Assuredly, I say to **you,** **this generation** *will by no means pass away till all these things take place. (Matt 24:34)*
(emphases added)

If we believe, as we so often hear, that *we* are in the "last days," one has to wonder—the "last days" of what? The last days of the Old Covenant? If so, then the "last days" have endured for nearly two thousand years—longer than the covenant itself! And how can we say that the Old Covenant has not completely passed away? What is left of it that is yet to pass away? Or are we in the last days of the world as we know it, waiting for the elements to be burned with fire and replaced with a new heavens and a new earth? Although these phrases are found in the Bible, are we required to understand them in a literal, physical sense? We think not, as we shall demonstrate in the coming chapters.

As untraditional and foreign as it sounds, the interpretation which best fits is that the last days spoken of in the Bible were the last days of the Old Covenant, which "passed away" in AD 70. Peter announced in ca. AD 30 (Acts 2) that they were in the last days. Thus the "last days" generation encompassed the forty years from AD 30-70. *That* was the generation which asked Jesus about the end times. *That* was the generation of which He spoke. *That* was the generation upon which "all these things" came to pass. In subsequent chapters we shall fortify this assertion. We offer these words from Partial Preterist Sproul:

> The great service preterism performs is to focus attention on two major issues. The first is the time-frame references of the New Testament regarding eschatological prophecy. The preterist is a sentinel standing guard against frivolous and superficial attempts to downplay or explain away the force of these references.
>
> The second major issue is the destruction of Jerusalem. This event certainly spelled the end of a crucial redemptive-historical epoch. It must be viewed as the end of some age. It also represents a significant visitation of the Lord in judgment and a vitally important "day of the Lord." Whether it was the *only* day of the Lord about which Scripture speaks remains a major point of controversy among preterists. (*The Last Days according to Jesus*, pp. 202-203; emphasis in original)

We note that Sproul is a Partial Preterist, believing in a yet-future coming of the Lord. We shall address this in coming chapters.

Apocalyptic Language

—ᵐ—

Behold, the day of the LORD comes,
Cruel, with both wrath and fierce anger,
To lay the land desolate;
And He will destroy its sinners from it.
For the stars of heaven and their constellations
Will not give their light;
The sun will be darkened in its going forth,
And the moon will not cause its light to shine.
Therefore I will shake the heavens,
And the earth will move out of her place,
In the wrath of the LORD of hosts
And in the day of His fierce anger.

The earth quakes before them,
The heavens tremble;
The sun and moon grow dark,
And the stars diminish their brightness.

Recognize these passages about the Tribulation? Are they from the Lord's Olivet discourse or the book of Revelation? Sorry, those are trick questions, which isn't fair. But don't they sound like a description of the Tribulation? Compare the above passages with these New Testament passages:

Immediately after the tribulation of those days the sun will be darkened, and the moon will not give its light; the stars will fall from heaven, and the powers of the heavens will be shaken. (Matt 24:29)

I looked when He opened the sixth seal, and behold, there was a great earthquake; and the sun became black as sackcloth of hair, and the moon became like blood. (Rev 6:12)

Then the fourth angel sounded: And a third of the sun was struck, a third of the moon, and a third of the stars, so that a third of them were darkened. A third of the day did not shine, and likewise the night. (Rev 8:12)

179

Then the temple of God was opened in heaven, and the ark of His covenant was seen in His temple. And there were lightnings, noises, thunderings, an earthquake, and great hail. (Rev 11:19)

Amazing similarities. However, our opening Old Testament passage was from Isaiah chapter 13, describing the Medes overthrowing the Babylonians. The second passage was from Joel chapter 2. Let's look closer at Isaiah chapter 13 (points to be emphasized have a **bold** font):

The burden against Babylon which Isaiah the son of Amoz saw.
"Lift up a banner on the high mountain,
Raise your voice to them;
Wave your hand, that they may enter the gates of the nobles.
I have commanded My sanctified ones;
I have also called My mighty ones for My anger;
Those who rejoice in My exaltation."
The noise of a multitude in the mountains,
Like that of many people!
*A tumultuous noise of **the kingdoms of nations gathered together!***
The Lord of hosts musters
The army for battle.
They come from a far country,
From the end of heaven;
The Lord and His weapons of indignation,
To destroy the whole land.
Wail, for the day of the Lord is at hand!
It will come as destruction from the Almighty.
Therefore all hands will be limp,
Every man's heart will melt,
And they will be afraid.
Pangs and sorrows will take hold of them;
They will be in pain as a woman in childbirth;
They will be amazed at one another;
Their faces will be like flames.
Behold, the day of the Lord comes,
Cruel, with both wrath and fierce anger,
To lay the land desolate;
And He will destroy its sinners from it.
For the stars of heaven and their constellations
Will not give their light;
The sun will be darkened in its going forth,

And the moon will not cause its light to shine.
"I will punish the world *for its evil,*
And the wicked for their iniquity;
I will halt the arrogance of the proud,
And will lay low the haughtiness of the terrible.
I will make a mortal more rare than fine gold,
A man more than the golden wedge of Ophir.
Therefore I will shake the heavens,
And the earth will move out of her place,
In the wrath of the Lord *of hosts*
And in the day of His fierce anger.
It shall be as the hunted gazelle,
And as a sheep that no man takes up;
Every man will turn to his own people,
And everyone will flee to his own land.
Everyone who is found will be thrust through,
And everyone who is captured will fall by the sword.
Their children also will be dashed to pieces before their eyes;
Their houses will be plundered
And their wives ravished.
"Behold, I will stir up the Medes against them,
Who will not regard silver;
And as for gold, they will not delight in it.
Also their bows will dash the young men to pieces,
And they will have no pity on the fruit of the womb;
Their eye will not spare children.
And Babylon, the glory of kingdoms,
The beauty of the Chaldeans' pride,
Will be as when God overthrew Sodom and Gomorrah.
It will never be inhabited,
Nor will it be settled from generation to generation;
Nor will the Arabian pitch tents there,
Nor will the shepherds make their sheepfolds there.
But wild beasts of the desert will lie there,
And their houses will be full of owls;
Ostriches will dwell there,
And wild goats will caper there.
The hyenas will howl in their citadels,
And jackals in their pleasant palaces.
Her time is near to come,
And her days will not be prolonged."

Note two things here: First, God is said to muster nations from the end of heaven to deliver judgment upon the Babylonians via foreign armies. Second, when we read this passage (especially the items in bold) do we believe that all of them happened literally when the Medes and Persians overthrew Babylon? We have never heard it taught that way. Consider Albert Barnes' commentary:

> **Isaiah 13:8.** *They shall be in pain as a woman that travaileth* This comparison is often used in the Scriptures to denote the deepest possible pain and sorrow, as well as the suddenness with which any calamity comes upon a people.

> **Isaiah 13:10.** *For the stars of heaven* This verse cannot be understood literally, but is a metaphorical representation of the calamities that were coming upon Babylon. The meaning of the figure evidently is, that those calamities would be such as would be appropriately denoted by the sudden extinguishment of the stars, the sun, and the moon. As nothing would tend more to anarchy, distress, and ruin, than thus to have all the lights of heaven suddenly and forever quenched, this was an apt and forcible representation of the awful calamities that were coming upon the people. Darkness and night, in the Scriptures, are often the emblem of calamity and distress. The revolutions and destructions of kingdoms and nations are often represented in the Scriptures under this image. (*Barnes' Notes*)

That certainly seems plausible; but then the question arises, "If these explanations are plausible here, why not in Matthew chapter 24 or in the book of Revelation?" In regard to the many prophetic Old Testament passages possessing similar language, there appears to be no controversy over their fulfillment despite the fact that theologians have found no historical evidence for the *"earth being moved from its place; the sun, moon and stars not giving forth their light; the heavens being rolled together as a scroll,"* etc. Moses Maimonides, whom Wikipedia describes as "by far the most influential figure in medieval Jewish philosophy," had this to say about the apocalyptic language under discussion:

> If we hear a person speaking whose language we do not understand, we undoubtedly know that he speaks, but do not know what his words mean; it may even happen that we hear some words which mean one thing in the tongue of the speaker, and exactly the reverse in our language, and taking the words in the sense which they have in our language, we imagine that the speaker employed

them in that sense. . . . The very same thing happens to the ordinary reader of the Prophets; some of their words he does not understand at all. . . . After this preliminary remark you will understand the metaphor frequently employed by Isaiah, and less frequently by other prophets, when they describe the ruin of a kingdom or the destruction of a great nation in phrases like the following: — "The stars have fallen," "The heavens are overthrown," "The sun is darkened," "The earth is waste, and trembles," and similar metaphors. . . . I do not think that any person is so foolish and blind, and so much in favour of the literal sense of figurative and oratorical phrases, as to assume that at the fall of the Babylonian kingdom a change took place in the nature of the stars of heaven, or in the light of the sun and moon, or that the earth moved away from its centre. For all this is merely the description of a country that has been defeated; the inhabitants undoubtedly find all light dark, and all sweet things bitter: the whole earth appears too narrow for them, and the heavens are changed in their eyes. He speaks in a similar manner when he describes the poverty and humiliation of the people of Israel, their captivity and their defeat, the continuous misfortunes caused by the wicked Sennacherib when he ruled over all the fortified places of Judah, or the loss of the entire land of Israel when it came into the possession of Sennacherib. (*Guide for the Perplexed*, pp. 204-205)

Yet in spite of both a scriptural and cultural precedent for nonliteral interpretations of apocalyptic language, many theologians assign literal interpretations to this same language in the New Testament when it is associated with the Second Coming. In his study of Bible prophecy, former pastor and evangelist John L. Bray searched extensively to acquire classic commentaries. In addition to many domestic libraries, his world-wide evangelistic meetings afforded him opportunities to search foreign libraries as well, including Cambridge, Oxford, and the British Museum. His studies led him to ask:

Can anyone tell me why we should consider all these passages in the Old Testament to be figurative language, but that in the New Testament they would have to be literal (that is, natural and physical)? Isn't it more logical to think that the writers of the New Testament (and Jesus) would naturally do the same as the Old Testament writers did, and use this kind of language metaphorically? Didn't the same God inspire the prophecies in both testaments? Why should He then deal with them differently? (*Matthew 24 Fulfilled*, p. 182)

Added to this is the fact that the timing passages, which we demonstrated earlier should be read at face value, are applied by many to some future generation rather than the generation to whom they were spoken. It seems that many in the church, when interpreting the Second Coming passages, have ignored biblical precedent in two areas: (1) the imminency (or timing) phrases; and (2) apocalyptic language (which determines the *nature* of His return). Lest the reader think that this scriptural precedent of apocalyptic language consists of only a couple of isolated passages, consider the following:

All the host of heaven shall be dissolved,
And the heavens shall be rolled up like a scroll;
All their host shall fall down
As the leaf falls from the vine,
And as fruit falling from a fig tree. (Isa 34:4; concerning the destruction of Idumea)

"When I put out your light,
I will cover the heavens, and make its stars dark;
I will cover the sun with a cloud,
And the moon shall not give her light.
All the bright lights of the heavens I will make dark over you,
And bring darkness upon your land,"
Says the Lord GOD. (Ezek 32:7-8; concerning the destruction of Pharaoh, king of Egypt)

The earth quakes before them,
The heavens tremble;
The sun and moon grow dark,
And the stars diminish their brightness.

The sun and moon will grow dark,
And the stars will diminish their brightness.
The LORD also will roar from Zion,
And utter His voice from Jerusalem;
The heavens and earth will shake;
But the LORD will be a shelter for His people,
And the strength of the children of Israel. (Joel 2:10; 3:15-16; concerning the judgment of God's enemies)

*"And it shall come to pass in that day," says the Lord G*ᴏᴅ,
*"That **I will make the sun go down at noon,**
And I will darken the earth in broad daylight . . . ."* (Amos 8:9;
concerning God's judgment against the house of Jacob)

*Then David spoke to the L*ᴏʀᴅ *the words of this song, on the day
when the L*ᴏʀᴅ *had delivered him from the hand of all his enemies,
and from the hand of Saul. And he said:*

*"In my distress I called upon the L*ᴏʀᴅ,
*And cried out to my God;
He heard my voice from His temple,
And my cry entered His ears.*
Then the earth shook and trembled;
The foundations of heaven quaked and were shaken,
Because He was angry.
Smoke went up from His nostrils,
And devouring fire from His mouth;
Coals were kindled by it.
He bowed the heavens also, and came down
With darkness under His feet.
He rode upon a cherub, and flew;
And He was seen upon the wings of the wind.
He made darkness canopies around Him,
Dark waters and thick clouds of the skies.
*From the brightness before Him
Coals of fire were kindled.*
The Lᴏʀᴅ **thundered from heaven,**
*And the Most High uttered His voice.
He sent out arrows and scattered them;
Lightning bolts, and He vanquished them.*
Then the channels of the sea were seen,
The foundations of the world were uncovered,
*At the rebuke of the L*ᴏʀᴅ,
*At the blast of the breath of His nostrils.
He sent from above, He took me,
He drew me out of many waters.
He delivered me from my strong enemy,
From those who hated me;*

For they were too strong for me." (2 Sam 22:7-18; David's description of the Lord delivering him from his enemies and the hand of
King Saul; cf. Ps 68:7-9; 144:5-6; Hab 3; Mic 1:3-4)
(emphases added)

Are you beginning to see a pattern emerging? The Jews used very
symbolic, figurative language when describing momentous events such
as battle victories, deliverance from enemies, nations falling, etc. In the
preceding chapters of 2 Samuel, which records the victories of which David
sings, there is no mention of any of these apocalyptic events happening in a
literal fashion. These figurative descriptions are merely a literary conven-
tion for describing God's judgment, whether predictive or after the fact.

There is no historical or scriptural reason to believe that this literary
style changed during the period of time between the Old and New
Testaments. In light of what we have seen concerning the fulfillment of
prophecy in a nonliteral (nonphysical) manner by John the Baptist, it
appears that this linguistic style was still used in Christ's day. Notice this
phrase from 2 Samuel 22:11:

And He was seen upon the wings of the wind . . . .

Was God literally seen? Did they see the "smoke from His nostrils" (v.9)?
If we can accept that this type of communication is typical of Jewish figu-
rative/apocalyptic language, then what about the following?

Behold, He is coming with clouds, and every eye will see Him
. . . .

Is not "coming with clouds" a lot like being "seen upon the wings of the
wind"? Aside from our own personal desire, is there any reason to believe
that "every eye will see Him" is any different from "He was seen upon
the wings of the wind"? Do you believe the last verse might be figurative
as well?

Be careful how you answer, because the last verse is not from the
Old Testament; it is from Revelation 1:7. Now what do you think? If you
have gone from being figurative to being literal, when did the change take
place? We have established already the New Testament use of figurative
language in the example of John the Baptist. In fact, a similar passage was
fulfilled by John the Baptist, of whom it was prophesied that *"the glory of
the Lord shall be revealed, and **all flesh shall see it together**"* (Isa 40:5).
How is that any different than *"every eye shall see him"*? Bray observes:

To "see" the Son of man coming in His kingdom does not mean that they would literally see Jesus physically coming from Heaven. The word is used more like as found in Matthew 5:8, "Blessed are the pure in heart: for they shall see God." Seeing God would not be literally seeing someone with the physical eye, for God cannot be seen in that way. God is "the invisible God" (Col 1:15). (See also 1 Tim 1:17). Moses forsook Egypt and "endured, as seeing him who is invisible" (Hebrews 11:27). (*Matthew 24 Fulfilled*, pp. 167-168)

If the Jews had for centuries used this kind of language to illustrate some form of national upheaval, should there not have been some instruction to the people that the same kind of language found in the Olivet discourse and the book of Revelation was to now be understood literally? We are talking about a major change in a culture's language and literary expression. Put yourself in the place of one of the disciples, taught from birth the Scriptures known as the Old Testament. Every time you hear about the sun going dark and the stars not shining, you associate these things with the demise of a nation under God's judgment. Now Jesus has just told you that the temple would be destroyed. He wept over the city because the people did not know the time of their visitation. He says that immediately after the tribulation of those days (during which the temple would be destroyed) the sun would be darkened, and the moon would not give its light; the stars will fall from heaven, and the powers of the heavens will be shaken. If you are one of the disciples, do you take that to mean that the sun will really be darkened, or do you think, "He's talking about an event as serious as what happened to those nations in the Old Testament"? Remember your Jewish mindset and background, and the fact that you have heard nothing that instructs you to understand this language differently. Do you think that the disciples believed Jesus was talking about literal astronomical phenomena, or was He describing God's wrathful judgment? Or imagine for a moment that amongst Jesus' audience were the prophets of old—Samuel, David, Isaiah, Ezekiel, etc. How do you suppose that they would have understood this very familiar language?

If the apocalyptic language associated with judgment in the Old Testament was never meant to be interpreted in a literal manner, Jesus should have told His listeners (and the author of Revelation his readers) that this same apocalyptic language was to now be taken in a literal sense. Consider again this chapter's opening passage from Isaiah, and how closely the language parallels that of Revelation, in the table on the following pages:

Isaiah 13	Revelation
4 The noise of a multitude in the mountains, Like that of many people! A tumultuous noise of the kingdoms of nations gathered together! The LORD of hosts musters The army for battle. 5 They come from a far country, From the end of heaven— The LORD and His weapons of indignation, To destroy the whole land.	16:14 For they are spirits of demons, performing signs, which go out to the kings of the earth and of the whole world, to gather them to the battle of that great day of God Almighty. 19:19 And I saw the beast, the kings of the earth, and their armies, gathered together to make war against Him who sat on the horse and against His army.
6 Wail, for the day of the LORD is at hand! It will come as destruction from the Almighty. 7 Therefore all hands will be limp, Every man's heart will melt, 8 And they will be afraid. Pangs and sorrows will take hold of them; They will be in pain as a woman in childbirth; They will be amazed at one another; Their faces will be like flames.	6:15-17 And the kings of the earth, the great men, the rich men, the commanders, the mighty men, every slave and every free man, hid themselves in the caves and in the rocks of the mountains, and said to the mountains and rocks, "Fall on us and hide us from the face of Him who sits on the throne and from the wrath of the Lamb! For the great day of His wrath has come, and who is able to stand?" 9:6 In those days men will seek death and will not find it; they will desire to die, and death will flee from them.

Isaiah 13	Revelation
9 Behold, the day of the LORD comes, Cruel, with both wrath and fierce anger, To lay the land desolate; And He will destroy its sinners from it.	**11:18** The nations were angry, and Your wrath has come, And the time of the dead, that they should be judged, And that You should reward Your servants the prophets and the saints, And those who fear Your name, small and great, And should destroy those who destroy the earth.
10 For the stars of heaven and their constellations Will not give their light; The sun will be darkened in its going forth, And the moon will not cause its light to shine.	**6:12-13** I looked when He opened the sixth seal, and behold, there was a great earthquake; and the sun became black as sackcloth of hair, and the moon became like blood. And the stars of heaven fell to the earth, as a fig tree drops its late figs when it is shaken by a mighty wind. **8:12** Then the fourth angel sounded: And a third of the sun was struck, a third of the moon, and a third of the stars, so that a third of them were darkened. A third of the day did not shine, and likewise the night.
13 Therefore I will shake the heavens, And the earth will move out of her place, In the wrath of the LORD of hosts And in the day of His fierce anger.	**6:14** Then the sky receded as a scroll when it is rolled up, and every mountain and island was moved out of its place.

Isaiah 13	Revelation
15 Everyone who is found will be thrust through, And everyone who is captured will fall by the sword.	**19:21** And the rest were killed with the sword which proceeded from the mouth of Him who sat on the horse. And all the birds were filled with their flesh.
19 And Babylon, the glory of kingdoms, The beauty of the Chaldeans' pride, Will be as when God overthrew Sodom and Gomorrah. **20** It will never be inhabited, Nor will it be settled from generation to generation; Nor will the Arabian pitch tents there, Nor will the shepherds make their sheepfolds there.	**18:21-22** Then a mighty angel took up a stone like a great millstone and threw it into the sea, saying, "Thus with violence the great city Babylon shall be thrown down, and shall not be found anymore." **18:8** Therefore her plagues will come in one day—death and mourning and famine. And she will be utterly burned with fire, for strong is the Lord God who judges her.
21 But wild beasts of the desert will lie there, And their houses will be full of owls; Ostriches will dwell there, And wild goats will caper there. **22** The hyenas will howl in their citadels, And jackals in their pleasant palaces. Her time is near to come, And her days will not be prolonged.	**18:2** And he cried mightily with a loud voice, saying, "Babylon the great is fallen, is fallen, and has become a dwelling place of demons, a prison for every foul spirit, and a cage for every unclean and hated bird!" **18:9-10** The kings of the earth who committed fornication and lived luxuriously with her will weep and lament for her, when they see the smoke of her burning, standing at a distance for fear of her torment, saying, "Alas, alas, that great city Babylon, that mighty city! For in one hour your judgment has come."

A comparison between God's judgment of physical Babylon in Isaiah chapter 13 and His judgment of spiritual Babylon in Revelation reveal amazing similarities. With this in mind, is it so far-fetched to believe that the book of Revelation is nothing more than an extensive prophecy of the destruction of Jerusalem, written in the established style of Jewish apocalyptic language? (We believe, and will continue to develop the premise, that the Babylon of Revelation represented apostate Israel of the last days' generation.) In fact, some have noted that only John's Gospel does not contain a record of Christ's Olivet discourse, which has obvious allusions to the destruction of Jerusalem. These scholars suggest that Revelation is John's divinely inspired, expanded version of what Christ delivered on the Mount of Olives. As Russell notes:

> Even a slight comparison of the two documents, the [Olivet] prophecy and the Apocalypse [Revelation], will suffice to show the correspondence between them. The *dramatis personae,* if we may so call them,—the symbols which enter into the composition of both,—are the same. What do we find in our Lord's prophecy? First and chiefly the Parousia; then wars, famines, pestilence, earthquakes; false prophets and deceivers; signs and wonders; the darkening of the sun and moon; the stars falling from heaven; angels and trumpets, eagles and carcasses, great tribulation and woe; convulsions of nature; the treading down of Jerusalem; the Son of man coming in the clouds of heaven; the gathering of the elect; the reward of the faithful; the judgment of the wicked. And are not these precisely the elements which compose the Apocalypse? This cannot be accidental resemblance—it is coincidence [i.e., the two coincide, or correspond], it is identity. What difference there is in the treatment of the subject arises from the difference in the method of the revelation. The [Olivet] prophecy is addressed to the ear, and the Apocalypse to the eye: the one is a discourse delivered in broad day, amid the realities of actual life—the other is a vision, beheld in a state of ecstasy, clothed in gorgeous imagery, with an air of unreality as in objects seen in a dream; requiring it to be translated back into the language of everyday life before it can be intelligible as actual fact. (*The Parousia,* pp. 375-376; brackets added)

If we were to take some of the individual Old Testament verses discussed previously and similar verses from New Testament prophecy, strip them of their references, and pull them from a hat one at a time, how would we determine which are literal and which are symbolic in their fulfillment? Are they not all describing national calamities? Are they not all "seeing" the Lord coming in judgment in the guise of foreign armies? Are they not all describing these events in earth-moving, heaven-falling terms? What happened between the times of Old Testament apocalyptic language and Jesus' Olivet discourse (which we are taught to interpret literally) that completely changed the Jewish style and understanding of prophetic language? In this we fear that we have gone beyond putting the veil back on, for even the Jews understood the nature of this language.

Coming in the Clouds

—⁓—

The reader may be surprised to learn that Jesus' Incarnation was not the only instance of God coming down to earth mentioned in the Bible. Consider the following example from the book of Judges:

> *Then Deborah and Barak the son of Abinoam sang on that day, saying:*
>
> *"When leaders lead in Israel,*
> *When the people willingly offer themselves,*
> *Bless the LORD!*
> *"Hear, O kings! Give ear, O princes!*
> *I, even I, will sing to the LORD;*
> *I will sing praise to the LORD God of Israel.*
> ***"LORD, when You went out from Seir,***
> ***When You marched from the field of Edom,***
> *The earth trembled and the heavens poured,*
> *The clouds also poured water;*
> *The mountains gushed before the LORD,*
> *This Sinai, before the LORD God of Israel."*
>
> . . .
>
> ***The LORD came down** for me against the mighty.*
>
> . . .
>
> *They fought from the heavens;*
> *The stars from their courses fought against Sisera."*
> (Judg 5:1-5, 13, 20)
> (emphasis added)

Notice v. 13, which says explicitly that "the LORD came down." Now some might be quick to say that He came in judgment, but not physically. Is not the book of Revelation also describing the Lord's judgment? In expecting a physical coming, are we not making the same mistake that the first-century Jews did in expecting their Messiah to physically deliver them from the Romans and to reign from Jerusalem? Note also that, just as in the example of David from the previous chapter "Apocalyptic

Language," the historic account in Judges seems to be a typical battle scene, while the ensuing song of praise describes the victory as "the LORD coming down." The following are additional examples of God "coming down":

> *And they heard the sound of the* LORD *God walking in the garden in the cool of the day, and Adam and his wife hid themselves from the presence of the* LORD *God among the trees of the garden.* (Gen 3:8)

> *But* **the** LORD **came down to see the city** *and the tower which the sons of men had built. And the* LORD *said, "Indeed the people are one and they all have one language, and this is what they begin to do; now nothing that they propose to do will be withheld from them. Come,* **let Us go down** *and there confuse their language, that they may not understand one another's speech."* (Gen 11:5-7)

> *And the* LORD *said, "Because the outcry against Sodom and Gomorrah is great, and because their sin is very grave,* **I will go down** *now and see whether they have done altogether according to the outcry against it that has come to Me; and if not, I will know."* (Gen 18:20-21)

> **Then God appeared to Jacob again**, *when he came from Padan Aram, and blessed him . . . . Then God went up from him in the place where He talked with him.* (Gen 35:9, 13)

> *And Joseph said to his brethren, "I am dying; but* **God will surely visit you**, *and bring you out of this land to the land of which He swore to Abraham, to Isaac, and to Jacob."* (Gen 50:24)

> *And the* LORD *said: "I have surely seen the oppression of My people who are in Egypt, and have heard their cry because of their taskmasters, for I know their sorrows. So* **I have come down to deliver them** *out of the hand of the Egyptians, and to bring them up from that land to a good and large land, to a land flowing with milk and honey . . . ."* (Exod 3:7-8)

> *And let them be ready for the third day. For on the third day* **the** LORD **will come down** *upon Mount Sinai in the sight of all the people.* (Exod 19:11)

> *So the* LORD *said to Moses: "Gather to Me seventy men of the elders of Israel, whom you know to be the elders of the people and officers over them; bring them to the tabernacle of meeting, that*

*they may stand there with you. Then **I will come down** and talk with you there.*" (Num 11:16-17)
(emphases added)

So we see that God has "come down" to man on many occasions, often in association with judgment or deliverance. As students of the Word, have we ever insisted that all of these "comings" were physical, bodily manifestations of God? We seem to have no problem understanding those comings as "spiritual" or "metaphorical" comings of God. We do not claim that God came down physically and delivered David and Deborah from their enemies, yet we must trust the Bible when it says that God came down in those instances. Maimonides observed:

> . . . the prophets, in referring to the ruin of a person, of a nation, or of a country, describe it as the result of God's great anger and wrath, whilst the prosperity of a nation is the result of God's pleasure and satisfaction. In the former case the prophets employ such phrases as "He came forth," "came down," "roared," "thundered," or "caused his voice to be heard"; also "He commanded," "said," "did," "made," and the like . . . . (*Guide for the Perplexed*, pp. 204-205)

Why, then, when the descriptions of Christ's Second Coming echo those same themes of judgment upon His enemies and deliverance of His people do we apply the physical nature of the Incarnation to it rather than the spiritual nature established by the precedent in the Old Testament? The reason that most people make this erroneous application is because Christ's physical body ascended into heaven, and He was said to be coming back in like manner:

> *Now when He had spoken these things, while they watched, He was taken up, and a cloud received Him out of their sight. And while they looked steadfastly toward heaven as He went up, behold, two men stood by them in white apparel, who also said, "Men of Galilee, why do you stand gazing up into heaven? This same Jesus, who was taken up from you into heaven, will so come in like manner as you saw Him go into heaven."* (Acts 1:9-11)

Based upon the statement of the angels, most believe the implication is that Jesus will return bodily. However, the Greek word for "so" (*houto*), means "in this way—referring to what precedes or follows." Thus, when Luke writes, "*This same Jesus, who was taken up from you into heaven, will **so** come in like manner as you saw Him go into heaven,*" the Scripture teaches that Jesus will come in like manner as He was taken up. But how was He taken up? "*. . . while they watched, He was taken up, and **a cloud received Him** out of their sight*" (emphasis added). While many in the Church focus on the observation that since Christ ascended bodily and, therefore, must return bodily, we believe that the other references to His coming and the use of *houto* here, place the emphasis on His returning *in the clouds*. If someone departs for a destination on a plane, and we are told that they are returning in the same manner as they left, do we understand that to mean that they would return in an identical physical condition (e.g., wearing the same clothes, arm still in a cast, etc.) or that they are coming back on a plane? The angel did not say that Jesus would return in the same *condition* that He left, but in the same *manner*. The focus is not on the condition of the traveler but on the *mode* of transportation — *in the clouds*! Notice how prevalent this theme is in Second Coming passages:

> *Then the sign of the Son of Man will appear in heaven, and then all the tribes of the earth will mourn, and they will see **the Son of Man coming on the clouds of heaven** with power and great glory.* (Matt 24:30)

> *Again the high priest asked Him, saying to Him, "Are You the Christ, the Son of the Blessed?" Jesus said, "I am. And you will see the Son of Man sitting at the right hand of the Power, and **coming with the clouds of heaven**."* (Mark 14:61-62)

> *Then we who are alive and remain shall be caught up together with them **in the clouds** to meet the Lord in the air.* (1 Thess 4:17)

> *Behold, **He is coming with clouds**, and every eye will see Him, even they who pierced Him. And all the tribes of the earth will mourn because of Him. Even so, Amen.* (Rev 1:7)

> *Then I looked, and behold, **a white cloud, and on the cloud sat One like the Son of Man**, having on His head a golden crown, and in His hand a sharp sickle.* (Rev 14:14)
> (emphases added)

Is this coming in the clouds something new to the early church, or had they heard the term before? Once again, we turn to the Old Testament:

> *He made darkness His secret place;*
> ***His canopy around Him was dark waters***
> ***And thick clouds of the skies.***
> *From the brightness before Him,*

His thick clouds passed with hailstones and coals of fire.
(Ps 18:11-12; emphasis added)

We remind the reader of the parallel passage from 2 Samuel 22 (discussed in the chapter "Apocalyptic Language") in which David used apocalyptic language to describe the Lord's delivering him from his enemies and Saul. David makes these statements in his song of thanksgiving, yet not one of these items is mentioned as a literal event in Samuel's historical accounts. However, we digress, for our current subject is coming in the clouds. Here are additional examples that once again highlight specific phrases with **bold** font:

He lays the beams of His upper chambers in the waters,
Who makes the clouds His chariot,
Who walks on the wings of the wind .... (Ps 104:3)

The burden against Egypt.
Behold, the L*ORD**** rides on a swift cloud,***
And will come into Egypt;
The idols of Egypt will totter at His presence,
And the heart of Egypt will melt in its midst. (Isa 19:1)

Blow the trumpet in Zion,
And sound an alarm in My holy mountain!
Let all the inhabitants of the land tremble;
For the day of the L*ORD**** is coming,***
For it is at hand:
A day of darkness and gloominess,
A day of clouds and thick darkness,
Like the morning clouds *spread over the mountains.* (Joel 2:1-2)

The L*ORD**** has His way***
In the whirlwind and in the storm,
And the clouds are the dust of His feet. (Nah 1:3b)

*The great day of the L*ORD *is near;*
It is near and hastens quickly.
*The noise of the day of the L*ORD *is bitter;*
There the mighty men shall cry out.
That day is a day of wrath,
A day of trouble and distress,
A day of devastation and desolation,
A day of darkness and gloominess,

A day of clouds and thick darkness . . . . (Zeph 1:14-15)
(emphases added)

So again we must ask ourselves, *When the early Christians (mostly Jewish converts) heard, or read, of Christ coming in the clouds to judge His enemies and deliver His saints, what images did their minds conjure up? Did they see the Mount of Olives splitting literally in two, the heavens rolling up like a scroll, and the stars falling from the sky, or did they see something else?* Almost all of the above passages describe God coming to various nations in judgment—judgments that occurred centuries before the New Testament era. There is nothing to indicate that any of the apocalyptic details literally happened, nor that anyone believed that they had. So what did happen? These nations were attacked, in various degrees, by foreign armies. Those armies, knowingly or not, were God's instruments of judgment against these nations:

> *Thus I will strengthen the arms of the king of Babylon, but the arms of Pharaoh shall fall down; they shall know that I am the* LORD*, when **I put My sword into the hand of the king of Babylon and he stretches it out against the land of Egypt.*** (Ezek 30:25)

> *Thus says the Lord GOD:*
> ***"I will also make a multitude of Egypt to cease***
> ***By the hand of Nebuchadnezzar king of Babylon."*** (Ezek 30:10)

> ***The** LORD **will bring the king of Assyria upon you** and your people and your father's house.* (Isa 7:17)

> ***Woe to Assyria, the rod of My anger***
> ***And the staff in whose hand is My indignation.***
> ***I will send him against an ungodly nation,***
> *And against the people of My wrath*
> *I will give him charge,*
> *To seize the spoil, to take the prey,*
> *And to tread them down like the mire of the streets.* (Isa 10:5-6)

> ***The** LORD **has raised up the spirit of the kings of the Medes.***
> ***For His plan is against Babylon to destroy it,***
> ***Because it is the vengeance of the** LORD,
> *The vengeance for His temple.* (Jer 51:11)

> ***You are My battle-ax and weapons of war:***
> ***For with you I will break the nation in pieces;***

With you I will destroy kingdoms . . . . (Jer 51:20)
(emphases added)

Again, what did the early church envision as the coming of the Lord in judgment? Remember our Lord's admonition to them:

> *But when you see Jerusalem surrounded by armies, then know that its desolation is near. Then let those who are in Judea flee to the mountains, let those who are in the midst of her depart, and let not those who are in the country enter her. For these are the days of vengeance, that all things which are written may be fulfilled. But woe to those who are pregnant and to those who are nursing babies in those days! For there will be great distress in the land and wrath upon this people. And they will fall by the edge of the sword, and be led away captive into all nations. And Jerusalem will be trampled by Gentiles until the times of the Gentiles are fulfilled.* (Luke 21:20-24)

Apostate Israel had played the harlot before God long enough. They had become His enemy, and the enemy of His new chosen people, the Church. He was about to come in judgment to them and destroy their city and temple, indicating a definitive end to the Old Covenant and confirming the New Covenant, which they had been persecuting, as the final stage of God's redemptive plan. In AD 70, after 3½ years (the "time, times and half a time"; the 1,260 days; and the 42 months of Revelation) of fighting, the Roman army was victorious. Concerning the temple, not one stone was left upon another.

The predisposition to interpret the Second Coming as having a nature more like the Incarnation than of the previous Old Testament examples, we believe, is due largely to the following three items:

- A misunderstanding of the nature of the New Covenant
- An erroneous interpretation of the angels' statement in Acts 1, "*This same Jesus, who was taken up from you into heaven, will so come in like manner as you saw Him go into heaven,*" which puts the focus on His physical body rather than on His being caught up in the clouds
- A mistaken belief that Christ, as the "first fruits" of the redeemed, requires that His physical, bodily resurrection be indicative of our future bodily resurrection, thus necessitating a more "physical" nature to the Second Coming

The first item was the subject of Part I of our study. We have addressed the second item in this chapter, as well as the chapter on apocalyptic language. Hopefully, the reader, if not convinced, at least admits that the New Testament language describing the Second Coming is strikingly similar to that of Old Testament comings, which generations of Christians have had no problem understanding in a spiritual, metaphorical sense. The third item is, admittedly, not an easy topic; still, we will endeavor to shed some light on it in a later chapter.

In light of the Old Testament examples of "comings of the Lord" and the apocalyptic language with which they are inextricably wrapped, we feel that a serious reconsideration is due regarding the nature of the Second Coming of Christ. Is not the book of Revelation a "revealing" of Christ coming in His glory, meting out judgment to His enemies and bringing deliverance to His people? And is not this "coming" also clothed in the same apocalyptic language that we have seen in the Old Testament? If we truly allow Scripture to interpret Scripture, it becomes clear that the Olivet discourse and the book of Revelation continue the Old Testament precedent of "comings of the Lord" in judgment and deliverance. The evidence favors His coming in the clouds of judgment, as opposed to touching down on earth bodily. Bray rightly asks,

> In Exodus 19 it states that on Mount Sinai "the LORD descended upon it in fire" (v. 18), "And the LORD came down upon mount Sinai, on the top of the mount (v. 20)." But no one saw Him in bodily form or shape. Did Jesus have to appear in bodily and physical form in AD 70 in order to "come" at that time? (*Matthew 24 Fulfilled*, p. 147)

Lest some think that by claiming a "spiritual" return of Christ, as opposed to a physical one, we are denying the physical, bodily resurrection of our Lord, we emphatically affirm our conformity to the doctrine of His bodily resurrection. Our focus here is not on the substance of our Lord as He ascended, but the *manner* in which He ascended — *in the clouds*. (As mentioned earlier, we will attempt to deal with the issue of the substance of our Lord's resurrected body and its implications in a later chapter.)

It may be argued that, regardless of the substance of our Lord's resurrected body, there is an undeniable emphasis as to the visual aspect of His return:

> *Now when He had spoken these things, while they watched, He was taken up, and a cloud received Him **out of their sight**. And*

> *while they looked steadfastly toward heaven as He went up,*
> *behold, two men stood by them in white apparel, who also said,*
> *"Men of Galilee, why do you stand gazing up into heaven? This*
> *same Jesus, who was taken up from you into heaven, will so come*
> *in like manner **as you saw Him go** into heaven."* (Acts 1:9-11)

> *Behold, He is coming with clouds, and **every eye will see Him,***
> *even they who pierced Him. And all the tribes of the earth will*
> *mourn because of Him. Even so, Amen.* (Rev 1:7)
> (emphases added)

That there seems to be a visual aspect to the Second Coming we do not deny; but how is this any different than "*the glory of the Lord shall be revealed, and **all flesh shall see it together***" being fulfilled during the ministry of John the Baptist? Similarly, Paul wrote Titus that *the grace of God that brings salvation **has appeared to all men*** (Titus 2:11; emphasis added). Surely we do not believe that every individual on the planet in Paul's day was made aware of God's grace.

Consider also the way that Jesus described to His disciples how He would be "seen" by them:

> *A little while longer and the world will see Me no more, but you*
> *will see Me. Because I live, you will live also. At that day you will*
> *know that I am in My Father, and you in Me, and I in you. He who*
> *has My commandments and keeps them, it is he who loves Me.*
> *And he who loves Me will be loved by My Father, and I will love*
> *him and manifest Myself to him. Judas (not Iscariot) said to Him,*
> *"Lord, how is it that You will manifest Yourself to us, and not to*
> *the world?" Jesus answered and said to him, "If anyone loves Me,*
> *he will keep My word; and My Father will love him, and We will*
> *come to him and make Our home with him."* (John 14:19-23)

Jesus said that the world would *not* see Him, but that His disciples would. Judas asked how this could be and Jesus responded that He and the Father would make Their home with them. We understand this to refer to the spiritual relationship between God and His children, not the act of dwelling in a physical house. The world would not see Him because the world did not have a relationship with Him. The "seeing" that the disciples would experience was one of spiritual insight using "*the eyes of their heart*" (Eph 1:18 NASB95).

We do not disallow that that first-century generation may have seen Christ in some bodily sense at His return. He showed Himself physically to many in order to establish the fact of His resurrection (1 Cor 15:4-8), so why not do the same to establish His return in judgment, especially to those who pierced Him? And we must not ignore the supernatural events that Josephus recorded during the destruction of Jerusalem:

> . . . for, before sun-setting, chariots and troops of soldiers in their armor were seen running about among the clouds, and surrounding of cities. Moreover, at that feast which we call Pentecost, as the priests were going by night into the inner [court of the temple,] as their custom was, to perform their sacred ministrations, they said that, in the first place, they felt a quaking, and heard a great noise, and after that they heard a sound as of a great multitude, saying, "Let us remove hence." (*Wars*, 5.5; brackets in original translation)

No Scriptures come to mind which would preclude Jesus from appearing to those upon whom judgment was falling, that they might know by Whom and why they were being judged. Who can say that those who pierced Him did not see Him in some form or fashion, only to realize that the Messiah, Whom they had rejected, had returned as Judge? (In agreement with Zechariah 12:10, we take "those who pierced Him" to mean the Jews who cried, "crucify Him, crucify Him," not necessarily the Roman soldiers who actually nailed Him to the cross.) Or who can say whether the Pharisees, who understood that the Lord's parables were spoken against *them*, realized that those parables were being fulfilled when the landowner came to slay His enemies and give the vineyard (kingdom) to another (Matt 21:33-44), and that, having rejected the wedding invitation, the King had sent out His armies to destroy them and burn up their city (Matt 22:1-10)? Or that the Sanhedrin that condemned Christ saw Him, as He said they would, *"at the right hand of the Mighty One and coming on the clouds of heaven"* (Matt 26:64)?

Being seen visibly does not necessitate a physical body. Christ could have been seen in His glorified body, just as Moses and Elijah were seen on the Mount of Transfiguration (Matt 17:3), and just as Elisha's servant saw a spiritual army (2 Kgs 6:17).

In areas where Scripture is silent or speaks little, we feel it wise to follow suit. Believing that the witness of Scripture, using apocalyptic language, argues for a spiritual return of Christ in the clouds of judgment, we feel constrained to speak no further on if, how, and by whom Christ was seen at His return.

Matthew 24

—m—

As we have progressed through our study, we have seen both systematically and scripturally the lack of support for a supposed future return of Christ to establish a physical kingdom. At the same time, we have established support for a Second Coming of Christ during the destruction of Jerusalem in AD 70. In this chapter, we turn our attention to our Lord's Olivet discourse. Although there are parallel passages in Mark and Luke, we will center our study on Matthew's account, as this is typically the primary text used by prophecy students.

As we mentioned earlier, we are not attempting a verse-by-verse exposition of the eschatological texts found in Daniel, Matthew 24, and Revelation; rather, we are attempting to provide an alternate framework to the current one upon which a future physical kingdom is built. (For an excellent verse-by-verse commentary on Matthew 24, we recommend John L. Bray's *Matthew 24 Fulfilled*.) The framework we seek is one that fits upon the foundation laid in Part I and provides a harmonization of all the various eschatological texts and their themes. That being said, we wish to look at two main points concerning Matthew 24: (1) the generation of Matthew 24 was the New Testament "last days" generation, and (2) the prophecies in Matthew 24 have been fulfilled.

This Generation

Although we have addressed this issue in the chapter "This Generation," we revisit it here because it is an integral part of Matthew 24. Of what generation was Jesus speaking in His Olivet address? Audience relevance would dictate that it was the same generation *to* whom He was speaking. However, two primary devices are commonly used to circumvent this understanding. The first device is the "redefinition" of the term *generation*. Some attempt to use an alternate meaning of the Greek *genea*, translating it "race." Thus, they say that what Jesus was saying was that the Jewish race wouldn't pass away before all these things came to pass. Although "race" is a possible meaning for *genea*, it is never translated that way in the Bible. As we have previously shown, other usages of *genea* in the Bible reveal that "race" is an untenable rendering. Others say that *genea* is not referring to the Jewish race in general, but to a particular kind of people—that is, a generation of wicked people. This position seems so tenuous as to barely warrant addressing. The implication is that Jesus is prophesying judgment, and then saying that the people who are to receive that judgment (i.e., those who are wicked) will not pass away until they receive it.

Provided below, we believe, is evidence that the generation to which Christ referred was His current generation. Regardless of possible definitions for the word *genea*, we feel that *genea* should be defined by the context. To point out that regardless of how *genea* can be translated, it was the hearers of Christ who were exhorted, warned, given signs, told what to do and what not to do, etc., we have emphasized certain pronouns (e.g., **YOU** and **YOUR**) in the text of Matthew 24. Notice that Christ continues to address the disciples directly throughout His entire discourse, implying that all of the warnings, signs, and instructions would apply to them:

> *1 Then Jesus went out and departed from the temple, and His disciples came up to show Him the buildings of the temple. 2 And Jesus said to them, "Do **YOU** not see all these things? Assuredly, I say to **YOU**, not one stone shall be left here upon another, that shall not be thrown down." 3 Now as He sat on the Mount of Olives, the disciples came to Him privately, saying, "Tell us, when will these things be? And what will be the sign of Your coming, and of the end of the age?" 4 And Jesus answered and said to them: "Take heed that no one deceives **YOU**. 5 For many will come in My name, saying, 'I am the Christ,' and will deceive many. 6 And **YOU** will hear of wars and rumors of wars. See that **YOU** are not troubled; for all these things must come to pass, but the end is not yet. 7 For nation will rise against nation, and kingdom against kingdom. And there will be famines, pestilences, and earthquakes in various places. 8 All these are the beginning of sorrows. 9 Then they will deliver **YOU** up to tribulation and kill **YOU**, and **YOU** will be hated by all nations for My name's sake. 10 And then many will be offended, will betray one another, and will hate one another. 11 Then many false prophets will rise up and deceive many. 12 And because lawlessness will abound, the love of many will grow cold. 13 But he who endures to the end shall be saved. 14 And this gospel of the kingdom will be preached in all the world as a witness to all the nations, and then the end will come. 15 Therefore when **YOU** see the 'abomination of desolation,' spoken of by Daniel the*

prophet, standing in the holy place" (whoever reads, let him under-stand), 16 "then let those who are in Judea flee to the mountains. 17 Let him who is on the housetop not go down to take anything out of his house. 18 And let him who is in the field not go back to get his clothes. 19 But woe to those who are pregnant and to those who are nursing babies in those days! 20 And pray that YOUR flight may not be in winter or on the Sabbath. 21 For then there will be great tribulation, such as has not been since the beginning of the world until this time, no, nor ever shall be. 22 And unless those days were shortened, no flesh would be saved; but for the elect's sake those days will be shortened. 23 Then if anyone says to YOU, 'Look, here is the Christ!' or 'There!' do not believe it. 24 For false christs and false prophets will rise and show great signs and wonders to deceive, if possible, even the elect. 25 See, I have told YOU before-hand. 26 Therefore if they say to YOU, 'Look, He is in the desert!' do not go out; or 'Look, He is in the inner rooms!' do not believe it. 27 For as the lightning comes from the east and flashes to the west, so also will the coming of the Son of Man be. 28 For wherever the carcass is, there the eagles will be gathered together.

29 "Immediately after the tribulation of those days the sun will be darkened, and the moon will not give its light; the stars will fall from heaven, and the powers of the heavens will be shaken. 30 Then the sign of the Son of Man will appear in heaven, and then all the tribes of the earth will mourn, and they will see the Son of Man coming on the clouds of heaven with power and great glory. 31 And He will send His angels with a great sound of a trumpet, and they will gather together His elect from the four winds, from one end of heaven to the other. 32 Now learn this parable from the fig tree: When its branch has already become tender and puts forth leaves, YOU know that summer is near. 33 So YOU also, when YOU see all these things, know that it is near—at the doors! 34 Assuredly, I say to YOU, this generation will by no means pass away till all these things take place. 35 Heaven and earth will pass away, but My words will by no means pass away. 36 But of that day and hour no one knows, not even the angels of heaven, but My Father only. 37 But as the days of Noah were, so also will the coming of the Son of Man be. 38 For as in the days before the flood, they were eating and drinking, marrying and giving in marriage, until the day that Noah entered the ark, 39 and did not know until the flood came and took them all away, so also will *the coming of the Son of Man be. 40 Then two men will be in the field: one will be taken and the other left. 41 Two women will be grinding at the mill: one will be taken and the other left. 42 Watch therefore, for **YOU** do not know what hour your Lord is coming. 43 But know this, that if the master of the house had known what hour the thief would come, he would have watched and not allowed his house to be broken into. 44 Therefore **YOU** also be ready, for the Son of Man is coming at an hour **YOU** do not expect. 45 Who then is a faithful and wise servant, whom his master made ruler over his household, to give them food in due season? 46 Blessed is that servant whom his master, when he comes, will find so doing. 47 Assuredly, I say to **YOU** that he will make him ruler over all his goods. 48 But if that evil servant says in his heart, 'My master is delaying his coming,' 49 and begins to beat his fellow servants, and to eat and drink with the drunkards, 50 the master of that servant will come on a day when he is not looking for him and at an hour that he is not aware of, 51 and will cut him in two and appoint him his portion with the hypocrites. There shall be weeping and gnashing of teeth."*

Another method designed to remove "this generation" from the last days of the Old Covenant is to divide Matthew 24 into two sections (as we have done above at v. 29). This is done because of the obvious references in it, and in the parallel accounts of Mark and Luke, to the destruction of Jerusalem in AD 70. Although the dividing point is debated (Terry cites six commentators, each with a different dividing point), the premise is that the events and the people referred to in the first section apply to the first-century generation and the destruction of Jerusalem, while the events and people of the second section apply to a yet-future generation at the Second Coming. This method's proponents are thus able to "have their cake and eat it too" by allowing the obvious prophecy of Jerusalem's destruction to stand while still maintaining their framework for a future return of Christ to a physical kingdom. Matthew Henry divides the discourse at v. 29, while Albert Barnes admits that it is sometimes difficult to tell to what particular subject—the destruction of Jerusalem or the final judgment—Jesus' remarks apply:

Matt 24:3:

[When shall these things be?] There are three questions here:

1. when those things should take place
2. what should be the signs of his own coming

3. what should be the signs that the end of the world was near

To these questions He replies in this and the following chapters. This He does, not by noticing them distinctly, but by intermingling the descriptions of the destruction of Jerusalem and of the end of the world, so that it is sometimes difficult to tell to what particular subject his remarks apply. The PRINCIPLE on which this combined description of two events was spoken appears to be, that "they could be described in the same words," and therefore the accounts are inter-mingled. A similar use of language is found in some parts of Isaiah, where the same language will describe the return from the Babylonian captivity, and deliverance by the Messiah. (*Barnes' Notes*)

In his book *What Happened in AD 70?*, Ed Stevens demonstrated that dividing Matthew's Olivet discourse to make Jesus refer to two different generations would wreak havoc on the parallel passage in Luke 17. Although Luke 17 is not an account of the Olivet discourse, Jesus taught much of the same material. In this particular address, Jesus answered the Pharisees' question regarding the coming kingdom and further instructed His disciples. While Matthew 24 is obviously one continuous discourse, if it does indeed address two different generations, then Jesus jumped back and forth confusingly between these two generations in Luke 17.

In our presentation of Matthew 24 above, we have shown a division between vv. 28 and 29 (although some commentators divide it between vv. 34 and 35), with vv. 1-28 relating to the destruction of Jerusalem and vv. 29-51 relating to a (supposedly) future generation. In the following presentation of Luke 17 we use the following emphases:

1. Portions of Luke that parallel the first section of the Matthew 24 text (addressing the New Testament generation) are in a **bold** font.

2. Parallels that are found in the second section of the Matthew 24 text (addressing a yet future generation) are <u>underlined</u>.

Using this method, we can see that if Jesus switched between two different generations once in Matthew 24, then he did it no less than four times in Luke 17! If this is indeed the case, how would His listeners be expected to keep things straight?

"Christ's Generation"

20 Now when He was asked by the Pharisees when the kingdom of God would come, He answered them and said, "The kingdom of God does not come with observation; 21 nor will they say, 'See here!' or 'See there!' For indeed, the kingdom of God is within you." 22 Then He said to the disciples, "The days will come when you will desire to see one of the days of the Son of Man, and you will not see it. 23 **And they will say to you, 'Look here!' or 'Look there!' Do not go after them or follow them. 24 For as the lightning that flashes out of one part under heaven shines to the other part under heaven, so also the Son of Man will be in His day.** 25 But first He must suffer many things and be rejected by this generation.

"Future Generation"

26 <u>And as it was in the days of Noah, so it will be also in the days of the Son of Man: 27 They ate, they drank, they married wives, they were given in marriage, until the day that Noah entered the ark, and the flood came and destroyed them all</u>. 28 Likewise as it was also in the days of Lot: They ate, they drank, they bought, they sold, they planted, they built; 29 but on the day that Lot went out of Sodom it rained fire and brimstone from heaven and destroyed them all. 30 Even so will it be in the day when the Son of Man is revealed.

"Christ's Generation"

31 **"In that day, he who is on the housetop, and his goods are in the house, let him not come down to take them away. And likewise the one who is in the field, let him not turn back.** 32 Remember Lot's wife. 33 Whoever seeks to save his life will lose it, and whoever loses his life will preserve it.

"Future Generation"

34 I tell you, in that night there will be two men in one bed: the one will be taken and the other will be left. 35 <u>Two women will be grinding together: the one will be taken and the other left. Two men will be in the field: the one will be taken and the other left."</u>

"Christ's Generation"

37 And they answered and said to Him, "Where, Lord?" So He said to them, **"Wherever the body is, there the eagles will be gathered together."** (Luke 17:20-37)

Luke 17:37 obviously belongs with the preceding verses, yet in Matthew's account many interpreters assign these statements to a completely different generation! Commentators, in order to separate the

AD 70 generation from a future Second Coming generation, disagree on where to divide Matthew 24—and this *after* one of the events has already taken place! If *we* are unable to discern which portions are fulfilled and which are predictive, one wonders how Jesus' listeners could discern, from their perspective, the near predictive from the far predictive. This is especially true of Luke 17, where Jesus supposedly switches generations *no less than four times!* When we recall that the disciples continually demonstrated their ignorance of Jesus' teachings and needed the simplest of parables explained to them, we can hardly imagine them "keeping up" with their Master as He traversed millennia in His answer to them. We agree with Bray, who states, "This division of time and events is made by interpreters of this passage, but was not made by the disciples themselves (nor Jesus)."

In order to demonstrate that we need not wait for future fulfillments of the "signs" of Matthew 24, we again provide portions of Matthew's text interspersed with their fulfillments from later biblical accounts and Josephus' account of the war leading up to the destruction of Jerusalem. The **bold** text highlights items in Matthew 24 and their corresponding fulfillments in these accounts:

Matthew 24:7
*. . . And there will be **famines**, pestilences, and earthquakes in various places.*

> *Then one of them, named Agabus, stood up and showed by the Spirit that there was going to be a great **famine throughout all the world, which also happened** in the days of Claudius Caesar.* (Acts 11:28)

> But the **famine** was too hard for all other passions, and it is destructive to nothing so much as to modesty; for what was otherwise worthy of reverence was in this case despised; insomuch that children pulled the very morsels that their fathers were eating out of their very mouths, and what was still more to be pitied, so did the mothers do as to their infants; and when those that were most dear were perishing under their hands, they were not ashamed to take from them the very last drops that might preserve their lives. (*Wars*, 5.10)

Matthew 24:9
*Then **they will deliver you up to tribulation and kill you**, and you will be hated by all nations for My name's sake.*

*At that time **a great persecution arose against the church** which was at Jerusalem; and they were all scattered throughout the regions of Judea and Samaria, except the apostles.* (Acts 8:1)

*Then he **killed James** the brother of John with the sword. And because he saw that it pleased the Jews, he proceeded further to **seize Peter** also.* (Acts 12:2-3)

*This I also did in Jerusalem, and **many of the saints I shut up in prison**, having received authority from the chief priests; and when **they were put to death**, I cast my vote against them.* (Acts 26:10)

Matthew 24:14
And this gospel of the kingdom will be preached in all the world as a witness to all the nations, and then the end will come.

*. . . of which you heard before in the word of the truth of **the gospel**, which has come to you, as it has also **in all the world** . . . .* (Col 1:5-6)

*. . . if indeed you continue in the faith, grounded and steadfast, and are not moved away from the hope of **the gospel** which you heard, which **was preached to every creature under heaven** . . . .* (Col 1:23)

*But they have not all obeyed the gospel. For Isaiah says, "Lord, who has believed our report?" So then faith comes by hearing, and hearing by **the word of God**. But I say, have they not heard? Yes indeed:*

*"Their sound has gone out **to all the earth**,*

*And their words **to the ends of the world**."* (Rom 10:16-18)

Matthew 24:23
*Then if anyone says to you, "Look, here is the Christ!" or "There!" do not believe it. 24 For **false christs** and **false prophets** will rise and show great signs and wonders to deceive, if possible, even the elect. 25 See, I have told you beforehand. 26 Therefore if they say to you, "Look, He is in the desert!" do not go out; or "Look, He is in the inner rooms!" do not believe it.*

*Dear children, this is the last hour; and as you have heard that the antichrist is coming, even now **many antichrists have come**. This is how we know it is the last hour.* (1 John 2:18 NIV)

*. . . because many **false prophets** have gone out into the world.* (1 John 4:1)

*Every spirit that confesses that Jesus Christ has come in the flesh is of God, and every spirit that does not confess that Jesus Christ has come in the flesh is not of God. And this is **the spirit of the Antichrist**, which you have heard was coming, and is now already in the world.* (1 John 4:2-3)

But there was an Egyptian **false prophet** that did the Jews more mischief than the former; for he was a cheat, and pretended to be a prophet also, and got together thirty thousand men that were deluded by him. (Wars, 2.5)

A **false prophet** was the occasion of these people's destruction, who had made a public proclamation in the city that very day, that God commanded them to get upon the temple, and that there they should receive miraculous signs of their deliverance. Now there was then **a great number of false prophets** suborned by the tyrants to impose on the people, who denounced this to them, that they should wait for deliverance from God. (Wars, 6.5)

Matthew 24:29
*Immediately after the tribulation of those days **the sun will be darkened, and the moon will not give its light; the stars will fall from heaven, and the powers of the heavens will be shaken.** 30 Then **the sign of the Son of Man will appear in heaven**, and then all the tribes of the earth will mourn, and they will see the Son of Man coming on the clouds of heaven with power and great glory. [We recall to the reader the apocalyptic language of the Jews used in describing judgment.]*

. . . for there broke out a prodigious storm in the night, with the utmost violence, and very strong winds, with the largest showers of rain, with continued lightnings, terrible thunderings, and amazing concussions and bellowings of the earth, that was in an earthquake. These things were a manifest indication that some destruction was coming upon men, when **the system of the world was put into this disorder**; and any one would guess that these wonders foreshowed some grand calamities that were coming. (*Wars*, 4.4)

Moreover, the eastern gate of the inner [court of the] temple, which was of brass, and vastly heavy, and had been with difficulty shut by twenty men, and rested upon a basis armed with iron, and had bolts fastened very deep into the firm floor, which was there made of one entire stone, was seen to be opened of its own accord about the sixth hour of the night. Now those that kept watch in the temple came hereupon running to the captain of the temple, and told him of it; who then came up thither, and not without great difficulty was able to shut the gate again. This also appeared to the vulgar to be a very happy prodigy, as if God did thereby open them the gate of happiness. But the men of learning understood it, that **the security of their holy house was dissolved** of its own accord, and that the gate was opened for the advantage of their enemies. So these publicly declared that **the signal foreshowed the desolation that was coming upon them**. Besides these, a few days after that feast, on the one and twentieth day of the month Artemisius, [Jyar,] a certain prodigious and incredible phenomenon appeared: I suppose the account of it would seem to be a fable, were it not related by those that saw it, and were not the events that followed it of so considerable a nature as to deserve such signals; for, **before sun-setting, chariots and troops of soldiers in their armor were seen running about among the clouds, and surrounding of cities**. Moreover, at that feast which we call Pentecost, as the priests were going by night into the inner [court of the temple,] as their custom was, to perform their sacred ministrations, they said that, in the first place, they felt a quaking, and heard a great noise, and after that they heard a sound as of a great multitude, saying, "Let us remove hence." (*Wars*, 6.5 — brackets in original)

Matthew 24:34

Assuredly, I say to you, this generation will by no means pass away till all these things take place. 35 Heaven and earth will pass away, but My words will by no means pass away.

*Now all these things happened to them [the Exodus generation] as examples, and they were written for **our [the New Testament generation's] admonition, upon whom the ends of the ages have come**. (1 Cor 10:11)*

But the end of all things is at hand . . . . (1 Pet 4:7)

Matthew 24:42

*Watch therefore, for you do not know what hour your Lord is coming. 43 But know this, that if the master of the house had known **what hour the thief would come**, he would have watched and not allowed his house to be broken into. 44 **Therefore you also be ready, for the Son of Man is coming at an hour you do not expect.***

*But you, brethren, are not in darkness, so that **this Day should overtake you as a thief**.* (1 Thess 5:4)

Matthew 24:45

*Who then is a faithful and wise servant, whom his master made ruler over his household, to give them food in due season? 46 Blessed is that servant whom his master, when he comes, will find so doing. 47 Assuredly, I say to you that he will make him ruler over all his goods. 48 **But if that evil servant says in his heart, "My master is delaying his coming,"** 49 and begins to beat his fellow servants, and to eat and drink with the drunkards, 50 the master of that servant will come on a day when he is not looking for him and at an hour that he is not aware of, 51 and will cut him in two and appoint him his portion with the hypocrites. There shall be weeping and gnashing of teeth.*

*. . . knowing this first: that scoffers will come in the last days, walking according to their own lusts, and saying, **"Where is the promise of His coming?** For since the fathers fell asleep, all things continue as they were from the beginning of creation."* (2 Pet 3:3-4)

*These are grumblers, complainers, walking according to their own lusts; and they mouth great swelling words, flattering people to gain advantage. But you, beloved, remember the words which were spoken before by the apostles of our Lord Jesus Christ: how they told you that **there would be mockers in the last time** who would walk according to their own ungodly lusts.* (Jude 16-18)

Double Fulfillment

Upon realizing the detail with which the destruction of Jerusalem in AD 70 fulfills the apocalyptic prophecies of Jesus and John, many resort to a double fulfillment scenario in order to maintain the promise of a future Second Coming. Thus, while admitting that the destruction of Jerusalem can be seen in these prophecies, they consider that event as a partial, or typical, fulfillment of the ultimate fulfillment to be realized in a future Second Coming. Concerning double fulfillment scenarios, Milton S. Terry wrote:

The hermeneutical principles which we have now set forth necessarily exclude the doctrine that the prophecies of Scripture contain an occult or double sense. It has been alleged by some that as these oracles are heavenly and divine we should expect to find in them manifold meanings. They must needs differ from other books. Hence has arisen not only the doctrine of a double sense, but of a threefold and fourfold sense, and the rabbis went so far as to insist that there are "mountains of sense in every word of Scripture." We may readily admit that the Scriptures are capable of manifold practical *applications*; otherwise they would not be so useful for doctrine, correction, and instruction in righteousness (2 Tim 3:16). But the moment we admit the principle that portions of Scripture contain an occult or double sense we introduce an element of uncertainty in the sacred volume, and unsettle all scientific interpretation. "If the Scripture has more than one meaning," says Dr. Owen, "it has no meaning at all." "I hold," says Ryle, "that the words of Scripture were intended to have one definite sense, and that our first object should be to discover that sense, and adhere rigidly to it . . . . To say that words *do* mean a thing merely because they *can* be tortured into meaning it is a most [dishonorable] and dangerous way of handling Scripture" (*Expository Thoughts on St. Luke*, vol. I, p. 383). "This scheme of interpretation," says Stuart, "forsakes and sets aside the common laws of language. The Bible excepted, in no book, treatise, epistle, discourse, or conversation, ever written, published, or addressed by any one man to his fellow beings (unless in the way of sport, or with an intention to deceive), can a double sense be found . . ." (*Biblical Hermeneutics*, pp. 493-494; emphasis in original)

Terry also commented on the difference between typology and double fulfillment:

Some writers have confused this subject by connecting it with the doctrine of type and antitype. As many persons and events of the Old Testament were types of greater ones to come, so the language respecting them is supposed to be capable of a double sense . . . . But it should be seen that in the case of types the language of the Scripture has no double sense. The types themselves are such because they prefigure things to come, and this fact must be kept distinct from the question of the sense of language used in any particular passage. (Ibid., p. 494)

Concerning double fulfillment in regard to Matthew 24, Terry commented:

The twenty-fourth [chapter] of Matthew, so commonly relied on to support this theory, has been already shown to furnish no valid evidence of either an occult or a double sense. (Ibid., p. 495)

As Terry noted, while Scripture has only one sense in matters of interpretation, it may have many applications. He provides further comment on this:

The precious words of promise to God's people find more or less [fulfillment] in every individual experience. But these facts do not sustain the theory of a double sense. The sense in every case is direct and simple; the applications and illustrations are many. Such facts give no authority for us to go into apocalyptic prophecies with the expectation of finding two or more meanings in each specific statement, and then to declare: This verse refers to an event long past, this to something yet future; this had a partial [fulfillment] in the ruin of Babylon, or Edom, but it awaits a grander [fulfillment] in the future. The judgment of Babylon, or Nineveh, or Jerusalem, may, indeed, be a type of every other similar judgment, and is a warning to all nations and ages; but this is very different from saying that the language in which that judgment was predicted was fulfilled only partially when Babylon, or Nineveh, or Jerusalem fell, and is yet awaiting its complete [fulfillment] . . . . To assume, in the absence of any hint, that we have an enigma, and in the face of explicit statements to the contrary, that any specific prophecy has a double sense, a primary and a secondary meaning, a near and a remote [fulfillment], must necessarily introduce an element of uncertainty and confusion into biblical interpretation. (Ibid., p. 495)

Bray also questions the double fulfillment scenario:

Some may say that while this passage does deal directly with the events of AD 70, there is also a "double fulfillment" which means that this will also happen in our future. But who says so? Who gives us the authority to say that there is to be another fulfillment beyond what Jesus said would take place back in His generation? These verses cannot be used to prove what will happen in our future at any future coming of Christ. (*Matthew 24 Fulfilled*, p. 85)

Preston writes:

Given the fact that no Old Testament prophet ever hinted that the events of AD 70 were to be typological of greater events beyond that event, it is additionally significant that no New Testament author ever stated that the events of AD 70 were typological! . . . Paul sets forth the truth that Christ is the *reality*, not the shadow! What Christ accomplished and established is not typological, but "the body," "the reality." . . . Jesus leaves no room for argumentation. He said that the events surrounding the end of that Old Covenant age would be the greatest ever. How then is it possible to argue that Christ's AD 70 parousia was simply typological? Logically, scripturally, textually, you cannot tenably make that argument. (*Fulfilled! Magazine*, Spring 2008, Vol. 3 Issue 1)

Lastly, we offer Russell's thoughts on double fulfillment:

There is another theory, however, by which many suppose that the credit of the apostles is saved, and yet room left for avoiding the acceptance of their apparent teaching on the subject of the coming of Christ. This is, by the hypothesis of a *primary* and *partial* [fulfillment] of their predictions in their own time, to be followed and completed by an *ultimate* and *plenary* [fulfillment] at the end of human history. According to this view, the anticipations of the apostles were not wholly erroneous. Something really did take place that might be called 'a coming of the Lord,' 'a judgment day.' Their predictions received a *quasi* [fulfillment] in the destruction of Jerusalem and in the judgment of the guilty nation. That consummation at the close of the Jewish age was a *type* of another and infinitely greater catastrophe, when the whole human race will be brought before the judgment seat of Christ and the earth consumed by a general conflagration. This is probably the view which is most commonly accepted by the majority of expositors and readers of the New Testament at the present day.

The first objection to this hypothesis is, that it has no foundation in the teaching of the Scriptures. There is not a scintilla of evidence that the apostles and primitive Christians had any suspicion of a twofold reference in the predictions of Jesus concerning the end. No hint is anywhere dropped that a primary and partial [fulfillment] of His sayings was to take place in that generation, but that the complete and exhaustive [fulfillment] was reserved for a future and far distant period. The very contrary is the fact. What can be more comprehensive and conclusive than our Lord's words, 'Verily I say unto you, This generation shall not pass, till ALL these things be fulfilled'? What critical torture has been applied to these words to extort from them some other meaning than their obvious and natural one! How has γενεα been hunted through all its lineage and genealogy to discover that it may not mean the persons then living on the earth! But all such efforts are wholly futile. While the words remain in the text their plain and obvious sense will prevail over all the glosses and perversions of ingenious criticism. The hypothesis of a twofold [fulfillment] receives no countenance from the Scriptures. We have only to read the language in which the apostles speak of the approaching consummation, to be convinced that they had one, and only one, great event in view, and that they thought and spoke of it as just at hand. (*The Parousia*, pp. 544-545; emphasis in original)

All efforts to see the generation referred to in Matthew 24 as any other than the one that heard the prophecy, we believe, is because that is what one *wants* to believe—not because the text plainly says so. Bray declares:

Our interpretation sees only past events in this passage. There is no double-fulfillment. There is no double-reference. There are no mixed-up passages which change the time factor. There is no "transition" verse separating the destruction of Jerusalem from another event 2,000 years or so in the future. Whatever passages elsewhere in the New Testament may teach a final coming of our Lord in resurrection and judgment power for all the world, they are not to be found in this chapter. (*Matthew 24 Fulfilled*, p. 108)

We remind the reader of the opening remarks that led to Christ's discourse and their parallels in Daniel:

Then Jesus went out and departed from the temple, and His disciples came up to show Him the buildings of the temple. And Jesus said to them, "Do you not see all these things? Assuredly, I say to you, not one stone shall be left here upon another, that shall not be thrown down." Now as He sat on the Mount of Olives, the disciples came to Him privately, saying, " Tell us, when will these things be? And what will be the sign of Your coming, and of the end of the age?" (Matt 24:1-3)

Then I, Daniel, looked; and there stood two others, one on this riverbank and the other on that riverbank. And one said to the man clothed in linen, who was above the waters of the river, "How long shall the fulfillment of these wonders be?" (Dan 12:5-6)

Both the disciples and Daniel had just heard amazing prophecies describing times of trouble and tribulation for their people. They both asked "what" and "when" these things were to be. Compare the response the angel gave to Daniel with the response Christ gave to His disciples:

Then I heard the man clothed in linen, who was above the waters of the river, when he held up his right hand and his left hand to heaven, and swore by Him who lives forever, that it shall be for a time, times, and half a time; and when the power of the holy people has been completely shattered, all these things shall be finished. Although I heard, I did not understand. Then I said, "My lord, what shall be the end of these things?" And he said, "Go your way, Daniel, for the words are closed up and sealed till the time of the end." (Dan 12:7-9)

But when you see Jerusalem surrounded by armies, then know that its desolation is near. Then let those who are in Judea flee to the mountains, let those who are in the midst of her depart, and let not those who are in the country enter her. For these are the days of vengeance, that all things which are written may be fulfilled. . . . Assuredly, I say to you, this generation will by no means pass away till all things take place. (Luke 21:20-22, 32)

The response to Daniel was that the words were sealed up until the time of the end. The response to the disciples was the Olivet discourse, in which Jesus said, "*Assuredly, I say to you, this generation will by no means pass away till all these things take place.*" Was He referring to a generation that was yet 2,000 years in their future? If so, why did He not tell His disciples that the words were still sealed up? Or, on the other hand, if "this generation" does not mean this generation, why was Daniel not told "*the end of these things shall be in this generation,*" just like the disciples were, instead of "*the words are sealed . . .*"? If the events foretold were 2,000 years away for the disciples and 2,500 years away for Daniel (who wrote approximately 500 years before Christ), what difference could those 500 years have made in the scheme of sealing and unsealing the prophecy? On the other hand, there is a striking similarity between Daniel's being told that *all things would be finished* when *the power of the holy people was completely shattered*, and Christ's prediction that the destruction of Jerusalem would witness the fulfillment *all things which were written*. The identity of these two prophecies with one another is further strengthened by the fact that Daniel's *time, times, and half a time*, correspond precisely with the 3 ½ year Roman siege which culminated in Jerusalem's destruction in AD 70.

If the disciples had their questions answered rather than being told that the words were sealed up, does that not indicate that the words were no longer sealed? Yet Daniel was told the words were sealed "*till the time of the end.*" Thus, we must assume that the generation to which Jesus ministered was in fact the "last days" generation living in the "*time of the end.*" It therefore makes sense that Jesus would say "*this generation will by no means pass away,*" especially when Peter, toward the end of that New Testament generation, writes, "*the end of all things is at hand*" (1 Pet 4:7). Daniel was told "*when the power of the holy people has been completely shattered, all these things shall be finished.*" How many "ends of all things" are there in the Bible? We believe that there is but one, and that Daniel, Jesus, and Peter are all referring to a single "end of all things." What was sealed to Daniel 500 years earlier was revealed in ca. AD 30 by Jesus to His disciples to be for their generation; it was also proclaimed by Peter in the mid-AD 60s to be "*at hand.*"

Note also that Daniel contains statements indicating that the fulfillments of those events were distant to him:

And the vision of the evenings and mornings
Which was told is true;
*Therefore **seal up the vision,***
For it refers to many days in the future. (Dan 8:26)

*But you, **Daniel, shut up the words, and seal the book until the time of the end**; many shall run to and fro, and knowledge shall increase.* (Dan 12:4)

On the contrary, Revelation contains statements proclaiming that the events were *at hand*:

*And he said to me, **"Do not seal the words of the prophecy of this book, for the time is at hand."*** (Rev 22:10)

*The Revelation of Jesus Christ, which God gave Him to show His servants—**things which must shortly take place**. . . . Blessed is he who reads and those who hear the words of this prophecy, and keep those things which are written in it; for **the time is near.*** (Rev 1:1, 3)

He who testifies to these things says, "Surely I am coming quickly."
(Rev 22:20)
(emphases added)

All prophecy students agree that the Books of Daniel and Revelation speak of the same events. In light of this fact, if (as we believe) Revelation was also written in the mid- to late-AD 60s, then the different instructions to Daniel and John regarding the sealing of their respective prophecies make perfect sense.

We believe that, in Christ's Olivet discourse, the generation *to* which He spoke was the same generation *of* which He spoke. Dividing His discourse, searching for alternate meanings for γενεα, and looking for double fulfillments of prophecy are devices used to wrestle the plain and clear meaning away from the text. Thus, arguments from the Olivet discourse for a future return of Christ are removed, and scriptural evidence is provided for His return during "that generation" as promised. Granted, this calls for sweeping changes in our understanding of the nature of His return. As with the apocalyptic language which describes that return, we believe that scriptural precedent supports these "sweeping changes."

Seventy Times Seven

—〰—

Having looked at the Olivet Discourse, we turn to the prophecy of Daniel's Seventy Weeks. While many studies on the topic involve intricate timelines and mathematics, we have kept these to a minimum, opting instead for a different approach. As we stated at the end of the first chapter of Part II, we are not providing expositional studies, but a new framework, built upon the scriptural foundation laid in Part I, to which expositional studies may be applied. Once the reader has apprehended this framework of eschatology, it is hoped that they will begin their own expositional studies. We are confident that the reader will find that the pieces fit this new paradigm, without being forced into place, much better than the Futurist paradigm. Although we do not launch directly into Daniel, we think that the reader will find this approach brings a harmony to Daniel's Seventy Weeks, as well as the last days, that has perhaps not been realized before. Let us, then, begin with Peter's question to Jesus regarding the scope of one's forgiveness:

> *Then Peter came to Him and said, "Lord, how often shall my brother sin against me, and I forgive him? Up to seven times?" Jesus said to him, "I do not say to you, up to seven times, but up to seventy times seven."* (Matt 18:21-22)

For some time we have pondered a theory regarding Peter's question. Had Peter, an uneducated fisherman, discovered the symbolic significance of seven as the number of completion (fullness)? Was he trying to impress his Master with his discernment? While it is just speculation on our part and inconsequential to the text, we were surprised that we were not alone in the matter:

> This indicates that Peter had indeed made excellent progress but that he had not yet arrived at true spiritual discernment. His suggestion of forgiving seven times went considerably beyond the maxims of the rabbis who admonished forgiveness three times but not four times, basing their position upon the word of God to Amos, "For three transgressions of Damascus and for four, I will not revoke the punishment" (Amos 1:4). Even Peter's relatively magnanimous forgiveness until seven times, however, fell

far short of Jesus' requirement of unlimited forgiveness. (*James Burton Coffman Commentary*)

Till seven times?—This being the sacred and complete number, perhaps his meaning was, Is there to be a limit at which the needful forbearance will be *full?* (*Jamieson, Fausset and Brown Commentary*; emphasis in original)

Imagine, however, Peter's dismay when Jesus not only does not confirm his deduction, but raises the number exponentially. Certainly no one can keep track of that many wrongs suffered at the hand of one person. Even if Christ had confirmed the initial number of seven, if one was keeping count, it could be argued that they were not forgiving at all (1 Cor 13:5). Most commentators put no significance on the number 490 (70 x 7) other than it is high enough to not be taken literally; rather, it teaches that we are to always forgive:

Christ did not mean that Christians should keep a ledger, exactly calculating a precise number such as 490, or using a variant reading, 70 times and 7. This simply means that a Christian must have the spiritual resources to keep on forgiving. Forgiveness of others was made a constant pre-condition of man's forgiveness by the Father, not only in these words of Jesus here, but upon other occasions as well. The business of forgiveness is so important that Christ immediately introduced one of his longest parables in order to reinforce the teaching and repeat the absolute necessity of forgiveness at the conclusion of it. (*James Burton Coffman Commentary*)

Christ's meaning is, that a man should be all the days, and every day of his life, forgiving those that sin against him, as often as they repent and acknowledge their fault; and that no time [limit] is to be set for the exercise of the grace of forgiveness; but as often as there are objects and occasions, though ever so many and frequent, it should be used; and which he illustrates by the following parable. (*The New John Gill Exposition of the Entire Bible;* brackets added)

Until seventy times seven—that is, so long as it shall be needed and sought: you are never to come to the point of refusing forgiveness sincerely asked. (*Jamieson, Fausset and Brown Commentary*; emphasis in original)

That this is the main point of Jesus' reply, we totally agree. Realizing, of course, that all Scripture is inspired—that not a jot or tittle will pass away without being fulfilled—could there be a deeper significance to Christ's statement? Although the number 490 is certainly large enough to preclude an individual from keeping track of grievances, it seems too specific to be simply an indeterminate large number. In fact, it seems that one thousand, or multiples thereof, is established in Scripture as the number which indicates an indeterminate large number, representing fullness or completeness. Consider the following:

> *May the Lord God of your fathers make you **a thousand** times more numerous than you are, and bless you as He has promised you!* (Deut 1:11)

> *Therefore know that the Lord your God, He is God, the faithful God who keeps covenant and mercy for **a thousand** generations with those who love Him and keep His commandments . . . .* (Deut 7:9)

> *If one wished to contend with Him,*
> *He could not answer Him one time out of **a thousand**.* (Job 9:3)

> *For every beast of the forest is Mine,*
> *And the cattle on **a thousand** hills.* (Ps 50:10)

> *For a day in Your courts is better than **a thousand**.*
> *I would rather be a doorkeeper in the house of my God*
> *Than dwell in the tents of wickedness.* (Ps 84:10)

> *A little one shall become **a thousand**,*
> *And a small one a strong nation.*
> *I, the Lord, will hasten it in its time.* (Isa 60:22)
> (emphases added)

Why did Jesus answer with *seventy* times seven, instead of a *thousand* times seven? It would have been more in line with biblical numerology. It certainly would not have changed the effect of the answer concerning forgiveness, except to heighten it. Could there be a secondary lesson communicated by seventy times seven? We believe so. We think that it is no coincidence that the same number, expressed by the same formula, is found in the book of Daniel:

> *Seventy weeks [sevens] are determined*
> *For your people and for your holy city. . . .* (Dan 9:24)

"Seventy sevens" is the same as "seventy times seven." Most Bible scholars agree that the "weeks" or "sevens" in this passage represent a "week" of years, that is, seven years:

> Seventy weeks are determined—The Jews had Sabbatic years, Lev 25:8, by which their years were divided into weeks of years, as in this important prophecy, each week containing seven years. The seventy weeks therefore here spoken of amount to four hundred and ninety years. (*Adam Clarke's Commentary*, Daniel 9:24)

> Bible scholars through the ages have seen 9:24 as a description of Christ's atonement for sin at Calvary and of his everlasting reign. Christ's work of salvation will, according to this interpretation, reach its fulfillment after three stages of prophecy—expressed as periods of weeks—have been fulfilled. Scholars generally agree that each "set of seven" (also translated "week") in this passage represents a "week of years," or seven years. . . . The Hebrew word that many Bible versions translate "week" (9:24) is actually seven; therefore, 9:24 literally reads "70 sevens." That the 70 sevens is actually 70 "weeks of years," or 490 years, seems logical in light of Jeremiah's earlier prophecies concerning the exile: The exile was to last 70 years (see Jer 25:11-12; 29:10), which, according to the chronicler, would make up for the 490 years during which Israel had failed to observe the Sabbath year (see 2 Chr 36:21; Lev 25:2-5; 26:34-35,43).
> (*Willmington's Bible Handbook*, Daniel 9:24)

In the case of Daniel, seventy sevens is referring to years, that is, seventy sets of seven years; thus, 490 years *are determined for your people and for your holy city.* Could it be that God had forgiven the Israelites each year at Yom Kippur (the Day of Atonement) for the 490 determined years—not just *until seven times, but until seventy times seven*—and then He would forgive them no more? Not only do we feel that this premise is possible, but as we shall see in our study, we feel that this is in fact what Jesus meant, and that when viewed from this perspective the seventy weeks of Daniel fit harmoniously with all that we have studied to this point. Alfred Edersheim made an interesting observation regarding the Day of Atonement ceremony of the "scapegoat":

> The lot having designated each of the two goats, the high-priest tied a tongue-shaped piece of scarlet cloth to the horn of the goat for Azazel—the so-called 'scape-goat'—and another round the throat of the goat for Jehovah, which then was to be slain. The

goat that was to be sent forth was now turned round towards the people, and stood facing them, waiting, as it were, till their sins should be laid on him, and he would carry them forth into 'a land not inhabited.' Assuredly a more marked type of Christ could not be conceived, as He was brought forth by Pilate and stood before the people, just as He was about to be led forth, bearing the iniquity of the people. And, as if to add to the significance of the rite, tradition has it that when the sacrifice was fully accepted the scarlet mark which the scape-goat had borne became white, to symbolize the gracious promise in Isaiah 1:18; but it adds that this miracle did not take place for forty years before the destruction of the Temple! (*The Temple: Its Ministry and Service*, p. 204)

According to tradition, says Edersheim, the scarlet cloth did not miraculously turn white for forty years before the destruction of the temple. Quoting from the Babylonian Talmud (Yoma 39b), Price adds to this:

Our Rabbis taught: During the last forty years before the destruction of the Temple the lot "for the Lord" did not come up in the right hand; nor did the crimson-colored string [suspended in the Temple to show the acceptance of the pascal sacrifice] become white; nor did the westernmost light shine; and the doors of the Temple would open by themselves, until R. Yohanan b. Zakkai rebuked them, saying: "Temple, Temple, why will you yourself be the alarmer? I know about you that you will be destroyed, for Zechariah b. Ido has already prophesied concerning you: 'Open your doors, O Lebanon, that the fire may devour your cedars'" (Zechariah 11:1).
(*The Coming Last Days Temple*, p. 82; brackets in original)

Counting back forty years from the year of the temple's destruction brings us to ca. AD 30, the years of Christ's ministry and crucifixion. Could it be that in crucifying their Messiah, the Jews had "filled up the measure of their sin," and that God had forgiven *until seventy times seven*, but would go no further? We turn now to Daniel's Seventy Weeks.

The Seventy Weeks of Daniel

Daniel was given the prophecy of the seventy sevens in answer to his prayers concerning the approaching end of the seventy years of Babylonian captivity, as prophesied by Jeremiah:

And this whole land shall be a desolation and an astonishment, and these nations shall serve the king of Babylon seventy years. (Jer 25:11)

In the first year of Darius the son of Ahasuerus, of the lineage of the Medes, who was made king over the realm of the Chaldeans—in the first year of his reign I, Daniel, understood by the books the number of the years specified by the word of the LORD through Jeremiah the prophet, that He would accomplish seventy years in the desolations of Jerusalem. Then I set my face toward the Lord God to make request by prayer and supplications, with fasting, sackcloth, and ashes . . . . O Lord, according to all Your righteousness, I pray, let Your anger and Your fury be turned away from Your city Jerusalem, Your holy mountain; because for our sins, and for the iniquities of our fathers, Jerusalem and Your people are a reproach to all those around us. (Dan 9:1-3, 16)

In this we can see a bit of parallel between Daniel's 490 and Jesus' 490. Daniel approached God for forgiveness for his people (his brothers) based upon the seventy years of Jeremiah's prophecy. God built upon the seventy, multiplying it by seven, to disclose the 490 years of forgiveness determined upon Israel. Peter, too, approached Jesus concerning forgiveness toward his brother(s), and based his question on the number seven. Jesus built upon the seven, multiplying it by seventy, to disclose the 490 times one is to forgive his brother.

The seventy years of Jeremiah's prophecy is itself based upon another 490-year period in Israel's history. When Israel came into the Promised Land, they were instructed to let the land observe a Sabbath—lay fallow—every seven years:

And the LORD spoke to Moses on Mount Sinai, saying, "Speak to the children of Israel, and say to them: 'When you come into the land which I give you, then the land shall keep a sabbath to the LORD. Six years you shall sow your field, and six years you shall prune your vineyard, and gather its fruit; but in the seventh year there shall be a sabbath of solemn rest for the land, a sabbath to the LORD. You shall neither sow your field nor prune your vineyard. What grows of its own accord of your harvest you shall not reap, nor gather the grapes of your untended vine, for it is a year of rest for the land.'" (Lev 25:1-5)

*You shall keep My Sabbaths and reverence My sanctuary: I am
the LORD . . . . But if you do not obey Me, and do not observe all
these commandments . . . I will bring the land to desolation, and
your enemies who dwell in it shall be astonished at it. I will scatter
you among the nations and draw out a sword after you; your land
shall be desolate and your cities waste. Then the land shall enjoy
its sabbaths as long as it lies desolate and you are in your enemies'
land; then the land shall rest and enjoy its sabbaths. As long as
it lies desolate it shall rest—for the time it did not rest on your
sabbaths when you dwelt in it.* (Lev 26:2, 14, 32-35)

Commentators tell us that Israel did not observe the Sabbath for the
land for 490 years. Therefore, God exacted the Sabbaths by force, sending
the Jews into captivity and causing the land to be desolate, as He had
warned them in Leviticus 26. This was the seventy-year captivity, prophesied by Jeremiah, which resulted because the land had missed seventy
sabbatical years:

In the 490 year time period between the accession of king Saul and
the Babylonian captivity, Israel did not observe the commanded
sabbaths for the land. The inspired writer of 2 Chronicles stated
categorically that the captivity lasted seventy years, "Until the
land had enjoyed its sabbaths: for as long as it lay desolate, it kept
sabbaths, to fulfill the threescore and ten years" (2 Chr 36:21)
. . . . One year out of every seven for 490 years equals exactly
"seventy years."

Also, notice in this connection that Daniel the prophet (Daniel
9:2), in the first year of the Median king Darius, took note of the
seventy years which God, according to the prophet Jeremiah,
would accomplish for the desolation of Jerusalem. "Furthermore,
Daniel's seventy prophetic weeks are based upon the seventy
years of the captivity (Daniel 9:2, 24)." (*James Burton Coffman
Commentary*)

Seventy years—(Jer 27:7). The exact number of years of
Sabbaths in four hundred ninety years, the period from Saul to the
Babylonian captivity; righteous retribution for their violation of
the Sabbath (Lev 26:34, 35; 2 Chr 36:21). The seventy years probably begin from the fourth year of Jehoiakim, when Jerusalem was
first captured, and many captives, as well as the treasures of the
temple, were carried away; they end with the first year of Cyrus,
who, on taking Babylon, issued an edict for the restoration of the

Jews (Ezra 1:1). Daniel's *seventy prophetic weeks* are based on the seventy years of the captivity (compare Dan 9:2, 24). (*Jamieson, Fausset and Brown Commentary*; emphasis in original)

Why did God say "enough is enough" after 490 years? Why wait until seventy Sabbaths had been missed? Why not after just 4—the symbolic number of the earth, or after 7—the symbolic number of completion—had been missed? Is it possible that the answer lies in Jesus' response to Peter's question, "*should I forgive my brother up to seven times?*"

*Jesus said to him, "I do not say to you, up to seven times, but **up to** seventy times seven . . .*

Could it be that God, in His infinite wisdom, has predetermined limits to which He will allow His grace to be presumed upon, and then His holiness demands that He act in judgment? He told Noah that "*His Spirit will not strive with man forever*" (Gen 6:3), and regarding this very captivity under discussion, Jeremiah told the people:

So the LORD could no longer bear it, because of the evil of your doings and because of the abominations which you committed. Therefore your land is a desolation, an astonishment, a curse, and without an inhabitant, as it is this day. (Jer 44:22)

This concept of a limit, of a set measure, is woven throughout the Scriptures:

*But in the fourth generation they shall return here, for **the iniquity of the Amorites is not yet complete**.* (Gen 15:16)

You have bought Me no sweet cane with money,
Nor have you satisfied Me with the fat of your sacrifices;
But you have burdened Me with your sins,
***You have wearied Me with your iniquities**.* (Isa 43:24)

"You have forsaken Me," says the Lord,
"You have gone backward.
Therefore I will stretch out My hand against you and destroy you;
***I am weary of relenting!**"* (Jer 15:6)

And in the latter time of their kingdom,
*When the **transgressors have reached their fullness**,*
A king shall arise,
Having fierce features,
Who understands sinister schemes. (Dan 8:23)

The iniquity of Ephraim is bound up;
His sin is stored up. (Hosea 13:12)

Fill up, then, the measure *of your fathers' guilt.* (Matt 23:32)

. . . and they do not please God and are contrary to all men,
forbidding us to speak to the Gentiles that they may be saved, so
as always to **fill up the measure of their sins**; *but wrath has come*
upon them to the uttermost. (1 Thess 2:15-16)
(emphases added)

For us it would be impractical, if not impossible, to keep track of 490 infractions; but for God it would be a simple task:

Are not five sparrows sold for two copper coins? And not one of
them is forgotten before God. But the very hairs of your head are
all numbered. Do not fear therefore; you are of more value than
many sparrows. (Luke 12:6-7)

He counts the number of the stars; He calls them all by name.
(Ps 147:4)

In the Old Testament, God allowed the Israelites to continue in disobedience for 490 years, and then used the Babylonians as His servants to take them into captivity. The city and the temple were destroyed. The land then enjoyed its Sabbaths for seventy years. It was toward the end of this seventy-year captivity that Daniel prayed, asking God to forgive them for their sins. God's answer was that there would now be another period of seventy determined for Israel, which in turn represented another period of 490 years.

Six items are listed which will be accomplished by the end of the seventy weeks. Attached to the six items, but not included in them, are the temple being destroyed and the land being made desolate once again—the very same things that occurred after the first 490-year period!

Seventy weeks are determined
For your people and for your holy city,
To finish the transgression,
To make an end of sins,
To make reconciliation for iniquity,
To bring in everlasting righteousness,
To seal up vision and prophecy,
And to anoint the Most Holy.
Know therefore and understand,

That from the going forth of the command
To restore and build Jerusalem
Until Messiah the Prince,
There shall be seven weeks and sixty-two weeks;
The street shall be built again, and the wall,
Even in troublesome times.
And after the sixty-two weeks
Messiah shall be cut off, but not for Himself;
And the people of the prince who is to come
Shall destroy the city and the sanctuary.
The end of it shall be with a flood,
And till the end of the war desolations are determined.
Then he shall confirm a covenant with many for one week;
But in the middle of the week
He shall bring an end to sacrifice and offering.
And on the wing of abominations shall be one who makes
desolate,
Even until the consummation, which is determined,
Is poured out on the desolate. (Dan 9:24-27)

The parallels do not end with just the destruction of the temple and the land becoming desolate. Consider the following:

Moreover all the leaders of the priests and the people transgressed more and more, according to all the abominations of the nations, and defiled the house of the LORD which He had consecrated in Jerusalem. And the LORD God of their fathers sent warnings to them by His messengers, rising up early and sending them, because He had compassion on His people and on His dwelling place. But they mocked the messengers of God, despised His words, and scoffed at His prophets, until the wrath of the LORD arose against His people, till there was no remedy. (2 Chr 36:14-16)

"And now, because you have done all these works," says the LORD, "and I spoke to you, rising up early and speaking, but you did not hear, and I called you, but you did not answer, therefore I will do to the house which is called by My name, in which you trust, and to this place which I gave to you and your fathers, as I have done to Shiloh." (Jer 7:13-14)

And the LORD has sent to you all His servants the prophets, rising early and sending them, but you have not listened nor inclined your ear to hear. (Jer 25:4)

Therefore, indeed, I send you prophets, wise men, and scribes: some of them you will kill and crucify, and some of them you will scourge in your synagogues and persecute from city to city . . . . (Matt 23:34)

"Hear another parable: There was a certain landowner who planted a vineyard and set a hedge around it, dug a winepress in it and built a tower. And he leased it to vinedressers and went into a far country. Now when vintage-time drew near, he sent his servants to the vinedressers, that they might receive its fruit. And the vinedressers took his servants, beat one, killed one, and stoned another. Again he sent other servants, more than the first, and they did likewise to them. Then last of all he sent his son to them, saying, 'They will respect my son.' But when the vinedressers saw the son, they said among themselves, 'This is the heir. Come, let us kill him and seize his inheritance.' So they took him and cast him out of the vineyard and killed him. Therefore, when the owner of the vineyard comes, what will he do to those vinedressers?"

They said to Him, "He will destroy those wicked men miserably, and lease his vineyard to other vinedressers who will render to him the fruits in their seasons."

Jesus said to them, "Have you never read in the Scriptures:

'The stone which the builders rejected
Has become the chief cornerstone.
This was the LORD's doing,
And it is marvelous in our eyes'?

Therefore I say to you, the kingdom of God will be taken from you and given to a nation bearing the fruits of it. And whoever falls on this stone will be broken; but on whomever it falls, it will grind him to powder." (Matt 21:33-44)

In both eras, God sent messengers to the Israelites for the purpose of warning them of their wicked ways. Instead of heeding the warnings the Israelites mistreated the messengers on both occasions. In the Old Testament, they filled up the measure of their sins by not observing the Sabbath for the land, for which God sent Babylon to make the land of Israel desolate. In the New Testament, they filled up the measure of their sins by killing the Lord of the Sabbath and His apostles, for which God sent the Romans to make spiritual Babylon (Israel) desolate. Let's look closer at the New Testament Israelites "filling up the measure of their sin":

*Therefore you are witnesses against yourselves that you are sons of those who murdered the prophets. **Fill up, then, the measure of your fathers' guilt.** Serpents, brood of vipers! How can you escape the condemnation of hell?* (Matt 23:31-33)

John Gill's commentary also speaks to the filling up the measure of the Jews' sin:

Fill ye up then the measure of your fathers.

Of their sins; for there were bounds and limits set how far they should proceed, and no further; as yet they had not got to the end of their iniquity: their fathers had gone great lengths in sin, but their iniquity was not yet full, as is said of the Amorites, (Genesis 15:16) these their sons were to fill it up. They had shed the blood of many of the prophets; and indeed there were none of them but they had persecuted and abused, in one shape or another: some they entreated shamefully, others they beat: some they stoned, and others they put to death with the sword, or otherwise; and now their children were about to fill the measure brimful, by crucifying the Son of God, which they were at this time meditating and contriving; and by persecuting and slaying his apostles, and so would bring upon them the vengeance of God. The Jews well enough understood these words, which were spoken to them in an ironical way, and expressing what they were about, and what they would hereafter do, and what would be the issue and consequence of it: they have a saying, that "the holy blessed God does not take vengeance on a man, until his measure is filled up"; according to (Job 20:22). Which the Chaldee paraphrase renders, "when his measure is filled up, then shall he take vengeance on him;" . . . .

As does Robertson's *Word Pictures*:

Fill ye up

The keenest irony in this command has been softened in some MSS [manuscripts] to the future indicative. "Fill up the measure of your fathers; crown their misdeeds by killing the prophet God has sent to you. Do at last what has long been in your hearts. The hour is come" (Bruce).

John Wesley's commentary:

Verse 32. *Fill ye up*—A word of permission, not of command: as if he had said, I contend with you no longer: I leave you to yourselves: you have conquered: now ye may follow the devices of your own hearts. *The measure of your fathers*—Wickedness: ye may now be as wicked as they.

By crucifying Christ, the heir of the vineyard, and killing His apostles, the New Testament Jews filled up the measure of sin for the second 490-year period. Judgment was now due upon *that* generation:

> **Fill up, then, the measure of your fathers' guilt.** *Serpents, brood of vipers! How can you escape the condemnation of hell? Therefore, indeed, I send you prophets, wise men, and scribes: some of them you will kill and crucify, and some of them you will scourge in your synagogues and persecute from city to city, that on you may come all the righteous blood shed on the earth, from the blood of righteous Abel to the blood of Zechariah, son of Berechiah, whom you murdered between the temple and the altar.* **Assuredly, I say to you, all these things will come upon this generation.** (Matt 23:32-36; emphasis added)

Notice, however, that the filling of the measure began way back in Genesis with Abel. "*All the righteous blood shed on the earth*" had come upon that generation. This 490-year period seems to address the entire span of wickedness prior to the gospel. Recall the six items that were to be accomplished by its end:

Seventy weeks [sevens] are determined
For your people and for your holy city,
To finish the transgression,
To make an end of sins,
To make reconciliation for iniquity,
To bring in everlasting righteousness,
To seal up vision and prophecy,
And to anoint the Most Holy. (Dan 9:24)

The list seems to speak of a very definitive end. Things are being wrapped up. We read of the end of sin and transgression, and the ushering in of everlasting righteousness. This is none other than the changing of the Covenants, from the Old Covenant of the Law—which was the strength of sin (1 Cor 15:56)—to the New Covenant of Grace, the everlasting righteousness of the Gospel.

67, 68, 69, . . . Gap . . . , 70?

Many people believe that there is a gap between the 69th and 70th weeks of Daniel, and that the 70th week, including the six items listed above, have yet to be fulfilled. We refer the reader to Mauro's treatment of the fulfillment of these items in *The Seventy Weeks and the Great Tribulation*. The following constitutes a brief summary of Mauro's treatment:

- *To finish the transgression*—by crucifying Christ, the Jews filled up the measure of their transgression, thus it was finished and judgment was due upon that generation
- *To make an end of sins*—Christ offered *one sacrifice for sins forever* (Heb 10:12), and *purged our sins* (Heb 1:3)
- *To make reconciliation for iniquity*—prior to Christ's atoning sacrifice, we were enemies of God; now we have been reconciled to Him (Rom 5:8-11)
- *To bring in everlasting righteousness*—the everlasting New Covenant provides a righteousness apart from the law of the Old Covenant, by which no flesh was justified [made righteous] (Rom 3:19-26)
- *To seal up vision and prophecy*—not a fulfilling, but a sealing up. This was part of the punishment upon national Israel, that both vision and prophet—eye and ear—were closed up, so that *seeing they would not see, and hearing they would not hear* (Isa 6:10; Acts 28:17-28; cf. Mic 3:1-7)
- *To anoint the Most Holy*—this is the pouring out of the Holy Spirit upon the Church at Pentecost, anointing the temple of the living God (2 Cor 6:16), the Most Holy

In *The End Times Controversy*, co-edited by Tim LaHaye and Thomas Ice, Ice writes a chapter dealing with the seventy weeks of Daniel and devotes several pages to defending a gap between the 69th and 70th weeks. He bases his argument on the 490 years of unobserved Sabbaths for the land, which led to the seventy-year Babylonian captivity. Stating that the Israelites were in the Promised Land for about 800 years prior to their captivity, Ice asserts that the 490 years of unobserved Sabbaths were not consecutive years. Thus there were gaps in the accumulation of those 490 years. He then says:

Why is this important? Because many of the critics of the literal interpretation of Daniel 9:24-27 insist that it is unreasonable to have gaps in that 490-year period. Of course, it is not, since there were many gaps in the 490-year period related to the Babylonian captivity. (*The End Time Controversy*, p. 320)

Note that according to Ice, a "literal" interpretation is one which contains gaps. We would counter, *What could be more "literal" than that the 70th week commenced immediately following the 69th week, just as the 69th followed the 68th, and so on?* Furthermore, if a truly "literal" interpretation is the goal, where is the word "gap" in this passage? Ice, in an attempt to refute Gary DeMar, who argues against any gaps in Daniel's weeks, writes:

> But he [DeMar] fails to observe the fact that the 490 years of Daniel 9:24-27 are derived from the 490 years of Israel's violation of the sabbatical years that were prescribed by God in His covenant with the nation. (Ibid., p. 321)

> Even though DeMar recognizes the cause for Daniel's prayer and Gabriel's subsequent revelation of the 70-weeks prophecy to Daniel, he fails to recognize that the 70-year captivity was based upon a 490-year period that contained multiple gaps of time. (Ibid., p. 322)

By claiming there are gaps in the 490-year period that led to Israel's captivity, Ice feels that he has established biblical precedence for gaps in prophetic time statements, most notably Daniel's seventy weeks. We feel that there are several errors in this supposition. The least of these is that Scripture does not record for us when Israel did and did not observe a Sabbath for the land. Therefore, one cannot say with absolute certainty that the 490 years in which they did not observe the Sabbath were not the last 490 *consecutive* years of their occupation of Canaan. In fact, this appears to be the understanding of the previously quoted commentaries of James Burton and Jamieson, Fausset and Brown.

Secondly, the fact that there may be gaps in the accumulation of the 490 years of sabbatical violation is a moot point. God decreed to Israel that they were to allow the land to observe a Sabbath every seven years, and if they did not, He would scatter them among the nations so that the land could enjoy its Sabbaths:

> *And the LORD spoke to Moses on Mount Sinai, saying, "Speak to the children of Israel, and say to them: 'When you come into the land which I give you, then the land shall keep a sabbath to the LORD. Six years you shall sow your field, and six years you shall prune your vineyard, and gather its fruit; but in the seventh year*

there shall be a sabbath of solemn rest for the land, a sabbath to the LORD. You shall neither sow your field nor prune your vine-yard. What grows of its own accord of your harvest you shall not reap, nor gather the grapes of your untended vine, for it is a year of rest for the land.'" (Lev 25:1-5)

You shall keep My Sabbaths and reverence My sanctuary: I am the LORD . . . . But if you do not obey Me, and do not observe all these commandments, . . . I will bring the land to desolation, and your enemies who dwell in it shall be astonished at it. I will scatter you among the nations and draw out a sword after you; your land shall be desolate and your cities waste. Then the land shall enjoy its sabbaths as long as it lies desolate and you are in your enemies' land; then the land shall rest and enjoy its sabbaths. As long as it lies desolate it shall rest for the time it did not rest on your sabbaths when you dwelt in it. (Lev 26:2, 14, 32-35)

God never prophesied how long He would let Israel continue in disobedience before they would be punished, nor did He put any type of time statement on the warning. All God said was, "*if you don't obey Me . . . I will bring the land to desolation.*" He never set a limit to the missed Sabbaths. The only reason that we know it was 490 years is because we know the length of the punishment that resulted. Therefore, since there is no time element in God's warning to Israel, there is nothing in which to place a "gap."

Next, Ice states that "the 490 years of Daniel 9:24-27 are derived from the 490 years of Israel's violation of the sabbatical years." This is only true by association and inference. Daniel 9:24-27 *never* makes mention of 490 years—it speaks only of seventy weeks. In fact, 490 years are *never* mentioned in *either* case, but are arrived at only by calculation. The 490 years of Daniel's prophecy are understood from the fact that the weeks do not consist of days but of years. Thus, in the strictest sense, the 490 years of Daniel are *not* derived from the 490 years of sabbatical violation. Rather, Daniel's seventy weeks are derived from Israel's seventy years of captivity, which were consecutive and contained no gaps. Because there was no gap during Israel's seventy years in captivity, there should be no gaps in the seventy sevens. We feel that Gabriel's message was divinely worded in such a manner as to compare two periods of seventy, not two periods of 490, which brings us to our final point.

That the seventy years of captivity were consecutive and without gaps is attested by Daniel's reason for interceding for his nation:

In the first year of Darius the son of Ahasuerus, of the lineage of the Medes, who was made king over the realm of the Chaldeans— in the first year of his reign I, Daniel, understood by the books the number of the years specified by the word of the LORD through Jeremiah the prophet, that He would accomplish seventy years in the desolations of Jerusalem. Then I set my face toward the Lord God to make request by prayer and supplications, with fasting, sackcloth, and ashes. (Dan 9:1-3)

Daniel set to prayer because he *understood* that the end of Jeremiah's prophesied seventy-year captivity was near. If there had been gaps in that seventy-year period, he would have been premature in his actions. Also worthy of note is Gabriel's statement concerning the seventy weeks decreed upon Daniel's people and holy city:

Know therefore and understand . . . . (Dan 9:25)

Just as Daniel could understand Jeremiah's prophecy of seventy years of captivity, so he was to understand Gabriel's prophecy of seventy weeks of years. Both prophecies were given for the purpose of understanding specific time frames. How could Daniel possibly *understand* the times decreed upon his people if those times had undisclosed gaps in them, especially when at least one gap is four times as long as the entire time span of the prophecy?

Even many Preterists see a need for a gap between the 69th and 70th weeks. This is because they see the destruction of Jerusalem in AD 70 as one of the events of the 70th week, which is separated by forty years from the fulfillments of Christ's first advent, which they place in the 69th week, in ca. AD 30-33. For example, Preston, King, and Ron McRay see the destruction of Jerusalem as belonging to the seventy weeks prophecy. Preston writes:

Now since Daniel tells us in no uncertain terms that 70 weeks were determined for the city and the temple, and since Denham admits this is referent to the doom of the temple it would seem inescapable that the fate of Jerusalem was encompassed within the fateful 70 weeks and therefore one cannot limit the prophecy to the passion of Jesus. . . . What is predicted cannot and does not exclude the determined fate of the city and the people. On the contrary the very fate of the city and people is at stake here. (*Seal Up Vision & Prophecy*, p. 18, 1991, Shawnee Printing Co.)

While King and McRay posit a gap between the 69th and 70th weeks in order to place the destruction of Jerusalem within that timeframe, Preston views the *entire 70 week period as a symbolic whole,* stating that: *Chronological exactness is not the point* (Ibid., p. 11).

While others may not be convinced of Mauro's interpretation, we favor it because we believe that any gap undermines the purpose for providing a prophetic timeline. If Daniel's Seventy Weeks continued uninterrupted through the four hundred silent years between Malachi and Matthew, how can we possibly entertain the thought that they would then be suspended and not address perhaps the most fertile forty years of biblical history? Daniel's weeks are broken into three sections—seven weeks, sixty-two weeks, and one week. If we can put a gap between sections two and three (weeks sixty-nine and seventy), why not put a gap between sections one and two (weeks 7 and 8)? We believe, and hope to demonstrate, that just as Daniel went to prayer because he understood the seventy *continuous* years of Jeremiah's prophecy, so the vision he received in answer to his prayer was one that could be understood by its readers as seventy continuous weeks of prophetic time.

We believe that the 70th week took place during the years of Christ's ministry, from the baptism of Christ, which marked the beginning of His public ministry, to 3½ years later (the midst of the week), when He was crucified. To maintain continuity in our study, we refer the reader to Mauro's *The Seventy Weeks and the Great Tribulation* for further treatment.

One of the major differences between the Futurist and Preterist understandings of Daniel's prophecy in 9:24-27 is *when* the Messiah is "cut off" in relation to the timeline. The prophecy states that this will take place *after* the 69th week (after seven weeks and sixty-two weeks). Many (if not most) Preterists would say that after the 69th week naturally comes the 70th week. Futurists, however, at this point abandon completely the timeline which was given to Daniel for the very purpose of *knowing and understanding* those events. As a result, they place the "cutting off" of the Messiah in some ethereal gap of time *after* the 69th week, yet *before* the 70th week. Mauro comments on the absurdity of a gap:

> Never since the world began has a described and "determined" measure of time, expressed in the way always used for that purpose (that is, by stating the number of time-units making up the complete measure) been treated according to the view we are now discussing. Never has a specified number of time-units, making

up a described stretch of time, been taken to mean anything but continuous or *consecutive time-units*. The Bible-usage in this regard will be shown presently. If, therefore, the period of the "seventy weeks" be an exception to a rule so universal and so *necessary*, we should at least require of those who maintain that view such clear and convincing proof as to leave no room for doubt.

. . .

We are bold, therefore, to lay it down as an absolute rule, admitting of no exceptions, that when a definite measure of time or space is specified by the number of units composing it, within which a certain event is to happen or a certain thing is to be found, the units of time or space which make up that measure are to be understood as running continuously and successively. "Seventy years" would invariably mean seventy *continuous* years; "seventy weeks" would mean seventy *continuous* weeks; "seventy miles" would mean seventy *continuous* miles.

If, for example, one journeying along a road were informed that, within seventy miles from a given point he would come upon certain specified things, as a hill, a tower, a stream, a mill, and the like, there is manifestly but one sense in which he could understand the statement. Suppose in such a case that he should proceed on his way for 69 miles without meeting any of the specified things, would he not confidently expect to find them in the one remaining mile of the 70? Suppose, however, he should traverse *that* mile without coming upon any of those things, would he not have a right to say he had been grossly and *intentionally* deceived? And would it set the matter right for the one who made the deceptive statement to say that the 70th mile *he* had in mind did not join on the 69th, but *was two thousand miles further on?* We say the deception in such case would be intentional; for if one uses an expression which has a definite and well-settled meaning, but gives to it in his own mind a very different meaning, *which he keeps to himself*, he can have had no other purpose than to mislead those who might act upon his words. (*The Seventy Weeks and the Great Tribulation*, pp. 94-95, 98-99; emphasis in original)

On the following pages we provide a comparison of Futurist and Preterist views of this passage from Daniel. Although we favor an interpretation without a gap, we are not dogmatic on the issue. If there is a gap, it must be confined to a period of time no longer than forty years as determined by Christ's declaration of "this generation" ca. AD 30 and the destruction of Jerusalem in AD 70. As we note in the comparison, regardless of one's eschatological position, the events of this passage cannot be viewed as strictly chronological. There are numerous times when the narrative "backtracks" to add detail to a previous item. For example, notice how in v. 25, after describing the coming of the Messiah after seven and sixty-two weeks, the latter portion of the verse goes back to provide additional data regarding the restoration of Jerusalem in the first seven weeks. In a similar manner Futurists must "go back" in their interpretation because they have the "antichrist" of v. 27 making a covenant with the Jews *after* the temple has been destroyed in v. 26! Thus, we can see that, regardless of one's view, it is inherent in the text for additional information to be given about previous events in the passage. Therefore, for Preterism to view Christ as the one confirming the covenant of the gospel apparently after the destruction of Jerusalem is not an anachronism.

Again, although there are differing views amongst Preterists, they all agree that the seventy weeks were fulfilled by, at the latest, AD 70. What follows is an annotated comparison between the typical Futurist and Preterist interpretations of Daniel 9:24-27. We consider the *italicized* portions of Daniel's prophecy as parenthetical, in that they provide additional information about Daniel's people and the Holy City, but are not specifically one of the six items to be fulfilled within the seventy weeks:

Futurist View

24 "Seventy weeks are determined
For your people and for your holy city,
To finish the transgression,
To make an end of sins,
To make reconciliation for iniquity,
To bring in everlasting righteousness,
To seal up vision and prophecy,
And to anoint the Most Holy.
25 Know therefore and understand,
That from the going forth of the command
To restore and build Jerusalem
Until Messiah the Prince,
There shall be seven weeks and sixty-two weeks;
The street shall be built again, and the wall,
Even in troublesome times.[this statement backtracks to the command to
'restore and build Jerusalem']
26 And after the sixty-two weeks [i.e., after the 69th week (483 years), yet
somehow not *during* the 70th week]
Messiah shall be cut off, but not for Himself;
And the people of the prince [a yet future Antichrist] who is to come
Shall destroy the city and the sanctuary [a future rebuilt temple (never
mentioned in the NT)].
The end of it shall be with a flood,
And till the end of the war desolations are determined.
27 Then he [the future Antichrist] shall confirm a covenant with many
for one week [allowing the Jews to reinstitute the sacrificial system
of the Law—this statement backtracks by reinstituting the sacrificial
system *after* the temple has been destroyed];
But in the middle of the [70th] week [separated by an indeterminate gap
from the 69th week]
He [the Antichrist] shall bring an end to sacrifice and offering [by
suspending his agreement].
And on the wing of abominations shall be one [the Antichrist] who makes
desolate [by entering the temple and declaring himself to be God—this
statement backtracks by desolating the temple after it is destroyed in v.
26],
Even until the consummation, which is determined,
Is poured out on the desolate."

242

Preterist View

24 "Seventy weeks are determined
For your people and for your holy city,
To finish the transgression,
To make an end of sins,
To make reconciliation for iniquity,
To bring in everlasting righteousness,
To seal up vision and prophecy,
And to anoint the Most Holy.
25 Know therefore and understand,
That from the going forth of the command
To restore and build Jerusalem
Until **Messiah the Prince**,
There shall be seven weeks and sixty-two weeks;
The street shall be built again, and the wall,
Even in troublesome times.[this statement backtracks to the command to
'restore and build Jerusalem']
26 And after the sixty-two weeks **[during the 70th week]**
Messiah shall be cut off, but not for Himself;
And the people [the Roman army] of the prince [can be either Titus as the
literal commander of the Roman army, or Messiah the Prince (v. 25) as
the spiritual commander (Matt 22:1-7)] who is to come [there is no time
indicator when he will come]
Shall destroy the city and the sanctuary [fulfilled in AD 70].
The end of it shall be with a flood,
And till the end of the war desolations are determined.
27 Then he **[Christ]** shall confirm a covenant **[the gospel—Matt 26:28]**
with many **[Rom. 5:15, 19]** for one week **[lit., in a week, i.e., the 70th**
week, the years of Christ's ministry—this statement backtracks to the
earthly ministry of Christ after the temple has been destroyed];
But in the middle of the week
He **[Christ]** shall bring an end to sacrifice and offering **[by offering**
Himself as the Lamb who takes away the sins of the world].
And on the wing of abominations shall be one [Titus and the Roman
armies] who makes desolate [by desecrating the Holy City and temple
complex by their presence, and their insignia of allegiance to Caesar],
Even until the consummation, which is determined,
Is poured out on the desolate."

The phrase *until the consummation* lends further support for separating the desolation of the temple from the six items of the 70th week. While all six items were to be fulfilled in the 70th week, the desolation of the temple and city appear to be a process (*even until*). This process began when Christ declared the Jews' house as desolate (Matt 23:38) and ended in AD 70. During this time period the author of Hebrews wrote that the Old Covenant was obsolete and ready to vanish away (Heb 8:13). When Christ was crucified, He put an end to sin, and made reconciliation for iniquity, thereby bringing an end to the need for sacrifice and offering:

For it is not possible that the blood of bulls and goats could take away sins. (Heb 10:4)

The next day John saw Jesus coming toward him, and said, "Behold! The Lamb of God who takes away the sin of the world!" (John 1:29)

Not with the blood of goats and calves, but with His own blood He entered the Most Holy Place once for all, having obtained eternal redemption. (Heb 9:12)

. . . not that He should offer Himself often, as the high priest enters the Most Holy Place every year with blood of another — He then would have had to suffer often since the foundation of the world; but now, once at the end of the ages, He has appeared to put away sin by the sacrifice of Himself. (Heb 9:25-26)

Christ offered Himself at the end of the Old Covenant age to put away sin. The blood of bulls and goats could not take away sin. They were merely a shadow of the Lamb of God who takes away the sin of the world. They were just an annual reminder and postponement until the Messiah was cut off, but not for Himself. When Christ offered Himself the whole typological system of the Old Covenant was made obsolete, and a new access to God was opened as indicated by the rending of the temple's veil (Matt 27:51). This is also why, after the crucifixion, the scarlet cloth did not turn white. Forgiveness was now found in Christ, not in the Pascal Lamb. After demonstrating how all six items of Daniel's prophecy were fulfilled during Christ's ministry in *The Seventy Weeks and the Great Tribulation*, Philip Mauro writes:

Furthermore, by running our eye rapidly over verses 25, 26 we see that the coming of Christ and His being "cut off" are announced as *the means whereby* the prophecy was to be fulfilled; and that there is added the foretelling of the destruction of Jerusalem by Titus the Roman "prince," and the "desolations" of Jerusalem, and the wars that were to continue through this entire age "unto the end." (pp. 53-54; emphasis in original)

Although the prophecy of the destruction of Jerusalem is given to Daniel at the same time as the prophecy of the 490 years, it is not one of the six items that were to take place within that time frame. We believe that it is attached to the prophecy of the seventy weeks because it was a momentous event that occurred to Daniel's people and holy city. The destruction of Jerusalem is closely tied with the six items of the seventy weeks as affirmed by Christ, who said that the judgment would come upon the generation to whom He was speaking—the generation that would fill up the measure of their sin:

> *Fill up, then, the measure of your fathers' guilt . . . so that upon you may fall the guilt of all the righteous blood shed on earth, from the blood of righteous Abel to the blood of Zechariah, the son of Berechiah, whom you murdered between the temple and the altar. Truly I say to you, all these things will come upon this generation. Jerusalem, Jerusalem, who kills the prophets and stones those who are sent to her! How often I wanted to gather your children together, the way a hen gathers her chicks under her wings, and you were unwilling. Behold, your house is being left to you desolate!* (Matt 23:32, 35-38 NASB95)

In a similar passage from Luke, we can see that Jesus is foreseeing the Roman conquest of Jerusalem in AD 70:

> *Now as He drew near, He saw the city and wept over it, saying, "If you had known, even you, especially in this your day, the things that make for your peace! But now they are hidden from your eyes. For days will come upon you when your enemies will build an embankment around you, surround you and close you in on every side, and level you, and your children within you, to the ground; and they will not leave in you one stone upon another, because you did not know the time of your visitation."* (Luke 19:41-44)

Josephus testified that the Romans built "banks" around the city, effectively hemming in the Jewish people in preparation for their destruction:

> He also at the same time gave his soldiers leave to set the suburbs on fire, and ordered that they should bring timber together, and raise banks against the city . . . . (*Wars*, 5.6)

... for they were come up from all the country to the feast of unleavened bread, and were on a sudden shut up by an army, which, at the very first, occasioned so great a straitness among them, that there came a pestilential destruction upon them, and soon afterward such a famine, as destroyed them more suddenly ... Now this vast multitude is indeed collected out of remote places, but the entire nation was now shut up by fate as in prison, and the Roman army encompassed the city when it was crowded with inhabitants. Accordingly, the multitude of those that therein perished exceeded all the destructions that either men or God ever brought upon the world. (*Wars*, 6.9)

Collectively, these events ended the coexistence of the two covenants. It was during the first portion of this "grace period" that the gospel was preached to the Jew first (Acts 13:46; Rom 1:16) because, as we shall see in the coming chapter, "All Israel Will Be Saved," God had *not* rejected His people. Salvation was still available to them, but on an individual basis, not on a national basis. The forty-year coexistence of the covenants was God's longsuffering, not willing that any should perish.

Seventy weeks are determined
*For **your** people and for **your** holy city* . . . .

Notice that God does not say *My* people and *My* holy city, but rather Daniel's. God was responding to Daniel's prayer, where he asked, "*O Lord, according to all Your righteousness, I pray, let Your anger and Your fury be turned away from **Your** city Jerusalem, **Your** holy mountain.*" Yet God tells Daniel that seventy weeks are determined upon *your* people and for *your* city. This is because *God's* holy people and holy city are not physical, but *spiritual*. Because the two covenants coexisted in the last days, the subjects of end-time prophecy include both physical and spiritual Israel, physical and spiritual kingdoms, and physical and spiritual temples, as noted by King:

It must be remembered that in the end-time, God is dealing with two Israels, two Jerusalems, and two temples, bringing salvation, blessing and glory to true spiritual Israel, and destruction, ruin, and everlasting shame to rebellious fleshly Israel. (*The Spirit of Prophecy*, p. 258)

For those who feel that there is an unwarranted delay for the Day of the Lord, from Daniel's 70th week (ca. AD 30) until AD 70, we believe that answer is found in properly applying the time statements of Daniel's prophecy. Although Daniel spoke of the desolation of the temple and the destruction of the city, the events are not tied to a specific week of the prophecy. The time-specific events prophesied by Daniel were events related to the Messiah's first coming. When the Messiah came, *He* gave the time statement for the Day of the Lord: *this generation.* Note that Jesus did not prophesy *immediate* judgment, but judgment within *that generation.* While the Day of the Lord could have come upon that generation at any time after Pentecost, it was stretched to the limits of what is considered commonly to be a biblical generation, that is, forty years. We believe the reason is twofold: (1) that as many as possible might repent and join the ranks of spiritual Israel; (2) that those of fleshly Israel who were unrepentant might "fill up the measure of their sins" by persecuting Christ's church till the end (1 Thess 2:14-16). Even as Christ hung upon the cross, He was interceding for His murderers:

> *Then Jesus said, "Father, forgive them, for they do not know what they do." And they divided His garments and cast lots.* (Luke 23:34)

Although judgment had been prophesied and could not be cancelled, it could be postponed, which is exactly what happened. By withholding the judgment of the Jews from the years of Christ's earthly ministry in ca. AD 30 until AD 70, God allowed the maximum amount of time for individual Jews to repent, even though they as a nation had rejected Him. This also gave the unrepentant the opportunity to confirm their stiff-necked rejection of Christ and *fill up the measure of their sins.* Bray agrees, writing:

> He gave them forty years to repent, and they did not. God cannot wait forever. The forty years were extra—thrown in for good measure to faithless Israel whose end should have come when they nailed Jesus to the cross! (*Matthew 24 Fulfilled*, p. 234)

According to the intercessory prayer of Jesus on the cross as well as Habakkuk's prayer, ". . . *in wrath remember mercy*" (Hab 3:2), God waited forty years to send judgment. If He had waited any longer, it would no longer have been carried out upon *that* generation:

> *The Lord is not slack concerning His promise, as some count slackness, but is longsuffering toward us, not willing that any should perish but that all should come to repentance.* (2 Pet 3:9)

Daniel was a Jew, and it was the Jewish people and the Jewish city that had the time determined upon them. As we saw in Part I, they were merely physical types of God's spiritual people and city, which is the Church. God's holy people are not of any particular national race:

> *There is neither Jew nor Greek, there is neither slave nor free, there is neither male nor female; for you are all one in Christ Jesus.* (Gal 3:28; see also Rom 10:12; Col 3:11)

At the changing of the covenants, the type was done away with and the antitype was established. The forty-year period from AD 30-70 was a transition period. This is why, in Daniel's prophecy, there is such a note of finality, a tone of "wrapping it all up." As we have discussed earlier, all of the Old Testament prophets were foretelling this time (Acts 3:24; 1 Pet 1:10-12). Daniel's prophecy foretold the end of the Old Covenant that dealt with his people, the Jews, and his city, Jerusalem. Jesus told His listeners that *they* were living in that end time:

> *So when* **you** *see the 'abomination of desolation,' spoken of by Daniel the prophet, standing where it ought not (**let the reader understand**), then let those who are in Judea flee to the mountains.* (Mark 13:14)

Matthew also inserts into Jesus' discourse the editorial note, *let the reader understand*. Are we to understand that the *readers* whom they had in mind were not their original audience, but those who would read their accounts some 2,000 years later? If this is the case, then the first readers of these Gospels must surely have been confused by the comment.

Why was there a general expectation of the Messiah by the Jews in Christ's day? Because they understood the prophecy of Daniel, the only prophecy in the Bible that has specific time indicators attached to it. Consider the following quote from Philip Mauro's *The Seventy Weeks and the Great Tribulation*:

> The message of Gabriel, found in Daniel 9:24-27, differs from all other prophecies in several particulars, and chiefly in that it contains a *measuring line* of "determined" length, whereby the years were to be measured from a given event (one of the great landmarks in Jewish history) down to the coming of the Messiah and the accomplishment of His work of redemption. The full length of that line was seventy "heptads," *i.e., sevens* (or "weeks") of years, making a total length of 490 years. The declared purpose of the prophecy (v. 24) was to foretell the *exact time* of the occurrence of certain things which are of supreme importance to mankind . . . in the light of this sure word of prophecy it is easy to see that,

when the Lord Jesus began preaching in Galilee, saying *"The time is fulfilled*, and the kingdom of God is at hand; repent ye, and believe the good news"* (Mark 1:14, 15), He was referring to "the time" measured out or "determined" in this prophecy, and that He was calling upon the people of Israel to "repent" and "believe," as the condition of receiving the new birth (John 3:3, 5) and thereby entering into the salvation of the kingdom of God. (pp. 112-113; emphasis in original)

The "time" of Daniel's prophecy was upon the Jews. Clearly the prophesied rebuilding of the temple had already been accomplished, so the only "time" left to be fulfilled was the 70th week. That week started with the baptism of Christ, and with the triumphant entry of Christ into Jerusalem they were now approaching the middle of the week. Bray cites this messianic expectation as the underlying cause for the Jews' revolt against Rome:

But this expectation was a main reason that the Jewish people were excited into the war with the Romans, thinking that they would soon have deliverance from the Romans through the Messiah. (*Matthew 24 Fulfilled*, p. 103)

Consider the following verses against the backdrop of Daniel's prophesied time:

*And suddenly they [the demons] cried out, saying, "What have we to do with You, Jesus, You Son of God? Have You come here to torment us before the **time**?"* (Matt 8:29)

*And He said, "Go into the city to a certain man, and say to him, 'The Teacher says, "My **time** is at hand; I will keep the Passover at your house with My disciples."'"* (Matt 26:18)

*Now after John was put in prison, Jesus came to Galilee, preaching the gospel of the kingdom of God, and saying, "**The time is fulfilled**, and **the kingdom of God is at hand**. Repent, and believe in the gospel."* (Mark 1:14-15)

*Hypocrites! You can discern the face of the sky and of the earth, but how is it you do not discern **this time**?* (Luke 12:56)

We have noted previously that the Jews understood they were on the threshold of Daniel's 70th week. Thus, they were experiencing "Messiah fever." The Gospels reveal to us the events of the 70th week of Daniel's prophecy. (The crucifixion's occurrence in the middle of the 70th week gives the appearance of an unaccounted for 3½-year period. Mauro reminds us that Daniel's prophecy is not dealing with years, but *weeks* of years. Thus, we do not need to account for the 490th year, only the 70th week. Mauro provides the parallel of Jesus predicting that He would be crucified and rise on the third day. Even though His resurrection took place early in the morning of the third day, we do not have a sense that the remainder of the day is "unaccounted for." Others believe that the final 3½ years encompassed the time when the gospel was preached to the Jews exclusively, from the crucifixion until the martyrdom of Stephen, or perhaps the conversion of Paul. This view is strengthened by the fact that Daniel was told a covenant would be *confirmed* with many (Dan 9:27), while the last verse of Mark records that the disciples went out and preached everywhere, the Lord working with them and *confirming* the word . . . .)

Could it be that it was against this backdrop of "the fullness of time" (Gal 4:4) that Jesus answered Peter's question about forgiveness with the same formula of Daniel's prophecy? In His answer, Jesus confirmed that forgiveness was more than just a one-time deal. But He also hinted that forgiveness had a limit and, by tying it in with Daniel's seventy sevens, indicated that the limit had been almost reached. By so doing, He called attention to what many seemed to have forgotten about Daniel's prophecy—that in addition to being the advent of the Messiah, it was also a time of judgment, as seen in the destruction of the city and the sanctuary. As in the days of Amos, the Day of the Lord was not what the Jews were expecting:

> *Woe to you who desire the day of the LORD!*
> *For what good is the day of the LORD to you?*
> *It will be darkness, and not light.*
> *It will be as though a man fled from a lion,*
> *And a bear met him!*
> *Or as though he went into the house,*
> *Leaned his hand on the wall,*
> *And a serpent bit him!*
> *Is not the day of the LORD darkness, and not light?*
> *Is it not very dark, with no brightness in it?*
> (Amos 5:18-20; cf. Mal 3:1-2)

Once we understand that the "end" of which the Bible speaks is not the end of the world (which we shall develop further in the next chapter), but rather the end of the Old Covenant age, the following passage from Daniel takes on a different perspective:

But you, Daniel, shut up the words, and seal the book until the time of the end; many shall run to and fro, and knowledge shall increase. (Dan 12:4)

We have already established that the New Testament era was the biblical "time of the end" (Acts 2:16-17; Heb 1:2; 1 John 2:18). This is confirmed by the fact that Daniel was told to seal up the book of prophecy until *the time of the end*, whereas John was told to not seal the words of the prophecy of Revelation, for the time was *at hand* (Rev 22:10). Therefore, the end-time increase of knowledge that Daniel speaks of must also be associated with the New Testament era. This is in stark contrast to the premise to which many hold today, believing that Daniel's increase in knowledge is a prophecy of the information age. We agree that knowledge has increased greatly in the last few decades. However, this type of increase is merely indicative of the natural progression of mankind, and knowledge will continue increasing at an exponential rate for as long as mankind remains. We feel that to associate Daniel's prophecy with this type of increase in knowledge is no different than saying "the population shall increase." With any increase in population, the number of descendants that can be produced increases exponentially (barring any major natural disasters or disease epidemics, of course). Furthermore, since "natural" knowledge increases with each succeeding generation, each generation might be justified in viewing theirs as witness of the fulfillment of Daniel's prophecy:

> Francis Bacon believed that the signs of the End included the distant voyages and the advancement in science seen in his time. He wrote,

> Nor should the prophecy of Daniel be forgotten, touching on the Last Ages of the world, "Many shall run to and fro, and knowledge shall be increased," clearly intimating that the thorough passage of the world (which by so many distant voyages seems to be accomplished, or in the course of accomplishment), and the advancement of sciences, are destined by fate, that is by the Divine Providence, to meet in the same age. (*The Day and the Hour*, by Francis X. Gumerlock, p. 149; 2000, American Vision)

We feel that for the phrase "knowledge shall increase" to be included in biblical prophecy, it should have a fulfillment that is more than just the natural progression of mankind. But can we find a "supernatural" increase in knowledge during the New Testament era? While we are not dogmatic on this issue, we believe these Scriptures from the chapter "The Veil of Moses" fit nicely:

> *. . . according to the revelation of the mystery kept secret since the world began but now made manifest . . . .* (Rom 16:25-26)

> *. . . and to make all see what is the fellowship of the mystery, which from the beginning of the ages has been hidden in God who created all things through Jesus Christ; to the intent that now the manifold wisdom of God might be made known by the church to the principalities and powers in the heavenly places . . . .* (Eph 3:9-10)

> *. . . how that by revelation He made known to me the mystery (as I have briefly written already, by which, when you read, you may understand my knowledge in the mystery of Christ), which in other ages was not made known to the sons of men, as it has now been revealed by the Spirit to His holy apostles and prophets . . . .* (Eph 3:3-5)

The fullness of Daniel's understanding of God's plan was sealed up until the time of the end. Could it be that the knowledge that would increase in the time of the end would be knowledge of God's plan of redemption, and not secular knowledge? Gary DeMar writes:

> It's most likely that the knowledge being described in Daniel 12:4 is related to the new covenant and the coming of the promised Redeemer. Since the focus of the Bible is on Jesus (Luke 24:25-27), we should expect that this is what God had in mind when the angel told Daniel that "the knowledge" will increase. What redemptive significance does a fatter set of encyclopedias have to do with God's redemptive plan for His People? (*Biblical Worldview Magazine*, Vol. 23, No. 10&11, Oct./Nov. 2007)

Jamieson, Fausset, and Brown see the statement that *many shall run to and fro* as the spreading of this increased understanding of the mysteries of God after they were unsealed to the New Testament apostles and prophets. They note that "running" is the characteristic mark of one who professes to have a divine communication to announce (Jer 23:21, "I have not sent these prophets, yet they *ran*"). Does this not fit with Peter's statement?

> *Of this salvation the prophets have inquired and searched carefully, who prophesied of the grace that would come to you, searching what, or what manner of time, the Spirit of Christ who was in them was indicating when He testified beforehand the*

sufferings of Christ and the glories that would follow. To them it was revealed that, not to themselves [it was sealed to them], but to us they were ministering the things which now have been reported [unsealed] to you through those who have preached [run to and fro] the gospel [the increase of knowledge] to you by the Holy Spirit sent from heaven—things which angels desire to look into. (1 Pet 1:10-12)

Conclusion

When Jesus told Peter that he was to forgive his brother up to 490 times (70 x 7), we believe that He was alluding to Daniel's 490 *determined years*. Thus, He was indicating the limit to God's patience and mercy, reaffirming that the judgment was at hand. The reason judgment was declared during Christ's ministry in the 70th week (ca. AD 30) upon *that* generation, but did not occur until AD 70, was because God displayed mercy in withholding the judgment as long as possible. This allowed all to hear the gospel, with as many as were willing to repent, and the remainder to fill up the measure of their sins. Had He waited any longer, the judgment would not have been upon the generation upon whom God said it would come, and it is impossible for God to lie (Heb 6:18). Thus we have the eschatology of Daniel in perfect harmony with our framework of the two covenants and their coexistence during the "last days" generation of the New Testament church.

A Comparison of the Two 490-Year Judgments

	Old Testament	New Testament
Warned by Prophets	2 Chr 36:14-16 Jer 25:4	Matt 23:34
Land Desolate	Jer 25:11	Luke 21:20
God uses a foreign army to destroy the temple	By the Babylonians 2 Chr 36:17-18	By the Romans Matt 24:1-2
Date of Destruction	10th of Ab	10th of Ab
Cup of Wrath	Jer 25:15-16	Rev 14:9, 16:19
Measure Filled Up	By not observing the Sabbaths	By not observing the Lord of the Sabbath

Revelation, AD 70, and the End of the World

—ιιι—

Even in light of an early date for Revelation, apocalyptic language, audience relevance, the Lord's numerous cloud comings, and the imminency passages, the reader may be asking, "What about the end of the world, and the new heavens and new earth? Isn't Revelation describing global judgments and catastrophes?" This, we agree, is a common perception of biblical end-times. The real question, however, is whether that perception is scripturally accurate. We have seen thus far that the focus of eschatology was upon God's redemptive plan and the prophesied transition from the Old to the New Covenant. Does the Bible also speak of global judgment and the end of the world? Or are we to fit the whole of eschatology into the events of AD 70? By "fitting" events into our eschatological framework, we do not mean "forcing" the events into our framework. Rather, we believe that when the common *mis*conception is rectified, an accurate interpretation of Scripture allows the pieces to fall into place naturally.

The End of the World vs. the End of the Age

We established previously that the "last days" referred to in the Bible were in fact the last days of the Old Covenant; but doesn't the Bible also speak of the end of the world? That depends on which translation of the Bible one uses. The phrase "end of the world" can be found in the Bible, primarily in the King James Version (KJV); however, "end of the world" is an unfortunate translation. Almost invariably, in passages that speak of the *end of the world*, or of the *world to come*, the Greek word translated "world" is *aion* (or *aioon*), from which we get our word "eon." While "world" may have had that connotation in 1611 when the KJV was first published, a more accurate contemporary English translation of this word is "age"; in fact, the New King James Version (NKJV) corrects the translational error of its predecessor. Below are some key passages that contrast the KJV's famous *end of the world* or *world to come* passages and their NKJV counterparts:

Matt 13:49

KJV: *So shall it be at the end of the **world**: the angels shall come forth, and sever the wicked from among the just . . . .*

NKJV: *So it will be at the end of the **age**. The angels will come forth, separate the wicked from among the just . . . .*

Matt 24:3

KJV: *And as he sat upon the mount of Olives, the disciples came unto him privately, saying, "Tell us, when shall these things be? and what shall be the sign of thy coming, and of the end of the **world**?"*

NKJV: *Now as He sat on the Mount of Olives, the disciples came to Him privately, saying, "Tell us, when will these things be? And what will be the sign of Your coming, and of the end of the **age**?"*

1 Cor 10:11

KJV: *Now all these things happened unto them for ensamples: and they are written for our admonition, upon whom the ends of the **world** are come.*

NKJV: *Now all these things happened to them as examples, and they were written for our admonition, upon whom the ends of the **ages** have come.*

Gal 1:4

KJV: *Who gave himself for our sins, that he might deliver us from this present evil **world**, according to the will of God and our Father . . . .*

NKJV: *. . . who gave Himself for our sins, that He might deliver us from this present evil **age**, according to the will of our God and Father . . . .*

Heb 9:26

KJV: *For then must he often have suffered since the foundation of the world [Gk. kosmos]: but now once in the end of the world hath he appeared to put away sin by the sacrifice of himself.*

NKJV: *He then would have had to suffer often since the foundation of the world [Gk. kosmos]; but now, once at the end of the ages, He has appeared to put away sin by the sacrifice of Himself.*
(emphases added)

Looking at the above passages from the KJV, it is easy to see from where the concept of the so-called "end of the world" originated. It is equally clear from the NKJV that the "world" that was ending was not the physical world, but rather the world (or age) of Judaism and the Old Covenant. Bray observes:

The Jewish people recognized two ages—the one in which they then lived (under the law), and the future age of the Messiah. "A common Jewish conception was that the appearing of the Messiah would close 'this age,' and introduce 'the coming age'—these phrases often occurring in the Talmud." (*An American Commentary on the New Testament*, John Broadus, p. 482)

Also interesting is the fact that only Matthew of the gospel writers used the expression "end of the age." We understand better about this when we realize, as many Bible scholars agree, that Matthew was writing primarily to Jewish people. The expression, "end of the world (age)," would certainly convey to them the idea of the end of their age, which to them would end with the coming of the Messiah. (*Matthew 24 Fulfilled*, pp. 19, 111)

In *The Typology of Scripture*, Patrick Fairbairn writes:

We find the designation of "the ends of the world" applied in Scripture to the Gospel-age; and that not so much in respect to its posteriority in point of time, as to its comparative maturity in regard to the things of salvation—the higher and better things having now come, which had hitherto appeared only in prospect or existed but in embryo. (p. 47, vol. 1)

This is in complete agreement with what we have already studied concerning the last days and the transition of the covenants. Yet, what about Peter's reference to the world being judged by fire and the elements melted by fervent heat?

For this they willfully forget: that by the word of God the heavens were of old, and the earth standing out of water and in the water, by which the world that then existed perished, being flooded with water. But the heavens and the earth which are now preserved by the same word, are reserved for fire until the day of judgment and perdition of ungodly men . . . . But the day of the Lord will come as a thief in the night, in which the heavens will pass away with a great noise, and the elements will melt with fervent heat; both the earth and the works that are in it will be burned up. Therefore, since all these things will be dissolved, what manner of persons ought you to be in holy conduct and godliness, looking for and hastening the coming of the day of God, because of which the heavens will be dissolved, being on fire, and the elements will melt with fervent heat? Nevertheless we, according to His promise, look for new heavens and a new earth in which righteousness dwells. (2 Pet 3:5-7, 10-13)

We will explore the heavens and earth passing away shortly. First, however, we will examine the elements melting with fervent heat. Are the elements to which Peter is referring the physical elements of this planet? Not necessarily. The Greek word for "elements" is *stoicheion*:

Strong's Greek Dictionary, NT: 4747

something orderly in arrangement, i.e. (by implication) a serial (basal, fundamental, initial) constituent (literally), proposition (figuratively): KJV—element, principle, rudiment.

While *stoicheion* can mean the physical elements of the universe, is that Peter's meaning? Consider the only other uses of *stoicheion* in the New Testament:

Even so we, when we were children, were in bondage under the **elements** *[stoicheion]* **of the world.** *But when the fullness of the time had come, God sent forth His Son, born of a woman, born under the law, to redeem those who were under the law, that we might receive the adoption as sons.* (Gal 4:3-5)

But now after you have known God, or rather are known by God, how is it that you turn again to the weak and beggarly **elements** *[stoicheion], to which you desire again to be in bondage? You observe days and months and seasons and years.* (Gal 4:9-10)

*Beware lest anyone cheat you through philosophy and empty deceit, according to the tradition of men, according to the basic **principles** [stoicheion] **of the world**, and not according to Christ.* (Col 2:8)

*Therefore, if you died with Christ from the basic **principles** [stoicheion] **of the world**, why, as though living in the world, do you subject yourselves to regulations—"Do not touch, do not taste, do not handle," which all concern things which perish with the using—according to the commandments and doctrines of men?* (Col 2:20-22)

*For though by this time you ought to be teachers, you need someone to teach you again the first **principles** [stoicheion] **of the oracles of God**; and you have come to need milk and not solid food.* (Heb 5:12)

The term "world" in the above passages comes from the Greek word *kosmos*, which means an "orderly arrangement." Can there be any doubt as to which "orderly arrangement" or "world" these authors had in view? Clearly Paul is juxtaposing bondage under the *elements* to a life redeemed from the Law. In the Galatians passage, several verses after Paul's first mention of *elements*, he writes that those who are turning again to the *elements* are observing days and months and seasons and years—all elements of the Law. In Colossians 2:8, he states that the principles of the world are according to the tradition of men, as opposed to the tradition of Christ. In vv. 20-22 he equates the basic principles of the world with the commandments and doctrines of men. The author of Hebrews uses *stoicheion* to describe the milk of the word of righteousness. Without a doubt, the physical elements of this planet are not the subject of these passages; rather the subjects are the elements of the "worlds" of either the Mosaic Law and the Old Covenant, or, as in Hebrews 5, the Gospel and the New Covenant. Why then should we seek to apply a different meaning to the term in Peter's writings? We believe that we should look for a meaning in line with the precedent established by the Scriptures above before we apply alternative meanings. Although the term *elements* may conjure up visions of the Periodic Table of Elements for us, what likely came to the mind of the first-century readers of Peter's letter? Josephus records four elements—earth, air, fire, and water. Did Peter's readers envision fire being burned up with fire? On the other hand, if we take the *elements* of Peter's letter to mean the elements of the Old Covenant, we have no problem seeing the fulfillment of his prophecy in AD 70, when Jerusalem and the temple—the undeniable icons of the Old Covenant—were indeed burned with fervent heat. We turn now to the historic accounts of Josephus, who describes the judgment of fire upon the "world" of Judaism:

> And now the soldiers had already put fire to the gates, and the silver that was over them quickly carried the flames to the wood that was within it, whence it spread itself all on the sudden, and caught hold on the cloisters. Upon the Jews seeing this fire all about them, their spirits sunk together with their bodies, and they were under such astonishment, that not one of them made any haste, either to defend himself or to quench the fire, but they stood as mute spectators of it only. However, they did not so grieve at the loss of what was now burning, as to grow wiser thereby for the time to come; but as though the holy house itself had been on fire already, they whetted their passions against the Romans. This fire prevailed during that day and the next also; for the soldiers were not able to burn all the cloisters that were round about together at one time, but only by pieces. (*Wars*, 6.4)

> But as for that house, God had, for certain, long ago doomed it to the fire; and now that fatal day was come, according to the revolution of ages; it was the tenth day of the month Lous, [Ab,] upon which it was formerly burnt by the king of Babylon . . . . While the holy house was on fire, every thing was plundered that came to hand, and ten thousand of those that were caught were slain; nor was there a commiseration of any age, or any reverence of gravity, but children, and old men, and profane persons, and priests were all slain in the same manner; so that this war went round all sorts of men, and brought them to destruction, and as well those that made supplication for their lives, as those that defended themselves by fighting. The flame was also carried a long way, and made an echo, together with the groans of those that were slain; and because this hill was high, and the works at the temple were very great, one would have thought the whole city had been on fire.

> Yet was the misery itself more terrible than this disorder; for one would have thought that the hill itself, on which the temple stood, was seething hot, as full of fire on every part of it, that the blood was larger in quantity than the fire, and those that were slain more in number than those that slew them; for the ground did no where appear visible, for the dead bodies that lay on it; but the soldiers

went over heaps of those bodies, as they ran upon such as fled from them.

And now the Romans, judging that it was in vain to spare what was round about the holy house, burnt all those places, as also the remains of the cloisters and the gates, two excepted; the one on the east side, and the other on the south; both which, however, they burnt afterward. They also burnt down the treasury chambers, in which was an immense quantity of money, and an immense number of garments, and other precious goods there reposited; and, to speak all in a few words, there it was that the entire riches of the Jews were heaped up together, while the rich people had there built themselves chambers [to contain such furniture]. (*Wars*, 6.5; brackets in original)

Accepting that the biblical precedent for the use of the Greek word *stoicheion* applies it to an orderly arrangement (Strong's)—chiefly that of the Old Covenant elements—and history records the physical representations of those elements being burned with fire, we see no need to look further for alternative interpretations. As Russell observes, Scripture does not require that Peter refers to the conflagration of the physical cosmos:

The imagery here employed by the apostle naturally suggests the idea of the total dissolution by fire of the whole substance and fabric of the material creation, not the earth only but the system to which it belongs; and this no doubt is the popular notion of the final consummation which is expected to terminate the present order of things. A little reflection, however, and a better acquaintance with the symbolic language of prophecy, will be sufficient to modify such a conclusion, and to lead to an interpretation more in accordance with the analogy of similar descriptions in the prophetic writings. First, it is evident on the face of the question that this universal conflagration, as it may be called, was regarded by the apostle as on the eve of taking place—"The end of all things is at hand" (1 Pet 4:7). The consummation was so near that it is described as an event to be "looked for, and hastened unto" (ver. 12.) It follows, therefore, that it could not be the literal destruction or dissolution of the globe and the created universe concerning which the spirit of prophecy here speaks. But that there was at the moment when this epistle was written an awful and almost immediate catastrophe impending; that the long-predicted "day of the Lord" was actually at hand; that the day did come, both *speedily* and *suddenly;* that it came "as a thief in the night;" that a fiery deluge of wrath and judgment overwhelmed the guilty land and nation of Israel, destroying and dissolving its earthly things and its heavenly things, that is to say, its temporal and spiritual institutions—is a fact indelibly imprinted on the page of history. (*The Parousia*, pp. 319-320; emphasis in original)

Russell notes, alluding to Josephus, the judgment upon the material structures of the Old Covenant is a fact imprinted indelibly on the page of history. In light of this and all we have studied concerning the transition of the covenants, we feel that Peter's expectations were wholly fulfilled. Bray concurs:

It hardly seems possible to me that "the heavens being on fire shall be dissolved" of 2 Peter 3:12 would have any different meaning than the "all the host of heaven shall be dissolved" of Isaiah 34:4. The latter refers to Bozrah and Idumea and their judgments (v. 6) at the day of the Lord's vengeance (v. 8). Both are symbolic expressions, neither of which refer to the actual heavens being burned up. (*Matthew 24 Fulfilled*, p. 238)

The New Heavens and New Earth

But what about Jesus declaring that *heaven and earth would pass away*? What about Peter's statement to his readers that they were, *according to His [God's] promise* (2 Pet 3:13), looking for new heavens and a new earth? Some see the promise to which Peter referred as that described in Isaiah 65:17:

For behold, I create new heavens and a new earth;
And the former shall not be remembered or come to mind.

Isaiah 65 speaks of God's elect receiving His blessings, while those who have rejected Him receive His judgments. In a coming chapter ("All Israel Will Be Saved"), we will see how Paul applied Isaiah 65:1-2 ("*I was found by those who did not seek Me*") to the Gentiles' acceptance of the gospel and to the Jews, as a nation, rejecting it ("*All day long I have stretched out My hands to a disobedient and contrary people*"). The elect, His Church, in which there is neither Jew nor Gentile (Gal 3:28) are the heirs according to the promise. Thus, the new heavens and new earth of Isaiah are contained in a passage that Paul associates with the gospel.

This is reminiscent of the author of Hebrews associating Jeremiah's new covenant (Jer 31:31ff) to the gospel (Heb 8). Isaiah 65 also states:

> *6 "Behold, it is written before Me:*
> *I will not keep silence, but will repay—*
> *Even repay into their bosom—*
> *7 Your iniquities and the iniquities of your fathers together,"*
> *Says the LORD,*
> *"Who have burned incense on the mountains*
> *And blasphemed Me on the hills;*
> *Therefore I will measure their former work into their bosom."*
> (Isa 65:6-7)

Here we see a parallel to Christ's statement to the scribes and Pharisees: *"Fill up, then, the measure of your fathers' guilt . . . that on you may come all the righteous blood shed on the earth"* (Matt 23:32, 35). Though Israel had been rebellious for generations, once their guilt was "filled up," God repaid it into their bosom, the iniquity of the sons and the fathers together upon *that* generation.

> *8 "As the new wine is found in the cluster,*
> *And one says, 'Do not destroy it,*
> *For a blessing is in it,'*
> *So will I do for My servants' sake,*
> *That I may not destroy them all.*
> *9 I will bring forth descendants from Jacob,*
> *And from Judah an heir of My mountains;*
> *My elect shall inherit it,*
> *And My servants shall dwell there."* (Isa 65:8-9)

The descendants that God will bring forth from Jacob—the heirs of God's mountains—are the elect, whom we have already seen to be *spiritual* Israel, i.e., the Church:

> *11 "But you are those who forsake the LORD,*
> *Who forget My holy mountain,*
> *Who prepare a table for Gad,*
> *And who furnish a drink offering for Meni.*
> *12 Therefore I will number you for the sword,*
> *And you shall all bow down to the slaughter;*
> *Because, when I called, you did not answer;*
> *When I spoke, you did not hear,*

But did evil before My eyes,
And chose that in which I do not delight." (Isa 65:11-12)

Remembering that, in God's eschatological picture, there are two Israels in view, physical and spiritual, we see in this portion of text His pronouncement of judgment upon physical Israel, which did not answer when He called. They had forsaken God; therefore, they were numbered for the sword and delivered to the slaughter, just as Jesus also prophesied:

O Jerusalem, Jerusalem, the one who kills the prophets and stones those who are sent to her! How often I wanted to gather your children together, as a hen gathers her brood under her wings, but you were not willing! See! Your house is left to you desolate . . . . (Luke 13:34-35)

In the following portion of Isaiah 65, we see a comparison of the two Israels:

13 Therefore thus says the Lord GOD:
"Behold, My servants shall eat,
But you shall be hungry;
Behold, My servants shall drink,
But you shall be thirsty;
Behold, My servants shall rejoice,
But you shall be ashamed;
14 Behold, My servants shall sing for joy of heart,
But you shall cry for sorrow of heart,
And wail for grief of spirit.
15 You shall leave your name as a curse to My chosen;
For the Lord GOD will slay you,
And call His servants by another name . . . ." (Isa 65:13-15)

As prophesied in v. 15, God slew physical Israel in AD 70; He also called spiritual Israel by another name:

And the disciples were first called Christians in Antioch. (Acts 11:26)

How is it that the elect, His servants, experience all of these blessings? As verse 17 demonstrates, the elect obtain these blessings by God's provision of a new heavens and a new earth in which they dwell: "*For behold, I create . . . .*" We could use the analogy of a parent describing the blessings that their children were to receive, *for behold, I have made you sole heirs in my will:*

17 "For behold, I create new heavens and a new earth;
And the former shall not be remembered or come to mind.
18 But be glad and rejoice forever in what I create;
For behold, I create Jerusalem as a rejoicing,
And her people a joy.
19 I will rejoice in Jerusalem,
And joy in My people;
The voice of weeping shall no longer be heard in her,
Nor the voice of crying.
20 No more shall an infant from there live but a few days,
Nor an old man who has not fulfilled his days;
For the child shall die one hundred years old,
But the sinner being one hundred years old shall be accursed.
21 They shall build houses and inhabit them;
They shall plant vineyards and eat their fruit.
22 They shall not build and another inhabit;
They shall not plant and another eat;
For as the days of a tree, so shall be the days of My people,
And My elect shall long enjoy the work of their hands.
23 They shall not labor in vain,
Nor bring forth children for trouble;
For they shall be the descendants of the blessed of the LORD,
And their offspring with them.
24 It shall come to pass
That before they call, I will answer;
And while they are still speaking, I will hear.
25 The wolf and the lamb shall feed together,
The lion shall eat straw like the ox,
And dust shall be the serpent's food.
They shall not hurt nor destroy in all My holy mountain," says the
LORD. (Isa 65:17-25)

Whereas the first portion of Isaiah 65 compares physical Israel and spiritual Israel (the elect), Isaiah focuses this passage about the new heavens and new earth on God's people, the elect (v. 22). Though many try to place this passage in a future physical kingdom, the New Testament—as we have previously established—does not speak of a future physical kingdom, nor of any age beyond the age of the everlasting New Covenant. That the new heavens and new earth refer to the spiritual kingdom of the gospel is not unheard of. Take note of Matthew Henry's commentary on this passage:

If these promises were in part fulfilled when the Jews, after their return out of captivity, were settled in peace in their own land and brought as it were into a new world, **yet they were to have their full accomplishment in the gospel church**, militant first and at length triumphant. The Jerusalem that is from above is free and is the mother of us all. **In the graces and comforts which believers have in and from Christ we are to look for this new heaven and new earth**. It is in the gospel that old things have passed away and all things have become new, and by it that those who are in Christ are new creatures, 2 Cor 5:17. It was a mighty and happy change that was described v. 16, that the former troubles were forgotten; but here it rises much higher: even the former world shall be forgotten and shall no more come into mind. Those that were converted to the Christian faith were so transported with the comforts of it that all the comforts they were before acquainted with became as nothing to them; not only their foregoing griefs, but their foregoing joys, were lost and swallowed up in this. The glorified saints will therefore have forgotten this world, because they will be entirely taken up with the other: For, behold, I create new heavens and a new earth. See how inexhaustible the divine power is; the same God that created one heaven and earth can create another. See how entire the happiness of the saints is; it shall be all of a piece; with the new heavens God will create them (if they have occasion for it to make them happy) a new earth too. The world is yours if you be Christ's, 1 Cor 3:22. **When God is reconciled to us, which gives us a new heaven, the creatures too are reconciled to us, which gives us a new earth.** The future glory of the saints will be so entirely different from what they ever knew before that it may well be called new heavens and a new earth, 2 Pet 3:13. Behold, I make all things new, Rev 21:5. (emphasis added)

Isaiah mentions the new heavens and new earth again at the end of chapter 66:

> 22 *"For as the new heavens and the new earth*
> *Which I will make shall remain before Me," says the* LORD,
> *"So shall your descendants and your name remain.*
> *23 And it shall come to pass*
> *That from one New Moon to another,*
> *And from one Sabbath to another,*

All flesh shall come to worship before Me," says the LORD.
24 "And they shall go forth and look
Upon the corpses of the men
Who have transgressed against Me.
For their worm does not die,
And their fire is not quenched.
They shall be an abhorrence to all flesh." (Isa 66:22-24)

Rather than assigning this passage to some future age beyond that of the gospel (of which the New Testament authors make no mention), we see vv. 22-23 as referring to the everlasting covenant:

. . . by so much more Jesus has become a surety of a better cove-
nant. Also there were many priests, because they were prevented
by death from continuing. But He, because He continues forever,
has an unchangeable priesthood. (Heb 7:22-24)

Now may the God of peace who brought up our Lord Jesus from
the dead, that great Shepherd of the sheep, through the blood of
the everlasting covenant . . . . (Heb 13:20)

This everlasting covenant is available to all flesh without restriction:

For you are all sons of God through faith in Christ Jesus. For
as many of you as were baptized into Christ have put on Christ.
There is neither Jew nor Greek, there is neither slave nor free,
there is neither male nor female; for you are all one in Christ
Jesus. And if you are Christ's, then you are Abraham's seed, and
heirs according to the promise. (Gal 3:26-29)

The corpses that were seen (v. 24) were not those of some future Battle of Armageddon, but those of the generation that filled up their transgressions against God by crucifying His Son and persecuting His apostles and prophets. Thus, the Isaiah passages regarding the new heavens and new earth do not need to be "forced" into some unknown future age; rather, they can be seen as having their fulfillment in the events of AD 70 and the consequent replacement of the Old Covenant. This agrees with both Jesus and Peter:

*For these are the days of vengeance, that **all things which are***
***written may be fulfilled**.* (Luke 21:22) [This would include Isaiah's "new heavens and new earth."]

*Of this salvation the prophets have inquired and searched carefully, who prophesied of the grace that would come **to you**, searching what, or what manner of time, the Spirit of Christ who was in them was indicating when He testified beforehand the sufferings of Christ and the glories that would follow. To them it was revealed that, **not to themselves, but to us** they were ministering the things which now have been reported to you through those who have preached the gospel to you by the Holy Spirit sent from heaven—things which angels desire to look into.* (1 Pet 1:10-12) [This passage further demonstrates that Old Testament prophecy was focused on the New Testament generation.]

There is another Scripture to which Peter may be referring as *His promise* of a new heavens and earth. Keeping in mind that Peter is writing shortly before his martyrdom (2 Pet 1:14-15) in ca. AD 67, and given the early date for the writing of Revelation, it is possible that Peter is quoting John:

Now I saw a new heaven and a new earth, for the first heaven and the first earth had passed away. Also there was no more sea. (Rev 21:1)

Again we must ask, are the physical heaven and earth in view here, or are they metaphors for the Old and New Covenants. We cannot deny that both Peter and John expected this new heavens and earth *shortly*, for the time was *at hand*. This fact argues against a physical interpretation, since nothing of its kind occurred within that time frame. In the coming pages we shall see that the Jews considered the temple to be a representation of the universe, and that the Holy of Holies, the Holy place, and the court of the priests represented heaven, the land, and the sea respectively. Although C. H. Spurgeon believed in a future physical new creation, consider his words regarding the changing of covenants:

Did you ever regret the absence of the burnt-offering, or the red heifer, or any one of the sacrifices and rites of the Jews? Did you ever pine for the feast of tabernacles, or the dedication? No, because, though these were like the old heavens and earth to the Jewish believers, they have passed away, and we now live under new heavens and a new earth, so far as the dispensation of the divine teaching is concerned. The substance is come, and the shadow has gone: and we do not remember it. (*Metropolitan Tabernacle Pulpit*, p. 354, vol. 37)

We add Bray's thoughts on Isaiah 51:16:

"And I have put my words in thy mouth, and I have covered thee in the shadow of mine hand, that I may PLANT THE HEAVENS, and LAY THE FOUNDATIONS OF THE EARTH, and say unto ZION, Thou art my people."

Planting the heavens and laying the foundations of the earth was symbolical language for Zion's becoming God's people. God did not literally plant the heavens and lay the foundations of the earth at this late date of writing. It has to be symbolical. Therefore, it is only logical that the shaking of the powers of the heavens (and the passing away of the heavens and earth afterward) would mean the utter end of Israel, the ending of what God had planted and set. (*Matthew 24 Fulfilled*, p. 126; emphasis in original)

Maimonides also observes that,

The Arabs likewise [as the Hebrew prophets] say of a person who has met with a serious accident, "His heavens, together with his earth, have been covered"; and when they speak of the approach of a nation's prosperity, they say, "The light of the sun and moon has increased," "A new heaven and a new earth has been created," or they use similar phrases. (*Guide for the Perplexed*, p. 204; brackets added)

Lastly, we come to the shaking of the heavens and earth in Hebrews 12:

See that you do not refuse Him who speaks. For if they did not escape who refused Him who spoke on earth, much more shall we not escape if we turn away from Him who speaks from heaven, whose voice then shook the earth; but now He has promised, saying, "Yet once more I shake not only the earth, but also heaven." Now this, "Yet once more," indicates the removal of those things that are being shaken, as of things that are made, that the things which cannot be shaken may remain. Therefore, since we are receiving a kingdom which cannot be shaken, let us have grace, by which we may serve God acceptably with reverence and godly fear. (Heb 12:25-28)

Concerning this shaking of the earth and the heavens, Russell wrote:

What, then, is the great catastrophe symbolically represented as the shaking of the earth and heavens? No doubt it is the overthrow and abolition of the Mosaic dispensation, or old covenant; the destruction of the Jewish church and state, together with all the institutions and ordinances connected therewith. There were "heavenly things" belonging to that dispensation: the laws, and statutes, and ordinances, which were divine in their origin, and might be properly called the "*spiritualia*" of Judaism—these were the *heavens*, which were to be shaken and removed. There were also "earthly things": the literal Jerusalem, the material temple, the land of Canaan—these were the *earth*, which was in like manner to be shaken and removed. The symbols are, in fact, equivalent to those employed by our Lord when predicting the doom of Israel. "Immediately after the tribulation of those days [the horrors of the siege of Jerusalem] shall the sun be darkened, and the moon shall not give her light, and the powers of the *heavens shall be shaken*" (Matt 24:29). Both passages refer to the same catastrophe and employ very similar figures; besides which we have the authority of our Lord for fixing the event and the period of which He speaks within the limits of the generation then in existence; that is to say, the references can only be to the judgment of the Jewish nation and the abrogation of the Mosaic economy at the Parousia. (*The Parousia*, pp. 289-290; emphasis and brackets in original)

Consider Bray's additional thoughts:

In Haggai 2:21-22 God said, "I will shake the heavens and the earth; And I will overthrow the throne of kingdoms, and I will destroy the strength of the kingdoms of heaven." Here we see the connection between shaking the heavens and earth, and the overthrow of kingdoms and powers.

In Deuteronomy 32:1, after the formation of Israel, God said, "Give ear, O ye heavens, and I will speak; and hear, O earth, the words of my mouth." To whom was God talking—the literal heavens and earth? No, He was talking to Israel. (*Matthew 24 Fulfilled*, pp. 225, 252)

Moreover, Josephus records how the temple (tabernacle) was a representation of the universe—the heavens and earth:

. . . for if any one do but consider the fabric of the tabernacle, and take a view of the garments of the high priest, and of those vessels which we make use of in our sacred ministration, he will find that our legislator was a divine man, and that we are unjustly reproached by others; for if any one do without prejudice, and with judgment, look upon these things, he will find they were every one made in way of imitation and representation of the universe. When Moses distinguished the tabernacle into three parts, and allowed two of them to the priests, as a place accessible and common, he denoted the land and the sea, these being of general access to all; but he set apart the third division for God, because heaven is inaccessible to men. And when he ordered twelve loaves to be set on the table, he denoted the year, as distinguished into so many months. By branching out the candlestick into seventy parts, he secretly intimated the Decani, or seventy divisions of the planets; and as to the seven lamps upon the candlesticks, they referred to the course of the planets, of which that is the number. The veils, too, which were composed of four things, they declared the four elements; for the fine linen was proper to signify the earth, because the flax grows out of the earth; the purple signified the sea, because that color is dyed by the blood of a sea shell-fish; the blue is fit to signify the air; and the scarlet will naturally be an indication of fire. Now the vestment of the high priest being made of linen, signified the earth; the blue denoted the sky, being like lightning in its pomegranates, and in the noise of the bells resembling thunder. And for the ephod, it showed that God had made the universe of four elements; and as for the gold inter-woven, I suppose it related to the splendor by which all things are enlightened. He also appointed the breastplate to be placed in the middle of the ephod, to resemble the earth, for that has the very middle place of the world. And the girdle which encompassed the high priest round, signified the ocean, for that goes round about and includes the universe. Each of the sardonyxes declares to us the sun and the moon; those, I mean, that were in the nature of buttons on the high priest's shoulders. And for the twelve stones, whether we understand by them the months, or whether we under-stand the like number of the signs of that circle which the Greeks call the Zodiac, we shall not be mistaken in their meaning. And for the mitre, which was of a blue color, it seems to me to mean heaven; for how otherwise could the name of God be inscribed upon it? That it was also illustrated with a crown, and that of gold also, is because of that splendor with which God is pleased. Let this explication suffice at present, since the course of my narra-tion will often, and on many occasions, afford me the opportunity of enlarging upon the virtue of our legislator. (*Antiquities of the Jews*, Book 3, Chapter 7)

Rabbi Joshua Berman makes some very thought-provoking observations in connecting the "heavens and earth" with the Jewish system:

The Sanctuary is the apex of *kedushah* [set apart to God—BLM] in the spatial realm. At its center lies the preeminent symbol of the covenant between God and Israel. . . . For Solomon, the Temple was not only a temple to God; it was a center that stood testimony to the covenantal bond between God and the Jewish people. . . . The account of the conclusion of the work of the Tabernacle bears a striking resemblance to the biblical description of the completion of the universe at the end of the sixth day of creation in Genesis:

Genesis 1-2	Exodus 39-40
And God saw all that he had made and behold it was very good. (1:31)	Moses saw all of the skilled work and behold they had done it; as God had commanded it they had done it. (39:43)
The heavens and earth and all of their array were completed. (2:1)	All the works of the Tabernacle of the Tent meeting was completed. (39:32)
And God completed all the work that He had done. (2:2)	And Moses completed the work. (40:33)
And God blessed . . . (2:3)	And Moses blessed . . . (39:43)
And sanctified it. (2:3)	And you shall sanctify it and all its vessels. (40:9)

What is the significance of the parallel between the conclusion of the account of creation and the conclusion of the Tabernacle works? On one level, creation ended on the Sabbath. On a second level, however, it only truly concluded once the Tabernacle work was completed. The composite parts of the physical works were completed on the sixth day of creation, but the ultimate purpose of these elements—to be dedicated to the service of God—is only realized once the Sanctuary is built, to serve as a universal focal point for the service of God. To be certain, the mere act of constructing the Sanctuary will accomplish nothing if the spiritual climate of the times is inappropriate for such activity. . . . When these conditions prevail, however, the presence of the Sanctuary represents the spiritual completion of the times and symbolizes the completion of the creation of the universe. . . . The notion that the erection of the Sanctuary completes the process of creation is conveyed explicitly in the midrash concerning the completion of the First Temple:

"All the work [that King Solomon had done in the House of the Lord] was completed (1 Kings 7:51"—scripture does not say *the work*, but *all the work*, which refers to the work of the six days of creation, as it says "[And God] completed all the work that He had planned to do" (Gen 2:2). Scripture does not say [*that He*] *had done*, but, [*that He*] *had planned to do*, implying that there was yet more work to do. When Solomon completed the Temple, God proclaimed: "Now the work of the heavens and the earth are complete (*shelemah*)." [When it says] "All the work was completed (*va-tashlem*)," it indicates why he was named Solomon (*Shelomoh*), for God completed (*hishlim*) the work of the six days of creation through him. [end of midrash quote—BLM]

The notion that man is a partner in the process of creation when he engages in the construction of the Tabernacle can be seen in the description of the capacities ascribed to Bezalel, chief artisan of the Tabernacle. Describing the creation of the universe, Proverbs 3:19-20 reads:

The Lord has founded the earth by *wisdom*;
He established the heavens by *understanding*;
By His *knowledge* the depths burst apart.

When God tells Moses that Bezalel is to oversee the Tabernacle works, He says: "See, I have singled out Bezalel the son of Uri the son of Hur of the tribe of Judah. I have endowed him with a divine spirit of *wisdom*, *understanding* and *knowledge* in every kind of craft (*melakhah*)" (Exod 31:2-3). As we assumed previously, the presence of terminology from one biblical section in another may be seen as intended to elucidate the meaning of that passage. When the author of Proverbs borrows terminology that, in another context, describes Bezalel's creative capacities and ascribes those same virtues to God as he created the universe, it may be read as a statement that Bezalel's creation of the Tabernacle is tantamount to God's creation of the universe. These parallels are reflected in the Talmud's statement that Bezalel knew how to create the heavens and earth. (*The Temple: Its Significance and Meaning Then and Now*, pp. 12-16; all emphases and brackets in original unless otherwise noted)

We are quick to acknowledge that these extrabiblical sources are not inspired, and we are not advocating interpreting the Bible based upon uninspired sources. However, by utilizing these sources we establish the audience relevance of particular terms and literary genres of the Bible. The task of the Bible student is not to ascertain how apocalyptic language, or terms such as "heavens and earth," are understood in 21st-century Western culture, but how they were understood in the times and culture in which they were written.

Although this understanding of the new heavens and earth is far removed from what much of Christianity believes, we feel that—when the Scriptures are allowed to speak for themselves—it is the most natural and straightforward interpretation. Moreover, those who believe that God will destroy the physical earth have apparently forgotten the following verses:

Surely the world is established, so that it cannot be moved. (Ps 93:1)

The world also is firmly established, It shall not be moved; (Ps 96:10)

One generation passes away, and another generation comes; But the earth abides forever. (Eccl 1:4)

You established the earth, and it abides. (Ps 119:90)

The Earth vs. the Land

Previously we saw how the translation of a particular Greek word has led to the general misunderstanding that the Bible speaks of the *end of the world*, when it was the *end of the age* that was in view. We turn our attention now to a similar situation, in which the Greek word γε (*ge*) can be translated as "earth" or "land." Russell addresses both of these issues:

We shall see that "the kingdom of God" is represented as arriving at its consummation at the period of the destruction of Jerusalem.

That event marks the denouement of the great scheme of divine providence, or economy, as it is called, which began with the call of Abraham and ran a course of two thousand years. We may regard that scheme, the Jewish dispensation, not only as an important factor in the education of the world, but also as an experiment, on a large scale and under the most favourable circumstances, whether it were possible to form a people for the service, and fear, and love of God; a model nation, the moral influence of which might bless the world. In some respects, no doubt, it was a failure, and its end was tragic and terrible; but what is important for us to notice, in connection with this inquiry, is that the relation of Christ, the Son of David and King of Israel, to the Jewish nation explains the prominence given in the Gospels to the Parousia, and the events which accompanied it, as having a special bearing upon that people. Inattention to this has misled many theologians and commentators: they have read "the earth," when only "the land" was meant; "the human race," when only "Israel" was intended; "the end of the world," when "the close of the age, or dispensation," was alluded to. At the same time it would be a serious mistake to undervalue the importance and magnitude of the event which took place at the Parousia. It was a great era in the divine government of the world: the close of an economy which had endured for two thousand years; the termination of one aeon and the commencement of another; the abrogation of the "old order" and the inauguration of the new. It is, however, its special relation to Judaism which gives to the Parousia its chief significance and import. (*The Parousia*, pp. 156-157)

Much confusion has arisen from the indiscriminate use of the word "world" as the translation of the different Greek words *aion*, *kosmos*, *oikoumene*, and *ge*. The unlearned reader who meets with the phrase "the end of the world," inevitably thinks of the destruction of the material globe, whereas if he read "conclusion of the age, or aeon," he would as naturally think of the close of a certain period of time—which is its proper meaning. We have already had occasion to observe that aion is properly a designation of *time*, an *age;* and it is doubtful whether it ever has any other signification in the New Testament. Its equivalent in Latin is *aevum*, which is really the Greek aion in a Latin dress. The proper word for the *earth*, or *world*, is kosmos, which is used to designate both the material and the moral world. Oikoumene is properly the *inhab-*

275

ited world, "the *habitable*," and in the New Testament refers often to the *Roman Empire*, sometimes to so small a portion of it as *Palestine*. Ge, though it sometimes signifies the earth generally, in the gospels more frequently refers to the *land* of Israel. Much light is thrown upon many passages by a proper understanding of these words. (Ibid., pp. 264-265; emphasis in original)

Everything in our study to this point has shown that biblical eschatology is focused upon the nation of Israel, the Church, and the period of covenantal transition. This is especially so when we realize that the Bible never speaks of the end of the world, as many think, but of the end of the age. In light of these facts, would not judgments and catastrophes on a global scale seem awkwardly out of place? The solution to properly determining the translation for the Greek word *ge* is found in using the eschatological framework that has proven to be consistent thus far. As Russell noted above, Christ's relation to the Jewish nation, as their Messiah and King, explains the bearing that His Second Coming has upon that people. Inattention to this has caused many to read "the earth," "the human race," and "the end of the world," when "the land," "Israel," and "the end of the age" were in view. Bray also notes:

The word "world" is from the Greek word "oikoumene" which meant the inhabited world as they knew it in their day and time. But usage of the word in that day meant different things to different peoples. To the Romans, it was the Roman Empire. To the Greeks, it meant all the countries where their language was spoken. But to the Jew, it meant primarily the land of Palestine with all of its tribes, and then later inclusive of all areas where their peoples were scattered. (*Matthew 24 Fulfilled*, p. 33)

Maimonides states:

Sometimes the prophets use the term "mankind" instead of "the people of a certain place," whose destruction they predict; e.g., Isaiah speaking of the destruction of Israel says, "And the Lord will remove man far away" (Isa. vi. 12). So also Zephaniah (i. 3, 4), "And I will cut off man from off the earth. I will also stretch out mine hand upon Judah." (*Guide for the Perplexed*, p. 205)

By not realizing that the focus of eschatology is upon Israel and the changing of the covenants, *ge* has often been translated "earth," when "land," specifically the land of Judea, is in view. This is especially true in the book of Revelation. In the KJV, in Matthew through Jude, nearly one-third of the occurrences of *ge* are translated "land." In Revelation, *not one* of the eighty uses is translated "land." Does this perhaps indicate a bias (possibly unintentional) on the part of the translators for a particular eschatological view? We are not proposing that all of these instances should be translated as "land," nor are we pretending to be qualified to determine which ones should. However, in light of the overwhelming support that biblical eschatology describes the changing of the covenants, would we not expect *ge* to refer to the environs of the Old Covenant? Thus, "land" would be the preferred translation, unless context demands the broader translation "earth."

With that in mind, we offer the reader several passages from Revelation that employ *ge*, with both possible translations. Once it is understood that "earth" is not necessarily the mandatory translation, but is rather determined by context, we feel that what seemed previously to be judgments on a perceived global scale can be rightfully put in their place in the lands and people of Israel:

> *Behold, He is coming with clouds, and every eye will see Him, even they who pierced Him. And all the tribes of the earth [land] will mourn because of Him. Even so, Amen.* (Rev 1:7)

Here we feel the context of *they who pierced Him* (not the Romans who drove the nails, but the Jews who cried, "Crucify Him!"), as well as mention of *the tribes*, speaks of Israel. Therefore, the land of Judea—not the entire earth—is in view.

> *Another horse, fiery red, went out. And it was granted to the one who sat on it to take peace from the earth [land], and that people should kill one another; and there was given to him a great sword.* (Rev 6:4)

> *And I looked, and I heard an angel flying through the midst of heaven, saying with a loud voice, "Woe, woe, woe to the inhabitants of the earth [land], because of the remaining blasts of the trumpet of the three angels who are about to sound!"* (Rev 8:13)

> *So the angel thrust his sickle into the earth [land] and gathered the vine of the earth [land], and threw it into the great winepress of the wrath of God.* (Rev 14:19)

> *Then I heard a loud voice from the temple saying to the seven angels, "Go and pour out the bowls of the wrath of God on the earth [land]."* (Rev 16:1)

Jesus pronounced woes upon the scribes and Pharisees (Matt 23), and said that the generation that would see all of these things (i.e., regarding the tribulation) was that of His contemporary Jewish audience. Thus, the judgments and wrath are not being poured out upon the entire earth, but upon the land of Judea, where that generation dwelt.

> *When He opened the fifth seal, I saw under the altar the souls of those who had been slain for the word of God and for the testimony which they held. And they cried with a loud voice, saying, "How long, O Lord, holy and true, until You judge and avenge our blood on those who dwell on the earth [land]?"* (Rev 6:9-10)

> *And in her was found the blood of prophets and saints, and of all who were slain on the earth [land]."* (Rev 18:24)

> *For true and righteous are His judgments, because He has judged the great harlot who corrupted the earth [land] with her fornication; and He has avenged on her the blood of His servants shed by her."* (Rev 19:2)

Jesus told the scribes and the Pharisees that upon *them* would come all the righteous blood shed on the earth [land] (Matt 23:35). The preceding verses from Revelation are John's vision of that judgment:

> *These have power to shut heaven, so that no rain falls in the days of their prophecy; and they have power over waters to turn them to blood, and to strike the earth [land] with all plagues, as often as they desire.* (Rev 11:6)

God warned Israel that if they turned from Him, He would send plagues upon *them* (Lev 26:13-21; Deut 28:15, 22, 58-61)—not upon the entire globe. Although we develop the theme of the plagues as God's judgment in the next chapter, it is important that we recognize John's vision of Revelation's plagues as referring to that very judgment.

Moreover, in Gentry's *Before Jerusalem Fell*, he establishes Nero as the Beast of Revelation, noting that, when written in Hebrew, the title Nero Caesar adds up to 666. Thus, we would say that from God's covenantal view those who worshipped the beast were not *all who dwelt on the globe*, but the covenant people who dwelt in the land of Judea and cried out, *"We have no king but Caesar!"* (John 19:15).

> *All who dwell on the earth [land] will worship him [the beast], whose names have not been written in the Book of Life of the Lamb slain from the foundation of the world.* (Rev 13:8)

278

Hanegraaff points out that the mark of the beast need not be physical, but rather symbolizes the allegiance or identity of the recipients to the Beast:

> The typology principle adds to our understanding by underscoring that the mark of the Beast is simply a parody of the mark of the Lamb. Just as the mark written on the foreheads of the 144,000 in Revelation 14 symbolizes identity with the Lamb, so the mark on the right hand and the forehead in Revelation 13 symbolizes identity with the Beast. (*The Apocalypse Code*, p. 11)

As we have seen previously, the eschatological judgments in the Bible are not the end of the world, but the end of the age—the end of the Old Covenant. Hopefully, we have also demonstrated that those same judgments were not expected upon the entire earth, but upon the land of Judea, the literal seat of the Old Covenant. We close this section with some select quotes from Russell, beginning with his commentary on the first trumpet judgment of Revelation 8:1:

> The standpoint of the Seer is still heaven, though the scene on which the main action of the piece is to take place is the earth, or rather the land. It cannot be too carefully borne in mind that it is Israel,—Judea, Jerusalem—on which the prophet is gazing. To roam over the breadth of the whole earth, and to bring into the question all time and all nations, is not only to bewilder the reader in a labyrinth of perplexities, but wholly to miss the point and purport of the book. "The Doom of Israel; or, the Last Days of Jerusalem," would be no unsuitable title for the Apocalypse. (*The Parousia*, p. 407)

> Secondly, the reader will observe the persons on whom the predicted woes are to fall—"the inhabiters of the land." As in chap. 6:10, so here, *ge* must be taken in a restricted sense, as referring to the land of Israel. The rendering of *ge* by *earth*, instead of *land*, and of *aion* by *world*, instead of *age*, have been most fruitful sources of mistake and confusion in the interpretation of the New Testament. With singular inconsistency our translators have rendered *ge* sometimes *earth*, sometimes *land*, in almost consecutive verses, greatly obscuring the sense. Thus in Luke 21:23, they render *ge* by *land*: "there shall be great distress in the land" [epi tes ges], being compelled to restrict the meaning by the next clause,—"And wrath upon *this* people." But in the next verse but one, where the very same phrase recurs,—'distress epi

tes ges,'—they render it "*upon the earth*." In the passage now before us the woes are to be understood as denounced, not upon the inhabitants of the globe, but of the *land*, that is, of Judea. (Ibid., p. 410; emphasis and brackets in original)

A very fruitful source of confusion and error in the interpretation of the New Testament is the capricious and uncertain way in which "ge" is rendered in our Authorised Version. Sometimes, though rarely, it has its proper meaning, *the land;* but more frequently it is translated *the earth,* and our translators never seem to have given themselves any trouble to inquire whether the word should be taken in its widest or in a more restricted sense. (Ibid., pp. 493-494; emphasis in original)

Although in this chapter we have focused primarily on the judgment which took place in Jerusalem and Judea, we note that some Preterists do see the end-time events as being of a more worldwide nature. By "world-wide" they mean the Roman world, not the entire globe. For example, Kurt Simmons notes:

In our previous article, we surveyed a catalogue of Roman disasters, detailing some of the retribution visited upon the world at Christ's coming. It was a time of universal tribulation: famines, wars, pestilences, storms, political upheavals, military and naval disasters, which rocked the world and shook it to its very foundations. Italy was ruined; it was leveled by the storms and blasts of civil war of those competing for the empire; there were five emperors in 1 yr. 22 days; hundreds of thousands of Romans died; fifty thousand perished in Vespasian's siege of Rome alone. The same year that saw Jerusalem and its temple destroyed saw Rome besieged and its temple destroyed. The two greatest temples in the world thus perished in heaven's outpouring of wrath upon the disobedience of man. (*The Sword & The Plow*, Vol. IX, Number III, April 2007, p. 4)

Revelation and AD 70

Even if we accept the early date for the writing of Revelation, and acknowledge that it is not referring to the end of the world or global judgments, we may still ask if this extravagant prophecy is to be understood as the destruction of just one city, namely, Jerusalem. Though there may be many reasons one may harbor doubts to this end, we list three counter-arguments that we feel are key to the issue:

- The nature of the apocalyptic language of the Jews, as we have seen, is highly symbolic and hyperbolic when describing God's judgment upon His enemies, and the deliverance of His people. Unfortunately, the modern Church has tended to literalize this language in Revelation.
- It is not just the destruction of Jerusalem that is in view, but the end of the Mosaic economy, a covenantal era, and a nation.
- There are few in the church today who realize the severity of the events surrounding the destruction of Jerusalem.

Having dealt with the first item in the chapter "Apocalyptic Language," we turn to the second item. We must realize that the nation and religious economy that ended in AD 70 had existed for some 1,500 years. When God watches over a people for that long, and then ultimately has to pour out His wrath upon them, should we expect anything less than the most extravagant, symbolic, and hyperbolic language to describe it? When we consider that the author of Exodus dedicated most of the book to the birth of Israel, should we not be surprised that there is a book dedicated to its death? We withhold further comment on the issue in favor of Russell's:

> In conclusion, we cannot help adverting to one other consideration, which we are persuaded has had much to do with the erroneous interpretation of this prophecy [Christ's Olivet discourse], viz., the inadequate appreciation of the importance and grandeur of the event which forms its burden—the consummation of the aeon age, and the abrogation of the Jewish dispensation.

> That was an event which formed an epoch in the divine government of the world. The Mosaic economy, which had been ushered in with such pomp and grandeur amidst the thunders and lightenings of Sinai, and had existed for well nigh sixteen centuries, which had been the divinely instituted medium of communication between God and man, and which was intended to realise a kingdom of God upon earth—had proved a comparative failure through the moral unfitness of the people of Israel, and was doomed to come to an end amid the most terrific demonstration of the justice and wrath of God. The temple of Jerusalem, for ages the glory and crown of Mount Zion—the sacred shrine, in whose holy place Jehovah was pleased to dwell—the holy and

beautiful house, which was the palladium of the nation's safety, and dearer than life to every son of Abraham—was about to be desecrated and destroyed, so that not one stone should be left upon another. The chosen people, the children of the Friend of God, the favoured nation, with whom the God of the whole earth deigned to enter into covenant and to be called their King—were to be overwhelmed by the most terrible calamities that ever befell a nation; were to be expatriated, deprived of their nationality, excluded from their ancient and peculiar relation to God, and driven forth as wanderers on the face of the earth, a byword and hissing among all nations. But along with all this there were to be changes for the better. First, and chiefly, the close of the one would be the inauguration of the reign of God. There were to be honour and glory for the true and faithful servants of God, who would then enter into the full possession of the heavenly inheritance. (This will be more fully unfolded in the sequel of our investigation.) But there was also to be a glorious change in this world. The old made way for the new; the Law was replaced by the Gospel; Moses was superseded by Christ. The narrow and exclusive system, which embraced only a single people, was succeeded by a new and better covenant, which embraced the whole family of man, and knew no difference between Jew and Gentile, circumcised and uncircumcised. The dispensation of symbols and ceremonies, suited to the childhood of humanity, was merged in an order of things in which religion became a spiritual service, every place a temple, every worshipper a priest, and God the universal Father. This was a revolution greater far than any that had ever occurred in the history of mankind. It made a new world; it was the "world to come," the oikoumene mellousa of Hebrews ii. 5; and the magnitude and importance of the change it is impossible to over-estimate. It is this that gives such significance to the overthrow of the temple and the destruction of Jerusalem: these are the outward and visible signs of the abrogation of the old order and the introduction of the new. The story of the siege and capture of the Holy City is not simply a thrilling historical episode, such as the siege of Troy or the fall of Carthage; it is not merely the closing scene in the annals of an ancient nation—it has a supernatural and divine significance; it has a relation to God and the human race, and marks one of the most memorable epochs of time. This is the reason why the event is spoken of in the Scripture in terms which to some appear overstrained, or to require some greater catastrophe to account for them. But if it was fitting that the introduction of that economy should be signalised by portents and wonders, earthquakes, lightenings, thunders, and trumpet-blasts—it was no less fitting that it should go out amid similar phenomena, fearful sights and great signs from heaven. Had the true significance and grandeur of the event been better apprehended by expositors, they would not have found the language in which it is depicted by our Lord extravagant or overstrained. (*The Parousia*, pp. 64-66; brackets added)

Bray states:

From the Jewish standpoint, when their city and temple were destroyed, and their entire land devastated, along with their religious sacrifices and ritualism, for them there could never be anything so tragic as that. Even their genealogies were lost, so that today Jewish people cannot trace their ancestries back. (*Matthew 24 Fulfilled*, p. 83)

In the PBS documentary *The Kingdom of David*, Rabbi Perry Netter comments on the implications of the destruction of the temple:

The destruction of the Temple in the year 70 was the greatest catastrophe and trauma to happen to the Jewish people, I would argue, until our own time of the holocaust. It was the center of the economic life of the Jewish people—as if the Federal Reserve was housed in the Temple. It was the center of the judicial life—the Supreme Court was housed in the Temple. It was the center of the religious life—as if the High Priest was the chief rabbi centered in that building. And in a matter of hours, it was gone. When the temple was destroyed, everything was gone. There was no other branch of government, because it was all invested in the priesthood, and the High Priest, and the temple.

Rabbi Netter believes (as do many in our era) that the Holocaust of World War II was a greater trauma to the Jewish people than was the destruction of the temple and the Jewish War. However, it can be argued that, although more individuals perished in World War II, their centers of economic, judicial, and religious life were not destroyed. Rather, those things had been *left desolate* to them since AD 70. Although the Holocaust was tragic beyond words and a blight on the record of mankind, neither a nation, a religious system, nor a dispensation of God ended at that time. When we consider what actually transpired at the destruction of Jerusalem, we should expect nothing less than the language of Revelation.

Our third item from above, and final point in this chapter, is what occurred in AD 70. When one begins to examine Josephus' account of those days, it will be found that the descriptions of Revelation are not so extravagant or overstrained, as Russell puts it. What follows, interspersed with Scripture, are various quotes from Josephus regarding the siege and destruction of Jerusalem:

Concerning the wicked generation (and remembering that judgment was upon apostate Israel for rejecting their Messiah), Josephus writes:

It is therefore impossible to go distinctly over every instance of these men's iniquity. I shall therefore speak my mind here at once briefly: —That neither did any other city ever suffer such miseries, nor did any age ever breed a generation more fruitful in wickedness than this was, from the beginning of the world. (*Wars*, 5.10)

And here I cannot but speak my mind, and what the concern I am under dictates to me, and it is this: I suppose, that had the Romans made any longer delay in coming against these villains, that the city would either have been swallowed up by the ground opening upon them, or been overflowed by water, or else been destroyed by such thunder as the country of Sodom perished by, for it had brought forth a generation of men much more atheistical than were those that suffered such punishments; for by their madness it was that all the people came to be destroyed. (*Wars*, 5.13)

Concerning false prophets and messiahs, Russell quotes Josephus: ". . . the country was full of robbers, magicians, false prophets, false Messiahs, and impostors who deluded the People with promises of great events" (p. 69, *The Parousia*). Another element of the tribulation of those days was famine (Matt 24:7, Rev 6:5-6):

But the famine was too hard for all other passions, and it is destructive to nothing so much as to modesty; for what was otherwise worthy of reverence was in this case despised; insomuch that children pulled the very morsels that their fathers were eating out of their very mouths, and what was still more to be pitied, so did the mothers do as to their infants; and when those that were most dear were perishing under their hands, they were not ashamed to take from them the very last drops that might preserve their lives: and while they ate after this manner, yet were they not concealed in so doing; but the seditious everywhere came upon them immediately, and snatched away from them what they had gotten from others; for when they saw any house shut up, this was to them a signal that the people within had gotten some food; whereupon they broke open the doors, and ran in, and took pieces of what they were eating almost up out of their very throats, and this by force: the old men, who held their food fast, were beaten; and if the women hid what they had within their hands, their hair was torn for so doing; nor was there any commiseration shown either to the aged or to the infants, but they lifted up children from the ground as they hung upon the morsels they had gotten, and shook them down upon the floor. (*Wars*, 5.10)

Now of those that perished by famine in the city, the number was prodigious, and the miseries they underwent were unspeakable; for if so much as the shadow of any kind of food did anywhere appear, a war was commenced presently, and the dearest friends fell a fighting one with another about it, snatching from each other the most miserable supports of life. Nor would men believe that those who were dying had no food, but the robbers would search them when they were expiring, lest any one should have concealed food in their bosoms, and counterfeited dying; nay, these robbers gaped for want, and ran about stumbling and staggering along like mad dogs, and reeling against the doors of the houses like drunken men; they would also, in the great distress they were in, rush into the very same houses two or three times in one and the same day. Moreover, their hunger was so intolerable, that it obliged them to chew everything, while they gathered such things as the most sordid animals would not touch, and endured to eat them; nor did they at length abstain from girdles and shoes; and the very leather which belonged to their shields they pulled off and gnawed: the very wisps of old hay became food to some; and some gathered up fibres, and sold a very small weight of them for four Attic [drachmae]. But why do I describe the shameless impudence that the famine brought on men in their eating inanimate things, while I am going to relate a matter of fact, the like to which no history relates, either among the Greeks or Barbarians? It is horrible to speak of it, and incredible when heard. (*Wars*, 6.3; brackets in original)

At this point Josephus goes on to describe a nursing mother who killed, roasted, and ate her son, and how even the Romans, when they heard of it, took pity upon the calamity that had fallen upon the Jews.

Wholesale carnage was also prophesied:

And unless those days were shortened, no flesh would be saved . . . . (Matt 24:22)

When He opened the fourth seal, I heard the voice of the fourth living creature saying, "Come and see." So I looked, and behold, a pale horse. And the name of him who sat on it was Death, and Hades followed with him. And power was given to them over a fourth of the earth [land], to kill with sword, with hunger, with death, and by the beasts of the earth. (Rev 6:7-8)

Consider the horrors that Josephus describes in the following passages, including the fact that over one million people perished:

Now the number of those that were carried captive during this whole war was collected to be ninety-seven thousand; as was the number of those that perished during the whole siege eleven hundred thousand, the greater part of whom were indeed of the same nation [with the citizens of Jerusalem], but not belonging to the city itself; for they were come up from all the country to the feast of unleavened bread, and were on a sudden shut up by an army, which, at the very first, occasioned so great a straitness among them, that there came a pestilential destruction upon them, and soon afterward such a famine, as destroyed them more suddenly . . . . Now this vast multitude is indeed collected out of remote places, but the entire nation was now shut up by fate as in prison, and the Roman army encompassed the city when it was crowded with inhabitants. Accordingly, the multitude of those that therein perished exceeded all the destructions that either men or God ever brought upon the world; (*Wars*, 6.9; brackets in original)

So all hope of escaping was now cut off from the Jews, together with their liberty of going out of the city. Then did the famine widen its progress, and devoured the people by whole houses and families; the upper rooms were full of women and children that were dying by famine, and the lanes of the city were full of the dead bodies of the aged; the children also and the young men wandered about the market-places like shadows, all swelled with the famine, and fell down dead, wheresoever their misery seized them. As for burying them, those that were sick themselves were not able to do it; and those that were hearty and well were deterred from doing it by the great multitude of those dead bodies, and by the uncertainty there was how soon they should die themselves; for many died as they were burying others, and many went to their coffins before that fatal hour was come. Nor was there any lamentations made under these calamities, nor were heard any mournful complaints; but the famine confounded all natural passions; for those who were just going to die looked upon those that were gone to rest before them with dry eyes and open mouths. A deep silence also, and a kind of deadly night, had seized upon the city; while yet the robbers were still more terrible than these miseries were themselves; for they brake open those houses which were no other than graves of dead bodies, and plundered them of what they had; and carrying off the coverings of their bodies, went out laughing, and tried the points of their swords in their dead bodies; and, in order to prove what metal they were made of they thrust some of those through that still lay alive upon the ground; but for those that entreated them to lend them their right hand and their sword to dispatch them, they were too proud to grant their requests, and left them to be consumed by the famine. Now every one of these died with their eyes fixed upon the temple, and left the seditious alive behind them. Now the seditious at first gave orders that the dead should be buried out of the public treasury, as not enduring the stench of their dead bodies. But afterwards, when they could not do that, they had them cast down from the walls into the valleys beneath. (*Wars*, 5.12)

And, indeed, why do I relate these particular calamities? while Manneus, the son of Lazarus, came running to Titus at this very time, and told him that there had been carried out through that one gate, which was intrusted to his care, no fewer than a hundred and fifteen thousand eight hundred and eighty dead bodies, in the interval between the fourteenth day of the month Xanthieus, [Nisan,] when the Romans pitched their camp by the city, and the first day of the month Panemus [Tamuz]. This was itself a prodigious multitude; and though this man was not himself set as a governor at that gate, yet was he appointed to pay the public stipend for carrying these bodies out, and so was obliged of necessity to number them, while the rest were buried by their relations; though all their burial was but this, to bring them away, and cast them out of the city. After this man there ran away to Titus many of the eminent citizens, and told him the entire number of the poor that were dead, and that no fewer than six hundred thousand were thrown out at the gates, though still the number of the rest could not be discovered; and they told him further, that when they were no longer able to carry out the dead bodies of the poor, they laid their corpses on heaps in very large houses, and shut them up therein; as also that a medimnus of wheat was sold for a talent; and that when, a while afterward, it was not possible to gather herbs, by reason the city was all walled about, some persons were driven to that terrible distress as to search the common sewers and old dunghills of cattle, and to eat the dung which they got there; and what they of old could not endure so much as to see they now used for food. When the Romans barely heard all this, they commiserated their case; while the seditious, who saw it also, did not repent, but suffered the same distress to come upon themselves; for they were blinded by that fate which was already coming upon the city, and upon themselves also. (*Wars*, 5.13; brackets in original)

Consider, too, the following parallels between Revelation and Josephus' accounts:

And the kings of the earth [land], the great men, the rich men, the commanders, the mighty men, every slave and every free man, hid themselves in the caves and in the rocks of the mountains, and said to the mountains and rocks, "Fall on us and hide us from the face of Him who sits on the throne and from the wrath of the Lamb!" (Rev 6:15-16)

So now the last hope which supported the tyrants, and that crew of robbers who were with them, was in the caves and caverns under ground; whither, if they could once fly, they did not expect to be searched for; but endeavored, that after the whole city should be destroyed, and the Romans gone away, they might come out again, and escape from them. This was no better than a dream of theirs; for they were not able to lie hid either from God or from the Romans. (*Wars*, 6.7)

In the same hour there was a great earthquake, and a tenth of the city fell. In the earthquake seven thousand people were killed, and the rest were afraid and gave glory to the God of heaven. (Rev 11:13)

. . . for there broke out a prodigious storm in the night, with the utmost violence, and very strong winds, with the largest showers of rain, with continued lightnings, terrible thunderings, and amazing concussions and bellowings of the earth, that was in an earthquake. These things were a manifest indication that some destruction was coming upon men, when the system of the world was put into this disorder; and any one would guess that these wonders foreshowed some grand calamities that were coming. (*Wars*, 4.4)

They had tails like scorpions, and there were stings in their tails. (Rev 9:10)

And great hail from heaven fell upon men, each hailstone about the weight of a talent. (Rev 16:21)

The engines, that all the legions had ready prepared for them, were admirably contrived; but still more extraordinary ones belonged to the tenth legion: those that threw darts [some translations of Josephus call these engines "scorpions"] and those that threw stones were more forcible and larger than the rest, by which they not only repelled the excursions of the Jews, but drove those away that were upon the walls also. Now the stones that were cast were of the weight of a talent, and were carried two furlongs and further. The blow they gave was no way to be sustained, not only by those that stood first in the way, but by those that were beyond them for a great space. As for the Jews, they at first watched the coming of the stone, for it was of a white color, and could therefore not only be perceived by the great noise it made, but could be seen also before it came by its brightness; accordingly the watchmen that sat upon the towers gave them notice when the engine was let go, and the stone came from it, and cried out aloud, in their own country language, THE STONE COMETH so those that were in its way stood off, and threw themselves down upon the ground; by which means, and by their thus guarding themselves, the stone fell down and did them no harm. But the Romans contrived how to prevent that by blacking the stone, who then could aim at them with success, when the stone was not discerned beforehand, as it had been till then; and so they destroyed many of them at one blow. (*Wars*, 5.6; brackets added)

And Jesus said to them, "Do you not see all these things? Assuredly, I say to you, not one stone shall be left here upon another, that shall not be thrown down." (Matt 24:2)

And where is now that great city, the metropolis of the Jewish nation, which was fortified by so many walls round about, which had so many fortresses and large towers to defend it, which could hardly contain the instruments prepared for the war, and which had so many ten thousands of men to fight for it? Where is this city that was believed to have God himself inhabiting therein? It is now demolished to the very foundations, and hath nothing but that monument of it preserved, I mean the camp of those that hath destroyed it, which still dwells upon its ruins . . . . (*Wars*, 7.8)

So total was the destruction of Jerusalem that Josephus wrote, ". . . there was no longer anything to lead those who visited the spot to believe that it had ever been inhabited." We encourage the reader to examine the accounts of Josephus for themselves, for there is too much to include in this brief section. We hope that these few passages have revealed the extent of the judgment of AD 70 and how they were "*the days of vengeance, that **all things which are written** may be fulfilled*" (Luke 21:22; emphasis added).

Before moving on, consider that the Romans were able to accomplish the destruction of Jerusalem by taking advantage of the infighting between various Jewish factions:

And now all the rest of the commanders of the Romans deemed this sedition among their enemies to be of great advantage to them, and were very earnest to march to the city, and they urged Vespasian, as their lord and general in all cases, to make haste, and said to him, that "the providence of God is on our side, by setting our enemies at variance against one another; that still the change in such cases may be sudden, and the Jews may quickly be at one again, either because they may be tired out with their civil miseries, or repent them of such doings." But Vespasian replied, that they were greatly mistaken in what they thought fit to be done, as those that, upon the theater, love to make a show of their hands, and of their weapons, but do it at their own hazard, without considering, what was for their advantage, and for their security; for that if they now go and attack the city immediately, they shall but occasion their enemies to unite together, and shall convert their force, now it is in its height, against themselves. But if they stay a while, they shall have fewer enemies, because they will be consumed in this sedition: that **God acts as a general of the Romans better than he can do, and is giving the Jews up to them** without any pains of their own, and granting their army a victory without any danger; that therefore it is their best way, while their enemies are destroying each other with their own hands, and falling into the greatest of misfortunes, which is that of sedition, to sit still as spectators of the dangers they run into, rather than to fight hand to hand with men that love murdering, and are mad one against another. . . . These men, therefore, trampled upon all the laws of men, and laughed at the laws of God; and for the oracles of the prophets, they ridiculed them as the tricks of jugglers; yet did these prophets foretell many things concerning [the rewards of] virtue, and [punishments of] vice, which **when these zealots violated, they occasioned the fulfilling of those very prophecies belonging to their own country**; for there was a certain ancient oracle of those men, that the city should then be taken and the sanctuary burnt, by right of war, when a sedition should invade the Jews, and their own hand should pollute the temple of God. Now while these zealots did not [quite] disbelieve these predictions, they made themselves the instruments of their accomplishment. (*Wars* 4.6; brackets in original)

Nay, indeed, while he [Titus] was assisting his father at Alexandria, in settling that government which had been newly conferred upon them by God, it so happened that **the sedition at Jerusalem was revived, and parted into three factions, and that one faction fought against the other; which partition in such evil cases may be said to be a good thing, and the effect of Divine justice.** Now as to the attack the zealots made upon the people, and **which I esteem the beginning of the city's destruction**, it hath been already explained after an accurate manner; as also whence it arose, and to how great a mischief it was increased. (*Wars* 5.1)

Now the warlike men that were in the city, and the multitude of the seditious that were with Simon, were ten thousand, besides the Idumeans. . . . The Idumeans that paid him homage were five thousand. . . . Jotre, who had seized upon the temple, had six thousand armed men under twenty commanders; the zealots also that had come over to him, and left off their opposition, were two thousand four hundred, and had the same commander that they had formerly, Eleazar, together with Simon the son of Arinus. Now, while these factions fought one against another, the people were their prey on both sides, as we have said already; and that part of the people who would not join with them in their wicked practices were plundered by both factions. Simon held the upper city, and the great wall as far as Cedron . . . he also held that fountain, and the Acra, which was no other than the lower city; But John held the temple, and the parts thereto adjoining, for a great way, as also Ophla, and the valley called "the Valley of Cedron;" and when the parts that were interposed between their possessions were burnt by them, they left a space wherein they might fight with each other; **for this internal sedition did not cease even when the Romans were encamped near their very wall.** But although they had grown wiser at the first onset the Romans made upon them, this lasted but a while; for they returned to their former madness, and separated one from another, and fought it out, and **did everything that the besiegers could desire them to do; for they never suffered any thing that was worse from the Romans than they made each other suffer**; nor was there any misery endured by the city after these men's actions that could be esteemed new. But it was most of all unhappy before it was overthrown, while those that took it did it a greater kindness for **I venture to affirm that the sedition destroyed the city, and the Romans destroyed the sedition**, which it was a much harder thing to do than to destroy the walls; so that **we may justly ascribe our misfortunes to our own people**, and the just vengeance taken on them to the Romans; as to which matter let every one determine by the actions on both sides. (*Wars* 5.6)

And who is there that does not know what the writings of the ancient prophets contain in them, - and particularly that oracle which is just now going to be fulfilled upon this miserable city? For they foretold that this city should be then taken when somebody shall begin the slaughter of his own countrymen. And are not both the city and the entire temple now full of the dead bodies of your countrymen? **It is God, therefore, it is God himself who is bringing on this fire, to purge that city and temple by means of the Romans, and is going to pluck up this city, which is full of your pollutions.** (*Wars* 6.2.1)
(emphases added)

We note that both Vespasian and Josephus considered this infighting by the Jewish factions to be God's way of delivering the city into the hands of the Romans. Is this not exactly how we see God delivering His enemies into the hands of others in the Old Testament?

Then Saul and all the people who were with him assembled, and they went to the battle; and indeed every man's sword [of the

Philistines] was against his neighbor, and there was very great confusion. (1 Sam 14:20)

When the three hundred blew the trumpets, the LORD *set every man's sword against his companion throughout the whole camp.* (Judg 7:22)

Now when they began to sing and to praise, the LORD *set ambushes against the people of Ammon, Moab, and Mount Seir, who had come against Judah; and they were defeated. For the people of Ammon and Moab stood up against the inhabitants of Mount Seir to utterly kill and destroy them. And when they had made an end of the inhabitants of Seir, they helped to destroy one another. So when Judah came to a place overlooking the wilderness, they looked toward the multitude; and there were their dead bodies, fallen on the earth. No one had escaped.* (2 Chr 20:22-24)

The burden against Egypt.
Behold, the LORD *rides on a swift cloud,*
And will come into Egypt;
The idols of Egypt will totter at His presence,
And the heart of Egypt will melt in its midst.
"I will set Egyptians against Egyptians;
Everyone will fight against his brother,
And everyone against his neighbor,
City against city, kingdom against kingdom.
The spirit of Egypt will fail in its midst." (Isa 19:1-3)

Splitting the Mount of Olives

Although not a New Testament passage, Zechariah's account of the Lord touching the Mount of Olives, causing it to split in two, is a flagship passage for many Futurists. Because there is no record of the Mount of Olives ever splitting in two, this passage *must* be future, they claim. Therefore, we will briefly examine this prophecy.

1 Behold, the day of the LORD *is coming,*
And your spoil will be divided in your midst.
2 For I will gather all the nations to battle against Jerusalem;
The city shall be taken,
The houses rifled,
And the women ravished.
Half of the city shall go into captivity,

But the remnant of the people shall not be cut off from the city.
3 Then the LORD will go forth
And fight against those nations,
As He fights in the day of battle.
4 And in that day His feet will stand on the Mount of Olives,
Which faces Jerusalem on the east.
And the Mount of Olives shall be split in two,
From east to west,
Making a very large valley;
Half of the mountain shall move toward the north
And half of it toward the south.
5 Then you shall flee through My mountain valley,
For the mountain valley shall reach to Azal.
Yes, you shall flee
As you fled from the earthquake
In the days of Uzziah king of Judah.
Thus the LORD my God will come,
And all the saints with You.
6 It shall come to pass in that day
That there will be no light;
The lights will diminish.
7 It shall be one day
Which is known to the LORD—
Neither day nor night.
But at evening time it shall happen
That it will be light.
8 And in that day it shall be
That living waters shall flow from Jerusalem,
Half of them toward the eastern sea
And half of them toward the western sea;
In both summer and winter it shall occur.
9 And the LORD shall be King over all the earth.
In that day it shall be— "The LORD is one,"
And His name one. (Zech 14:1-9)

The first point to notice is that Zechariah is speaking of the Day of the LORD. As we have seen in our study so far, the New Testament saints expected the Day of the LORD, the casting out of Ishmael, and the passing away of the Old Covenant in *their* generation. Therefore, if we cannot find a place for Zechariah's prophecy within those confines, then we must assume that he is referring to another Day of the LORD, for which we have found no other scriptural support.

Yet Zechariah 14:2 describes nations being gathered against Jerusalem, the city being taken, houses rifled, women ravished and people going into captivity. Have we not read accounts of these very things from Josephus' pen concerning the destruction of Jerusalem? Who is the remnant that God shall not cut off? Who constituted the remnant in the days of Elijah and in the days of Paul? Those who had not bowed their knee to Baal and those who were the elect according to grace (Rom 11:4-5). The remnant is, and always has been, spiritual Israel.

The next several verses describe the LORD fighting against those nations and standing upon the Mount of Olives. When the Mount of Olives splits in two, His people shall flee through the valley that is created; thus the Lord will come and all His saints with Him. Do we not have in these verses another example of apocalyptic language, describing the LORD coming in judgment upon His enemies and delivering His people? Consider Micah's prophecy concerning Jerusalem's earlier destruction:

> *The word of the Lord that came to Micah of Moresheth in the days of Jotham, Ahaz, and Hezekiah, kings of Judah, which he saw concerning Samaria and Jerusalem.*

> *. . . For behold, the Lord is coming out of His place;*
> *He will come down*
> *And tread on the high places of the earth.*
> *The mountains will melt under Him,*
> *And the valleys will split . . . .* (Mic 1:1, 3-4)

Did the mountains melt and valleys split when Jerusalem was conquered by the Assyrians? Some may argue that Zechariah's description is too specific to be apocalyptic language. The foundations of the earth moving, the heavens shaking, yes, but a specifically named mountain splitting in half? To this rebuttal, we ask what of the mountains and valleys mentioned in the prophecy fulfilled by John the Baptist?

> *Every valley shall be exalted*
> *And every mountain and hill brought low;*
> *The crooked places shall be made straight*
> *And the rough places smooth . . . .* (Isa 40:4)

As the Messiah's forerunner, a Jewish prophet who was to preach the soon-to-arrive kingdom of God to the Jews, would not those mountains and valleys have been understood to be those of the environs of Jerusalem? And yet we know that no geographical upheavals occurred as a result of John the Baptist's ministry.

On the other hand, is there not a parallel between the prophecy of Isaiah regarding those mountains and valleys and Zechariah's description before us? Do not the geographical hindrances to physical travel represent the encumbrances of the Law, which had shut up all men under sin and kept them in custody until the faith of the New Covenant was revealed (Gal 3:22-23 NASB)? The lowering of the mountains, the raising of the valleys, and the splitting of the Mount of Olives represent the removing of the bondage of the law. Those who labored and were heavy laden under its encumbrances could now cast it aside and take upon themselves the yoke of the gospel of Christ, which was easy and the burden of which was light. (There is another possible fulfillment to this prophecy. As we shall see in the chapter "The Veiled Generation," during the initial stages of the Roman siege of Jerusalem, Cestius inexplicably withdrew his troops, allowing the Christians, who saw *Jerusalem surrounded by armies*, to *flee to the mountains*. Luke 21:20-21.)

And is not Zechariah 14:5 (*Thus the LORD my God will come And all the saints with You*) reminiscent of other passages which refer to the Second Coming?

> *. . . so that He may establish your hearts blameless in holiness before our God and Father at the coming of our Lord Jesus Christ with all His saints.* (1 Thess 3:13)

> *Now Enoch, the seventh from Adam, prophesied about these men also, saying, "Behold, the Lord comes with ten thousands of His saints . . . ."* (Jude 14)

> *Now I saw heaven opened, and behold, a white horse. And He who sat on him was called Faithful and True, and in righteousness He judges and makes war . . . . And the armies in heaven, clothed in fine linen, white and clean, followed Him on white horses.* (Rev 19:11, 14)

Moving on from here, we read that there will be no light, and the lights will diminish, in a day known to the LORD. Is this any different from that great and terrible judgment of which "*no one knows the day or hour, not even the angels, nor the Son, but the Father alone*" (Matt 24:36), in which "*the sun will be darkened, and the moon will not give its light, and the stars will fall from heaven*" (Matt 24:29)?

But at evening time it shall happen
That it will be light. (Zech 14:7)

Josephus records that at 3 am on the 8th of Nisan, so great a light shone round the altar and the holy house, it appeared to be bright daytime for half an hour (*Wars*, 6.5). Whether this is the fulfillment of the above verse, or if it refers to the "night" of the Old Covenant passing and the day of salvation dawning (Rom 13:11-12), we can still find the events within the scope of AD 70.

The final portion of our passage speaks of living waters flowing from Jerusalem. As we have studied previously, these are the living waters of the gospel of Christ, flowing not from physical Jerusalem but from the Church, which is the heavenly Jerusalem (Rev 21:9-10). Thus, we feel that Zechariah spoke not of a yet-future literal splitting of the Mount of Olives, but rather maintained the precedent of the prophets' use of apocalyptic language to describe the various days of the LORD. Moreover, we see nothing in this passage, either literal or spiritual, for which the events of AD 70 cannot account.

Conclusion

If we allow ourselves to entertain, if only for conjecture, the premise of an early date for the composition of Revelation, the picture that comes into focus is astounding. It suddenly fits into the scope of the rest of biblical eschatology—God's redemptive plan and the changing of the covenants. Two things result from allowing Revelation to fit naturally in place as the judgment that was to "*shortly come to pass*" upon the Jews of the New Testament generation. There is no longer a need to remove the Olivet discourse from the generation to which it was delivered, and there is no need for an indeterminate gap in the specific time line of Daniel's seventy weeks. We have seen that Josephus' exhaustive records provide many detailed examples of fulfillments for Revelation's prophecies.

Even in light of apocalyptic language, however, some may demand a point-by-point analysis of the seals, trumpets, vials, etc., in a historical setting before they reconsider their eschatology. Nevertheless, we must remember that we are nearly two thousand years removed from the events, and despite a historical record of them, we do not possess an *inspired* record. On the other hand, in the case of David being delivered from his enemies, we have both apocalyptic language (e.g., 2 Samuel 22) *and* a historical record of the events described (the preceding chapters of 1 & 2

Samuel), each written by an inspired author. To those who would demand a point-by-point analysis of Revelation, we would ask to be shown from the exploits of David when the foundations of Heaven were shaken; when smoke went up from God's nostrils and devouring fire proceeded from His mouth; when He rode upon a cherub and was seen on the wings of the wind; when the channels of the sea were seen and the foundations of the earth were uncovered. If we do not demand a point-by-point analysis of these instances of apocalyptic and hyperbolic language, why should we demand one for Revelation?

The Veiled Generation

In Part I, we concluded several chapters with a supporting illustration of Old Testament typology. In similar fashion, this concluding chapter of Part II is a study of the Old Testament typology of the "last days" generation of the New Testament Church. We feel that it dovetails all of the elements in this section of our study and provides scriptural "foreshadowing" of the eschatological framework that we have already presented. Because we have covered much ground in this section, and the typology of the New Testament generation is so rich, this chapter is somewhat lengthy; nevertheless, we feel that the reader's efforts will be rewarded.

As we understand it, there are two basic classes of biblical "types." First are those that Scripture defines for us. Jesus described Moses' lifting up of the brass serpent in the wilderness as a type of His being lifted up on the cross (John 3:14). Jesus also described Jonah's three days and nights in the belly of a "great fish" as a type of His three days and nights in the belly (heart) of the earth, that is, in a tomb (Matt 12:40). Paul described Adam as a type of Christ (Rom 5:14), whom he called the "last Adam" (1 Cor 15:45).

The second class of types contains those that the reader discerns, although Scripture does not declare them specifically. These we might consider "uninspired" types—meaning not that the original text providing the type is uninspired, but rather that the interpretation of the type is uninspired and not declared specifically in the Scriptures for us. (This definition of "uninspired" can also be applied to extraneous details relating to the first class of types which, while not found explicitly in Scripture, can be discerned by the reader). For example, we have yet to discover anywhere in the Bible that defines or describes the patriarch Joseph as a type of Christ, yet we would be hard-pressed to deny the fact. Consider the following:

- Both were despised by their siblings
- Both came up alive from the earth, which was supposed to hold them in death (Joseph from the pit; Jesus from the tomb)
- Both became servants in a foreign land (Joseph in Egypt; Jesus on earth)

- Both paid the penalty for sins they did not commit
- Joseph was exalted to the right hand of Pharaoh; Jesus was exalted to the right hand of the Father
- During the famine in Egypt, relief was found only by going to Joseph; relief for our souls' spiritual famine is found only in Christ

In the following pages, we will explore how the first generation of national Israel, which experienced the Exodus first-hand, is a type of the first generation of spiritual Israel as depicted in the New Testament era. This type is established explicitly in Scripture for us by Paul in 1 Corinthians 10:

Moreover, brethren, I do not want you to be unaware that all our fathers were under the cloud, all passed through the sea, all were baptized into Moses in the cloud and in the sea, all ate the same spiritual food, and all drank the same spiritual drink. For they drank of that spiritual Rock that followed them, and that Rock was Christ. But with most of them God was not well pleased, for their bodies were scattered in the wilderness.

Now these things became our examples, to the intent that we should not lust after evil things as they also lusted. And do not become idolaters as were some of them. As it is written, "The people sat down to eat and drink, and rose up to play." Nor let us commit sexual immorality, as some of them did, and in one day twenty-three thousand fell; nor let us tempt Christ, as some of them also tempted, and were destroyed by serpents; nor complain, as some of them also complained, and were destroyed by the destroyer. Now all these things happened to them as examples, and they were written for our admonition, upon whom the ends of the ages have come.

Therefore let him who thinks he stands take heed lest he fall.
(1 Cor 10:1-12)

The word "examples" in verses 6 and 11 is the Greek word τυπος (*tupos*; Strong's 5179). This same word is translated "type" in Romans 5:14, which states that Adam is "a *type* of Him [Christ] who was to come." What is *not* established in the 1 Corinthian passage is how much detail to read into the type. However, when Paul, inspired by the Holy Spirit writes, "*all* these things happened to them as examples" (types), we feel that the precedent is to include, rather than exclude, details (cf. Rom 15:4).

The premise presented here is that not only was the first generation of national Israel a picture-perfect type of the first generation of spiritual Israel, but that it fits best when considered from a Preterist viewpoint, which is the framework that has been established thus far. While "uninspired" types or details should not establish doctrine, often these various types or details help elucidate a particular subject. They bring out subtle nuances, sometimes expanding our perspective. Perhaps, on rare occasions, they may even tip the scale of indecision one way or another. We will let the reader be the judge, noting the following comments by Patrick Fairbairn and Hank Hanegraaff:

> Still the relation between type and antitype, when pursued through all its ramifications, may produce as deep a conviction of design and preordained connection, as can be derived from simple prophecy and its fulfillment, though, from the nature of things, the evidence in the latter case must always be more obvious and palpable than in the former. (*The Typology of Scripture*, p. 107, vol.1, Fairbairn)

> Far from being peripheral, typology is central to the proper interpretation of the infallible Word of God. One cannot fully grasp the meaning of the New Testament apart from familiarity with the redemptive history and literary forms of the Old Testament. Likewise, the New Testament shines its light on the Old Testament and reveals the more complete significance of God's redemptive work in and through the nation of Israel. This relationship between the Testaments is in essence typological. Thus, as eschatology is the thread that weaves the tapestry of Scripture into a glorious mosaic; typology is the material out of which that thread is spun. (*The Apocalypse Code*, p. 170, Hanegraaff)

The End of the Ages

Now all these things happened to them as examples, and they were written for our admonition, upon whom the ends of the ages have come. (1 Cor 10:11)

When Preterists read the above passage, they take the phrase "*upon whom the ends of the ages have come*" at face value, just like the phrases "*at hand,*" "*this generation,*" etc., that we have previously explored. The end of the age of Judaism and its accompanying Mosaic Law had come upon those first-century readers, culminating in the destruction of Jerusalem in AD 70.

The first question that jumps out at us is what are *all these things*? From the context of this verse, we see that *all these things* were the experiences of the early Israelites: their deliverance from the bondage of Egypt and their march through the wilderness prior to entering the Promised Land. The Apostle Paul admonishes the first-century Christians (spiritual Israel) to learn from the example of the physical Israelites: *"Therefore let him who thinks he stands take heed lest he fall."* Up to this point, we could consider Paul's admonition one of general diligence concerning their Christian walk, indeed even one that speaks through the ages to us. *Don't fall into the same pitfalls; don't trip on the same stumbling blocks as those who have walked this path before you; learn from their mistakes,* he seems to be saying. We might compare this passage with similar admonitions of Paul:

> *For this reason we also, since the day we heard it, do not cease to pray for you, and to ask that you may be filled with the knowledge of His will in all wisdom and spiritual understanding; that you may walk worthy of the Lord, fully pleasing Him, being fruitful in every good work and increasing in the knowledge of God . . . .* (Col 1:9-10)

> *. . . as you know how we exhorted, and comforted, and charged every one of you, as a father does his own children, that you would walk worthy of God who calls you into His own kingdom and glory.* (1 Thess 2:11-12)

Yet, why does Paul insert the phrase *"upon whom the ends of the ages have come"* into 1 Corinthians 10:11? Is it merely an aside, or is it one of Paul's many doctrinal embellishments for which his writings are known? Neither possibility would detract from the significance of the passage as an admonition to our Christian walk.

We propose, however, that the Holy Spirit inspired Paul to include that phrase because there is much more for us to discover here. The theme we wish to develop is this: Paul was writing to the final generation of *his* age—a generation that had just been delivered permanently from the bondage of sin by the death and resurrection of Christ (rendering obsolete the temporary forgiveness provided by animal sacrifice); a generation that was going through a period of spiritual testing and poised to enter the spiritual Promised Land. To admonish and encourage them to *take heed lest they fall*, he uses the example of a previous generation that too had been delivered from bondage (Egypt), went through testings in the wilderness, and was standing poised to enter the physical Promised Land. Just as Moses—a type of Christ—presented to Israel the Promised Land which they refused to enter, so Christ—the prophet to come, like unto Moses (Deut 18:15)—presented to Israel their Messiah. Unfortunately, like their forefathers, the New Testament generation refused to enter "through the veil of His flesh" (Heb 10:19-20) into the true Holy of Holies, the spiritual Promised Land. Christ came to His own and His own did not receive Him (John 1:11). Just as God decreed judgment on Moses' generation, which died off approximately 40 years after refusing to enter the physical Promised Land while their innocent offspring entered in, Christ decreed judgment on His generation, which also died off approximately 40 years after refusing their Messiah, allowing faithful Israel (the Christian church) to enter the spiritual Promised Land.

Granted, at face value the passage before us is already a serious admonition toward a diligent Christian walk, an admonition we can apply to our own walk. However, in light of the above proposal, can you envision how much more weight the passage carries? Paul is not just saying "*walk in a manner worthy of the Lord*"; he is saying "*the end is come upon us, don't stumble now, don't be like those who failed to enter in.*" Compare this to how the author of Hebrews admonishes his readers by the same example (cf. Jude 5ff):

Therefore, as the Holy Spirit says:

"Today, if you will hear His voice,
Do not harden your hearts as in the rebellion,
In the day of trial in the wilderness,
Where your fathers tested Me, tried Me,
And saw My works forty years. Therefore I was angry with that generation,
And said, 'They always go astray in their heart,
And they have not known My ways.' So I swore in My wrath,
'They shall not enter My rest.'"

Beware, brethren, lest there be in any of you an evil heart of unbelief in departing from the living God; but exhort one another daily, while it is called "Today," lest any of you be hardened through the deceitfulness of sin. For we have become partakers of Christ if we hold the beginning of our confidence steadfast to the end, while it is said:

"Today, if you will hear His voice, Do not harden your hearts as in the rebellion."

For who, having heard, rebelled? Indeed, was it not all who came out of Egypt, led by Moses? Now with whom was He angry forty years? Was it not with those who sinned, whose corpses fell in the wilderness? And to whom did He swear that they would not enter His rest, but to those who did not obey? So we see that they could not enter in because of unbelief. (Heb 3:7-19)

This passage is even more pertinent, in that it was written to the Hebrews, i.e., Jewish believers. Here the author is telling them to exhort one another, so that they do not depart from God. He is, in essence, saying, *"our forefathers made a similar journey, and failed to enter His rest—don't do the same."* That generation learned that *"it is a fearful thing to fall into the hands of the living God"* (Heb 10:31; cf. Num 14:36-37). The author is telling them to not be among the portion of their generation destined to suffer the same consequence, of whom we read earlier: *"they shall go forth and look upon the corpses of the men who have transgressed against Me"* (Isa 66:24).

Some might point out that, unlike the 1 Corinthians passage, there is no "end of the age" timestamp in this Hebrews passage. Yet, all we have to do is go forward seven chapters:

And let us consider one another in order to stir up love and good works, not forsaking the assembling of ourselves together, as is the manner of some, but exhorting one another, and so much the more as you see the Day approaching. (Heb 10:24-25)

What day did they see approaching? The Day of the LORD, the end of the Old Covenant, and the "crossing over the Jordan into the Promised Land." Let us dig deeper and see what we can discover.

The Big Picture

It has long been recognized that the journey of the Israelites from Egyptian bondage to arrival in the Promised Land is an overview (or synopsis) of the believer's spiritual journey. The Egyptian bondage represents the bondage to sin prior to salvation. The Israelites were technically freed when their oppressors drowned in the Red Sea. This is a picture of the believer's salvation; the Israelites going down into the sea and then coming back up out of the sea can also be a picture of baptism, which often accompanies a new believer's confession of faith. The journey through the wilderness represents the bulk of the believer's spiritual life, filled with the blessings and provisions of God, with times of testing, with new revelation of who God is and how He wants to interact with the believer. The Promised Land represents heaven, and the Jordan River, which must be crossed, represents death. (Some Preterists would take issue with the Jordan representing death, believing that after Christ consummated the New Covenant by His return in AD 70, all subsequent believers enter into the fullness of the "Promised Land" upon conversion (i.e., acceptance of the New Covenant). Although we will touch upon this matter in Part III, the purpose of this volume is to introduce the general framework of Preterism, not debate the various nuances within it.)

When we think of this overview of the believer's spiritual journey, the tendency is to think of Gentile believers. In a general sense the overview can fit all believers in all ages. However, we believe the specific type, or foreshadow, applies to the physical and spiritual Jews of the New Testament era. Consider the following:

> *For I am not ashamed of the gospel of Christ, for it is the power of God to salvation for everyone who believes,* **for the Jew first** *and also for the Greek.* (Rom 1:16)

> *... but to those who are self-seeking and do not obey the truth, but obey unrighteousness—indignation and wrath, tribulation and anguish, on every soul of man who does evil,* **of the Jew first** *and also of the Greek; but glory, honor, and peace to everyone who works what is good,* **to the Jew first** *and also to the Greek.* (Rom 2:8-10)

> *But He answered and said, "I was not sent except to the* **lost sheep of the house of Israel."** (Matt 15:24)

> *These twelve Jesus sent out and commanded them, saying: "Do not go into the way of the Gentiles, and do not enter a city of the Samaritans. But go rather to the* **lost sheep of the house of Israel."** (Matt 10:5-6)

> *"You are sons of the prophets, and of the covenant which God made with our fathers, saying to Abraham, 'And in your seed all the families of the earth shall be blessed.'* **To you first**, *God, having raised up His Servant Jesus, sent Him to bless you, in turning away every one of you from your iniquities."* (Acts 3:25-26)

*Then Paul and Barnabas grew bold and said, "It was necessary that the word of God **should be spoken to you first**; but since you reject it, and judge yourselves unworthy of everlasting life, behold, we turn to the Gentiles." (Acts 13:46)*
(emphases added)

Although salvation is available to both Jew and Gentile, God offered it first to the Jews. This, we believe, was because they had been the custodians of the existing stage of God's redemptive plan, which foreshadowed the next stage. Therefore, it was only fitting that they should be given first choice of moving into the next and final stage of God's redemptive plan. The fact that most of the Jews did not accept the offer was what brought Paul great sorrow:

I tell the truth in Christ, I am not lying, my conscience also bearing me witness in the Holy Spirit, that I have great sorrow and continual grief in my heart. For I could wish that I myself were accursed from Christ for my brethren, my countrymen according to the flesh, who are Israelites, to whom pertain the adoption, the glory, the covenants, the giving of the law, the service of God, and the promises; of whom are the fathers and from whom, according to the flesh, Christ came, who is over all, the eternally blessed God. Amen. (Rom 9:1-5)

To be sure, there were Jewish converts; but when it came to accepting Christ as their promised Messiah, as a nation the Jews cried out, *"Crucify Him!"* Though there were two spies, Joshua and Caleb, who believed that God would deliver the Promised Land to Israel, as a nation the Israelites cried out, *"It would have been better for us to serve the Egyptians than that we should die in the wilderness"* (Exod 14:12).

Therefore, although the general typology of the Exodus generation can apply to all believers of all ages, we feel that the specific typology belongs to the last generation of national Israel and the first generation of spiritual Israel, both of whom coexisted as the "last days" generation. Not only do the events parallel each other, they seem more like mirror images, one a reflection of the other. Let us look at some examples in further detail.

Moses

In the Exodus generation, both Moses and Joshua are seen as types of Christ. While Moses personifies the "savior" aspect of Christ, delivering

Israel from bondage, Joshua personifies the "conquering warrior" aspect of Christ, vanquishing his enemies and bringing his people into their final destination. While Moses brought out, Joshua led in. We would like to propose that Moses is a type of Christ in His first coming, while Joshua is a type of Christ in His Second Coming. We offer the following support for this premise from the Scriptures.

Moses alluded to the typology between Christ and himself when he stated, *"The LORD your God will raise up for you a Prophet like me from your midst, from your brethren"* (Deut 18:15). Christ also alluded to the connection between them when He said, *"As Moses lifted up the serpent in the wilderness, so must the Son of Man be lifted up"* (John 3:14). Let us examine the similarities:

First, the very name of Moses denotes the concept of "drawing out," or deliverance:

> *And the child grew, and she brought him to Pharaoh's daughter, and he became her son. So she called his name Moses, saying, "Because I drew him out of the water."* (Exod 2:10)

Adam Clarke's Commentary says:

> maashah (OT: 4871) signifies "to draw out," and Mosheh (OT: 4872) is the person drawn out.

The Old Testament uses *maashah* two other times:

> *He sent from above, He took me,*
> *He drew [maashah] me out of many waters.* (2 Sam 22:17)

> *He delivered [maashah] me from my strong enemy,*
> *From those who hated me,*
> *For they were too strong for me.* (Ps 18:17)

We find it fascinating that Moses' very name foretold his ministry, his purpose in life. The same is true of the Prophet whom Moses prophesied would be "like" him, whom God raised up centuries later:

> *And she will bring forth a Son, and you shall call His name JESUS, for He will save His people from their sins."* (Matt 1:21)

Again, we turn to *Adam Clarke's Commentary*:

> Jesus, the same as Joshua, Yᵃhowshuwa' (OT: 3091), from yaasha' (OT: 3467), he saved, delivered, put in a state of safety.

Already we see a connection to Joshua, which we will address shortly. However, notice that the name Jesus means "*he saved, delivered.*" Just as with Moses, Jesus' very name foretold his ministry, his purpose in life; but there is much more than just what is in a name. We wish to stress, however, that the purpose of this section is not an in-depth study of Moses as a type of Christ, for that would be a separate study in itself. Rather, the intent here is to demonstrate that the typology of Moses centers on Christ's ministry in His *first* coming.

Because of Pharaoh's fear of the Israelites growing in number and threatening his kingdom, he decreed the murder of all newborn male Israelite babies. Born during the time of this decree, Moses escaped death when his mother placed him afloat in a reed basket on the Nile River. There, Pharaoh's daughter discovered and adopted him. In short, Moses escaped death by going to Egypt. Likewise, Herod feared that the prophesied Messiah would incite the Israelites to rise up against his kingdom. He too issued a decree calling for the murder of all male Israelite infants. Jesus, in His first coming, came during this decree. How did He escape? Joseph and Mary fled to Egypt with Him!

On the night of the Israelites' deliverance from Egypt, Moses instituted the Passover. This is probably the most poignant of the types of Christ associated with Moses. Here, we see a lamb brought into the home to live with the family prior to the appointed time of sacrifice. During this time, the lamb was examined to determine that it was without blemish and, therefore, a suitable sacrifice. Once killed, its blood was collected in a bowl and, with a hyssop branch, applied to the family's doorway in three places—the top and both sides. No doubt, as the hyssop branch, dripping with blood, moved from the bowl to the top, and to each side of the doorway, some blood fell on the ground at the base of the doorway, creating a fourth spot of blood. When the Lord's angel of death passed through the land to kill the firstborn, those homes that had the blood on their doorways would be "passed over." John the Baptist testifies to the connection of the Passover lamb and Christ:

> *The next day John saw Jesus coming toward him, and said, "Behold! The Lamb of God who takes away the sin of the world!"*
> (John 1:29)

As Christ dwelt among His people, He was examined closely by the religious leaders, but they could not catch Him in anything (Matt 22:15-46). Even Pilate said, "I find no fault in Him" (John 19:4). Christ was a suitable sacrifice. In His crucifixion, we see the blood on His head from the crown of thorns, and on each hand and on His feet from the nails, the same positions as the doorways in Goshen. His blood, applied to the "doorways of our hearts," removes our sins, causing spiritual death to pass over us. There is much more to say about this, but we must move on.

Though Moses and the Israelites had left Egypt, they were not truly free until they came up out of the Red Sea. Though Christ's death provided deliverance from sin, it did not become effective until His resurrection: *"And if Christ is not risen, your faith is futile; you are still in your sins!"* (1 Cor 15:17). Interestingly enough, Christ rose from the tomb on the same day of the Jewish calendar that Moses and the Israelites came up out of the Red Sea!

For the sake of expediency, we provide the following types and anti-types as cursory looks, with little introduction or commentary:

- Moses cast a tree into the bitter waters, causing them to become sweet. Jesus became cursed of God because He was hanged on a tree (Deut 21:22-23; Gal 3:13). However, the cross of Christ, cast into the bitter waters of our lives, changes them into the sweetness of salvation.

- During Moses' administration, the Israelites received manna from heaven (Exod 16). Christ was the true manna from heaven (John 6:48).

- When the Israelites cried out for water, Moses struck the rock and water poured forth (Exod 17:6). Christ, the Rock of our salvation, was struck for us in order that He could provide us with living water (1 Cor 10:4).

- When Joshua led the Israelites into battle against Amalek, they prevailed only while Moses had his hands stretched out. When his hands grew heavy, Aaron and Hur stood on either side of him and held his hands out for him (Exod 17). Likewise, we can only prevail against the battle of sin in our lives through the outstretched hands of the crucified Christ (Matt 27:38).

- Through Moses, God instituted the covenant of the Law (Exod 19ff). Through Christ, God instituted the New Covenant (Matt 26:28; Heb 9:15).

- Moses was the mediator of the Old Covenant (Exod 20:19). Christ is the Mediator of the New Covenant (1Tim 2:5).

- God instituted the Ten Commandments through Moses (Exod 20). God instituted a new commandment through Christ (John 13:34).

- God instituted the priesthood through Moses (Exod 28-29). God installed Christ as our High Priest (Heb 4:14).

- On various occasions, the people refused to recognize Moses as their leader and deliverer (Exod 2:14; Num 16:3). Likewise, Christ was not accepted by the Jews as their leader and deliverer (John 19:15).

Time does not permit us to look into the numerous types of Christ in the tabernacle, its services, the various sacrifices, etc. We hope that what has been presented here is adequate to demonstrate that, as a type of Christ, Moses was specifically a type of Christ's first coming, finding its climax in His death and resurrection.

Because he disobeyed the Lord, God did not allow Moses to lead the Israelites into Canaan. At the end of his life, God told him to ascend the mountain so that he could look over the Jordan River and see the Promised Land. There he died and was "gathered to his people." Here we see a picture of the ascension of Christ into heaven at the close of His earthly ministry. Both Moses and Jesus gave farewell addresses to their followers, then ascended from them, leaving them poised to enter a "promised land."

Joshua

Since Moses is considered by many to be the greatest leader in the history of the Jews, we might not expect the life of Joshua to be as typologically rich as that of Moses. However, we are not left wanting.

As with Moses, we begin with the name. As already noted, the name *Jesus* is the Greek equivalent of the Hebrew *Joshua*. Thus, Jesus and Joshua shared a name. Let us look once more at *Adam Clarke's Commentary*:

Jesus, the same as Joshua, Y^{a}howshuwa' (OT: 3091), from yaasha' (OT: 3467), he saved, delivered, put in a state of safety.

Just as Moses saved, delivered, and led the Israelites into a state of safety from their life of bondage, so Joshua saved, delivered, and led the Israelites into a state of safety from their enemies.

There is a twofold aspect to the Second Coming of Christ which we believe Joshua typifies. These two facets are: (1) the leading of the people into the Promised Land; and (2) the vanquishing of His enemies.

1. Leading the People into the Promised Land

As the miracle of the parting of the Red Sea equates with the miracle of spiritual rebirth, so the miracle of crossing the Jordan during its flood stage equates with the miracle of the translation of the saints. In each case, a physical miracle typifies a spiritual miracle. A change in physical state of the body (from one shore of the water to the other) typifies a change in the spiritual state of the body.

As we established previously, both Canaan and Heaven were/are "Promised Lands," places of bounty and of final rest. Thus, entering Canaan was a type of entering heaven. Prior to the destruction of the Old Covenant no one could enter heaven (Heb 9:8). Therefore, the dead went to a temporary holding place known as Sheol in Hebrew, or Hades in Greek. Preterists believe that the righteous dead were brought into the throne room of heaven at Christ's Second Coming in AD 70. To our knowledge, there were only three ways for true believers to enter the spiritual dimension of the afterlife: (1) translation (bypassing death), as is commonly understood of Enoch and Elijah; (2) physical death; or (3) being among those raptured away at Christ's Second Coming (though we use the term *rapture*, we note that Preterism does not typically define that event in the same manner as most Futurists. We will discuss this in a later chapter). While translation into the spiritual realm is extremely rare (we acknowledge that some Preterists do not believe Enoch and Elijah actually bypassed physical death), it is appointed for men to die once and then face the final judgment (Heb 9:27). Once again, while the analogy of "crossing over Jordan" can apply to all three modes in a general sense, we believe that the New Testament writers applied it specifically to their generation. This was the generation "*upon whom the end of the ages had come*" and who could "*see the Day approaching.*" The author of Hebrews admonished his readers by the specific example of the Israelites failing to enter Canaan in order to prevent them from doing the same.

Both generations had the gospel, the "good news," preached to them. The Israelites had the promise of entering Canaan, but it did not profit them because they did not believe the gospel in faith. Likewise, an individual must believe the gospel of Christ with faith in order to enter Christ's rest:

Therefore, since a promise remains of entering His rest, let us fear lest any of you seem to have come short of it. For indeed the gospel was preached to us as well as to them; but the word which they heard did not profit them, not being mixed with faith in those who heard it. For we who have believed do enter that rest . . . . (Heb 4:1-3)

But without faith it is impossible to please Him, for he who comes to God must believe that He is, and that He is a rewarder of those who diligently seek Him. (Heb 11:6)

Here, we see both generations poised to enter their respective Promised Lands and their final rest, their entrance fully dependent upon their response to the gospel preached to them.

We have considered previously many of the Second Coming passages which describe what the Church was expecting in the chapter "This Generation." Thus, we know that the rapture is that aspect of Christ's Second Coming when Christ comes for His church, and takes them to the place He has prepared (we again note that the nature of the rapture will be further discussed in Part III). So, in Joshua's leading Israel into Canaan we see a foreshadowing of Christ's leading His church into heaven.

2. Enemies Vanquished

As we mentioned earlier, the Second Coming of Christ was twofold. Not only did He lead His church into the Promised Land (1 Thess 4:16-17), He also vanquished His enemies (2 Thess 1:7-10). We see the same in the actions of Joshua, who not only led Israel into Canaan but also led them in battle to vanquish their enemies before them. (This is not to say that there are enemies of God in heaven. All types and analogies break down at some point. We believe that the point here is the twofold aspect to Joshua's ministry and its foreshadowing of the twofold aspect of Christ's Second Coming.)

Throughout Scripture, Christ is portrayed by two diametrically opposed animals—the lion and the lamb. In His first coming, He came as the Lamb of God. Remember John the Baptist's declaration, *"Behold! The Lamb of God."* At Christ's Second Coming, He came as the Lion of the tribe of Judah to pounce upon and vanquish His enemies. True to form, the characters of Moses and Joshua correspond with Christ's actions. As it is written, *"Moses was very humble, more than all men who were on the face of the earth*" (Num 12:3). Moses had the character of a lamb. Joshua, on the other hand, was a warrior, a commander in battle. He had the character of a lion. Recall the Israelites' battle against Amalek: Joshua commanded the battle, even though Moses, interceding on the hilltop, was still their leader. Then, of course, recall the famous battle of Jericho and the subsequent battles to rid Canaan of its evil inhabitants.

God even revealed Himself differently to Moses than Joshua. He revealed Himself to Moses as "*the God of Abraham, Isaac and Jacob*" and the "*I AM that I AM*" (Exod 3:6, 14). To Joshua, He revealed Himself as "*Commander of the army of the LORD*" (Josh 5:14). Having seen the type in Joshua, let us look at the antitype in Christ:

> . . . *since it is a righteous thing with God to repay with tribulation those who trouble you, and to give you who are troubled rest with us when the Lord Jesus is revealed from heaven with His mighty angels, in flaming fire taking vengeance on those who do not know God, and on those who do not obey the gospel of our Lord Jesus Christ. These shall be punished with everlasting destruction from the presence of the Lord and from the glory of His power, when He comes,* **in that Day**, *to be glorified in His saints and to be admired among all those who believe, because our testimony among you was believed.* (2 Thess 1:6-10; emphasis added)

Here we see the term "*that Day*," which is synonymous with "*the Day*" of Hebrews 10. Look closely at what happens when Christ comes in *that Day*: (1) He will "*give rest to those who are troubled*"—this is the deliverance of the saints; and (2) He will "*take vengeance on those who do not know God*"—this is the vanquishing of His enemies. Two events, one Day. Two aspects of the Second Coming, one Second Coming. Let us look again at the passage from Hebrews in a fuller context:

> *And let us consider one another in order to stir up love and good works, not forsaking the assembling of ourselves together, as is the manner of some, but exhorting one another, and so much the more as you see* **the Day** *approaching. For if we sin willfully after we have received the knowledge of the truth, there no longer remains a sacrifice for sins, but a certain fearful expectation of judgment, and fiery indignation which will devour the adversaries.* (Heb 10:24-27; emphasis added)

Why were the Hebrews exhorted to encourage one another? So that they might enter God's rest! If they did not enter His rest, what was the alternative? *"Fiery indignation which will devour the adversaries."* Once again, two events, one Day. Consider two final verses pertaining to Christ as a warrior at His Second Coming:

> *Now out of His mouth goes a sharp sword, that with it He should strike the nations. And He Himself will rule them with a rod of iron. He Himself treads the winepress of the fierceness and wrath of Almighty God. . . . And the rest were killed with the sword which proceeded from the mouth of Him who sat on the horse. And all the birds were filled with their flesh.* (Rev 19:15, 21)

Do you see the twofold aspect of Christ's Second Coming—*entering in* and *judgment*? We stress this point because many attempt to separate the events of the rapture/entering in from those of the judgment. This, we believe, is because, despite recognizing the Preterist eschatological framework in Scripture and, therefore, assigning the last days and Christ's Second Coming to the New Testament generation and the destruction of Jerusalem, they have failed to realize the spiritual nature of the New Covenant and kingdom fully. These "Partial" Preterists are still looking for a future, physical return of Christ to fulfill a physical resurrection of the dead and a truly universal judgment for all of humankind. While they believe that "a coming of Christ" occurred in the framework of the destruction of Jerusalem in AD 70, thus fulfilling the imminency passages, they still look for a "third" coming of Christ to bring about the final resurrection and judgment. (Most Partial Preterists do not consider Christ's coming in judgment in AD 70 to be *the* Second Coming, but rather *a* "judgment coming." Thus, they look for a future, "third" coming which they define as the "Second Coming.")

We believe that the above passages, as well as many similar ones, teach otherwise. Granted, though there is one "Day," it is not a 24-hour day. Although the gathering of the elect happened "in a moment, in the twinkling of an eye," the judgment was a process lasting approximately 3½ years, as described in Revelation. Similarly, the crossing of the Jordan (entering Canaan) was a relatively brief event, while the vanquishing of Israel's enemies took decades. We believe that the typology before us confirms this as well, in that one person carries out both events simultaneously. The leading of the Israelites into Canaan and the subsequent vanquishing of Israel's enemies by Joshua go hand-in-hand. You cannot have one without the other. While the events of the first and second comings of Christ are obviously separate and typified by different people (Moses and Joshua), the two facets of the Second Coming cannot be separated, either in type

314

or antitype. The Full Preterist framework that we have been presenting fits perfectly with the teaching of the New Testament and the typology of the Old Testament, while a Partial Preterist framework calls for a "third coming" of Christ, which must be forced into the New Testament's eschatological framework, and ultimately rejects the Old Testament typology of the veiled generation. We feel that the fulfilled promises of Joshua and Jesus to their respective generations during Joshua's leadership and Christ's Second Coming further strengthen this premise:

> *Not a word failed of any good thing which the L*ORD *had spoken to the house of Israel. All came to pass.* (Josh 21:45)

Since Joshua is a type of Christ in His Second Coming, we see this thought echoed in the events surrounding the destruction of Jerusalem in the days of Christ's Second Coming:

> *But when you see Jerusalem surrounded by armies, then know that its desolation is near . . . . For these are the days of vengeance, that all things which are written may be fulfilled.* (Luke 21:20, 22)

Let us briefly, then, summarize this section. Moses personifies the first coming of Christ. In him, we see the Lamb of God who takes away the sins of the world. We see the deliverance from the bondage of sin through the death and resurrection of Christ. Joshua personifies the Second Coming of Christ. In him, we see the Lion of the tribe of Judah who leads His people into the Promised Land and vanquishes His enemies. These two facets of one Second Coming occurred simultaneously in the first century.

The Timing

In our estimation, from a Preterist perspective, this is one of the most compelling portions of the typology. After spending about two years in the desert, receiving the Law and establishing the tabernacle and its Priesthood, the Israelites were poised to enter Canaan. As we read above, they did not mix the promise with faith and failed to enter. God became angry with that generation (those 20 years old and older) and made Israel wander in the desert another 38 years, until that generation had all died. Consider this commentary from the book of Hebrews:

> *For who, having heard, rebelled? Indeed, was it not all who came out of Egypt, led by Moses? Now with whom was He angry forty years? Was it not with those who sinned, whose corpses fell in the*

wilderness? And to whom did He swear that they would not enter His rest, but to those who did not obey? So we see that they could not enter in because of unbelief. (Heb 3:16-19)

Is there any question with whom God was angry or who died in the wilderness? The same generation to whom God said, "I am angry with you," is the one that perished in the wilderness. Likewise, it was "this generation" (Matt 24:34) to whom Jesus said they would see "all these things." It is almost as if the author of Hebrews is saying, "Is there any doubt as to which Old Testament generation received the judgment of God and did not enter His rest? Neither should there be any doubt as to which generation Jesus was referring." In both cases the generation that *heard* the judgment pronounced also *saw* the judgment delivered.

God, angry with the Old Testament generation for forty years, allowed it to perish in the wilderness. Is it mere coincidence that forty years after the Jews rejected their Messiah, over one million of Christ's generation died during the siege of Jerusalem and, concerning the temple, not one stone was left upon another?

Is it just coincidence that the New Testament authors saw the approaching Day and admonished the Church with the example of a previous generation that had missed their "day"? God did not withhold judgment upon the Old Testament generation until some future date. As we are vividly told, "their corpses fell in the wilderness." To say that the corpses that fell in AD 66-70, with all of the accompanying tribulations, were not a fulfillment of Christ's prophecies is to take a piece that is perfectly fitted in the puzzle and force it into another place in which it does not belong.

An Adulterous Generation

Notice what kind of generation Christ said sought for a sign: an "adulterous" generation (Matt 12:39). The theme of Israel as an adulterous nation is found throughout Scripture. Why this term? Because Israel was "betrothed" to God at Mount Sinai:

I remember you,
The kindness of your youth,
The love of your betrothal,
When you went after Me in the wilderness,
In a land not sown. (Jer 2:2)

"Return, O backsliding children," says the LORD; *"for I am married to you."* (Jer 3:14)

"When I passed by you again and looked upon you, indeed your time was the time of love; so I spread My wing over you and covered your nakedness. Yes, I swore an oath to you and entered into a covenant with you, and you became Mine," says the Lord GOD. (Ezek 16:8)

Therefore, God viewed Israel's unbelief and worship of foreign gods as adultery or fornication. We will further develop this theme later in this chapter under the heading "The Judgment of Plagues: The Wilderness Generation and Revelation's Mystery Babylon."

The book of Revelation depicts this adulterous generation of Christ's day as the great harlot. Its most egregious act of harlotry was the rejection of the One to Whom they had been betrothed: their Messiah, the Bridegroom. As in the parable of the Wedding Supper, they refused to attend; in their stead, the Groom invited others. Why is Israel's unbelief and wandering after other gods couched in terms of moral infidelity? Because there is only one scriptural justification for divorce: adultery. It was during the delivery of the Law to Moses at Mount Sinai when Israel was betrothed to God; sadly, the divorce became final in AD 70! (It may be argued that the Jews themselves finalized the divorce when they cried, "We have no king but Caesar!")

When God told the Israelites that they would not enter Canaan, but would die in the wilderness, they suddenly reconsidered. However, God said that it was too late. As in the days of Noah, when God shut the door to the Ark, the invitation was closed (Matt 24:38-39). Despite God's warning, the Israelites attempted to battle against the inhabitants of Canaan—and were soundly defeated (Num 14:39-45). Similarly, Christ's generation missed their invitation as well:

Now as He drew near, He saw the city and wept over it, saying, "If you had known, even you, especially in this your day, the things that make for your peace! But now they are hidden from your eyes. For days will come upon you when your enemies will build an embankment around you, surround you and close you in on every side, and level you, and your children within you, to the ground; and they will not leave in you one stone upon another, because you did not know the time of your visitation." (Luke 19:41-44)

To summarize: Israel's first generation stood at the threshold of entering the Promised Land, but failed to do so due to their unbelief. God pronounced judgment upon *that* generation and allowed *that* generation to perish within forty years—the span of a biblical generation—of His decree. Hinging upon their judgment was their children's entrance into Canaan. There was no long span of time between the judgment of the rebellious generation and the entrance into the Promised Land by those who had not shown unbelief.

Likewise, the last generation of national Israel stood at the threshold of entering the Promised Land, via a new covenant mediated by their Messiah, but failed to do so as a result of their unbelief. God pronounced judgment upon *that* generation and *that* generation perished in AD 70. Within forty years of His decree—the span of a biblical generation—judgment was complete. Hinging upon their judgment was the Church's (spiritual Israel's) entrance into the kingdom of Heaven. There was no long span of time between the judgment of the rebellious generation and the entrance into the Promised Land by those who believed in the Messiah.

The Offspring

The children of that rebellious Old Testament generation represent the New Testament Church. These believing children of an unbelieving generation entered the Promised Land—Canaan. Likewise, the Church—the believing children of an unbelieving generation—entered the spiritual Promised Land:

> *But your little ones, whom you said would be victims, I will bring in, and they shall know the land which you have despised.* (Num 14:31)

> *Men and brethren, sons of the family of Abraham, and **those among you who fear God**, to you this word of this salvation has been sent . . . . And we declare to you glad tidings—that promise which was made to the fathers. God has fulfilled this for **us their children**, in that He has raised up Jesus.* (Acts 13:26, 32-33; emphasis added)

The Jews' ancient forefathers rejected God's original promise. God was now offering a new promise, the Glad Tidings, to the believing children of the current generation, the Church. Christ Himself illustrated this

318

promise in His parable of the wicked vinedressers, who beat the servants of the landowner and killed his son. What was the result?

> *"Therefore I say to you, the kingdom of God will be taken from you and given to a nation bearing the fruits of it. And whoever falls on this stone will be broken; but on whomever it falls, it will grind him to powder." Now when the chief priests and Pharisees heard His parables, they perceived that He was speaking of them. But when they sought to lay hands on Him, they feared the multitudes, because they took Him for a prophet.* (Matt 21:43-46)

The chief priests and Pharisees *knew* that this parable was spoken against them, yet they would soon reject the chief cornerstone and, as in Luke's parallel account, kill the Beloved Son. The Owner would take from them the vineyard and the kingdom and give it to others—the Christian Church. The unbelieving Jews would not enter in, but the "next generation" would. The first-century church—the "children" of the fathers—was that next generation:

> *Coming to Him as to a living stone, rejected indeed by men, but chosen by God and precious, you also, as living stones, are being built up a spiritual house, a holy priesthood, to offer up spiritual sacrifices acceptable to God through Jesus Christ. Therefore it is also contained in the Scripture,*
>
> *"Behold, I lay in Zion*
> *A chief cornerstone, elect, precious,*
> *And he who believes on Him will by no means be put to shame."*
> *Therefore,* **to you who believe**, *He is precious; but to those who are disobedient,*
> *"The stone which the builders rejected*
> *Has become the chief cornerstone,*
> *And,*
> *A stone of stumbling*
> *And a rock of offense."*
>
> *They stumble, being disobedient to the word, to which they also were appointed. But* **you are a chosen generation**, *a royal priesthood, a holy nation,* **His own special people** *... who were once not a people but are* **now the people of God** *....* (1 Pet 2:4-9a, 10a; emphasis added)

The first-century Christians were given the kingdom of God (the vineyard). They accepted what the Jews, as a nation, had rejected. They were now "*His own special people*," fulfilling the typology of the Jews, who had been "*a special treasure above all the peoples on the face of the earth . . .*" (Deut 7:6). They entered the Promised Land that God offered to a previous "chosen people," just as in the days of Moses:

> *But your little ones, whom you said would be victims, I will bring in, and they shall know the land which you have despised.* (Num 14:31)

Where did the offspring of the rebellious generation go while God judged that generation? Into the wilderness, until the time came for them to enter the Promised Land. When the Christians saw Jerusalem surrounded by armies in preparation to execute the righteous judgment of God, to where did they flee and await their redemption that was drawing nigh? Into the wilderness!

> *But when you see Jerusalem surrounded by armies . . . let those who are in Judea flee to the mountains . . . .* (Luke 21:20-21)

Josephus records how Cestius, in the very early stages of the Roman siege upon Jerusalem, retreated for no apparent reason:

> And now the seditious, insomuch that many of them ran out of the city, as though it were to be taken immediately; but the people upon this took courage, and where the wicked part of the city gave ground, thither did they come, in order to set open the gates, and to admit Cestius as their benefactor, who, **had he but continued the siege a little longer, had certainly taken the city;** but it was, I suppose, owing to the aversion God had already at the city and the sanctuary, that he was hindered from putting **an end to the war that very day**. It then happened that Cestius was not conscious either how the besieged despaired of success, nor how courageous the people were for him; and so he recalled his soldiers from the place, and by despairing of any expectation of taking it, without having received any disgrace, **he retired from the city, without any reason in the world.** (*Wars*, 2.19; emphasis added)

William Whiston, the translator of Josephus' works quoted above, makes the following observation concerning Cestius' strange behavior:

> There may another very important, and very providential, reason be here assigned for this strange and foolish retreat of Cestius; which, if Josephus had been now a Christian, he might probably have taken notice of also; and that is, the affording the Jewish

Christians in the city an opportunity of calling to mind the prediction and caution given them by Christ about thirty-three years and a half before, that "when they should see the abomination of desolation" [the idolatrous Roman armies, with the images of their idols in their ensigns, ready to lay Jerusalem desolate,] "stand where it ought not;" or "in the holy place;" or, "when they should see Jerusalem encompassed with armies," they should then "flee to the mountains." By complying with which those Jewish Christians fled to the mountains of Perea, and escaped this destruction. Nor was there, perhaps, any one instance of a more unpolitic, but more providential conduct than this retreat of Cestius, visible during this whole siege of Jerusalem; which yet was providentially such a "great tribulation, as had not been from the beginning of the world to that time; no, nor ever should be." (*Wars*, 2.19, footnote; brackets in original)

We note also in the previous quote from Josephus, himself a Jew, that he realized that God had an aversion to the city and the sanctuary.

Joshua and Caleb

Just as we will never know what the conquest of Canaan would have been like if Israel had marched in the first time, so we will never know how events would have unfolded if Israel, as a nation, had received their Messiah. These national rejections resulted in national judgments in both cases. However, even in both judgments, God showed mercy. God did not judge those who believed His promise with their respective generations.

Joshua and Caleb were the only two individuals from their rebellious generation who entered Canaan (Num 14:30). They had faith that God would deliver the land into their hands. Because they were willing to enter, God allowed them to enter, although they had to wait until God carried out His judgment on the remainder of their generation.

In the same manner, though the Jews as a nation rejected Christ as Messiah, many Jews did receive Him and were counted among the believers (Acts 14:1; 17:1-4, 10-12; 18:4; 21:20). Like Joshua and Caleb, these Jews did not enter heaven at the moment of their belief; they had to wait until Christ came in judgment on their generation, at which time He led the true Church into the true Promised Land.

The Judgment of Plagues: The Wilderness Generation and Revelation's Mystery Babylon

Plagues seem to be God's judgment of choice in matters of infidelity, whether physical or spiritual. When Abram introduced Sarai to Pharaoh as his sister, God sent a plague on Pharaoh's house after he attempted to add her to his harem (Gen 12:17). Consider also the judgment upon an unfaithful wife, according to the Law:

When he has made her drink the water, then it shall be, if she has defiled herself and behaved unfaithfully toward her husband, that the water that brings a curse will enter her and become bitter, and her belly will swell, her thigh will rot, and the woman will become a curse among her people. (Num 5:27)

Is that not a plague on an individual level? Thus, we should not be surprised to see plagues as judgments upon Israel because, as we have seen, Israel was betrothed to God at Mount Sinai (Jer 2:2; 3:14; Exod 24:3). Yet even as Moses was up on the mount obtaining the final "marriage papers," the people had already begun their harlotries, making a golden calf and worshipping it. As a result, God, who is a jealous God (Exod 20:5), sent a plague among them:

So the LORD plagued the people because of what they did with the calf which Aaron made. (Exod 32:35)

Thus, when the Israelites did not trust God to bring them into the Promised Land, God viewed that as an act of infidelity, killing the ten remaining (and disbelieving) spies with a plague:

*And your sons shall be shepherds in the wilderness forty years, and bear the brunt of your **infidelity**, until your carcasses are consumed in the wilderness . . . . Now the men whom Moses sent to spy out the land, who returned and made all the congregation complain against him by bringing a bad report of the land, those very men who brought the evil report about the land, **died by the plague** before the LORD.* (Num 14:33, 36-38; emphasis added)

Israel also played the harlot with Baal of Peor and was subsequently judged with a plague:

They joined themselves also to Baal of Peor,
And ate sacrifices made to the dead.
Thus they provoked Him to anger with their deeds,
And the plague broke out among them. (Ps 106:28-29)

As God continued establishing the Israelites as a nation, He warned them that if they turned from Him, they would suffer His wrath, which included plagues:

> *"But if you do not obey Me, and do not observe all these command-ments, and if you despise My statutes, or if your soul abhors My judgments, so that you do not perform all My commandments, but break My covenant, I also will do this to you: I will even appoint terror over you, **wasting disease and fever** which shall consume the eyes and cause sorrow of heart. . . . Then, if you walk contrary to Me, and are not willing to obey Me, I will bring on you **seven times more plagues**, according to your sins."* (Lev 26:14-16, 21)

> *"But it shall come to pass, if you do not obey the voice of the LORD your God, to observe carefully all His commandments and His statutes which I command you today, that all these curses will come upon you and overtake you . . . The LORD will make **the plague** cling to you until He has consumed you from the land which you are going to possess."* (Deut 28:15, 21)

> *"If you do not carefully observe all the words of this law that are written in this book, that you may fear this glorious and awesome name, THE LORD YOUR GOD, then the LORD will bring upon you and your descendants **extraordinary plagues—great and prolonged plagues—and serious and prolonged sicknesses**. Moreover He will bring back on you all the diseases of Egypt, of which you were afraid, and they shall cling to you. Also **every sickness and every plague**, which is not written in this Book of the Law, will the LORD bring upon you until you are destroyed."* (Deut 28:58-61)

(emphases added)

Surely, all nations (and individuals) deserve God's wrath and judg-ment. Yet, would we not expect more loyalty from a spouse over and above other relatives and acquaintances? Would we not also expect God to require more loyalty from Israel, than from other nations? After all, He chose them over and above any other people:

> *For you are a holy people to the LORD your God; the LORD your God has chosen you to be a people for Himself, a special treasure above all the peoples on the face of the earth.* (Deut 7:6)

Israel was a special treasure *above all the peoples on the face of the earth.* God had warned them of the penalty of turning from Him.

Furthermore, in Ezekiel 16 God describes Jerusalem's rebellion against Him as adultery:

> *And in all your abominations and acts of harlotry you did not remember the days of your youth, when you were naked and bare, struggling in your blood. . . . You are an adulterous wife, who takes strangers instead of her husband.* (Ezek 16:22, 32)

In light of these facts, does it not make sense that the plagues of Revelation are God's delivering on His promise to Israel alone and not the whole world? Was the whole world betrothed to God? Absolutely not. Therefore, it was impossible for the world to be unfaithful to Him in the sense that Israel was. Did Jesus say to the world, "You have missed the day of your visitation?" Again, no. While the gospel is available to all the nations, only Israel was a special treasure above all the peoples on the face of the earth. Therefore, God warned only Israel of the consequences of spiritual infidelity; thus, the subsequent plagues were visited upon them. *You only have I known of all the families of the earth; Therefore I will punish you for all your iniquities* (Amos 3:2). God did not warn them of just run-of-the-mill plagues; He warned them about "*seven times more plagues, extraordinary plagues—great and prolonged plagues, and every plague, which is not written in this Book of the Law, will the* LORD *bring upon you until you are destroyed.*" Does this not sound like the intensity of the plagues in Revelation? Is it pure coincidence that Leviticus 26 warns of four sevenfold judgments, and in Revelation we see four sevenfold judgments delivered?

<u>Judgment Warned:</u>

> *And after all this, if you do not obey Me, then I will punish you* **seven times** *more for your sins.* (Lev 26:18)

> *Then, if you walk contrary to Me, and are not willing to obey Me, I will bring on you* **seven times** *more plagues, according to your sins.* (Lev 26:21)

> *And if by these things you are not reformed by Me, but walk contrary to Me, then I also will walk contrary to you, and I will punish you yet* **seven times** *for your sins.* (Lev 26:23-24)

> *And after all this, if you do not obey Me, but walk contrary to Me, then I also will walk contrary to you in fury; and I, even I, will chastise you* **seven times** *for your sins.* (Lev 26:27-28)

<u>Judgment Delivered:</u>

*I watched as the Lamb opened the first of the **seven seals**.* (Rev 6:1 NIV)

*Then the seven angels who had the **seven trumpets** prepared to sound them.* (Rev 8:6)

*I saw in heaven another great and marvelous sign: seven angels with the **seven last plagues**—last, because with them God's wrath is completed.* (Rev 15:1)

*Then I heard a loud voice from the temple saying to the seven angels, "Go, pour out the **seven bowls** of God's wrath on the earth [land]."* (Rev 16:1)
(emphases added)

Is it possible that Revelation's judgments are the fulfillment of God's warnings to Israel in Leviticus 26? Some may argue that the seven last plagues and the seven bowls of wrath are one and the same—thus there are really only three sevenfold judgments. However, we note that some commentators believe that there is only one sevenfold judgment in Revelation, which is portrayed several different ways. We find it more than coincidence that Leviticus mentions four "seven times" judgments, and Revelation mentions four sevenfold judgments. In light of this, can Babylon, the great harlot of Revelation, be any other than the final generation of Israel, which was so taken by her other "lovers" that she failed to recognize the One to Whom she was betrothed? Before they had even entered the Promised Land, God told Moses that the Israelites would play the harlot, and that His anger would come upon them in **that day**:

*And the LORD said to Moses: "Behold, you will rest with your fathers; and this people will rise and play the **harlot** with the gods of the foreigners of the land, where they go to be among them, and they will forsake Me and break My covenant which I have made with them. Then My anger shall be aroused against them in **that day**, and I will forsake them, and I will hide My face from them, and they shall be devoured. And many evils and troubles shall befall them, so that they will say in **that day**, 'Have not these evils come upon us because our God is not among us?' And I will surely hide My face in **that day** because of all the evil which they have done, in that they have turned to other gods.* (Deut 31:16-18; emphasis added)

What was foretold in Deuteronomy is revealed in Revelation, for it depicts the "*many evils and troubles*" that befell the nation of Israel for their harlotries:

So he carried me away in the Spirit into the wilderness. And I saw a woman sitting on a scarlet beast which was full of names of blasphemy, having seven heads and ten horns. The woman was arrayed in purple and scarlet, and adorned with gold and precious stones and pearls, having in her hand a golden cup full of abominations and the filthiness of her **fornication**. (Rev 17:3-4)

After these things I saw another angel coming down from heaven, having great authority, and the earth was illuminated with his glory. And he cried mightily with a loud voice, saying, "Babylon the great is fallen, is fallen, and has become a dwelling place of demons, a prison for every foul spirit, and a cage for every unclean and hated bird! For all the nations have drunk of the wine of the wrath of **her fornication**, *the kings of the earth have* **committed fornication with her**, *and the merchants of the earth have become rich through the abundance of her luxury." And I heard another voice from heaven saying,* **"Come out of her, my people, lest you share in her sins, and lest you receive of her plagues**. *For her sins have reached to heaven, and God has remembered her iniquities. Render to her just as she rendered to you, and repay her double according to her works; in the cup which she has mixed, mix double for her. In the measure that she glorified herself and lived luxuriously, in the same measure give her torment and sorrow; for she says in her heart, 'I sit as queen, and am no widow, and will not see sorrow.' Therefore* **her plagues** *will come in one day—death and mourning and famine. And she will be utterly burned with fire, for strong is the Lord God who judges her.* (Rev 18:1-8)
(emphases added)

Consider also Christ's warning to the disciples:

"But when you see Jerusalem surrounded by armies, then know that its desolation is near. Then let those who are in Judea flee to the mountains, let those who are in the midst of her depart, and let not those who are in the country enter her. For these are the days of vengeance, that all things which are written may be fulfilled."
(Luke 21:20-22)

Does that not sound like *"Come out of her, my people, lest you share in her sins, and lest you receive of her plagues"* (Rev 18:4)? The Christians did come out of her when they saw the Roman armies surrounding Jerusalem. They fled into the wilderness, as we have noted earlier. Consider also the fact that the Babylon of Revelation is guilty of the blood of the saints:

> *And on her forehead a name was written: MYSTERY, BABYLON THE GREAT, THE MOTHER OF HARLOTS AND OF THE ABOMINATIONS OF THE EARTH [LAND]. I saw the woman, drunk **with the blood of the saints and with the blood of the martyrs of Jesus.** And when I saw her, I marveled with great amazement.* (Rev 17:3-6)

> *"Rejoice over her, O heaven, and you **holy apostles and prophets, for God has avenged you on her!"** . . . And in her was found the blood of prophets and saints, and of all who were slain on the earth [land]."* (Rev 18:1-8, 20, 24) (emphases added)

Jesus told the scribes and Pharisees of His day that they would be guilty of *"all the righteous blood shed on the earth [land], from the blood of righteous Abel to the blood of Zechariah . . ."* (Matt 23:35). In Revelation 18:24, John states that in Babylon was found the blood of all who were slain on the earth [land], and that plagues were coming upon her. How can Babylon be anything but Jerusalem and the apostate Jews, whose house was left unto them desolate? *For it cannot be that a prophet should perish outside of Jerusalem* (Luke 13:33). After the Christians fled into the wilderness came the *days of vengeance* when *all things which are written were fulfilled.* God avenged His saints in AD 70. The harlot was utterly burned with fire (Rev 18:8). We have seen previously from the accounts of Josephus how the Romans utterly burned and destroyed Jerusalem.

In *Revelation: Four Views*, Gregg notes some of the interpretations that Futurists apply to Revelation 17's *MYSTERY, BABYLON THE GREAT*:

> Many, including Ryrie, Gaebelein, and Ironside, agree with Walvoord, who understands the harlot to be a religious entity, a coalition of apostate churches, head-quartered in Rome and, most probably, dominated by the Vatican . . . . Other commentators interpret Babylon principally in political, cultural, or commercial terms, a representative of the anti-God systems of man in any age.

> Elsewhere in Scripture, the word harlot, when not speaking of an actual woman, generally **refers to apostate Judaism,** and alludes

to the practice of spiritual adultery, usually including the worship of idols, as Walvoord writes:

The symbolism of spiritual adultery is not ordinarily used of heathen nations who know not God, but always of people who outwardly carry the name of God while actually worshipping and serving other gods. (pp. 401-403; emphasis added)

If the term harlot, in a spiritual sense, applies generally to apostate Judaism and is not used ordinarily of heathen nations who know not God (e.g., Rome), why look for the meaning of *MYSTERY, BABYLON* outside of those parameters, especially since it was the nation of Israel who was betrothed to God—and thus the only nation qualified to commit spiritual adultery—and who also refused the "wedding invitation"? Hanegraaff notes, "In biblical history only one nation is inextricably linked to the moniker 'harlot.'" (*The Apocalypse Code*, p. 119)

Gregg quotes Gaebelein, who identifies the harlot with Romanism, in reference to the phrase *drunk with the blood* of God's people:

The inquisition, the torture-chambers, the countless victims who were burned to death and cruelly tortured, the unspeakable horrors of centuries of violence and murder come to our minds as we read this description. (*Revelation: Four Views*, p. 407)

Perhaps those events come to the minds of Futurists, but we must ask how the horror of *centuries* of violence can be applied to events which Revelation states *must shortly come to pass* (1:1), whose *time was near* (1:3), were *about to come* (3:10 NASB95) and *must shortly take place* (22:6)? Even with a late date for the writing of Revelation, centuries of horror cannot be forced to fit within these time statements. Conversely, Jesus said, "*Jerusalem, Jerusalem, the **one who kills the prophets** . . . your house is left to you desolate*" (Matt 23:37-38). Preston writes:

. . . and significantly, one of the cities is the "*new* Jerusalem." Does this not of itself indicate that John is contrasting the *old Jerusalem* with the *new*? It certainly seems incongruous to contrast a *new Jerusalem* with ancient *Rome*, or any other city that could ever be classified as an *old Jerusalem*!

In Revelation, the Harlot City Babylon thinks herself to have a chosen special relationship, i.e. that of *wife* "I am no widow!" What other city in all the world might make the claim that she was, at least once, married to Jehovah? That can only refer to Old

Covenant Jerusalem. (*Like Father, Like Son, On Clouds of Glory*; p. 194; emphasis in original)

If *MYSTERY, BABYLON* is not apostate Israel, how can the blood of all the righteous be found in two different entities (Matt 23:34-36; Rev 18:24)? Returning briefly to the typology of Saul and David with the physical and spiritual Jerusalems, we observe that when Samuel anointed David as king *the Spirit of the Lord came upon him from that day forward*, while Saul was troubled by an evil spirit (1 Sam 16:13-14 NASB). Likewise, God anointed spiritual Jerusalem (the Church) on Pentecost, while physical Jerusalem (spiritual Babylon) became *a habitation of demons, a prison for every foul spirit* (Rev 18:2).

Consider also the fact that spiritual Jerusalem has physical Jerusalem as its antithesis: one is heavenly, the other earthly; one above, the other below; one free, the other in bondage. What, then, corresponds to the characteristic of spiritual Jerusalem being the Bride of Christ? Surely, it must be the harlot Babylon! Thus we see two female representatives in the spiritual and physical Jerusalems—the faithful Bride and the unfaithful bride. In light of the fact that the Bible is a revelation of God's redemptive plan, and that eschatology focuses on the "last days" of the Old Covenant and the transition to the New, we feel that physical Jerusalem—and only physical Jerusalem—qualifies as the harlot Babylon.

So once again, we see type and antitype in the first and last generations of national, physical Israel. The first generation saw the plagues sent upon Egypt because Pharaoh would not let God's people (His bride-to-be) go to Him. God is a jealous God. The last generation received the plagues because they had rejected the Bridegroom. God is a jealous God.

Pre- and Post-National Jews

Israel became a nation once again in 1948. This is one of the cornerstones of many Futurists' eschatology. Futurists believe now that Israel exists once again as a nation, the prophetic time clock, which was allegedly paused during their nonexistence, has once again restarted. The judgments and Christ's Second Coming discussed above can now take place. Everything that happened in AD 70 was just a "partial judgment," or perhaps a "type" of the final judgment, but it wasn't the real or final deal.

However, just because the world recognizes Israel as a nation, does that mean that God also recognizes them as such? Not necessarily. In fact, we believe that Scripture prohibits God from recognizing Israel as a covenant nation ever again! We have already seen that Israel was symbolically married to God (Jer 2:2, 3:14). We know that God judged the nation as a harlot, and that Israel did not attend the great wedding supper (Matt 22:1-13). As in the parable, God sent out armies against the Jews, the murderers were destroyed, and their city was burned. While the term "divorce" is not used concerning the final generation of Israel, it is implied by the fact that God the Son is presented with a bride (the Church) in Revelation (Rev 19:7-8; 21:2, 9). As stated previously, God had scriptural grounds to divorce national Israel:

> *"And I say to you, whoever divorces his wife, except for sexual immorality, and marries another, commits adultery; and whoever marries her who is divorced commits adultery."* (Matt 19:9)

Israel had been playing the harlot for centuries. Rejecting her Messiah, the Bridegroom, was the last straw. The kingdom (vineyard) was taken from her and given to another. Never do we see the kingdom (vineyard) returning to the original vinedressers. Who is the new bride?

> *For I have betrothed you to one husband, that I may present you as a chaste virgin to Christ.* (2 Cor 11:2b; cf. Eph 5:22-23)

The new bride is the Church! We stated above that God's own Word prohibits Him from recognizing the nation of Israel ever again as His special, chosen people. Why do we believe this? Because of what the author of Hebrews writes:

> *Seeing then that we have a great High Priest who has passed through the heavens, Jesus the Son of God . . . .* (Heb 4:14)

Jesus is our High Priest. As a High Priest, He can only marry a certain type of bride:

> *He who is the high priest among his brethren . . . shall take a wife in her virginity. A widow or a divorced woman or a defiled woman or a harlot—these he shall not marry; but he shall take a virgin of his own people as wife.* (Lev 21:10, 13-14)

National Israel certainly does not meet the qualifications. However, according to Paul, the Church does:

> *For I am jealous for you with godly jealousy. For I have betrothed you to one husband, that I may present you as a chaste virgin to Christ.* (2 Cor 11:2)

Lest we think that Israel could ever be "reconciled" *as a nation* to God, consider the following:

> *When a man takes a wife and marries her, and it happens that she finds no favor in his eyes because he has found some uncleanness in her, and he writes her a certificate of divorce, puts it in her hand, and sends her out of his house, when she has departed from his house, and goes and becomes another man's wife, if the latter husband detests her and writes her a certificate of divorce, puts it in her hand, and sends her out of his house, or if the latter husband dies who took her as his wife, **then her former husband who divorced her must not take her back to be his wife** after she has been defiled; for that is an abomination before the Lord . . . .* (Deut 24:1-4; emphasis added)

According to Scripture, Christ, as the fulfillment of the typology of the high priest, can never take the nation of Israel back to Himself as a special people. Furthermore, the Church is betrothed to God forever:

> *And it shall be, in that day,*
> *Says the LORD,*
> *That you will call Me "My Husband."*
> *I will betroth you to Me forever;*
> *Yes, I will betroth you to Me*
> *In righteousness and justice,*
> *In lovingkindness and mercy;*
> *I will betroth you to Me in faithfulness,*
> *And you shall know the LORD.*
> *Then I will say to those who were not My people,*
> *"You are My people!"*
> *And they shall say, "You are my God!"* (Hos 2:16, 19-20, 23)

It may be argued that the above teaches that God will indeed restore and remarry (betroth) Israel. This is true to a degree. At first, this passage appears to be speaking of physical, national Israel. However, Peter applies this to the Church, establishing definitively the Church as God's chosen people. Thus, the Church is the spiritual fulfillment of what national Israel typified originally:

> *Therefore, to you who believe, He is precious; but to those who are disobedient,*
> *The stone which the builders rejected*
> *Has become the chief cornerstone,*

And,
"A stone of stumbling
And a rock of offense."
They stumble, being disobedient to the word, to which they also
were appointed. But you are a chosen generation, a royal priest-
hood, a holy nation, His own special people . . . **who were once**
not a people but are now the people of God *. . . .* (1 Pet 2:7-9a,
10a; emphasis added)

The Church consists of individuals who are *new creations* (2 Cor
5:17), therefore Christ is not taking back a former wife. National Israel
was divorced, whereas spiritual Israel is betrothed forever. We believe
that these verses teach that God can never restore the physical nation of
Israel to "chosen people" status again. Does this mean that God prohibits
Jews from entering the kingdom? Absolutely not! Jews can enter on an
individual basis like everyone else, just not on a *national* basis. This was
discussed under the heading "Joshua and Caleb," and will be further developed in the chapter "All Israel Will Be Saved." All peoples make up the
Church. She is spiritual Israel and the spiritual seed of Abraham:

There is neither Jew nor Greek, there is neither slave nor free,
there is neither male nor female; for you are all one in Christ
Jesus. And if you are Christ's, then you are Abraham's seed, and
heirs according to the promise. (Gal 3:28-29)

Although the Romans destroyed the nation of Israel in AD 70, individual Jews did survive the war. They survive even to this day, dispersed
throughout the world; of course, as one might imagine, the bloodline must
be extremely diluted. Indeed, Bray writes:

The Encyclopedia Brittanica (1973), vol. 12, page 1054, actually
states: "The Jews As A Race: The findings of physical anthro-
pology show that, contrary to the popular view, there is no Jewish
race. Anthropometric measurements of Jewish groups in many
parts of the world indicate that they differ greatly from one another
with respect to all important physical characteristics." . . . Being a
Jew has nothing to do with race. Sammy Davis Jr. became a Jew.
Elizabeth Taylor became a Jew when she married Eddie Fisher. In
June of 1991 Tom Arnold and Roseanne Barr, the T.V. entertainer,
renewed publicly their wedding vows, and he was celebrating his
conversion to Judaism. . . . In Israel they have a peculiar law which
says what their government says is a Jew. I quote this from Funk
and Wagnall's New Encyclopedia, vol. 14, p. 214: "In 1970 the

Israeli Knesset adopted legislation defining a Jew as one born of a Jewish mother or convert." It matters not who the father is, nor to what race he belongs. And a convert can be from any race. So you see, we are not talking about a "race" of people when we talk about the Jewish people. (*Matthew 24 Fulfilled*, pp. 206-207)

This certainly raises questions regarding the connection, if any, between modern "Jews" and those of biblical times. While today there may not be any Jews in the biblical sense, there were Jews who survived the Roman war. Similarly, there were individual Jews before Israel became a nation. Abram was called a "Hebrew" (Gen 14:13) as were his offspring (Exod 2:11). Israelites were called Hebrews until that term was replaced by the term "Jews" in the postexilic period. Israel did not become a nation until God delivered unto them the Law, which told them how to be a nation:

Now the LORD had said to Abram . . . . I will make you a great nation." (Gen 12:1, 2)

Now therefore, if you will indeed obey My voice and keep My covenant, then you shall be a special treasure to Me above all people; for all the earth is Mine. And you shall be to Me a kingdom of priests and a holy nation. (Exod 19:5-6)

Once again we see the first and last generations of national Israel mirroring each other, in that there are individual Jews (Hebrews) on both sides of them — prenational Hebrews (Abraham to Moses) and postnational Jews (post-AD 70). Just as God had a chosen people (Abraham to Moses) before He coalesced them into a nation, He continues to have a chosen people (the Church) after Israel was dissolved as a nation.

What about all the speculation concerning the restored nation of Israel and her plans to rebuild the temple? Like the rebellious generation in Moses' day, they are trying to force their way in after the window of opportunity has passed. Others received what God offered to them originally. God took the kingdom from Saul and gave it to David, never to be returned to Saul. God took the vineyard (kingdom) from the original vinedressers and gave it to others, never to be returned. God extended the wedding banquet invitation to others, never to be reoffered to those who initially refused it. Preston makes the interesting observation that present-day Israel has been attacked numerous times on her feast days. Interestingly enough, this never happened while she remained in a faithful covenant relationship with God.

On Wednesday, 3-27-02, a suicide bomber walked into a hotel in Israel and killed himself, and over 20 Israelis. . . . In 1967 the Arab league, led by Egypt, attacked Israel on *Yom Kippur*, the *Day of Atonement*. This is one of Israel's most holy days. . . . Instead of proving that Israel remains as God's chosen people, the attack in 1967, and the recent attack on Passover [prove], indubitably, that Israel is not in covenant relationship with Jehovah! Read Exodus 34:23f: "Three times in the year all your men shall appear before the Lord, the Lord God of Israel. For I will cast out the nations before you and enlarge your borders; nether will any man covet your land when you go up to appear before the Lord your God three times in the year." The promise here is simple and profound. As long as Israel was in covenant relationship with Jehovah, her enemies would not attack her during the holy feast days. (*Like Father, Like Son, On Clouds of Glory*, pp. 121-122)

Again, we wish to note that we view this position as "fulfilled theology" rather than "replacement theology." We do not believe that Israel was "wiped off the table" and that God started over with the New Covenant. Rather, just as a butterfly cannot come into existence without the caterpillar metamorphosing, so the New Covenant could not come into being apart from the Old. Was the caterpillar "replaced"? No, it became the butterfly. Likewise, the Old Covenant had always pointed to the New; that was always God's ultimate goal. When the New Covenant emerged from the Old, what remained physically was just a cocoon, that which had effected the transformation. The old system of types and shadows, like the cocoon, was no longer needed.

Conclusion

Now all these things happened to them as examples [types], and they were written for our admonition, upon whom the ends of the ages have come. (1 Cor 10:11)

For whose admonition were these things written? The New Testament generation to whom Paul was writing! This is not to say that other generations cannot profit from the examples as well; but is it going too far to suggest that Paul is actually saying that Exodus and Numbers were written for his generation? Just as John wrote to his readers, "*but these have been written that you may believe that Jesus is the Christ, the Son of God; and that believing you may have life in His name*" (John 20:31 NASB), so

Paul is saying *"these things were written . . ."* to admonish *his* generation. Consider Fairbairn's thoughts:

> A relation so formed, and subsisting to any extent between Old and New Testament things, evidently presupposes and implies two important *facts*. It implies, first, that the realities of the Gospel, which constitute the antitypes, are the ultimate objects which were contemplated by the mind of God, when planning the economy of His successive dispensations. And it implies, secondly, that to prepare the way for the introduction of these ultimate objects, He placed the Church under a course of training, which included instruction by types, or designed and fitting resemblances of what was to come. (*The Typology of Scripture*, p. 47, vol. 1)

Why did Paul feel the need to admonish his generation? Because the end of the ages had come upon them. What did that mean to them? According to the book of Hebrews, they were about to enter God's rest. They could see *the Day* approaching. How many of these things served as examples? ALL OF THEM! It appears that all these things happened by divine appointment to provide an example to the final generation of national Israel and the first generation of spiritual Israel. Even though there were many lessons to be learned from the Israelites' two-year journey toward Canaan, we believe that the emphasis here is on the fact that they did *not* enter, as well as the details surrounding that fact. Paul's generation was on the brink of becoming the spiritual antitype (fulfillment) of the natural type. Again, from Hebrews:

> And all these, having obtained a good testimony through faith, did not receive the promise, God having something better for us, that they should not be made perfect apart from us. (11:39-40)

Who are "all these"? The heroes of the faith described in Hebrews 11. What promise did they not receive? The final rest of which the author has been speaking. Who is the "us" in this passage? Not you and me! It is the generation to whom the epistle of Hebrews was written.

Paul could have used other wicked generations in Scripture as examples to warn against rejecting God, e.g., Noah's generation, Sodom and Gomorrah, etc. Why not use these examples? After all, Christ did (Matt 24:37-39; Luke 17:28-30)! First, although wicked, they were not *adulterous*. Second, those other generations lacked the detail and would only apply in a general sense, whereas *all* the details of the Exodus generation—including the timing—were types of the New Testament generation.

The first and last generations fit each other detail for detail, mirror reflections of one another. Together they form a set of matched bookends. Look at one and you can see the image of the other. To put a twist on a familiar passage, *"the first shall be last, and the last shall be first."*

Nevertheless, the details *only* mirror each other from the framework of Preterist eschatology, especially in their timing. To apply these details to a Futurist perspective, one would have to distort the reflection, as in a carnival mirror. As we stated at the outset, typology does not establish doctrine. Yet, can it tip the scale of indecision? It is most certainly an interesting question that we hope serves as food for thought. Only you, the reader, can decide that.

The underlying theme of this chapter is that the typology of the first generation of national Israel fits perfectly the last generation of national Israel (and, by implication, the first generation of spiritual Israel), but *only* if one is willing to accept the Preterist viewpoint that Christ did indeed come in AD 70, although not in a physical sense, as is usually taught. Scripture supports a nonphysical coming of the Lord, as we studied previously in the chapter "Coming in the Clouds." Preterists believe that Scripture maintains nonphysical as the *rule* concerning the Lord's coming in judgment, whereas a physical coming would be the *exception*. Indeed, many may gladly receive the details of this typological study demonstrating the Old Testament Exodus generation was a prophetic type of the New Testament "last days" generation, with the exception of one item: the return of Christ in *that* generation.

Because of this exception, we feel that this last point is the crown jewel of this chapter:

> *So I have come down to deliver them out of the hand of the Egyptian, and to bring them up from that land to a good and large land, to a land flowing with milk and honey . . . .* (Exod 3:8)

This is God speaking to Moses at the burning bush. He is going to deliver the Israelites out of Egypt, and bring them into Canaan. More importantly, here we have, presented at face value, Scripture that says, *"The Lord came down."* It was not physical, although much happened in the physical realm as evidence of His coming down. This is exactly what Full Preterists believe happened in AD 70. Christ returned, delivered His saints, and judged His enemies. At the risk of being repetitive, we must say that in this framework—and *only* in this framework—all of the details of our study harmonize perfectly. How can we believe the Scriptures when they tell us that the Lord came down in deliverance/judgment in the first generation, and yet refuse to believe them when they tell us that He would do the very same to the last (His) generation, especially when we see virtually identical events taking place?

Some may argue that God only came down to the burning bush as a *physical* apparition, and from there He worked through Moses (and Joshua) to accomplish the rest. This is precisely what happened in AD 70. According to Josephus, there *were* physical apparitions in the sky (chariots of fire, bright lights in the middle of the night, etc.) and God worked through the Roman armies to accomplish the rest.

God, according to Scripture, did come down in the first generation of national Israel, and He promised to do the same in the last generation. Scripture records for us the deliverance of God's people and the judgment of His enemies through a nonphysical coming in Exodus. There is no denying it. Why should we expect any different type of coming to accomplish the very same things in the last generation? *If we are willing to receive it* by removing the veil, we see the Exodus generation typifies the New Testament generation detail for detail. If we are *not* willing to receive it, how do we explain away all of those details? *Perhaps in the same way that the Jews explain away all the details of the coming Messiah that Christ fulfilled in His first coming.* Is it possible that Christianity, in general, is doing the same thing to Christ's Second Coming that the Jews did to His first?

There is a saying that goes something like this: *God said it, I believe it, that settles it!* Someone has taken it a step further and said, *God said it, and whether I believe it or not, that settles it!* To this, we give a hearty "Amen." Jesus said that He would return to *that* (His) generation, and *that* generation would see *all these things.* The Holy Spirit taught the New Testament Church about the *things to come.* Every inspired writer in the New Testament described the Second Coming as *near, at hand, soon,* etc. To explain away these statements and apply them to an event millennia away is to call into question the very inspiration of the New Testament. King states:

> Any interpretation, therefore, that removes the coming of Christ as taught in the gospels, the epistles, and Revelation from the time and events of that generation, **unwittingly denies the inspiration of God's word**, and builds a false concept of God's eternal purpose with respect to the end-time. (*The Spirit of Prophecy,* p. 262; emphasis added)

We have demonstrated the scriptural precedent for apocalyptic language—including cloud-comings—and for audience relevance. Undeniably, *God has said it!* Therefore, as unpalatable as some of the implications may seem at first, we believe *that settles it!* Now the only question is, *do we believe it?* Are we willing to receive it? Will we be persuaded by the voice of the majority, which flirts with calling Jesus and the New Testament authors mistaken or ignorant, or will we say with Paul, *"Let God be true but every man a liar"* (Rom 3:4)? Even R. C. Sproul recognizes that "what is at stake here is the authority of Jesus, and **we must be consumed with maintaining his authority**." (*The Last Days according to Jesus*, p. 158; emphasis added)

Summary to Part II

—ᛞ—

Having laid the foundation of the nature of the New Covenant in Part I, we have built our eschatological framework upon it in Part II. The framework that fits that foundation most naturally and harmoniously is the eschatological position of Full Preterism. Admittedly, much of this framework is foreign to what we may have understood previously regarding the events and nature of the Second Coming of Christ. Though foreign, we believe that none of it is forced to fit, but rather falls into place naturally when we allow Scripture to interpret Scripture and follow the precedents set forth therein. This, we feel, cannot be said of a Futurist eschatological framework. Although we may have rearranged completely the pieces of the reader's eschatological puzzle, we believe that they now fit fully in place, revealing the picture that was meant by our Lord and the Bible's inspired authors concerning the "last days." Any other arrangement of the pieces is due to man's forcing them into place to display the picture *he* desires to see. This has been the theme of this section, and we summarize it as follows:

1. The New Testament is replete with statements indicating that the return of Christ—the Day of the Lord—would occur within the lifetime of the New Testament generation (see the Appendix for 101 references). Those who believe that He did not return in that generation must resort to numerous devices to "explain" the multitude of imminency passages:

    a. Wordplay is used on several fronts. The events of Revelation, which the author declared would "shortly come to pass," are not seen as happening soon, but speedily. Every possible nuance of the Greek is employed to show that "this generation" is *not* the generation being addressed. Because of the pervasive New Testament teaching of an imminent return of Christ, even the word *imminent* (which is not found in the New Testament) is redefined, so that it does not mean "about to happen," but "certain to happen," without any intervening events necessary to be fulfilled first.

b.   Jesus is said to jump back and forth between His contemporary generation and some future generation in His descriptions of the last days and the coming of the Son of Man—all with no indication to His listeners that He is traversing millennia in His discourse.

c.   Time statements are so distorted by multiplying factors (a day is as a thousand years) and gaps that one wonders what purpose they serve at all. Instead of being cornerstones that determine the nature and scope of their respective prophecies, they end up as inconvenient details that must be twisted around preconceived scenarios.

d.   Because Jesus said that some of His disciples would live to see Him coming in the glory of His Father with His angels in His kingdom (Matt 16:27-28), we are told that they witnessed it on the Mount of Transfiguration, or at His resurrection, or on the Day of Pentecost.

All of these devices, and several others, are forcing alternate meanings upon the time statements. But why grasp at every possible remedy to explain away the time statements, when ONE explanation accounts for every last one of them—Christ returned when He said He would, and as the New Testament authors taught that He would, in that very generation?! Note also that, while Christ introduced the "spiritual" nature of fulfillment of the second coming of Elijah with the qualifier "if you are willing to receive it," nowhere in the New Testament do we read "if you are willing to receive it" as a qualifier of a time statement.

2.   Revelation has obvious parallels to Christ's Olivet Discourse, which was given to His generation to forewarn of the judgment that would soon come upon them. During the Olivet Discourse, Christ connected the events He described with Daniel's Seventy Weeks. Concerning the dating of Revelation, if we allow for an early authorship, then we see Revelation falling into step with Christ's Olivet Discourse and Daniel's Seventy Weeks as judgment upon *that* generation. If, however, we move the date of Revelation past AD 70, then the generation of Matthew 24 and Daniel's Seventy Weeks are disjointed. Matthew's "this generation" can no longer mean "this generation," and Daniel's Seventy Weeks can no longer be consecutive. However, if we heed Gentry's warning, and do not let the voice of man (i.e., the early church fathers' *external* evidence for a late date) quiet the voice of

God (i.e., Revelation's *internal* evidence for an early date), then Revelation fits the imminent judgment taught throughout the New Testament, and Matthew 24 and Daniel's Seventy Weeks are not distorted. That notwithstanding, Gentry has soundly "quieted" the voice of man in this matter and quite capably demonstrated the early date for Revelation from all sides.

3. Because of unfortunate translation errors the Bible has been perceived as describing the end of the world and judgments of global proportions. Equally unfortunate is the fact that, after modern translations have helped to rectify this, many continue trying to force the rest of eschatology into these same previously held misconceptions. The Bible does not speak of the end of the *world*, but rather the end of the *age*. The arena in which this took place was not the entire earth, but the land of Judea. Christ did not pronounce woes upon Caesar and the Romans, nor the Greeks, but rather upon the scribes, Pharisees, and apostate Jews of His generation. It was the nation of Israel—who killed the prophets and, eventually, the Son of God—upon whom judgment was impending, not the entire human race. The "last days" were the last days of the Old Covenant, the end of the Mosaic age. They were the transition period between the covenants, the days that ALL the prophets had foretold (Acts 3:24).

4. The apocalyptic language of the Jews is highly symbolic and hyperbolic. This is demonstrated by numerous passages from the Old Testament, where typical battle scenes and judgments, which were historically fulfilled, were described by songs of praise that speak in earth-shaking, heaven-moving terms. This type of Old Testament language is understood for what it is and taken in stride. Yet when the same language is employed by Jesus and John, the unwarranted popular precedent is to force literal interpretations upon the text. The fact that the Old Testament precedent of apocalyptic language carries through to the New Testament is witnessed by the geography of Judea: The literal (physical) valleys, hills, and crooked places were not transformed during the ministry of John the Baptist, who also was not the literal (physical) Elijah. Jesus and John were Jews, and their listeners and readers were either Jewish or heavily influenced by the Jewish culture. Therefore their use of apocalyptic language would not be foreign to their audiences, but instead would be expected, especially considering the gravity of the events which they were describing. What *would* be foreign to their audience would be the idea that this language,

without so much as a hint to them, was to now be understood in a literal manner, breaking all scriptural precedent with which the audience would be familiar. On the other hand, the natural fit is that this language maintains the symbolic and hyperbolic nature it did in the Old Testament. Thus, in both testaments, it is used to describe God's judgment, the fall of a nation, and the transference of kingdoms.

5. In addition to breaking the Old Testament precedent for apocalyptic language, many also break the Old Testament precedent for "comings of the Lord"—specifically, coming with the clouds in judgment. Once again, we take in stride the many instances in the Old Testament where God is said to have "come down" and been seen in the "clouds of judgment." Yet when the New Testament says that "He is coming with clouds" (Rev 1:7); that we shall meet Him "in the clouds" (1 Thess 4:17); that when He ascended He was received by a cloud and would return in like manner (Acts 1:9, 11); the action of many is to completely ignore the cloud association and focus solely on the fact that He was visibly seen as He ascended, therefore asserting He will be visibly seen when He returns. Yet there can be no denying that one of the major aspects of His return was judgment upon His enemies, just as in the Old Testament cloud comings of the Lord, which are not understood as being physical "comings." Again, we do not deny the possibility that Christ was visibly manifested to certain of His enemies during that judgment period; but when the misconception of a physical kingdom of God is removed (the focus of Part I), then the only text which lends itself to a physical return of Christ is that of Acts 1. When taken together with other New Testament passages, we feel Acts 1 is speaking of His return *in the clouds*, as opposed to visibly. We must emphasize again that by holding this view we are by no means denying the bodily resurrection of Christ.

6. Many develop elaborate schemes of double fulfillment in order to maintain an eschatology that acknowledges the relationship of the destruction of Jerusalem to prophecy, and yet holds out for a future ultimate fulfillment of these same prophecies. However, if we can say that the land of Palestine is still promised to the Jews, that there are "last days" yet to be experienced, and that *"all things which are written"* are yet to be ultimately fulfilled—in spite of Scripture that clearly states that all of these things are historically fulfilled—then it may be reasonable for us to expect another incarnation, crucifixion, and resurrection, in spite of the

Scriptures that clearly state that those events also are historically fulfilled. There is just as much right for one as for the other. To those who say that the events of AD 70 were merely typological of future fulfillments, we would say that if Christ were to appear again in our future, there would undoubtedly be aspects of that appearance which would not meet the expectations of some. They would claim that it was merely a typological or partial fulfillment and continue waiting for what they want to see. Instead of looking for fulfillments that fit our expectations, perhaps we should fit our expectations to the fulfillments taught in the Scriptures. Modern Jews who fit their expectations to the Scriptures and acknowledge Christ as the promised Messiah are called Messianic Jews (or more accurately, Christians, for in Christ there is neither Jew nor Gentile). Jews who are still looking for fulfillments that fit their expectations are still waiting for the Messiah.

7. Many in Christendom are unfamiliar with the events of the destruction of Jerusalem and the historical, theological, and national significance of those events. This has led to the perception that the destruction of Jerusalem and the end of the Old Covenant do not rise to the grand scale of the prophecies of Jesus and John. As we have shown, it was not just the destruction of a city; it was the end of an economy, the end of a nation in the eyes of God, and judgment upon those who killed the very Son of God. Josephus' records reveal that the events accompanying the destruction of Jerusalem were of a far grander scale than most have realized. These facts, along with the symbolism of apocalyptic language, bring a harmonious balance between the prophecies and the events.

8. Lastly, this framework of eschatology is confirmed to us by the typology of "the veiled generation." Paul, by divine inspiration, reveals that the Exodus generation was a "type" of his generation, prepared beforehand as an illustration for them. The many details of this type quite obviously fit Paul's generation best if we view them from the framework of Preterist eschatology.

We remind the reader that the Old Testament prophecies, such as Ezekiel's temple and Isaiah's New Heavens and Earth, which the Church teaches as being yet in our future, were claimed by the inspired authors of the New Testament to be for *their* generation (Acts 3:24; Rom 15:4; Heb 11:39-40; 1 Pet 1:10-12; Matt 11:13; Luke 21:22).

Though all the pieces of the eschatological puzzle fit perfectly and naturally within the framework presented in this section, we are sympathetic with the reader in realizing they may be quite foreign to one's own beliefs. But we must ask ourselves, which do we prefer: a framework that fits naturally in our own beliefs, but is foreign to the teaching of Scripture; or one which is foreign to our beliefs, but fits naturally with what Scripture teaches? If we rely on feelings, then we will be in the same position as the Jews who didn't "feel" that Christ was the Messiah.

In light of all of this, one wonders what God must think about the millions of dollars Christians send to Israel in an effort to reestablish the *ministry of death*—that obsolete covenant which He Himself brought to an end. One needs only to enter a phrase such as "Christian support of Israel" in an Internet search engine to see the many ministries involved in this effort. After *"it pleased Him to crush His only begotten Son, putting Him to grief by rendering Him as a guilt offering"* (Isa 53:10 NASB), do we think that we honor Him by supporting the reestablishment of those sacrifices which He replaced when *"He offered Himself once for all"* (Heb 7:27)? Furthermore, the author of Hebrews states, *"For here we have no continuing city, but we seek the one to come"* (Heb 13:14). This same author makes clear that the "city" to come is not a physical city, that is, a rebuilt Jerusalem:

> *For he [Abraham] waited for the city which has foundations, whose builder and maker is God. . . . But now they desire a better, that is, a heavenly country. Therefore God is not ashamed to be called their God, for He has prepared a city for them.* (Heb 11:10, 16)

While Old Testament passages may be wrested from their context to support a future temple and kingdom, the inspired authors of the New Testament gave not so much as a hint that this was how those passages were to be interpreted, nor did they contain any such hint in their own writings.

In the opening paragraph of this section, we proposed that while Christianity recognizes the "speck" in the eye of the Jews, in that the Jews failed to recognize Christ in His first coming, Christianity may very well have a "speck" in its own eye regarding the Second Coming. We close this section with a quote from King:

> But what is the reaction of people today when told that Christ came the second time in the end of the Jewish age? It is the same as that of a Jew when told Christ came the first time. He doesn't believe it, even though he knows that time-wise that was when the

Messiah was to come. But why doesn't he believe Christ came then? Simply because Christ was not in person, purpose, and work what the Jews thought he should be; therefore, they are still waiting for one to come who will fulfill their **earthly desires and concepts**.

Any careful and thoughtful student of God's Word can readily see that the church was taught to look for the Second Coming of Christ in that same generation of his first coming. Time-wise, we know his Second Coming was then at hand (James 5:8). But many do not believe that he came then. Why? Because that Second Coming of Christ was not in manner, purpose, and result what they think it should be, therefore they are waiting for a Second Coming that will meet **their demands and fulfill their expectations**. (*The Spirit of Prophecy*, p. 101; emphasis added)

We must follow wherever the argument leads.

Socrates

Part III

Beyond the Veil

When you have eliminated the impossible, whatever remains, however improbable, must be the truth.

Sherlock Holmes

Completing the Structure

—ɯ—

U sing the analogy of a house, we laid the foundation in Part I, and erected the framework in Part II. What remains is to apply the finishing exterior to the structure. While a tract of homes may have many houses with the same floor plan, it is the different exterior styles and colors that individualize them. In a similar manner, most Preterists hold to the foundation and framework presented thus far. It is in how they apply various doctrines to this framework, such as the final resurrection, the rapture of the Church, the ministry of the Holy Spirit, etc., that their individuality is expressed.

Even though there may be several options available for the same floor plan in a tract of homes, some particular options may be so to the disliking of prospective buyers, that they turn away before learning that other options are available. They certainly have no inclination as to the soundness of the foundation and framework of the homes, having not even left the car to take a closer look. The same holds true for Preterism. Some of the positions held by various Preterists strike the newcomer so negatively that they never take the time to consider the soundness of the foundation and framework upon which they are built. It is for this reason we have structured our study in the manner we have. It is hoped that the reader has recognized the soundness of the foundation upon which Preterism is built and was therefore willing to at least examine the framework. However, we are careful to acknowledge that although much of Preterism's framework may be foreign to our beliefs, we must not dismiss "exterior applications" solely because they are foreign to our beliefs or strike us negatively.

While we all desire to live in homes with sound foundations and frameworks, we are most keenly aware of the finishing touches. After all, that is where we live—not in the house that has exceptional framing or a less than perfect foundation, but in that home with the beautiful brick siding, or that one with the ugly shade of purple. The finishing touches either catch our eye or turn it. Similarly, in eschatology, there are certain doctrines that are "finishing touches," which either catch our eye or turn it. When Preterists tell others that their belief that Christ returned in AD 70 is based upon imminency passages, apocalyptic language, cloud comings, etc., these "foundational" items are quickly glossed over in favor of discussing the "finishing touches"—"so you mean we're in the new heavens and new earth now? What happened to the rapture of the Church? This is the kingdom of God? What about the resurrection of the dead, and the judgment throne of God?"

Certainly these are important questions; but if the foundation of Preterism is sound, we hope that the reader is willing to exercise patience in considering the various "finishing touches," as well as the discipline necessary to remove previous biases. In this last section of our study, our intent is not so much to finish the structure, but to present the reader with some of the "options" available. Our reasons are threefold: (1) to leave off from our study now without the mention of some of these implications, we feel, would leave the reader hanging; (2) to do justice to these topics would require another book, and; (3) though we may favor some options over others, our own studies in these matters are ongoing, thus we hesitate to say too much.

It is our hope that as acceptance of the doctrine of Preterism grows and more scholarship comes to the field, those with more qualified minds (at least more qualified than this writer) will take up the torch and help illuminate these areas.

The Millennium

—ɯ—

In the chapter "The Dating of Revelation," we mentioned that eschatological views regarding the date of Revelation are not necessarily tied to a specific view on the Millennium. However, since the topic of the Millennium is so integral to one's eschatological position, we feel it should not be left unmentioned. Because the topic of the Millennium is so enigmatic, in no way do we claim to have the last word or even a definite position. We merely provide the reader with some points to consider that call into question some popular concepts regarding the Millennium, while presenting plausible possibilities for it to fit within the framework of Preterism.

Before exploring possibilities of what the Millennium is, we must establish what it is *not*. Crucial to this process is recognizing that Revelation 20 is the *only* chapter in the Bible in which the Millennium is mentioned. Reminding the reader of the apocalyptic and highly symbolic language of Revelation, we provide the full text of chapter 20 below:

> *Then I saw an angel coming down from heaven, having the key to the bottomless pit and a great chain in his hand. He laid hold of the dragon, that serpent of old, who is the Devil and Satan, and bound him for a thousand years; and he cast him into the bottomless pit, and shut him up, and set a seal on him, so that he should deceive the nations no more till the thousand years were finished. But after these things he must be released for a little while. And I saw thrones, and they sat on them, and judgment was committed to them. Then I saw the souls of those who had been beheaded for their witness to Jesus and for the word of God, who had not worshiped the beast or his image, and had not received his mark on their foreheads or on their hands. And they lived and reigned with Christ for a thousand years. But the rest of the dead did not live again until the thousand years were finished. This is the first resurrection. Blessed and holy is he who has part in the first resurrection. Over such the second death has no power, but they shall be priests of God and of Christ, and shall reign with Him a thousand years. Now when the thousand years have expired, Satan*

*will be released from his prison and will go out to deceive the
nations which are in the four corners of the earth [land], Gog
and Magog, to gather them together to battle, whose number is
as the sand of the sea. They went up on the breadth of the earth
[land] and surrounded the camp of the saints and the beloved city.
And fire came down from God out of heaven and devoured them.
The devil, who deceived them, was cast into the lake of fire and
brimstone where the beast and the false prophet are. And they will
be tormented day and night forever and ever. Then I saw a great
white throne and Him who sat on it, from whose face the earth and
the heaven fled away. And there was found no place for them. And
I saw the dead, small and great, standing before God, and books
were opened. And another book was opened, which is the Book of
Life. And the dead were judged according to their works, by the
things which were written in the books. The sea gave up the dead
who were in it, and Death and Hades delivered up the dead who
were in them. And they were judged, each one according to his
works. Then Death and Hades were cast into the lake of fire. This
is the second death. And anyone not found written in the Book of
Life was cast into the lake of fire.*

Notice that there is no mention of the "*wolf dwelling with the lamb,
the lion eating straw like the ox,*" and "*a little child leading them*" (Isa 11
& 65). Nor does it say "*no more shall an infant from there live but a few
days,*" or that "*they shall build houses and inhabit them, they shall plant
vineyards and eat their fruit*" (Isa 65). These are just a few of the conditions that are popularly assigned to the Millennial reign of Christ. But by
what scriptural precedent? Yes, Isaiah 65 speaks of new heavens and a new
earth (v. 17), but as we have previously seen, this speaks prophetically of
the New Covenant. The old heavens and earth were the universe, the spiritual "world" of the Judaic Old Covenant. The Isaiah passage continues:

*But be glad and rejoice forever in what I create;
For behold, I create Jerusalem as a rejoicing,
And her people a joy.
I will rejoice in Jerusalem,
And joy in My people;
The voice of weeping shall no longer be heard in her,
Nor the voice of crying.* (Isa 65:18-19)

Jesus prophesied the destruction of physical Jerusalem, but never its
rebuilding. In Galatians 4, Paul equates physical Jerusalem with Hagar,

who was to be "cast out." We have established the spiritual nature of the New Covenant in Part I and demonstrated that the New Testament authors, after Pentecost, never allude to a future physical kingdom or temple. On the other hand, Paul says in Galatians 4 that the saints of the New Covenant belong to the Jerusalem which is above. The author of Hebrews says that the saints have come to the *heavenly Jerusalem* (Heb 12:22). Therefore, the Jerusalem of Isaiah 65 (and parallel passages) is not a rebuilt physical city existing in the future.

After describing the Millennial period in Revelation 20, in the next chapter John is shown the Lamb's wife, "*the holy Jerusalem descending out of heaven*" (v. 10). Those who have not removed the veil of Moses are still looking for physical fulfillments of these and similar passages where God speaks of establishing Israel and building Jerusalem. The New Testament authors never speak of any age after that of the New Covenant; rather, they state that the New Covenant is *everlasting*. As King points out from Paul's typology of Ishmael, Isaac, and the two covenants, Abraham did not have a third son. (We have previously noted, according to Genesis 25:1, that Abraham actually did have a third son, by his second wife Keturah. However, if there was to be an age after the present Christian age of the New Covenant, what better opportunity for Paul to work that into his analogy of mothers, sons, and covenants? Here is a third son, by a third mother, and yet Paul emphasizes only two.) Because there is no scriptural evidence for an age beyond the Gospel age, the only place to find a yet future physical fulfillment is in the Millennial reign of Christ. Mauro's comment regarding this is worth repeating:

> This view [that Ezekiel's temple relates to Millennial times] is characteristic of that peculiar system of interpreting the Scriptures [dispensationalism] which we are examining in the present volume; for, according to the principles thereof, all difficulties in the prophetic Word, and all problems of like nature are solved by the simple expedient of postponing their fulfillment to the Millennial age. Thus the Millennium becomes the convenient and promiscuous dumping place of all portions of Scripture which offer any difficulty; and the unhappy consequence is that many prophecies which were fulfilled at the first coming of Christ, or are being fulfilled in this age of the gospel, and many Scriptures, such as the Sermon on the Mount, which apply directly to the saints of this dispensation, are wrenched out of their proper place, and are relegated to a distant future, much to the loss of the people of God and to the dislocation of the Scriptures as a whole.

The "postponement" system doubtless owes the popularity it enjoys to the circumstance that its method is both safe and easy. It is *safe* because, when a fulfillment of prophecy is relegated to the Millennium, it cannot be conclusively refuted until the time comes. All date-setting schemes owe their measure of popularity to the same fact. It is *easy* because it relieves the Bible student of the trouble of searching for the meaning and application of difficult passages. (*The Hope of Israel: What Is It?*, pp. 114-115; emphasis in original)

According to Mauro, many prophecies that are being fulfilled in this age of the gospel are wrenched out of their proper place. That these and other passages might refer to the gospel of the New Covenant is not new, nor is this suggestion merely a device used to "fit" them into this framework. We looked previously at Matthew Henry's commentary on Isaiah 65:17-25 concerning the new heavens and new earth. Consider his commentary on a similar passage from Isaiah 11:6-9:

> *"The wolf also shall dwell with the lamb,*
> *The leopard shall lie down with the young goat,*
> *The calf and the young lion and the fatling together;*
> *And a little child shall lead them.*
> *The cow and the bear shall graze;*
> *Their young ones shall lie down together;*
> *And the lion shall eat straw like the ox.*
> *The nursing child shall play by the cobra's hole,*
> *And the weaned child shall put his hand in the viper's den.*
> *They shall not hurt nor destroy in all My holy mountain,*
> *For the earth shall be full of the knowledge of the LORD*
> *As the waters cover the sea."* (Isa 11:6-9)

Unity or concord, which is intimated in these figurative promises, that even *the wolf shall dwell peaceably* with *the lamb*; men of the most fierce and furious dispositions, who used to bite and devour all about them, shall have their temper so strangely altered by the efficacy of the gospel and grace of Christ that they shall live in love even with the weakest and such as formerly they would have made an easy prey of. So far shall the sheep be from hurting one another, as sometimes they have done (Ezek 34:20-21), that even the wolves shall agree with them. Christ, who is our peace, came to slay all enmities and to settle lasting friendships among his followers, particularly between Jews and Gentiles: when multitudes of both, being converted to the faith of Christ, united in one sheep-fold, then the wolf and the lamb dwelt together; the wolf did not so much as threaten the lamb, nor was the lamb afraid of the wolf. *The leopard shall not* only not tear the kid, but shall *lie down with her*: even *their young ones shall lie down together*, and shall be trained up in a blessed amity, in order to the perpetuating of it. *The lion* shall cease to be ravenous and *shall eat straw like the ox*, as some think all the beasts of prey did before the fall. *The asp* and *the cockatrice* shall cease to be venomous, so that parents shall let their children *play* with them and *put their hands* among them. A generation of vipers shall become a seed of saints, and the old complaint of *homo homini lupus—man is a wolf to man*, shall be at an end. Those that inhabit the holy mountain shall live as amicably as the creatures did that were with Noah in the ark, and it shall be a means of their preservation, for *they shall not hurt nor destroy* one another as they have done. . . . **This is fulfilled in the wonderful effect of the gospel upon the minds of those that sincerely embrace it**; it changes the nature, and makes those that trampled on the meek of the earth, not only meek like them, but affectionate towards them. When Paul, who had persecuted the saints, joined himself to them, then the *wolf dwelt with the lamb*. (bold emphasis added)

Here Henry sees the wolves and lambs not as the literal animals, but as metaphors for men of different natures. We note that Jesus made a similar comparison:

Beware of false prophets, who come to you in sheep's clothing, but inwardly they are ravenous wolves. (Matt 7:15; cf. Zeph 3:3)

Behold, I send you out as sheep in the midst of wolves. Therefore be wise as serpents and harmless as doves. (Matt 10:16)

Can there be a clearer illustration of this than the conversion of Paul? As a "Pharisee of Pharisees" he ravaged the lambs of God. After his conversion, however, this former "wolf" did indeed lay down with the lambs, as it was said, "He who formerly persecuted us now preaches the faith he once tried to destroy" (Gal 1:23). The Church even enjoyed a period of peace when this "wolf" lay down with the "lambs" (Acts 9:31). Consider also that both Jesus and John the Baptist called the Pharisees a "brood of vipers" (Matt 12:34; 3:7). Mauro provides further insight as to the nature of the Millennium:

In the interpretation of the above passage [Rev 20], the principal question to be decided is: *in what realm* do the described events take place? Are they in the realm of *the natural*, or in that of the *spiritual*? They who locate them in the realm of the natural, in other words who make them a part of this earth's history, must of necessity postpone them to a future era, regardless of whether they place Christ's Second Coming before the Millennium or after; for certainly no such events as are here described have as yet transpired on earth. But, for those who locate the scenes and events of the Millennium in the realm of the unseen things, there is no such necessity. According to their understanding of the passage those scenes and events may be already past, or they may be going on now. (*The Hope of Israel: What Is It?*, p. 242)

Applying this idea [that there is an unseen spiritual dimension coexisting with the visible physical dimension] to the case of a prophecy whereof we know of no fulfillment, it is evident that we may do with it either of two things: (1) we may locate the fulfillment in another realm of space, or (2) we may locate it in another era of time. And specifically, we may either (1) assume its fulfillment to be in this realm of the natural and visible at a *future era of time*, or we may (2) assume its fulfillment to be at this present time (or in a time already past) in *another region of space*. The first of these alternatives is that which is usually chosen; the reason being that it is far easier for us to conceive of a future era of time where the same state of things with which we are familiar is still going on, than to conceive of a realm co-existent with this where a state of things of a spiritual kind subsists. Yet the latter explanation is obviously as satisfactory and sufficient as the former. And what we claim for it is that it has solid support in the Scripture; whereas the postponement of the prophecies concerning Israel, Zion and Jerusalem to a yet future era is contrary to clear statements of the word of God. (*The Hope of Israel: What Is It?*, p. 244; emphasis in original)

In regard to the view that a future Millennium is the seventh and final day in the "week" of world history, corresponding to the seven days of creation, Mauro quotes Dr. T. P. Stafford:

Dr. Stafford points out (and it is important to take note of this) that the author of Revelation did not adopt or share in any degree whatever, the then current Jewish expectation of a millennium of

Jewish ascendency over the Gentiles, and of world-wide peace and plenty. And he quotes Adam Smith's *Life and Letters of St. Paul* to the effect that the early Christian imagination proceeded upon the Jewish notion that the history of the world was to last for six ages, corresponding to the six days of Creation. And that "just as the six days of creation were succeeded by a day of rest, so the six ages will be followed by the Millennium, a thousand years of peace. By and by the idea arose that each of the past ages had lasted a thousand years; and hence it was reckoned that the year 1000 A. D., would terminate the current age and witness the Lord's Advent and the final Judgment."

As to this Dr. Stafford comments as follows:

"That there was a Jewish expectation of a millennium of some kind, and that it has had some influence upon Christian eschatology, is freely admitted. But that this Jewish notion is found in the New Testament is denied. This false idea, like many other false ideas, has come into Christian thought from Judaism, but does not belong there."

In proof of this Dr. Stafford points out that our Lord Himself was a martyr to His outspoken "nonconformity to Jewish notions," and to the fact that He was a complete contradiction to their ideas of the Messiah; "that Paul's life-long fight was against Jewish notions;" and that he "saved Christianity from the ruin which the Jewish party in the first churches would have brought upon it." And rightly he says: **"The idea of a civil government on earth for a thousand years is not found in a single utterance of Jesus, Paul or Peter; much less that Christ is going to 'set it up' when He returns."**
(Ibid., pp. 245-246; emphasis added)

As one can see, we must erase from the "blackboard" of our minds the misconceptions regarding the Millennium, before we can begin to formulate its possible fulfillments. We summarize this "erasing of the blackboard" as follows:

- Revelation 20 is the *only* chapter in the Bible that contains descriptions of the Millennium. All other descriptions are added as a result of individual interpretation and/or eisegesis
- The New Testament authors *never* speak of any age to come other than that of the Gospel age, which is declared to be everlasting

- Details other than those found in Revelation 20 which are assigned to the Millennium (e.g. Isa 11, 65) are the result of a desire for a "physical" fulfillment of passages which pertain to the New Covenant
- These other passages have been understood by others (e.g., Barnes, Henry) as pertaining to the Gospel age

Having addressed what the Millennium is *not*, we return to Revelation 20 to see what it is:

- The binding of Satan
- The martyred souls reigning with Christ
- The releasing of Satan to deceive the nations and gather them against the camp of the saints and the beloved city
- Satan thrown into the lake of fire
- The judgment of the dead

With these items in mind, we now turn our attention to a possible interpretation for the Millennium as described in Revelation 20. When we recognize the spiritual realm in which the Millennium takes place, those scenes and events, as Mauro stated, may be already past or they may be going on now. Thus, some see the Millennium as figurative of the Church age and the gospel's effect upon mankind, based upon the following:

- The New Testament authors speak of no other age than the coming Church age
- The binding of Satan, Christ judging His enemies and reigning, are elements of the Gospel age
- "A thousand" is representative of the completeness or fullness of an item

Others see it as that period when the Covenants coexisted, the "last days" generation, the span of approximately forty years. While many may think it preposterous to make forty years equal a thousand years (even though they have no problem making one day equal a thousand years), those who hold this view remind us of the hermeneutic of audience relevance. Revelation was written by a Jew, to a largely Jewish audience, in the apocalyptic language of the Jews. Therefore we must try to ascertain what the Jewish perspective of a Millennium was in that day.

It seems that, according to ancient commentaries and literature, the Jewish concept of the duration of the Millennium, viewed commonly as a transition period between the ages, was much different than that conceived by modern Christians. Whereas modern Christianity sees the Millennium as a period of at least a thousand years (and maybe much more, as in the Amillennial view), the Jews saw it as *maybe* a thousand years, but perhaps much less. Some actually believed it would be a 40-year period. In *Case Dismissed: Rebutting Common Charges Against Preterism*, Dr. Randall E. Otto documents this view:

> While this interim period of the messianic age was placed at four hundred years in 4 Ezra 7:28 and Apocalypse of Baruch 29-30, "older traditions concerning the days of the Messiah fix a very short interval for the interim period, namely, forty years ...." Similarly, the Qumran materials indicate such a period, as, for instance, the Damascus Document: "from the day of the gathering in of the unique teacher, until the destruction of all the men of war who turned back with the man of lies, there shall be about forty years" (CD xx, 14-15), and a Commentary on Ps 37:10: "I will stare at his place and he will no longer be there. Its interpretation concerns all the evil at the end of the forty years, for they shall be devoured and upon the earth no wicked person will be found" (p. 63)

Thus, when the New Testament saints read Revelation, they quite possibly had a different mental image of the Millennium than we do. The view in which the Millennium is considered a transition period sees the binding of Satan as taking place during Christ's earthly ministry. This is evidenced by His power to cast out demons:

> *And if I cast out demons by Beelzebub, by whom do your sons cast them out? Therefore they shall be your judges. But if I cast out demons by the Spirit of God, surely the kingdom of God has come upon you. Or how can one enter a strong man's house and plunder his goods, unless he first binds the strong man? And then he will plunder his house.* (Matt 12:27-29)

> *And He said to them, "I saw Satan fall like lightning from heaven. Behold, I give you the authority to trample on serpents and scorpions, and over all the power of the enemy, and nothing shall by any means hurt you."* (Luke 10:18-19)

> *Now is the judgment of this world; now the ruler of this world will be cast out.* (John 12:31)

> *... how God anointed Jesus of Nazareth with the Holy Spirit and power, and how he went around doing good and healing all who*

were under the power of the devil, because God was with him. (Acts 10:38 NIV)

The reigning of the martyred souls with Christ is seen as being in the spiritual realm, where Paul says that the New Testament saints were currently reigning with Christ:

> . . . *which He worked in Christ when He raised Him from the dead and seated Him at His right hand in the heavenly places, far above all principality and power and might and dominion, and every name that is named, not only in this age but also in that which is to come. And He put all things under His feet, and gave Him to be head over all things to the church, which is His body, the fullness of Him who fills all in all.* (Eph 1:20-23)

> *But God, who is rich in mercy, because of His great love with which He loved us, even when we were dead in trespasses, made us alive together with Christ (by grace you have been saved), and raised us up together, and made us sit together in the heavenly places in Christ Jesus . . . .* (Eph 2:4-6)

The releasing of Satan to deceive the nations and gather them against the beloved city is seen as occurring ca. AD 65-70, when heavy persecution broke out against Christians from both Nero and the Jews. While many understand the *beloved city* to be Jerusalem, we must remember King's observation that there are two Jerusalems in God's eschatology. Is the *beloved city* physical Jerusalem or spiritual Jerusalem? Our first clue is in the title *beloved city*, for we know that physical Jerusalem was not beloved in God's sight. Rather, Jesus wept over it and pronounced its desolation because it was the city that killed the prophets and stoned those who were sent to her. Even as far back as Daniel, God called the Jews and Jerusalem, "Daniel's people" and, "Daniel's holy city," not His (Dan 9:24). Our second clue is that it is the camp of the saints. The saints are the children of promise and of the Jerusalem above (Gal 4:26-28), that is, the heavenly Jerusalem (Heb 12:22). Preston comments on a similar passage from Zechariah:

> It will be noted of course, that the prophet also says that the Lord would fight *for* Jerusalem (12:8). How can this strange paradox be explained? How could the prophet say on the one hand that the city would be destroyed, with two-thirds of the people killed, and only a remnant remain, and then turn around and say that Jerusalem would be defended by Jehovah (Zech 12:8)? The answer is to be

found in two Biblical truths, the doctrine of the Two Cities, i.e. the Two Jerusalems, and the doctrine of the *remnant*. (*Like Father, Like Son*, p. 150)

Next we see that fire comes down from God and devours these armies which have surrounded the beloved city. This is not physical Jerusalem being delivered, for God sent the Roman armies to lay her waste. Rather, as we studied in "The Two Covenants and the Two Sons of Abraham," the fleshly seed of Abraham persecuted the spiritual seed—the Jews persecuted the Christians. The fire that God sent was upon physical Jerusalem, in part because they had "surrounded" the camp of the saints. King also makes the observation that the nations that gathered together, Gog and Magog, are as numerous as the sand of the sea. This is the same description used to describe the fleshly seed of Abraham (Gen 22:17). This confirms that the fire from God is coming upon physical Jerusalem, who killed the prophets, persecuted the Church, and to whom judgment was due. Both Amos and Moses agree:

You only have I known of all the families of the earth;
Therefore I will punish you for all your iniquities. (Amos 3:2)

And the LORD *said to Moses: "Behold, you will rest with your fathers; and this people will rise and play the harlot with the gods of the foreigners of the land, where they go to be among them, and they will forsake Me and break My covenant which I have made with them. Then My anger shall be aroused against them in that day, and I will forsake them, and I will hide My face from them, and they shall be devoured. And many evils and troubles shall befall them, so that they will say in that day, 'Have not these evils come upon us because our God is not among us?' And I will surely hide My face in that day because of all the evil which they have done, in that they have turned to other gods."* (Deut 31:16-18)

By recognizing the beloved city as *spiritual* Jerusalem, and the nations that are destroyed by God as *physical* Jerusalem, the battle scene is brought back into focus with the rest of Revelation, where we see God's judgment upon apostate Israel. It might be argued that physical Jerusalem fails to qualify for the term "nations." However, it appears that David may have made a similar use of the term in connection with Saul's men, as well as the companions of Peter and John regarding the crucifixion:

*To the Chief Musician. Set to "Do Not Destroy." A Michtam of
David **when Saul sent men, and they watched the house in order
to kill him.***

Deliver me from my enemies, O my God;
Defend me from those who rise up against me.
Deliver me from the workers of iniquity,
And save me from bloodthirsty men.
For look, they lie in wait for my life;
The mighty gather against me,
Not for my transgression nor for my sin, O LORD.
They run and prepare themselves through no fault of mine.
Awake to help me, and behold!
You therefore, O LORD God of hosts, the God of Israel,
*Awake to punish **all the nations**;*
Do not be merciful to any wicked transgressors.
Selah
At evening they return,
They growl like a dog,
And go all around the city.
Indeed, they belch with their mouth;
Swords are in their lips;
For they say, "Who hears?"
But You, O LORD, shall laugh at them;
*You shall have **all the nations** in derision.* (Ps 59:1-8)

*So when they heard that, they raised their voice to God with one
accord and said: "Lord, You are God, who made heaven and earth
and the sea, and all that is in them, who by the mouth of Your
servant David have said:*
*'**Why did the nations rage,***
And the people plot vain things?
The kings of the earth took their stand,
And the rulers were gathered together
Against the LORD and against His Christ.'
*For truly against Your holy Servant Jesus, whom You anointed,
**both Herod and Pontius Pilate, with the Gentiles and the people
of Israel, were gathered together** to do whatever Your hand and
Your purpose determined before to be done."* (Acts 4:24-28)
(emphases added)

If Herod, Pilate, the Gentiles, and the people of Israel can constitute "nations" and "kings of the earth," cannot the Jewish and Neronian persecutions of the saints constitute nations being gathered against spiritual Jerusalem?

The casting of Satan into the lake of fire takes place in AD 70 at the Second Coming of Christ and the consummation of the New Covenant. The final resurrection and judgment of the dead, having one of the spiritual interpretations described in the next chapter, occur at this time also.

Although the preceding was a very brief overview, one can see that there is enough scriptural support to at least warrant its consideration for further study. Naturally, there are objections to the view, one of which is the inspired use of the term *thousand years*. The Jewish understanding of this time period notwithstanding, as we stated in the chapter "Seventy Times Seven," a thousand seems to represent fullness or completeness. If the forty years of the last day's generation was the time described by Revelation 20, why did the Holy Spirit inspire John to write "thousand years," as opposed to "generation"? But we must remember the apocalyptic and highly symbolic language of Revelation, as well as the fact that "thousand" often seems to represent a figurative number in Scripture. (There may be literal uses in certain measurements and in human and animal population counts. However, many of these multiples of "thousand" are rounded off, as indicated by the expression "about." For example, on the Day of Pentecost *about* three thousand souls were added to the Church. It is therefore likely that many other multiples of "thousand" are also rounded off, leaving a relative few instances in which a thousand is precisely one thousand.)

If we understand a thousand to represent fullness or completeness, it is interesting to note that although the preflood patriarchs had very long life spans, none of them attained a thousand years. Timothy Martin and Jeffrey Vaughn postulate that the long life spans of the preflood patriarchs are figurative, and the fact that none of them attained a thousand years is representative of the fallen state in which they lived. In contrast, they note that the first generation of redeemed New Covenant saints is said to reign with Christ for a thousand years:

> The thousand years is a life-span signifying eternal life. John's millennium (the fulfillment of Isaiah 65:20) is ultimately rooted in the apocalyptic life-spans in early Genesis (as [are] so many other things we find in Revelation). The patriarchs, blessed as they were to live in covenant with God, *never* lived a 1000 years. The

comparison to the millennium can hardly be missed. All those who receive the final redemption from the Adamic curse, "the death," live *symbolically* for 1000 years.

Just as the apocalyptic life-spans in Genesis reference the single lives of individual patriarchs, so it is with the millennial life-span. The millennium references one generation (40 years). Though many have seen that the 1000 years is a symbolic number, they have not seen the *source* of the millennium in the long life-spans referenced in early Genesis and Isaiah 65:20. The millennium is surely symbolic, but it is important to recognize what John's symbolism references—the eternal life the first Christians received through faith in Jesus Christ. If this is correct, then John's millennium can *only* be applied to the 40 years of that generation. *To apply it to a literal thousand years (or ongoing thousands of years) is to miss John's point altogether.* (*Beyond Creation Science*, p. 414; emphasis in original)

Another problem area is the casting of Satan into the lake of fire. If this is the case, many wonder to what we are to ascribe evil and apparent demonic activity in our present world. But we must remember that the power associated with the Devil in Revelation 20 is not that of evil in general (e.g., temptation), but "the second death"—that is, spiritual death. As we shall see in the chapter "Is This All There Is?" whereas the Old Covenant only foreshadowed the promised eternal spiritual life, the New Covenant delivers it. When Christ rose from the grave with the keys of death and Hades (Rev 1:18), Satan no longer had that power. Thus we might say that this aspect of his power and influence has been cast into the lake of fire. Although his "bark" of temptation may still exist, his "bite" of spiritual death has been muzzled. That is, spiritual life is now available, death having been conquered for those who accept it. Those who do not receive the gift of spiritual life remain spiritually dead.

Again we note that a particular eschatological position does not necessarily dictate any one millennial view. Returning to our analogy of a tract home, we see the Millennium as the paint delivered to the construction site. That it is for our project there is no doubt. Likewise, we know that the Millennium also belongs with our eschatology. But we must determine whether the paint is all interior—that is, unseen from the outside—or exterior as well—seen from the outside, but only as an accent of the underlying construction. Do the events of the Millennium take place wholly in the spiritual realm, unseen in the physical, or are there visible "accents" of it in the physical while largely shaped in the spiritual realm? As Postmillennialist Mauro states, there may be ongoing aspects of the Millennium in our present Church Age. Even Preterist Russell struggled with fitting the whole of the Millennium within the AD 70 time frame.

On the other end of the spectrum is Kurt Simmons, president of the *Bimillennial Preterist Association*, who posits not only that the Millennium fits within the AD 70 time frame, but that there are *two* millennial periods described in Revelation 20. Simmons believes that the binding of Satan (Rev 20:3) and the reign of saints (Rev 20:4) represent two separate nonliteral thousand year periods and delineates these in his book *The Consummation of the Ages*.

We also must not lose sight of the fact that the Bible is dealing with God's redemptive plan, and that eschatology is focused on the casting out of Ishmael and the transition of the covenants. With this in view, should we not expect the Millennium to fit within this paradigm, rather than assigning it to some disjointed era of which *none* of the New Testament authors speak? Regardless of how much of the Millennium is realized in either the spiritual or physical realms, since there is no scriptural precedent to detach it from the eschatology of the "last days" generation, we feel compelled to find its fulfillment in that time frame. Certainly there is no justification for creating additional "ages" and physical kingdoms that are mentioned nowhere else in the New Testament.

While there will always be controversy and disagreements over what exactly the Millennium is, we feel that properly recognizing what it is *not* removes the major obstacles to fitting it within the framework of Preterist eschatology.

The Resurrection

It is sown a physical body, it is raised a spiritual body. If there is a physical body, there is also a spiritual body. (1 Cor 15:44 RSV)

It is sown a natural body, it is raised a spiritual body. There is a natural body, and there is a spiritual body. (1 Cor 15:44)

Literal, Physical, and Spiritual

In all of the doctrines that we have discussed, the meanings people assign to the terms *literal*, *physical*, and *spiritual* can be a source of great confusion. This is especially true of the resurrection. It is our understanding that there are three primary views of the resurrection:

The Literal Physical

This is the traditional view and is held by most Futurists and Partial Preterists. They believe that the resurrected spiritual body is a reconstituted physical body, still consisting of the physical elements of this material world but transformed in such a manner that it is now capable of existing in the spiritual realm as well as the physical. They point to Christ's resurrected body as seen during the forty days between His resurrection and ascension as proof of this. Since Christ is the first fruits of those raised from the dead, they believe we will have a body similar to His. Gentry attests to this in his April 2003 website article "Christ's Resurrection and Ours:"

> This is why the tomb and His burial clothing were found empty: His physical body had departed from them. The gospels present the resurrected Christ in a material body that could be touched and handled, which still had the wounds of the cross, which could be clung to, and could eat food. . . . in that He is the "first-fruit" He represents the rest, just as the Old Testament offering of the first part of the harvest represented the whole harvest (cp. Rom. 11:16). Christ's resurrection represents our own. . . . Thus, once

we determine the nature of Christ's resurrection, we understand the nature of our own. If Christ was physically raised from the dead, then so shall we, for He is the "first-fruits" of our resurrection. The only way around our physical resurrection is to deny Christ's physical resurrection.

The Full Preterist vantage point that all prophecy was fulfilled in the New Testament generation would require that physical graves were opened in AD 70 and that resurrected physical bodies ascended into heaven. Since there is no evidence this took place, Preterists who hold this physical view are forced to look toward a yet-future resurrection, hence the "Partial Preterist" label attributed commonly to them. As we shall demonstrate, we feel that the literal physical view is untenable.

However, not all Futurists insist upon a physical resurrection of believers. Futurist Murray J. Harris, professor of New Testament exegesis and theology at Trinity Evangelical Divinity School, wrote a scholarly work on resurrection. In *From Grave to Glory: Resurrection in the New Testament*, Harris deals in depth with the concepts of a spiritual body, the continuity between believers' physical bodies and resurrection bodies, and the continuity between Christ's resurrection body and the resurrection bodies of believers. Harris concludes that *there is no identity between the molecular structure of the physical and spiritual bodies of believers* . . . . (*From Grave to Glory*, p. 436, 1990 Acadamie Books, Zondervan Publishing House)

While we affirm that Christ was bodily (physically) resurrected, and that He is the first fruits of those who are resurrected after Him, we believe that this "first fruits/harvest" logic is oversimplified. First, it is important to distinguish between being "resurrected" and being "raised from the dead." Being raised from the dead is merely a reestablishment of physical life, of being restored to a predeath condition. (In using the term "merely," we do not mean to downplay the miracle of someone's being raised from the dead; but when one considers the vast difference between a second chance for a few more years in the natural realm in light of being transformed and ushered into the spiritual realm for eternity, being raised from the dead pales in comparison with being resurrected.) Resurrection, on the other hand, involves a supernatural change that allows us immediate and intimate access to the presence of God. As a case in point, Jesus was not the first person to be raised from the dead. However, He was the first person to experience resurrection, *never to die again*. Harris writes:

We are here gently probing a mystery, for Jesus was the first person to rise immortal in a spiritual body. (Ibid., p. 142)

Everyone else who was raised from the dead eventually died again. Christ not only rose *from* the dead, but He possessed power *over* death as the holder of the keys of Hades and Death (Rev 1:18).

The Literal Spiritual

Many Full Preterists hold the view that there was a literal resurrection of the dead in AD 70, but that individuals were raised with spiritual bodies. Thus, while the physical graves remained unopened, the spiritual grave (Sheol/Hades) gave up its righteous dead. In the same manner, post-AD 70 believers that have died shed their earthly tent and received a building (i.e., spiritual body) from God (2 Cor 5:1), in which they were ushered into heaven. Thus the final resurrection is a past event concerning biblical prophecy, but ongoing on an individual basis in the everlasting New Covenant. Since the receiving of the resurrection body and putting on immortality take place at physical death, this view is sometimes called the Immortal Body at Death (IBD) view. Even though these Preterists believe that individuals are resurrected, this view still calls for a nonphysical understanding of the resurrection body.

The Spiritual Corporate/Covenantal

This view, held by some Full Preterists, posits that the resurrection is not a literal resurrection of either physical or spiritual bodies, but rather that the various resurrection terms are metaphorical for the "death," or the laying down, of the Old Covenant, and the receipt, or "putting on," of the New Covenant. Thus the resurrection is not seen as a change in the *substance* of an individual's body, but rather as a change in their *stance* before God. The natural conclusion of the Corporate view is that, subsequent to AD 70 and the change of the covenants, believers are now received into the resurrected body of Christ at their regeneration when they are "born again" into the New Covenant, which imparts immortality and incorruption. These Preterists believe that we (as Christians) have our immortal bodies now, hence the term Immortal Body Now (IBN) view.

We should note that these differing resurrection views are not mutually exclusive. Preston writes:

Resurrection is multi-faceted reality in scripture. There is a corporate concept, (i.e. the resurrection of Israel, Ezek 37), the individualistic perspective, (Rom 6, Eph 2, Col 2, etc.), and the Hadean realm (Rev 20), involved as well. Thus, to speak of resurrection in a monolithic way, limited to a single idea, is, we believe, misguided. (*Like Father, Like Son, On Clouds of Glory*, p. 338)

Even some Futurists, such as Harris, see corporate and individual aspects to a believer's resurrection:

On the issue of the time of believers' spiritual resurrection, we must distinguish four stages: the resurrection of Christ itself; the corporate identification of Christians with their representative Head; the individual identification of Christians with their risen Lord; the consequent state of resurrection life. We may suggest that corporately believers were actually raised with Christ, in the divine estimation, when Christ the representative Man was raised, but that only at their regeneration when they are personally united with the risen Christ does the truth of resurrection with Christ become a reality of individual experience. That is, in regeneration what was actually achieved by Christ is applied personally. (*Grave to Glory*, p. 189)

We shall explore these different resurrection concepts further after laying some foundational points.

The Time of the Resurrection

The reason that Full Preterists look for alternative meanings for the resurrection (alternative to tradition, not to Scripture) is the presence of certain time statements associated with the Resurrection. Martin and Vaughn write:

The Old Testament contains the promises of resurrection. Both Ezekiel 37-38 and Daniel 12 give prophecies to old covenant Israel of a coming resurrection. We can demonstrate this fact directly from the New Testament. The Jews had an expectation of the resurrection as shown by what Martha said to Jesus:

Martha answered, "I know he will rise again in the resurrection at the last day." (John 11:24 NIV)

Martha did not get this teaching from the New Testament; her belief in the coming resurrection even preceded the ministry of Christ, long before any New Testament books were written! Her belief in resurrection had its origins in the old covenant promises.

That demonstrates that the resurrection is past, for the old covenant *has passed away*. Paul made it absolutely clear that not one of God's promises could fail (Rom 9:6). How is it possible, then, to believe that the old covenant has ended, but some of the promises it contained *remain unfulfilled?* The idea that the resurrection remains in our future implies that God's old covenant resurrection promise to Israel (Ezek 27-38; Dan 12) *failed.* If the resurrection remains in our future, then the old covenant passed away without some of its promises coming to pass. The resurrection is a promise to old covenant Israel. This is a strong indication that the resurrection is in our past, not in our future.

. . .

Theologians have long made a connection between Daniel's book of prophecy and Revelation. This means that if it can be proved that Revelation was fulfilled in the first century, culminating with the destruction of Jerusalem, then we have *prima facie* evidence that Daniel is fulfilled historically at the same time. Since Daniel speaks of the resurrection, this alone would place the resurrection in our distant past.

Daniel 12 provides a key prophecy about the resurrection:

At that time Michael, the great prince who protects your people, will arise. There will be a *time of distress* such as has not happened from the beginning of nations until then. But at that time your people—everyone whose name is found written in the book—will be delivered. *Multitudes who sleep in the dust of the earth will awake: some to everlasting life, others to shame and everlasting contempt.* Those who are wise will shine like the brightness of the heavens, and those who lead many to righteousness, like the stars for ever and ever. (Dan 12:1-3 NIV)
(*Beyond Creation Science*, pp. 404, 406; emphases in original)

We have argued previously that the New Testament generation was truly the "last days" generation: they were living in the last days, looking for the Day of the Lord, and the end of all things that were at hand for them. The end of the age was upon them, and it was in this "time of the end" that the angel told Daniel he would arise:

> *But you, go your way till the end; for you shall rest, and will arise*
> *to your inheritance at the end of the days.* (Dan 12:13)

If we put the resurrection in our future, we create two "times of the end"—one in AD 70 and another in the future. Furthermore, the angel's statement *Multitudes who sleep in the dust of the earth will awake: some to everlasting life, others to shame and everlasting contempt* is very similar to a statement of Christ's:

> *Do not marvel at this; for the hour is coming in which all who are*
> *in the graves will hear His voice and come forth—those who have*
> *done good, to the resurrection of life, and those who have done*
> *evil, to the resurrection of condemnation.* (John 5:28-30)

Yet Christ stated that the time for that resurrection was during His generation (John 5:25). Daniel 12 also puts the abomination of desolation in the timeframe of the resurrection, and Jesus told His disciples that *they* would see the abomination of desolation (Matt 24:15). The clear inference is that the resurrection would also take place during their lifetimes.

In addition to Daniel's passage, Paul quotes other related Old Testament passages in 1 Corinthians 15:

> *So when this corruptible has put on incorruption, and this mortal*
> *has put on immortality, then shall be brought to pass the saying*
> *that is written: "Death is swallowed up in victory."*
> *"O Death, where is your sting?*
> *O Hades, where is your victory?"*
> *The sting of death is sin, and the strength of sin is the law. But*
> *thanks be to God, who gives us the victory through our Lord Jesus*
> *Christ.* (1 Cor 15:54-57)

> *He will swallow up death forever* . . . . (Isa 25:8)

> *I will ransom them from the power of the grave;*
> *I will redeem them from death.*
> *O Death, I will be your plagues!*
> *O Grave, I will be your destruction!*
> *Pity is hidden from My eyes.* (Hos 13:14)

Are not these passages in Isaiah and Hosea part of the "all things which are written" that were fulfilled in AD 70? If they are not, how many other things that were written were not fulfilled? By what standard do we make that determination? (As an aside, note that Paul applies Hosea's resurrection passage to the believers in the Church, not to physical/national Israel!)

Unless it can be demonstrated clearly from Scripture that Daniel's "time of the end" resurrection was not a part of the "end of all things" of which Peter spoke, and that the Isaiah and Hosea passages are not amongst the "all things which are written" that were fulfilled during the "days of vengeance," then we *must* place the general resurrection of the dead (whatever that entails) within the AD 70 timeframe. Although many have attempted to demonstrate that the resurrection is yet future, we remain unconvinced. Therefore, even though the graves of the saints are not empty, we believe in faith that the resurrection has indeed taken place.

"Resurrection" vs. "Raised from the Dead"

Scripture illustrates the difference between resurrection and being raised from the dead using the examples of Lazarus and Jesus:

So Jesus, again being deeply moved within, came to the tomb. Now it was a cave, and a stone was lying against it. Jesus said, "Remove the stone." Martha, the sister of the deceased, said to Him, "Lord, by this time there will be a stench, for he has been dead four days." Jesus said to her, "Did I not say to you that if you believe, you will see the glory of God?" So they removed the stone. Then Jesus raised His eyes, and said, "Father, I thank You that You have heard Me. I knew that You always hear Me; but because of the people standing around I said it, so that they may believe that You sent Me." When He had said these things, He cried out with a loud voice, "Lazarus, come forth." The man who had died came forth, bound hand and foot with wrappings, and his face was wrapped around with a cloth. Jesus said to them, "Unbind him, and let him go." (John 11:38-44 NASB95)

Now on the first day of the week Mary Magdalene came early to the tomb, while it was still dark, and saw the stone already taken away from the tomb. So she ran and came to Simon Peter and to the other disciple whom Jesus loved, and said to them, "They have taken away the Lord out of the tomb, and we do not know where they have laid Him." So Peter and the other disciple went forth, and they were going to the tomb. The two were running together; and the other disciple ran ahead faster than Peter and came to the tomb first; and stooping and looking in, he saw the linen wrappings lying there; but he did not go in. And so Simon Peter also came, following him, and entered the tomb; and he saw the linen wrappings lying there, and the face-cloth which had been on His head, not lying with the linen wrappings, but rolled up in a place by itself. So the other disciple who had first come to the tomb then also entered, and he saw and believed. For as yet they did not understand the Scripture, that He must rise again from the dead. (John 20:1-9 NASB95)

Notice that Jesus asked for the stone to be rolled away from Lazarus' tomb. Why? So that Lazarus could come out of the tomb. The stone was also rolled away from Jesus' tomb, but we know that this was not necessary for Him to exit the tomb. Why? Because He was able, in His resurrected body, to pass through material objects:

Then, the same day at evening, being the first day of the week, when the doors were shut where the disciples were assembled, for fear of the Jews, Jesus came and stood in the midst, and said to them, "Peace be with you.". . . And after eight days His disciples were again inside, and Thomas with them. Jesus came, the doors being shut, and stood in the midst, and said, "Peace to you!" (John 20:19, 26)

Harris summarizes the difference between being raised from the dead and resurrection:

There is also an implicit contrast between the circumstances of the revival of Lazarus and those of Jesus' resurrection. Both died, Lazarus as a result of illness (John 11:1-4), Jesus at his own volition (John 10:18). In each instance a stone sealed the tomb, but in one case it was removed by natural means (John 11:38-41), in the other, by supernatural means (John 20:1, by implication). Both were bound in graveclothes when buried, but whereas Lazarus needed others to unbind him when he emerged from the tomb (John 11:44), Jesus left his own burial cloths intact in his grave as a sign of his resurrection (John 20:5-7). Both rose from the dead, Lazarus with a new lease of physical life (John 12:2, 10), Jesus as the possessor of a transformed body (John 20:17, 19-20, 26). (*Grave to Glory*, p. 91)

Jesus did not need the stone rolled away to leave the tomb. He could have simply passed through it as He did the walls/doors of the disciples' room in which they gathered. So why was the stone rolled away? According to Harris, it was not so that Jesus could get out, but so that the disciples *could get in*. Why was that important? Because inside they saw something that made them (at least John) believe. Believe what? That Jesus had been resurrected from the underworld of Sheol/Hades, for they had not yet understood the Scripture:

Now on the first day of the week, very early in the morning, they, and certain other women with them, came to the tomb bringing the spices which they had prepared. But they found the stone rolled away from the tomb. Then they went in and did not find the body of the Lord Jesus. And it happened, as they were greatly perplexed about this, that behold, two men stood by them in shining garments. Then, as they were afraid and bowed their faces to the earth, they said to them, "Why do you seek the living among the dead? He is not here, but is risen! Remember how He spoke to you when He was still in Galilee, saying, 'The Son of Man must be delivered into the hands of sinful men, and be crucified, and the third day rise again.'" And they remembered His words. Then they returned from the tomb and told all these things to the eleven and to all the rest. It was Mary Magdalene, Joanna, Mary the mother of James, and the other women with them, who told these things to the apostles. And their words seemed to them like idle tales, and they did not believe them. But Peter arose and ran to the tomb; and stooping down, he saw the linen cloths lying by themselves; and he departed, marveling to himself at what had happened. (Luke 24:1-12)

When we combine the above accounts of John and Luke, we see that the women were telling the apostles that an angel had told them that Jesus had risen, recalling to them the teaching of Jesus regarding His resurrection on the third day. The apostles thought it nonsense, that is, until Peter and John went to the tomb. John went away *believing*, and Peter left *marveling*. What did they see that caused them to believe the report of the women?

And so Simon Peter also came, following him, and entered the tomb; and he saw the linen wrappings lying there, and the face-cloth which had been on His head, not lying with the linen wrappings, but rolled up in a place by itself. So the other disciple who had first come to the tomb then also entered, and he saw and believed. (John 20:6-8 NASB95)

But Peter arose and ran to the tomb; and stooping down, he saw the linen cloths lying by themselves; and he departed, marveling to himself at what had happened. (Luke 24:12)

Something about the linen wrappings caused the apostles to believe, not that Jesus' body had been removed, but that He had risen from the dead. According to Hatikva Ministries' Joseph Good, the answer lies in the procedure for preparing a body for burial. Strips of linen are coated with a gummy aromatic substance and additional spices, and then wrapped around the body:

> *Then they took the body of Jesus, and bound it in strips of linen with the spices, as is the custom of the Jews to bury.* (John 19:40)

The result was similar to what we see with mummies in classic horror films. The entire body is wrapped with strips of linen, except the face, which has a separate cloth laid over it:

> *When He had said these things, He cried out with a loud voice, "Lazarus, come forth." The man who had died came forth, bound hand and foot with wrappings, and **his face was wrapped around with a cloth**.* (John 11:43-44)

> *And so Simon Peter also came, following him, and entered the tomb; and he saw the linen wrappings lying there, and the **face-cloth** which had been on His head, not lying with the linen wrappings, but rolled up in a place by itself.* (John 20:6-7 NASB95) (emphases added)

Notice that although Lazarus was able to walk out of his tomb, indicating that his limbs were wrapped individually, he also needed to have his wrappings removed by others:

> *Jesus said to them, "Unbind him, and let him go."* (John 11:44)

Even if Jesus had unwrapped Himself, or had been unwrapped by someone else (an angel perhaps), how would a pile of wrappings indicate to Peter and John that He had risen, as opposed to His body having been stolen? What did they see in the placement of those linens that caused them to "*believe*" and "*marvel*"? Again, according to Joseph Good, when the aromatic gums with which the linens are coated begin to dry, they form a soft cast around the body. Not so firm that, as with Lazarus, a person could not walk after four days, but firm enough that if a body were somehow able to pass miraculously through them, they would retain the general shape of the body. In fact, one might believe that they were still looking at a body save for one item—the face cloth was removed from the wrappings, revealing a hollow soft cast in the shape of a body:

. . . and he saw the linen wrappings lying there, and the face-cloth which had been on His head, not lying with the linen wrappings, but rolled up in a place by itself. (John 20:7 NASB95)

Harris concurs:

It is particularly from the fourth gospel's account of the discovery of the "empty" tomb that we learn that the tomb was not completely empty: the body had gone, but the graveclothes remained. When "the other disciple" (John himself) saw that the tomb was open and empty and perceived the significance of the burial clothes, he "believed" (John 20:8). What prompted his faith was not only the presence of the clothes—no grave robbers had been at work—but also their position. The linen wrappings that had encircled the body had collapsed under the weight of the aromatic spices embedded in their folds, and the headcloth that had passed over his head and under his chin was not lying flattened like the linen wrappings but remained twirled up in its folds, turbanlike, in a place by itself, where Jesus' head had lain (John 20:6-7). Jesus' body had miraculously passed through the graveclothes, leaving them undisturbed. He had not needed someone to unwind the strips of linen to set him free, as Lazarus had before him (John 11:44). (*Grave to Glory*, pp. 388-389)

This demonstrates the difference between being raised from the dead and being resurrected. Lazarus needed his wrappings removed—Jesus passed through His wrappings just as He did the tomb and the closed doors of the room in which the apostles were staying.

Christ's Resurrected Body

Although Christ was resurrected in the same body in which He ministered and died, it was manifestly different from the body that was laid in the tomb. Those familiar with the processes of scourging and crucifixion (as depicted in Mel Gibson's *The Passion of the Christ*) are aware of how mutilating it is to the human body. The scourging process could strip the flesh down to the bone, oftentimes revealing inner organs. Some victims, not surviving this process, never made it to the cross. Scripture also tells us that all of Christ's bones were out of joint (Ps 22:14); that His beard was plucked (Isa 50:6); His visage was marred more than any man (Isa 52:14). The mutilated body that was laid in the tomb was no doubt unrecognizable even to those closest to Him.

Yet the resurrected body in which Christ revealed Himself to His followers had only two sets of wounds remaining from that horrendous act—the nail scars in His hands and feet, and the wound from the spear in His side—and even these had to be *shown* to His followers. Other than these wounds, in none of the accounts of His postresurrection appearances is there so much as a hint of additional residual marks from His preliminary scourging. Obviously, most of the damage done to His body during His scourging and crucifixion had been undone at His resurrection; but why most of the damage and not all of it? Certainly, it was not due to a shortage of divine power on God's part to complete the process. The preserving of those wounds was deliberate and with purpose: they remained as purposeful testimonies and doubtless identifications to the disciples that they were indeed beholding their crucified Master. The nail scars identified Him with crucifixion, while the wound in His side identified Him as a particular victim of crucifixion—their Lord and Master! Again, we quote Harris:

> As the possessor of a spiritual body which had remarkably different properties from any "body" the disciples already knew, Jesus faced the challenge of proving his reality and introducing his disciples to a phenomenon beyond their experience and imagination. Not surprisingly, when Jesus suddenly appeared among the disciples (Luke 24:36 = John 20:19), they at first imagined he was a bodiless spirit who had returned from the unseen world and assumed a visible form as a ghost (Luke 24:37). To calm their fears and assure them of his identity, he invited them to look at the scars from his crucifixion and thus know "that it is I myself," to handle him and so understand that he was no bodiless spirit (Luke 24:39). (*Grave to Glory*, p. 145)

The resurrection of Christ's crucified body demonstrated to them that He was not appearing in the form of a new and second incarnation, nor as a Spirit manifesting Himself physically as angels might, but as the One who has the power over death, who could lay down His life and take it up again (John 10:18).

The question then arises, was Christ resurrected in His physical body because that is the nature of *all* resurrected bodies, or was it expressly for demonstrating His resurrection from spiritual death to His followers? The essence of spiritual death (and life) belongs to the spiritual dimension, which is invisible to us. Therefore, how would one demonstrate victory over spiritual death to those whose primary existence and experience was in the physical dimension? Without some tangible evidence in the physical realm, it would have been a matter of total faith. Yet the disciples were of *little faith* (Matt 8:28; 14:31; 16:8). On the other hand, Christ's raising of His physical body from death, never to die again, would certainly increase one's faith that He had also conquered *spiritual* death, the true enemy. We believe that the following passage illustrates this principle:

> *Then behold, they brought to Him a paralytic lying on a bed. When Jesus saw their faith, He said to the paralytic, "Son, be of good cheer; your sins are forgiven you." And at once some of the scribes said within themselves, "This Man blasphemes!" But Jesus, knowing their thoughts, said, "Why do you think evil in your hearts? For which is easier, to say, 'Your sins are forgiven you,' or to say, 'Arise and walk'? But that you may know that the Son of Man has power on earth to forgive sins"—then He said to the paralytic, "Arise, take up your bed, and go to your house." And he arose and departed to his house.* (Matt 9:2-7)

Jesus could just as easily have forgiven the man's sins without healing him; but how would anyone have truly known that Jesus had actually forgiven this cripple's sins? We believe that the paralytic's sins were in fact forgiven the moment Jesus declared them as such (dependant, of course, on Christ's death and resurrection). However, rather than marveling and rejoicing over this fact, the scribes considered Jesus to be a blasphemer. They didn't believe that Jesus had actually forgiven the paralytic's sins, but that He has blasphemed by claiming to be able to do so. Therefore, Jesus had to provide for them tangible proof that He had that supernatural power.

Jesus demonstrated His power to forgive sins—an action that is unseen because it occurs in the spiritual realm—by healing the man's paralysis. The power exhibited in the visible, physical realm was a testimony of the power exercised in the invisible, spiritual realm. We feel that this same principle is true of Christ's resurrection: He could have, just as easily, conquered spiritual death while leaving His physical body in the tomb.

Even if Christ's resurrection was physical because, as some believe, that is the nature of all resurrected bodies, we feel that what Christ exhibited during those forty days prior to His ascension (He was touched, handled, ate) is but a facet of the true nature of a resurrected body. Are not angels capable of the same things?

Do not forget to entertain strangers, for by so doing some have unwittingly entertained angels. (Heb 13:2)

Now the two angels came to Sodom in the evening, and Lot was sitting in the gate of Sodom. When Lot saw them, he rose to meet them, and he bowed himself with his face toward the ground. And he said, "Here now, my lords, please turn in to your servant's house and spend the night, and wash your feet; then you may rise early and go on your way." And they said, "No, but we will spend the night in the open square." But he insisted strongly; so they turned in to him and entered his house. Then he made them a feast, and baked unleavened bread, and they ate. (Gen 19:1-3)

It would appear that the actions of Christ during the days between His resurrection and ascension were nothing more than what angels have done. How was it, then, that the disciples knew that He was not an angel, or that it was not just His spirit manifesting physically as do angels? They knew by the crucifixion scars on His person in addition to the empty tomb! Those scars were the only link between His crucified body and His resurrected body.

With the empty tomb, Jesus' scars affirmed that He had the power to lay down His life and the power to take it up again. The empty tomb was merely the evidence of a *greater* spiritual resurrection; although the tomb of Lazarus was empty (for a time), it demonstrated Christ's power over physical death only. Christ's resurrection, on the other hand, demonstrated His power over both physical *and* spiritual death:

The Resurrection was not simply an occurrence in the spiritual world, for the empty tomb stands at the intersection of the spiritual and the material and shows that these two categories are reconcilable. (*Grave to Glory*, p. 121)

Resurrection may therefore be described as an event that occurred simultaneously within history and beyond history. (Ibid., p. 104)

Unfortunately, Futurists do not seem to understand that this physical body in which Christ was seen for forty days, which they are so fixated upon as the first fruits of the resurrection, was but a facet of what His resurrected body is:

But we see Jesus, who was made a little lower than the angels, for the suffering of death crowned with glory and honor, that He, by the grace of God, might taste death for everyone. (Heb 2:9)

. . . when He had by Himself purged our sins, sat down at the right hand of the Majesty on high, having become so much better than the angels, as He has by inheritance obtained a more excellent name than they. (Heb 1:3-4)

Christ, after being made a little lower than the angels in His incarnation, has, in His resurrection, become *so much better than* they are. Why, then, do we look at the "mere" angelic features of Christ's resurrected body and build our doctrine of the resurrection of the saints upon them? Certainly in becoming *so much better* than the angels, we would expect a body capable of much more than just being able to eat or be touched and handled. We all accept the fact that when angels manifest themselves as men it is a very limited representation of their nature. Would it not follow, then, that the nature of the preascension body of Christ, Who is *so much better than the angels*, would also be only a limited representation of the nature of His resurrected body? Yet many in the Church point to that limited representation and say *that is what we shall be like.* Is not the physical body that Christ took on during His incarnation the "earthly" nature that Paul speaks of?

The first man was of the earth, made of dust; the second Man is the Lord from heaven. As was the man of dust, so also are those who are made of dust; and as is the heavenly Man, so also are those who are heavenly. And as we have borne the image of the man of dust, we shall also bear the image of the heavenly Man. (1 Cor 15:47-49)

We already bear the image of the man of dust; Christ Himself took on this image in His Incarnation. Yet compared to His previous glorious existence, the incarnation was an act of humbleness, not one of exaltation:

Let this mind be in you which was also in Christ Jesus, who, being in the form of God, did not consider it robbery to be equal with God, but made Himself of no reputation, taking the form of a bondservant, and coming in the likeness of men. (Phil 2:5-7)

Is Christ's resurrected physical body "*the image of the heavenly Man*" that all resurrected saints are to bear? Should we not expect something more along the lines of Christ's existence *before* He "*made Himself of no reputation?*"

In support of this is the inspired testimony of the apostle John, the beloved apostle, who, as he stood at the foot of the cross, was the only male disciple willing to identify with Christ at His death. Thus, we would not be surprised if John might have spent more time with the resurrected Christ than many others did. He, perhaps more than anyone, would have been familiar with the nature of Christ's resurrected body. Yet, despite this, he wrote the following:

> *Beloved, now we are children of God; and it has not yet been revealed what we shall be, but we know that when He is revealed, we shall be like Him, for we shall see Him as He is.* (1 John 3:2)

The fact *we shall be like Him* agrees with the teaching that Christ is the first fruits. Therefore, His resurrected nature is an indication of the nature of those who follow. Nevertheless, notice that John also says, "*it has not yet been revealed what we shall be.*" This flies in the face of what Partial Preterism and Futurism teach. Some say that what we shall be *has* been revealed and point to that same forty-day period that John witnessed as that revealing. How can His body that was touched, handled, clung to, and able to eat, be the nature of our resurrected bodies, when, according to John, that nature "*had not been revealed yet?*" In addition, when John states, ". . . *for we shall see Him as He is,*" it implies that, thus far, they (including John) had not experienced Christ as He really is. The opening verses of John's first epistle strengthen this fact:

> *That which was from the beginning, which we have heard, which we have seen with our eyes, which we have looked upon, and our hands have handled, concerning the Word of life—the life was manifested, and we have seen, and bear witness, and declare to you that eternal life which was with the Father and was manifested to us—that which we have seen and heard we declare to you, that you also may have fellowship with us; and truly our fellowship is with the Father and with His Son Jesus Christ.* (1 John 1:1-3)

We find it strange indeed that Partial Preterists and Futurists point to the preascension nature of Christ's resurrected body and insist that it is the revealing of the resurrection first fruits, thus claiming that we indeed know what we shall be like. All of this when the inspired words of John claim that, despite experiencing the reality of Christ's resurrected body, "*it has not yet been revealed what we shall be.*" Partial Preterists and Futurists construct a resurrection scenario that is contrary to Scripture and, subsequently, accuse Full Preterists of everything from ignorance to heresy because Full Preterists do not adhere to their particular resurrection theology. At the same time, they deny that the nature of the resurrection of the dead is primarily "spiritual." If John's experience with the risen Lord allowed him to question honestly the true nature of resurrection ("*it has not yet been revealed what we shall be"*), why is it that Partial Preterists and Futurists rule out a primarily spiritual resurrection? According to John's statement, and the fact that Christ's body was seen by many between His resurrection and ascension (1 Cor 15:4-8), we *must* rule out Christ's physical body as an example of what our own resurrection body shall be like.

There is another description of Christ's resurrected body that, strangely enough, is never put forth as a representation of what we shall be like at our resurrection:

> *I was in the Spirit on the Lord's Day, and I heard behind me a loud voice, as of a trumpet . . . . Then I turned to see the voice that spoke with me. And having turned I saw seven golden lampstands, and in the midst of the seven lampstands One like the Son of Man, clothed with a garment down to the feet and girded about the chest with a golden band. His head and hair were white like wool, as white as snow, and His eyes like a flame of fire; His feet were like fine brass, as if refined in a furnace, and His voice as the sound of many waters; He had in His right hand seven stars, out of His mouth went a sharp two-edged sword, and His countenance was like the sun shining in its strength. And when I saw Him, I fell at His feet as dead. But He laid His right hand on me, saying to me, "Do not be afraid; I am the First and the Last. I am He who lives, and was dead, and behold, I am alive forevermore. Amen. And I have the keys of Hades and of Death."* (Rev 1:10, 12-18)

Why is it that this description of the resurrected Christ is not put forth as His true first fruits nature, which we, as the harvest to follow, will achieve? We cannot deny that Christ is the one in view here. It is obviously after His resurrection, for He says, "*I . . . was dead, and behold, I am alive forevermore.*" Here Christ appears in such a glorious manner that John does not seem to recognize Him. Jesus must tell him who He is. Again, we do not desire to diminish nor demean any aspect of the resurrected Christ, but of the two descriptions, which is more glorious and exalted? Certainly Christ's divinity is on display here, something which we will never achieve. Yet when John declares that what we shall be has not yet been revealed, can we not suppose that at least a degree of this glory might be in store for us?

Partial Preterist C. Jonathin Seraiah takes issue with this interpretation:

What, therefore, does John mean when he says that "we shall see him as he is" (1 John 3:2)? John here uses a particular Greek word for "we shall see" that he has used at other times in this letter. The same word also appears over thirty times in the gospel of John. The predominant usage by John refers to physical sight. In the first epistle of John, there is not a single reference that refers to anything other than physical sight (1:1-3 is especially powerful in this idea). The weight of the evidence for John's usage of this word is that he means that we shall physically "see him as he is" "when he appears" physically, before the eyes of all men. We must remember here that only a select few actually saw the risen Christ (Acts 10:40-41). Equally important is the fact that John himself only saw a "vision" of Christ in Revelation 1:12-16, it was not truly Christ "as he is" (unless one supposes that He just did a really good job of speaking with a sword in His mouth [Rev 1:16]). (*The End of All Things: A Defense of the Future*, pp. 187-186, 1999 by Canon Press)

We do not argue that this description of Christ certainly has "vision-like" qualities; but is this because the appearance is truly a vision or because the actual appearance of the glorified Christ is so overwhelming to the natural senses that our limited minds can only perceive Him with vision-like quality? Does one fall as a dead man at the feet of a vision? Moreover, if it was a vision, and not truly Christ "as he is," as Seraiah asserts, does that not imply that Christ is representing Himself in a vision as more glorious than He is in His actual resurrected, "physical" body?

We must not forget that Paul had contact with this glorious, postascension form of Christ. Blinded by a bright light on the road to Damascus (Acts 9:3), Christ taught Paul personally (Gal 1:11-12) and caught him up into the third heaven in some manner, where Paul heard inexpressible things (2 Cor 12:2-4). As Harris notes:

> . . . although he does not explicitly say so, undoubtedly Paul found in his own conversion encounter with the risen Christ the conclusive evidence of the existence of the spiritual body. At that time he saw Jesus (Acts 9:27; 1 Cor 9:1). (*Grave to Glory*, p. 194)

Paul likely had this in mind when he wrote:

> *For our citizenship is in heaven, from which we also eagerly wait for the Savior, the Lord Jesus Christ, who will transform our lowly body that it may be conformed to **His glorious body**, according to the working by which He is able even to subdue all things to Himself.* (Phil 3:20-21; emphasis added) [We note that the

Corporate view sees "His glorious body" as the corporate Body of Christ, His Church.]

When we combine Paul's statement of being *conformed to His glorious body* with John's statement that *it has not yet been revealed what we shall be*, we feel that our resurrection bodies must fall somewhere between Christ's postresurrection body and His appearance to John on Patmos.

The Empty Tomb

The final hurdle for a *spiritual* resurrection (of any kind) is Christ's empty tomb. If His tomb is empty because His physical body was raised, should not the saints, as the harvest following His first fruits example, also be raised physically and therefore have empty graves? It begs the question: How far do we carry the analogy of first fruits and harvest? (Compare this with Romans 6:5: How much were we/they in the likeness of His death?) Are all the saints to be raised with nail scars in their hands and feet? Are we to maintain some of our personal scars from this life, but not all of them? Because our Adamic body is from the dust, to the dust it shall return:

In the sweat of your face you shall eat bread
Till you return to the ground,
For out of it you were taken;
For dust you are,
And to dust you shall return. (Gen 3:19)

Because of Christ's sinless nature, His body did not return to the dust—therefore Scripture already demonstrates to us the dissimilarities between the bodies of the first fruits and the harvest:

For You will not leave my soul in Sheol,
Nor will You allow Your Holy One to see corruption. (Ps 16:10)

For David, after he had served his own generation by the will of God, fell asleep, was buried with his fathers, and saw corruption; but He whom God raised up saw no corruption. (Acts 13:36-37)

Harris quite adeptly points out the dissimilarities between Christ's resurrection body and that of believers:

Basic similarities between Christ's resurrection and ours do not exclude significant differences. . . . It is clear, therefore, that in certain areas relating to the person and work of Jesus, his resurrection was unique and distinctive. (p. 219, *Grave to Glory*)

Whether we view the resurrection of Christ as the cause, the pledge, or the pattern of believer's resurrection, there need not be a precise identity between the two. Basic similarities do not exclude significant differences. Several of these differences stem from the distinctiveness of Christ's person and work. Although believers first acquire immortality through their resurrection (1 Cor 15:53-54), when Christ rose from the grave he regained the immortality that he had surrendered when he became "obedient to death" (Phil 2:8; Rev 1:18). Only of Christ can it be said that he "became a life-giving spirit" (1 Cor 15:45) through his resurrection, or that his coming to life vindicated him as the suffering Son of Man (Luke 24:26, 46) and established him as the prince of life and conqueror of death (Acts 2:24-28; Rev 1:18). Only of Christ is it true that resurrection meant his designation as "Son of God in power" (Rom 1:4) and as universal Lord and Judge (Acts 17:31; Rom 14:9; Eph 1:20-21). And only Christ needed to reappear on earth to convince his disciples that he had indeed risen from his tomb and was the all-sovereign Lord. (*Grave to Glory*, pp. 409-411)

When Christ existed in the spiritual realm (Heb 10:5) prior to His incarnation in a physical body, it is widely held that He appeared in human form in what are known as "theophanies," or more accurately, "Christophanies" (manifestations of God in general and Christ, respectively; see Gen 18 and Josh 5:13-15). We can deduce two things from this: (1) a physical, earthly body is not necessary in the spiritual realm, and (2) *without* a physical body, Christ was presumably able to perform all of the events that we see Him doing after His resurrection in His preascension body. Does this not open the door for the saints to be raised spiritually, yet still be capable of all the characteristics of Christ's preascension resurrected body?

Christ did not need His physical body to return to heaven. Surely, the nail holes and spear wound could have been healed (and thus absent) in His resurrected body, just as His torn flesh, plucked beard, and displaced joints were. Why, then, was Christ resurrected in a body He did not need, and one that still displayed wounds that could have been healed completely? We feel that it was to demonstrate to His followers that He was not just a spirit or ghost (Luke 24:37-39), but that He had the power to lay His life down and the power to take it up again (John 10:18). The nature of Christ's body prior to His ascension was not to demonstrate to us the *nature* of our resurrected body, but rather to show that He had conquered spiritual (not just physical) death, thereby demonstrating the *guarantee* of our resurrection.

As Harris observes, "The risen Lord or his rising from the dead is the guarantee of the bodily resurrection of all his followers" (*Grave to Glory*, p. 223).

Joseph's empty tomb in Egypt illustrates this well. Although God told the Israelites that He would bring them to the Promised Land, when Moses appeared initially before Pharaoh, he asked only that Pharaoh allow the Israelites to go three days' journey into the wilderness to sacrifice to the LORD their God (Exod 3:18; 5:3; 7:16; 8:1; 8:20). Even when Pharaoh began to negotiate conditions for letting the Israelites go, Moses maintained that they were going three days' journey into the wilderness (8:25-27). When Pharaoh finally did let them go, it was to *serve the Lord as you have said*—that is, three days' journey into the wilderness (Exod 12:31). Yet, when Pharaoh was told that the Israelites had fled, he claimed to have lost his workforce of slaves:

> *Now it was told the king of Egypt that the people had fled, and the heart of Pharaoh and his servants was turned against the people; and they said, "Why have we done this, that we have let Israel go from serving us?"* (Exod 14:5)

Why did Pharaoh and the Egyptians assume that the Israelites had fled and were not coming back after three days of serving the LORD in the wilderness? It quite possibly could be because of the following:

> *... Moses took the bones of Joseph with him, for he had placed the children of Israel under solemn oath, saying, "God will surely visit you, and you shall carry up my bones from here with you."* (Exod 13:19)

As he was dying, Joseph told his brothers that God would visit them and bring them out of the land of Egypt into the land which He had sworn to Abraham, Isaac, and Jacob (Gen 50:24-25). In fulfillment of the oath under which Joseph had placed his brothers, Moses gathered Joseph's bones. Moses would not have done that if he and the Israelites would be going back to Egypt after three days. Therefore, Joseph's empty tomb was a sign that God was delivering the Israelites from bondage and they were indeed on their way to the Promised Land.

Likewise, we feel that Jesus' empty tomb was (and is) evidence to all Christians (especially those living in the first century) that we have been delivered from spiritual bondage and are on our way to the spiritual Promised Land, Heaven. We also note that, of all the Israelite tombs in Egypt, only one (Joseph's) need be emptied as evidence of the Israelites freedom from Egyptian bondage. Likewise, of all the Christian tombs through the ages, only one—Christ's—need be emptied as evidence that we have been freed from spiritual bondage.

Therefore, just because the graves of the saints remain occupied does not mean that there could not have been a resurrection of the dead, for it is a misunderstanding of the nature of the resurrected body that has led to the assumption that physical bodies will rise out of their earthly graves. The resurrected physical body that most of the Church insists on is far too limiting for what our resurrection bodies will actually be like. Rather than physical bodies that are "supercharged" in order to exist in the spiritual realm, we believe that our resurrection bodies are spiritual, with the capability of manifesting themselves in the physical realm, just as angels are able to. Just as seeing an angel in the form of man would not reveal the surpassing and glorious existence he possesses in the spiritual realm, so Christ's resurrected form as a man did not reveal His surpassing and glorious existence as described in Revelation 1. Harris notes:

> No New Testament writer broaches the subject of the anatomical or physiological constitution of the spiritual body. Details of its anatomy or physiology were of no more consequence to Paul and the early Christians than was the geography of heaven. (*Grave to Glory*, p. 194)

Thus, we believe that our resurrected bodies are not physical bodies with spiritual capabilities, but substantial, spiritual bodies with physical capabilities. While at first glance that might appear to be two ways of saying the same thing, it is not, for the latter far surpasses the former.

For example, was Jesus man becoming God, or God becoming man? Even though He was both God and Man, He was God who became Man, not man who became God. Likewise, the resurrection body is not the physical body exhibiting spiritual qualities, but a new spiritual body that can exhibit physical qualities. We might say, in a loose sense, that the resurrection is the process of the incarnation in reverse. To have a physical body implies the limitations that come with it. To say that God transforms that body so that it no longer has those limitations—capabilities yes, limitations no—we believe, is to say that the body is no longer physical. Still a body of substance, yes, but not a physical one, just as Paul says, "*There is a natural body, and there is a spiritual body*" (1 Cor 15:44).

In addition to this, what possible purpose would physical bodies serve in the spiritual dimension? When we realize that the kingdom of God is spiritual and not a physical kingdom on this earth, there is no purpose for physical bodies in the resurrection. Thus, the graves of the saints did not need to be emptied, nor did bodies need to float up to heaven, in order for the resurrection to have taken place.

Spiritual Resurrection

We have mentioned previously that, within the spectrum of Preterist doctrine, there are those who consider themselves Partial Preterists and those who consider themselves Full Preterists. The dividing point between the two is their respective interpretations regarding the general resurrection of the dead and final judgment. Full Preterists believe that *all* Bible prophecy is fulfilled (Luke 21:22), except for the ongoing aspects of the everlasting covenant (e.g., Mark 13:30-32; Heb 13:20). This dictates a nonphysical interpretation for the resurrection of the dead. Even though Partial Preterists believe that Christ came in judgment in AD 70, because they hold that the Bible teaches a physical resurrection of the dead and coming of Christ, they believe that there is yet to be a final physical coming of Christ, accompanied with a physical resurrection and judgment. As such, most Partial Preterists believe that the last few chapters of Revelation are yet to find fulfillment in human history.

The traditional/physical resurrection view has believers' graves opening, the reconstitution of their physical bodies, and their subsequent flight to Heaven. Since this did not occur in AD 70 (nor does it occur at the death of a believer post-AD 70), Full Preterism requires that the resurrection body have a more "spiritual" nature to it. This is where Futurism and Partial Preterism clash with Full Preterism. As a prime example, in Gentry's "Christ's Resurrection and Ours" article he labels Full Preterists as "hyper-preterists" and calls their spiritual interpretation of the resurrection "a new gnosticism."

It cannot be overstated that the resurrection is a crucial point for the acceptance of Full Preterism, as R. C. Sproul notes:

> The great weakness of full preterism—and what I regard to be its fatal flaw—is its treatment of the final resurrection. If full preterism is to gain wide credibility in our time, it must overcome this obstacle. (*The Last Days according to Jesus*, p. 203)

We would note that several Preterists have addressed Sproul's concerns from various resurrection perspectives, including: Dan Harden's

Overcoming Sproul's Resurrection Obstacles; John Noē's *Your Resurrection Body and Life: Here, Now, and Forever*; Randall Otto's *Case Dismissed: Rebutting Common Charges Against Preterism*. Sproul, a Partial Preterist, is not alone in his reservations about a spiritual interpretation of the resurrection and rapture endorsed by most Full Preterists. In his article, "A Closer Look at the 'AD 70 Theory' of Last Things," Olan Hicks writes:

> But God said, "Behold I make all things new." The truth is, as Paul said in 1 Cor 15:50, "Flesh and blood cannot inherit the kingdom of God, nor does corruption inherit incorruption." This mortal must put on immortality and this corruptible must put on incorruption. (vv. 52-53). In Max King's largest book he spends over 250 pages trying to explain away this entire chapter. When it takes that much "explaining" to support a theory, you know that theory has serious problems.

The book to which Hicks refers is King's *The Cross and the Parousia of Christ*, and King's theory is only one of several spiritual interpretations of the resurrection of the dead. It is our understanding that within Preterism there are two major views of the resurrection (each containing several variations): the *corporate resurrection* (Immortal Body Now) view and the *individual resurrection* (Immortal Body at Death) view. The corporate view does not see the resurrection as applying primarily to individuals, but rather to the corporate body of Christ. King notes:

> It is easy for commentators, who understand 1 Cor 15 to teach the resurrection of **physical bodies**, to substitute freely the plural **bodies** where Paul used the singular **body**, and to speak of **dead bodies** (even **corpses**) where Paul speaks of **the dead**, without any thought of a difference in meaning. There is, however, a difference that is crucial in following Paul's pattern of argumentation. Verse 35, for example, is an illustration of what we are saying. After the question, "How are the dead raised," Paul adds, "and with what body (not **bodies**) do they come?" What is the difference whether the singular body or the plural bodies is used? The claim that it makes no difference, that it is purely a matter of grammatical variation, is based on the assumption that Paul is thinking primarily of individuals. But what if Paul was thinking first and foremost of body from a collective or corporate viewpoint, which was quite common in Hebrew thought? In that case, the focus would be on the **singular collective** in which the destiny of the

many is determined. From this viewpoint, that which always is in the foreground in Paul's motif is **the body** rather than **bodies**.

This is illustrated further in verses 42-44 where Paul is answering the question of verse 35, "With what body do they (the dead) come?" He continues his use of the collective singular. "So also is the resurrection of the dead . . . It is sown a natural body." Paul is not thinking of a sowing of individual bodies one by one from Adam to Christ (or beyond Christ), but of the sowing of the **one body** that is inclusive of all who are bound up together within one common mode of somatic existence. (*The Cross and the Parousia of Christ*, pp. 549-550; emphases in original)

Similarly, McRay sees the forty-year transition period as the time when God transformed His people from a physical body into a spiritual body, that is, from the body of Moses to the Body of Christ (*The Last Days?*, p. 61, 1990, Kingdom Press). As mentioned previously, proponents of a corporate resurrection believe that the resurrection did not entail a change in the *substance* of a person's physical body, but rather a change in their spiritual *stance* before God. Some see this change as the corporate body of Old and New Testament believers resurrecting out of the Old Covenant into the New Covenant, as Preston explains:

Now if the Old Law was a ministration of death what would deliverance from that death be? Would it be life from the dead? Would it be resurrection? And if the Old Law was concerned with "carnal ordinances" Heb 9:10, and "things made with hands" but was to give way to the incorruptible Word of the Gospel, 1 Pet 1:23, would that not be a change from corruptibility to incorruptibility, 1 Cor 15:53? ("Resurrection" article at www.eschatology.org)

A suitable term for this view would be "Covenantal Resurrection," which would fall in the Corporate Resurrection category. King's corporate resurrection, while certainly founded on the changing of the covenants, seems to encompass more than just a change of covenant. As noted above, he takes 250 pages to explain the resurrection mentioned in 1 Corinthians 15, which is an indication that the view is not easily understood. In fact, King himself doubted whether the Corinthians ever truly understood the corporate view that Paul was attempting to explain to them (at least according to King's understanding):

Who can say if the Corinthians, in their lifetime, ever fully understood the meaning of Christ's resurrection and its bearing upon their own gospel resurrection, much less the subsequent resurrection of "the dead?" (*The Cross and the Parousia*, p. 750)

Preterists who hold a Corporate Resurrection view interpret 2 Corinthians 5:1, in which Paul speaks of our earthly tent being torn down and of our receipt of a new building from God, of the corruptible putting on incorruption and the mortal putting on immortality, etc., as a metaphor for change between the Old and New Covenants. The earthly tent, or tabernacle, is the temple of the Old Covenant, while the building from God is the Church, the temple of the New Covenant.

Other Preterists believe that the resurrection of the saints is realized on an individual basis (although many will admit readily that, while there exists a corporate sense to the resurrection, they see it as secondary). These Preterists do not see present-day saints as having already received their resurrected bodies, having put on immortality in this life, but rather as receiving a spiritual body in the life to come.

When we consider the spiritual nature of the New Covenant we must wonder about the insistence on a physical body in the resurrection. Concerning the resurrection body, Paul wrote:

It is sown a natural body, it is raised a spiritual body. There is a natural body, and there is a spiritual body. (1 Cor 15:44)

He does not say that it is sown a natural body and *changed* into a spiritual body. He says that there are *two* bodies—a natural one and a spiritual one. Harris deals with this in depth:

> . . . biochemists inform us that during a seven-year cycle the molecular composition of our bodies is completely changed. Even during our present life the continuity between the body now possessed and the body possessed seven years ago resides in personality, not materiality. . . . In a similar way, we suggest, the link between the Christian's successive forms of embodiment—the physical, then the spiritual—lies in the same identifiable *ego*. Just as there is a historical continuity—an identity—between our present body and the body we had at birth, so there will be a historical continuity— an identity of identifiable personal characteristics—between the present body and the resurrection body.
>
> . . . But is not God able to gather together, sort out, and reassemble the scattered particles of decomposed or incinerated corpses, so that the resurrection body will have the same molecular structure

as the body that was laid in the grave or cremated? Indeed he is. And, of course, such a miracle, though awe-inspiring, would be less amazing than God's original creation of matter "out of nothing." But even if God were to follow this procedure on the morning of the resurrection, the material identity would still not be complete or absolute, for in the course of natural processes there has been an ongoing movement of the same material particles from one living organism to another, so that the reconstruction of persons as they were at the time of their death would necessarily involve the fresh creation of at least some material particles. And what of persons who were deformed throughout life or who were fatally injured in an accident. Will they rise with their deformities or their injuries? And will children be eternally assigned to childhood?

All these considerations make it inevitable that we reject the notion that resurrection involves the regaining of exactly the same material particles of which our physical bodies were composed at the time of death. The majority of Christian scholars, both ancient and modern, concur in rejecting this notion. (*Grave to Glory*, pp. 199-201; emphasis in original)

Although the link between the physical body and the spiritual body is not in identical material particles, there is real continuity between the two in that the same "person" finds expression in two successive but different types of body. (Ibid., p. 238)

. . . I argue that there is no identity between the molecular structure of the physical and spiritual bodies of believers . . . . (Ibid., p. 436)

According to the IBD view, upon death we exchange the physical body, which cannot inherit the kingdom of God, for a spiritual one, which can.

Now we know that if the earthly tent we live in is destroyed, we have a building from God, an eternal house in heaven, not built by human hands. (2 Cor 5:1 NIV)

However, the spiritual is not first, but the natural, and afterward the spiritual. The first man was of the earth, made of dust; the second Man is the Lord from heaven. As was the man of dust, so also are those who are made of dust; and as is the heavenly Man, so also are those who are heavenly. And as we have borne the image of the man of dust, we shall also bear the image of the heavenly Man. (1 Cor 15:46-49)

This image of the heavenly Man which we shall bear, we feel is more analogous to the description of Christ in the first chapter of Revelation than of His manifested appearances prior to His ascension. The fact that Christ existed in heaven prior to His incarnation demonstrates that His physical body was not necessary for Him to return to heaven at His ascension. This lends credence to the premise that His physical body was resurrected only to demonstrate His power over death and the grave. Christ's resurrection power allows us to exchange our physical bodies for spiritual ones—an exchange that the saints prior to the Parousia were unable to experience because of their particular place in both human and redemptive history: thus the angel's declaration at the consummation of the New Covenant, *"Blessed are the dead who die in the Lord from now on"* (Rev 14:13).

Conclusion

The resurrection is clearly a complex issue. Volumes can and have been written about it. We recommend the following books and articles for further reading on the various views:

Corporate view: Max R. King's *The Cross and the Parousia of Christ*; Samuel Frost's *Exegetical Essays on The Resurrection of the Dead*

Covenantal view: Don K. Preston's "The Resurrection" article (www.eschatology.org)

Immortal Body at Death (IBD) view: Daniel Harden's *Overcoming Sproul's Resurrection Obstacle;* Ed Stevens' *Questions about the Afterlife*; Steve and Tom Kloske's *The Second Coming: Mission Accomplished*

While we favor the IBD view, we are not dogmatic on this particular issue, as we are still studying and formulating our own views. Obviously, the corporate/covenantal views are not without proponents who can define and defend them ably. We recommend, however, that those who decry anything but a literal physical resurrection take a closer look at the foundation upon which their view is built, for to us a literal physical resurrection appears contrary to Scripture. If we can be *"crucified with Christ and buried with Him through baptism,"* but *"nevertheless live"* (cf. Gal 2:20; Rom 6:4) in a spiritual sense, can we not also be *"resurrected in His likeness"* (Rom 6:5) in a spiritual sense?

If Futurists and Partial Preterists were to reexamine the basis upon which a literal *physical* resurrection is founded and consider the possibilities of a literal *spiritual* resurrection, the doors to more accepting and fruitful dialogue might be opened. Additionally, Partial Preterists might find that there is no need for an awkward "third" coming of Christ in a future final judgment and resurrection.

Because this resurrection discussion has been rather didactic, we close with the following thoughts from Harris in order to bring this sacred subject back into perspective:

> Before we begin any detailed discussion of the event we call the resurrection of Jesus Christ, it is appropriate for all of us reverently to stand back, slip off the shoes of our human pride, and remember that the ground under our feet is indeed sacred. For even when we have tried our utmost to understand rightly all the New Testament narratives that describe this unparalleled event, we must confess our inability as mere mortals to fully penetrate the mystery of Christ's resurrection to immortality. (*Grave to Glory*, p. 371)

> Inevitably, when we set ourselves a task such as this and are investigating a topic such as Christ's resurrection, we soon discover that we are probing a mystery that defies human understanding and mocks human language. (Ibid., p. 440)

> In reality we are dealing here with one of the ultimate mysteries of the universe—the relation of matter of "body" to spirit—so that all these hypotheses are at best accommodations to human language. (Ibid., p. 375)

The Partial or the Perfect

—◆—

Just as the size and placement of a window can restrict one's view from a home, so the framework of one's position on the "partial or perfect" can restrict their perspective on other doctrines. The terms "partial" (also described as first fruits and pledge), and "perfect" (also described as harvest and fullness) come from 1 Corinthians:

> *For we know in part and we prophesy in part.* **But when that which is perfect has come, then that which is in part will be done away.** *When I was a child, I spoke as a child, I understood as a child, I thought as a child; but when I became a man, I put away childish things. For now we see in a mirror, dimly, but then face to face. Now I know in part, but then I shall know just as I also am known.* (1 Cor 13:9-12)

> *For we know that the whole creation groans and labors with birth pangs together until now. Not only that, but we also who have* **the firstfruits of the Spirit,** *even we ourselves groan within ourselves, eagerly waiting for the adoption, the redemption of our body.* (Rom 8:22-23)

> *Now He who establishes us with you in Christ and anointed us is God, who also sealed us and gave us the Spirit in our hearts as a* **pledge.** (2 Cor 1:21-22 NASB95)

> *For indeed while we are in this tent, we groan, being burdened, because we do not want to be unclothed but to be clothed, so that what is mortal will be swallowed up by life. Now He who prepared us for this very purpose is God, who gave to us the Spirit as a* **pledge.** (2 Cor 5:4-5 NASB95)

> *In Him, you also, after listening to the message of truth, the gospel of your salvation—having also believed, you were sealed in Him with the Holy Spirit of promise, who is given* **as a pledge of our inheritance,** *with a view to the redemption of God's own posses-sion, to the praise of His glory . . . . Do not grieve the Holy Spirit*

397

of God, by whom you were sealed for the day of redemption. (Eph
1:13-14; 4:30 NASB)
(emphases added)

While the New Testament saints were already partakers of many
aspects of the New Covenant and kingdom of God, they were waiting for
a fuller experience (sometimes referred to theologically as the "already/
not yet"). This is illustrated in the following topics, where Scriptures are
given which indicate the *partial* measure already being experienced by the
New Testament saints, and the *perfect* measure expected by them. (The
information presented here is based upon the book by Ian Harding, *Taken
to Heaven in AD 70.*)

Salvation:

Partial:

*For by grace you **have been saved** through faith; and that not of
yourselves; it is the gift of God . . . .* (Eph 2:8)

Perfect:

*Do this, knowing the time, that it is already the hour for you
to awaken from sleep; for **now salvation is nearer to us than
when we believed**. The night is almost gone, and the day is near.
Therefore let us lay aside the deeds of darkness and put on the
armor of light.* (Rom 13:11-12 NASB95)

Righteousness/Justification:

Partial:

*Therefore, **having been justified** by faith, we have peace with God
through our Lord Jesus Christ . . . .* (Rom 5:1)

Perfect:

*For we through the Spirit, by faith, are **waiting for the hope of
righteousness**.* (Gal 5:5 NASB95)

Resurrection:

Partial:

*But God, being rich in mercy, because of His great love with which
He loved us, even when we were dead in our transgressions, **made***

*us alive together with Christ (by grace you have been saved), **and raised us up with Him**, and seated us with Him in the heavenly places in Christ Jesus . . . .* (Eph 2:4-6 NASB95)

Perfect:

*Now God has not only raised the Lord, but **will also raise us up** through His power.* (1 Cor 6:14 NASB95)

Redemption:

Partial:

In Him we have redemption *through His blood, the forgiveness of our trespasses, according to the riches of His grace . . . .* (Eph 1:7 NASB95)

Perfect:

*. . . who is given as a pledge of our inheritance, **with a view to the redemption** of God's own possession, to the praise of His glory.* (Eph 1:14 NASB95)
(emphases added)

From a Preterist perspective the "perfect" has come and there is no longer any "already/not yet" aspect to the Scripture (except for ongoing portions of the everlasting covenant). The question then is, *after* the Second Coming, when do new converts receive their fullness? Is it upon their conversion, or upon their death? There are Preterists on both sides of the issue. In fact, narrowing the issue to two sides is probably an oversimplification. The Resurrection and, as we shall see, The Rapture, are also intertwined with the partial and perfect. The first-century saints obviously had something prior to AD 70 (the partial), and received something more at Christ's Second Coming (the perfect).

Some Preterists argue that the New Covenant was fully consummated in AD 70, and that post-AD 70 believers receive that fullness of the New Covenant upon conversion. Based upon the spiritual nature of the New Covenant, they hold that statements which speak of our beholding God face to face, of reigning with Christ, of putting on incorruption and immortality, etc., are to be understood in a spiritual or covenantal sense, and not interpreted literally. As stated in "The Resurrection" chapter, the natural conclusion here is that if we receive all of this at conversion, then salvation is equated with having our resurrection bodies and having put on immortality.

Others would say that if we are living in the fullness of the New Covenant—the "perfect" that the apostles were expecting—then we should have more insight of the Scriptures, better prayer lives, and holier walks than they did, for they were only living in a first fruits experience. Since this is obviously not the case, these Preterists argue that we also must be living in a first fruits experience, which means that we will receive our fullness upon death. In Revelation 14, at the consummation of the New Covenant, a voice from heaven proclaims, " . . . *blessed are the dead who die in the Lord from now on*" (v. 13). Preterists on this side of the issue would point out that it is those who *die* in the Lord, not those who *believe* in the Lord from now on. This is because up until the consummation of the New Covenant in AD 70 the righteous dead were not in the full presence of God. They had not received the promise, but were waiting to receive it along with the New Testament saints at the consummation of the New Covenant and return of Christ (Heb 11:39-40). But "*blessed are the dead who die in the Lord from now on*" after the consummation, because there is no longer any waiting period in Sheol/Hades. Upon their deaths they immediately receive the fullness of the Covenant.

Still others would say that the New Covenant was fully consummated at Pentecost and that the "perfect" anticipated by the saints was being raptured to heaven in a literal sense. In this view we would not have better prayer lives or understanding of the Scripture because we are living in the same first fruits (partial) capacity that they were. We will attain the "perfect" upon our individual deaths.

Those (or at least some) who believe that we now have our resurrection bodies, also believe that what the Bible describes as the Heavenly state—that place where God dwells—is a description of God dwelling with us in the salvation experience. Thus they claim that we have "Heaven now."

While perhaps not all who hold to a corporate resurrection view would say that we are in Heaven now, most believe that all of the descriptions of the New Jerusalem and Heaven are metaphors for what the Church has today in the fullness of the New Covenant. King asks the question,

> What is the meaning of "in heaven?" It generally is understood as referring to the eternal destiny of man following the end of the Christian age. In this view, entering heaven is associated with resurrection from physical death in connection with the destruction of this world. Without question, heaven is the eternal abode of redeemed man, but the biblical meaning of heaven in these

passages [1 Pet 1:3-5; Col 1:3-6] is missed when it is placed in contrast to **planet earth**. In redemptive history, the contrast is between two worlds, aeons, or modes of life as determined by the two covenants. It is not the passing of the earth but the Old Covenant kosmos that determines the destiny of man in terms of "heavenly things" or "things in the heavens."

. . .

Because of the tendency to interpret the heavenly realm spatially, to see it as **other worldly** in terms of that which is beyond human existence, the preparation that Jesus talked about seldom is seen as occurring on earth in connection with His body, the church. But it is precisely here that the quickening, transforming Spirit accomplished that which Jesus said would be done in His going away and coming again. Jesus' return (His presence or arrival) occurred through the covenantal transforming ministry of the Spirit. . . . The Spirit is not sent as a replacement for Christ, but as the transforming power through which the presence of Christ is progressively mediated unto His own, until "we all come . . . unto the measure of the stature of the fullness of Christ" (Eph 4:13). Reaching this "fullness of Christ" equals conformity to His image (Rom 8:29; Phil 3:20, 21; Col 1:15-19), and therefore has the meaning of consummated entrance into His presence—**into the holiest of all**.

. . .

It is important to take note of the contrasting terminology **earthly** and **heavenly** which is descriptive of the nature of the two contrasting covenantal aeons. It is a mistake to see the heavenly things or heavenly house as **other-worldly** in the sense of something that is beyond the New Covenant age. (*The Cross and The Parousia*, pp. 678-679, 559-560, 585; all emphases in original)

This is not to say that Preterists who hold Corporate or Covenantal Resurrection views do not believe in a greater existence for us after death:

"We are not saying that there is no beyond, that man will not, at physical death, enter unto a mode of being that transcends biological existence with its limitations." (*The Cross and The Parousia*, p. 685)

Preston, a Covenantal Resurrection advocate, also believes in a "beyond," while putting the traditional biblical descriptions of Heaven in our present realm:

> I used to look at Revelation 21 and 22 as a description of Heaven. . . . I believe Heaven is so much better, and so much greater, than even that [which] is presented in Revelation 21 and 22, that we can't even begin to imagine it and fathom it. (*Transition Period and the Millennium*, audio tape #6)

So we see that one's views of the resurrection and the partial and the perfect are inseparably linked. If we hold a Corporate/Covenantal Resurrection view, then we are living in the perfect today. Biblical terms that we traditionally associated with Heaven and the "afterlife" become metaphors for our present experiences in the New Covenant. Whatever may be in store for us on the other side of physical death, it is not described in the Bible:

> In tying the change of the living and resurrection of the dead to the full outworking of covenantal change, the objection may be raised that this leaves unanswered the composition or make-up of man beyond his biological demise, whether saved or lost. This obviously is true, but is this just cause for alarm? Do we have the right to pervert the meaning of that which is revealed in an effort to go beyond and discover things known only to God (Deut. 29:29)? Was not the Bible written for creaturely man, for man as he is now, in this stage of existence? What greater evidence is needed that God is both able and willing to sustain life forever, in whatever form He chooses, than the full, complete and perfect life that we now have in Christ through the covenantal change effected by His death and resurrection? Is it not enough to know that in this manner, "God hath given to us eternal life, and this life is in his Son" (1 John 5:11)? (*The Cross and The Parousia*, p. 594)

On the other hand, if we receive our resurrection bodies and put on immortality at physical death, then we are now living in a "partial" condition, since we will receive more later. This does not mean that the New Covenant, nor any aspect of salvation, is incomplete. Rather, as Ian Harding states, we are unable to experience the fullness of life in Christ while in these physical bodies:

. . . the Christian has the capacity for only a firstfruit or deposit experience of God's new covenant salvation while in the mortal body. (*Taken to Heaven in AD 70*, p. 23)

When saints, such as the apostles John and Paul, and prophets such as Ezekiel, Daniel and Isaiah, received a small vision into God's glory-realm, they fell down as dead men, depleted of all strength. While on this earth in earthly bodies and imperfect capacities, man can only cope with a deposit/firstfruit measure of the coming glory. (Ibid., p. 62)

One can easily see that it would take another book to fully address this issue. Our intent here is to give a very brief introduction to the differing views, giving the reader a broad picture of Preterism. It is our further hope and prayer that, based upon the soundness of the foundation and framework, the reader will desire to search out these matters for further contemplation. Perhaps he or she will be the very one we mentioned earlier, who will take up the torch and illuminate the truths that are yet to be discovered.

The Rapture

—ᴍ—

C losely tied to one's view on the partial and perfect (and the resurrection) is their view of the rapture—the catching away of the saints at the Second Coming. Although we used the term "rapture" in the chapter "The Veiled Generation," most Preterists do not interpret the rapture in the manner popularized by teachings such as those found in the *Left Behind* series of novels. Rather than a physical catching away of the saints, many believe that it is a reference to being spiritually "gathered" into the New Covenant (or the spiritual kingdom). While it is our understanding that most Preterists hold to a spiritual interpretation of the rapture, in the last several years there has been a growing number of Preterists that support a physical catching away of the New Testament saints. This view is presented by Edward E. Stevens in his book *Expectations Demand a First Century Rapture* as well as in Ian Harding's *Taken to Heaven in AD 70*. A literal rapture is not a new concept within Preterism, having been postulated by earlier Preterists such as J. Stuart Russell, E. Hampdon-Cook, Richard Weymouth, William S. Urmy and Milton Terry.

While many Preterists feel that a physical rapture is too radical of a departure from the spiritual nature of the New Covenant, others feel that it more adequately explains the expectations of the New Testament saints. A third view, the Process View, sees problems with both the spiritual and literal rapture views. They are among those noted in the previous chapter who take issue with present-day Christians experiencing the perfect here on earth. They also struggle with the concept of a literal rapture in AD 70. Therefore, they believe that, subsequent to AD 70, individual believers are "raptured" at their deaths. We will briefly examine the three views.

Spiritual Rapture

Those that hold to a spiritual/covenantal nature of the rapture use the example of being born-again, which Paul describes as a translation:

> *He has delivered us from the power of darkness and translated us into the kingdom of the Son . . . . (Col 1:13)*

Obviously this deliverance from the power of darkness and translation into the kingdom of His Son takes place on a spiritual plane. Therefore we should expect nothing different when the saints are *translated* into the fullness of that kingdom at the Second Coming of Christ. This is further supported by other uses of the term "gather":

> *O Jerusalem, Jerusalem, the one who kills the prophets and stones those who are sent to her! How often I wanted to **gather** your children together, as a hen gathers her chicks under her wings, but you were not willing!* (Matt 23:37; emphasis added)

Here, it is claimed, the gathering Jesus intended was that of being gathered into His spiritual kingdom, not into one physical locale. Therefore, the gathering of the rapture is also seen as being gathered into His spiritual kingdom. One of the primary rapture texts being 1 Thessalonians 4:13-18, we offer that passage and a few of King's comments to illustrate the spiritual interpretation:

> *But I do not want you to be ignorant, brethren, concerning those who have fallen asleep, lest you sorrow as others who have no hope. For if we believe that Jesus died and rose again, even so God will bring with Him those who sleep in Jesus. For this we say to you by the word of the Lord, that we who are alive and remain until the coming of the Lord will by no means precede those who are asleep. For the Lord Himself will descend from heaven with a shout, with the voice of an archangel, and with the trumpet of God. And the dead in Christ will rise first. Then we who are alive and remain shall be caught up together with them in the clouds to meet the Lord in the air. And thus we shall always be with the Lord. Therefore comfort one another with these words.* (1 Thess 4:13-18)

Caught up in a Cloud. "Then we which are alive and remain shall be caught up together with them in the clouds, to meet the Lord in the air:" Clouds, in biblical language, are symbolic of God's majesty, power, and presence. It is a figure of speech denoting the glory and the elevated position of the saints on that day of vindication. (See Matt 13:43; Rom 8:18; Col 3:4). Also, Christ is pictured as coming in the clouds, denoting his power and glory that would be manifested in that day.

To meet the Lord in the Air. This gathering of the saints to Christ in the air, to ever be with him there, has been no small problem to the "literalists." But *air* is a symbol of the heavenly or spiritual realm wherein the government of God is exercised. Concerning Satan, (before he was cast out) it was said that he was the prince of the power of the *air*. (Eph 2:2; 6:11). But Christ conquered Satan and cleansed the "air" and restored man to his rightful dominion of life and righteousness, and so shall we ever be with the Lord . . . .The thought is the glorious reunion of Christ and his saints as promised in John 14:1-3 and Matthew 24:31. (*The Spirit of Prophecy*, pp. 206-207; emphasis in original)

Being caught up together in the clouds to meet the Lord in the air simply is accommodative language denoting the end-of-the-age gathering together of God's elect (Eph 1:10). In a parallel text dealing with the AD 70 fall of Jerusalem, Christ revealed that He would ". . . send his angels with a great sound of a trumpet, and they shall gather together his elect from the four winds, from one end of heaven to the other" (Matt 24:31). The point is that all of God's elect (both the first fruit saints and historical Israel) would be gathered as one new creation in Christ in the final end of the old dispensation. This is the point in the so-called *rapture* text (1 Thess 4). To insist on a literal reading of that which is clearly symbolic (apocalyptic) language is to miss the spiritual truths contained in such passages. (*The Cross and The Parousia*, p. 641; emphasis in original)

We believe . . . that the departure of Christ from the Old Covenant kosmos to prepare a place in the coming New Covenant kosmos from which He appears the second time apart from sin to receive His disciples unto Himself, is the biblical exposition of the "rapture" of the saints at the end of the age. (Ibid., pp. 702-703)

Literal Rapture

There are others who feel that Preterists, after having championed the hermeneutic of audience relevance for the *timing* of the Second Coming, have abandoned it when it comes to the *substance* of the Second Coming, citing what the New Testament saints were expecting:

- To be where Christ is (John 14:3)
- To be united with previously deceased saints (1 Thess 4:17)
- To have their bodies changed, redeemed, and transformed to be like Christ's glorious body (Phil 3:21)

- To be like Christ (1 John 3:2)
- To appear with Him in glory (Col 3:4)

A spiritual interpretation of the rapture, they argue, does not fulfill these expectations of the early church. To illustrate the literal interpretation of the rapture we offer select quotes from Stevens in which he comments on the phrase *caught up* from the 1 Thessalonians 4 passage:

> Some figurative-rapturists assert that the "snatching" is not a "catching up" of living saints at the parousia, but rather a post-AD 70 process of taking of their souls/spirits to heaven after they die. But Paul says the living (and the dead with them) are snatched then, not just their souls at death later. The only way they could make this fit their theory would be to assume that all these living saints were martyred right at the time of Christ's parousia in AD 70 and therefore their souls were "snatched" at the time of the parousia. But if they lived on beyond the AD 70 parousia and died later after AD 70, then something is drastically wrong with either Paul's statements here or our interpretation of them. He said the "living and remaining ones" would be snatched, not their souls after death. This is an event which occurs to the living at the parousia, not a process that only begins to occur to the souls of those saints who die after the parousia from AD 70 onwards. (*Expectations Demand A First Century Rapture*, pp. 114-115, by Edward E. Stevens—International Preterist Association)

> 1 Thess 4 is literally talking about the dead saints in Hades being raised out of Hades. Then those who are still alive and remained alive until the parousia would be "snatched away" or "caught up" together with them (v. 17) into the air (the spiritual realm where the angels were active) where Christ had just "descended" (v. 16) with His angels. It says that Christ would "descend from heaven" and meet them "in the clouds" and "in the air." (Ibid., p. 118)

Ian Harding argues that both deceased and living saints had been promised the same expectations of glory, to be realized by both groups at the same time—Christ's Parousia:

- *Those believers who had died* before the time of the Parousia, expected to be gathered to Christ at the Parousia and to inherit fully their eternal inheritance . . . .

- *Those believers who were alive* at the time of the Parousia, *also* expected to be gathered to Christ at the Parousia and to inherit fully the same eternal inheritance.

- Both deceased and living believers prior to AD 70, all, together, on the occasion of the Parousia, expected to receive the fulfillment of the promised consummate measure of new covenant blessings . . . which would see them totally delivered from remaining on earth in mortal bodies carrying a legacy of fallenness, and totally delivered into a permanent glorified state with the glorified Christ and the Father in heaven. (*Taken to Heaven in AD 70*, pp. 145-146)

(emphases in original)

The Process View

Steve and Tom Kloske support the Process View in their book *The Second Coming: Mission Accomplished.* The following notes are excerpted from a message delivered by David Curtis at Berean Bible Church (www. BereanBibleChurch.org):

Then [Gk. epeita] we who are alive and remain shall be caught up together with them in the clouds to meet the Lord in the air. And thus we shall always be with the Lord. (1 Thess 4:17)

This is the verse that the physical rapture theory comes from. A little time spent looking at the Greek words should quickly dispel many false notions.

Let's start with the first word in the verses—the word "then." Normally, when a sequence of events is described, the simple word *eita* "then" is used. *Eita* is best translated as "at that time" or "next." *Eita* is used to indicate an immediate sequence. But in our text, the Greek word is not *eita* but *epeita*, which is essentially the same Greek word with an "*epi*" prefix. This has the effect of affixing the word "after" to the word "then," and the best translation becomes "after then," "after that," or "after that time," and thereby doesn't include the idea of right after.

Let's look at some other uses of *epeita* to get a clearer idea of its meaning:

Then (epeita) after three years I went up to Jerusalem to see Peter, and remained with him fifteen days. (Gal 1:18)

Then (epeita) after fourteen years I went up again to Jerusalem with Barnabas, and also took Titus with me. (Gal 2:1)

In Galatians 1:18 the word "then" (*epeita*) involved at least three years later, while in 2:1 it involved fourteen years. The point is that the form of the word for "then" used in 1 Thessalonians 4:17 is not the form *eita*, meaning: "right after," but *epeita*, meaning: "after that time."

Then (after that time) *we who are alive and remain shall be caught up together with them in the clouds to meet the Lord in the air. And thus we shall always be with the Lord.*

What would be the point of saying *"the dead in Christ will rise first,"* if the living were to be also caught up and changed at almost the same time? Paul is saying that at the return of Christ the dead in Christ will be resurrected, after that time the living will be "caught up" with them in the clouds at their physical death.

The words "caught up" are [from] the Greek word *harpazo*, it means: "to snatch away." [We note here that the word *harpazo* has no directional indicators, such as "up" or "away." These have been added by translators—BLM] This is where the word "rapture" comes from. But certainly being "caught up" means something different than a levitation of the physical body from earth up into the atmosphere of the sky. Remember, this being "caught up" happens some time after the second coming.

Harpazo could refer to the body being "caught up" but it could also refer to the Christian being "caught up" without the body. It is used this way in:

I know a man in Christ who fourteen years ago; whether in the body I do not know, or whether out of the body I do not know, God knows; such a one was caught up (harpazo) to the third heaven. And I know such a man; whether in the body or out of the body I do not know, God knows; how he was caught up (harpazo) into Paradise and heard inexpressible words, which it is not lawful for a man to utter. (2 Cor 12:2-4)

Paul doesn't know whether the body was involved in this man's "snatching away." The body isn't necessary, then, in the *harpazo* event, or Paul wouldn't have expressed this uncertainty. We know that Paul didn't mean that living Christians would be caught up in their living, physical bodies at the Second Coming of Christ because this never happened. Christians were still around on the earth after the Second Coming, as history plainly tells us.

Paul says that those who were alive at the Second Coming will *later be caught up together* with the dead who were raised, to meet the Lord in the air.

It is not the physical body that is raptured. It is the Christian himself who is raptured as he leaves his body behind at physical death and moves into the spiritual realm (the "air"). The dead believers were resurrected when Christ returned, and all other Christians would be caught up at their physical death. The writer of Hebrews wrote:

And as it is appointed for men to die once, but after this the judgment . . . . (Heb 9:27)

We won't escape physical death, we all have an appointment with it. But when we do die physically, we are "raptured" into the heavenly realm, *"And thus we shall always be with the Lord"* (1 Thess 4:17).

Once again, it would take a book to fully explore this issue. (Indeed, Preterist books dealing with just the rapture are now being written.) Since our primary objective in this volume is to introduce and establish the foundation and framework of Preterism rather than conduct an exhaustive study on all of its implications, we will leave off here.

All Israel Will Be Saved

—⚹—

And so all Israel will be saved, as it is written:

"The Deliverer will come out of Zion,
And He will turn away ungodliness from Jacob;
For this is My covenant with them,
When I take away their sins." (Rom 11:26-27)

We turn our attention now to Paul's statement in Romans 11:26 that *"all Israel will be saved."* If this is referring to national, fleshly Israel, does that not fly in the face of everything we have seen so far about the Old Covenant passing away and finding its fulfillment in the New? Up to this point, everything has harmonized concerning the transition from the Old to the New Covenant. Each item has seen a physical type in the Old Covenant, which coexisted with its spiritual fulfillment during the transition period, and then finally passed away. For national Israel to continue on (or reemerge) in the New Covenant disrupts the pattern that has so perfectly repeated itself thus far.

This is not to say that Jews cannot be saved, for salvation is to the Jews first (Rom 1:16). Because the early Church was almost exclusively Jewish, the problem is not with Jews being saved, but rather with the Jewish *nation* being saved. How can the type and the antitype coexist for any longer than the transition period? If the type does not pass away, then it cannot properly be considered a type, for by definition a type is something that imperfectly foreshadows an ultimate fulfillment. We remind the reader of Goppelt's words, "The type is not essentially a miniature version of the antitype, but is a prefiguration in a different stage of redemptive history that indicates the outline or essential features . . . of the future reality and that loses its own significance when that reality appears" (quoted in Hanegraaff, *The Apocalypse Code*, p. 173).

Yet apart from this passage in Romans 11, everything else about fleshly and spiritual Israel fits perfectly into the pattern that we have seen in the other elements of the covenants. Is there an alternative to all *fleshly (national)* Israel being saved? We remind the reader that there are two

413

Israels in biblical eschatology (Rom 9:6-8). In fact, Paul's statement that *they are not all Israel who are of Israel* lies at the beginning of the passage (Rom 9-11), which deals first with Israel's rejection of Christ and then with *all Israel* being saved. We also note that this section of Scripture contains deep, theological concepts and, because of this, is a source of endless controversy, not just over the subject at hand, but also over the predestination issue. Therefore, we are certainly not claiming to have the "last word" in this area, but desire only to bring out the points which we feel refute the notion that all *national* Israel shall be saved, as is popularized by certain Futurist views. There are differing interpretations of this passage within Preterism, and we present the following material as one possibility.

Throughout these three chapters in Romans, Paul intermittently uses the term "Israel" to refer to either national/fleshly Israel or spiritual/elect Israel. Although many interpret Paul's conclusion that all Israel will be saved as pertaining to *national* Israel, Paul's opening remarks, and several others throughout the passage, would seem to indicate otherwise:

> *I tell the truth in Christ, I am not lying, my conscience also bearing me witness in the Holy Spirit, that **I have great sorrow and continual grief in my heart. For I could wish that I myself were accursed from Christ for my brethren, my countrymen according to the flesh,** who are Israelites . . . .* (Rom 9:1-4)

> *Isaiah also cries out concerning Israel:*

> *"Though the number of the children of Israel be as the sand of the sea,*

> **The remnant will be saved.**
> *For He will finish the work and cut it short in righteousness,*
> *Because the LORD will make a short work upon the earth."*

> *And as Isaiah said before:*

> **"Unless the LORD of Sabaoth had left us a seed,**
> **We would have become like Sodom,**
> **And we would have been made like Gomorrah."** (Rom 9:27-29)

> **Brethren, my heart's desire and prayer to God for Israel is that they may be saved.** (Rom 10:1)

> *But Isaiah is very bold and says:*
> *"I was found by those who did not seek Me;*
> *I was made manifest to those who did not ask for Me."*

But **to Israel he says:**

"All day long I have stretched out My hands
*To **a disobedient and contrary people**."* (Rom 10:20-21)

For I speak to you Gentiles; inasmuch as I am an apostle to the
*Gentiles, I magnify my ministry, if by any means I may **provoke to***
***jealousy those who are my flesh** and **save some of them**.* (Rom
11:13-14)

And they [fleshly Israel, represented by the natural branches]
*also, **if they do not continue in unbelief**, will be grafted in, for*
*God is able to graft them in **again**.* (Rom 11:23-24)
(emphases added)

Paul is clearly anguishing over *national* Israel—his *countrymen*
according to the flesh—because they were *a disobedient and contrary*
people and only a *remnant would be saved*. Therefore:

- Paul had *great sorrow and continual grief*
- Paul actually wished that he was *accursed from Christ* for his
  brethren
- his *heart's desire and prayer to God for Israel is that they may be*
  saved
- he tried by *any means* to *provoke to jealousy* his fellow Jews in the
  hope that, *if* they did *not continue in unbelief*, he might *save **some***
  of them

Paul goes so far as to say that he wishes that he could be *accursed from*
Christ for the sake of his brethren! Does that sound like the heartfelt cry of
a person who believed that all his physical countrymen would be saved?
These passages give absolutely no hint that all national/physical Israel
will be saved. Quite the contrary, they emphatically declare the source of
Paul's *continual grief*—all physical Israel would *not* be saved. Are we to
believe, then, that one verse (11:26) totally negates all these others? But if
all *national* Israel is not saved, just exactly who is *all Israel*, and how are
they all saved?

*And **so** all Israel will be saved, as it is written:*
"The Deliverer will come out of Zion,
And He will turn away ungodliness from Jacob;
For this is My covenant with them,
When I take away their sins." (Rom 11:26-27; emphasis added)

Notice that the verse does *not* say, "And *then* all Israel will be saved," but says, "And *so* all Israel will be saved." This is no small matter, for the context is not saying that after the preceding event(s), *then* all Israel will be saved, but rather, in the manner described by the preceding event(s), **so** all Israel will be saved. The Greek word translated **so** is ουτο:

Strong's Greek Dictionary NT: 3779

houto (hoo'-to); or (before a vowel) houtos (hoo'-toce); adverb from NT: 3778; **in this way (<u>referring to what precedes or follows</u>):**

KJV—after that, **after (in) this manner**, as, **even (so)**, for all that, **like (-wise)**, no more, **on this fashion** (-wise), **so (in like manner)**, **thus**, what.
(emphases added)

Consider these usages of ουτο by Paul elsewhere in Romans:

*Therefore, as through one man's offense judgment came to all men, resulting in condemnation, even **so** through one Man's righteous act the free gift came to all men, resulting in justification of life. For as by one man's disobedience many were made sinners, **so** also by one Man's obedience many will be made righteous.* (Rom 5:18-19)

*. . . as sin reigned in death, even **so** grace might reign through righteousness to eternal life through Jesus Christ our Lord.* (Rom 5:21)

*Therefore we were buried with Him through baptism into death, that just as Christ was raised from the dead by the glory of the Father, even **so** we also should walk in newness of life.* (Rom 6:4)

*For the death that He died, He died to sin once for all; but the life that He lives, He lives to God. **Likewise** you also, reckon yourselves to be dead indeed to sin, but alive to God in Christ Jesus our Lord.* (Rom 6:10-11)

*I speak in human terms because of the weakness of your flesh. For just as you presented your members as slaves of uncleanness, and of lawlessness leading to more lawlessness, **so** now present your members as slaves of righteousness for holiness.* (Rom 6:19)

*But what does the divine response say to him? "I have reserved for Myself seven thousand men who have not bowed the knee to Baal." Even **so** then, at this present time there is a remnant according to the election of grace.* (Rom 11:4-5)

*For as we have many members in one body, but all the members do not have the same function, **so** we, being many, are one body in Christ, and individually members of one another.* (Rom 12:4-5) (emphases added)

It is easy to see from the above examples how the word **so** is often used as a "hinge" between an illustration and that which is being illustrated:

- As judgment came to all men, so the free gift came to all men
- As many were made sinners, so many will be made righteous
- As sin reigned in death, so grace reigns in righteousness
- As Christ died to sin, so [likewise] we should die to sin
- As we have been slaves of uncleanness, so now be slaves of righteousness
- As there was a remnant in Elijah's day, so there was a remnant in Paul's day
- As our physical bodies have many members, so the Body of Christ has many members

What, then, is the other half of the "hinge" for Romans 11:26? It is verse 25:

*25 For I do not desire, brethren, that you should be ignorant of this mystery, lest you should be wise in your own opinion, that blindness in part has happened to Israel until **the fullness of the Gentiles has come in.** 26 And **so** all Israel will be saved, as it is written:*

"The Deliverer will come out of Zion,
And He will turn away ungodliness from Jacob;
27 For this is My covenant with them,
When I take away their sins." (Rom 11:25-27; emphasis added)

What does the other half of the "hinge" tell us? The manner by which all Israel will be saved is by the fullness of the Gentiles coming in! Barnes acknowledges this connection, but unfortunately associates the coming in of the Gentiles as a prerequisite to all Jews being saved rather than the *manner* in which all Israel is saved:

[**And so**] That is, in this manner; or when the great abundance of the Gentiles shall be converted, then all Israel shall be saved.
[**All Israel**] All the Jews. (Barnes' Notes, Romans 11:26)

We know that Gentiles are not part of fleshly Israel, but of spiritual Israel (the remnant) in whom there is neither Jew nor Greek (Gal 3:28). But this implies that *Israel* of v. 26 is spiritual Israel, while the *Israel* of v. 25 is physical (national) Israel. We have already read Paul's definition of spiritual Israel earlier in Romans:

> *But it is not that the word of God has taken no effect. For they are not all [spiritual] Israel who are of [physical] Israel, nor are they all children because they are the seed of Abraham; but, "In Isaac your seed shall be called." That is, those who are the children of the flesh [physical Israel], these are not the children of God [spiritual Israel]; but the children of the promise are counted as the seed.* (Rom 9:6-8)

But is it not convoluted to change the meaning of a word from one verse to the next, we might ask? Perhaps, except that we see Paul has already established the precedent in Romans 9:6-8 above. Jesus did the same when He said, *let the dead bury their own dead* (Matt 8:22). Consider too the following passage by Paul, in which he is also describing a mystery (note that Paul is the only author in the epistles that uses the term *mystery*, and that it is intricately bound up with the subject of the Church):

> *"For this reason a man shall leave his father and mother and be joined to his wife, and the two shall become one flesh." This is a great mystery, but I speak concerning Christ and the church.* (Eph 5:31-32)

Here Paul takes a passage which is explicitly dealing with husbands and wives, and says that he is speaking of Christ and the Church. He has poured a spiritual meaning into a physical term in order to illustrate a point. We believe that he is doing the same thing in Romans 9-11, moving back and forth between physical and spiritual Israel. Indeed, no one struggles with the fact that, in Romans 9:6, Paul applies different meanings to the term Israel in the same sentence:

> *For they are not all [spiritual] Israel who are of [physical] Israel . . . .*

The fact that Paul is not referring to all of national Israel's salvation is supported by his other statements in this section of Scripture at which we looked previously. Why was Paul experiencing such sorrow over his countrymen (physical Israel), if he knew that *all physical Israel* was going to be saved? Why was he ready to give up his salvation (be accursed from Christ) for something that was going to happen anyway? His sorrow makes sense, however, if the *all Israel* being saved is spiritual Israel and not Paul's countrymen according to the flesh. Michael Horton notes:

> In the latter part of Romans, Paul wrote that "all Israel will be saved" (11:26). A bit earlier he wrote that only "a remnant chosen by grace" (11:5) will be saved out of Israel. He then proceeds to show us that "all Israel is saved" via an elect remnant. (*Putting Amazing Back Into Grace*, p. 106)

As we have seen, the remnant included both Jews and Gentiles (Greeks). But if *fleshly* Israel was not going to be saved, what do we make of the fact that Paul says that God has not rejected His people?

> *I say then, has God cast away His people? Certainly not! For I also am an Israelite, of the seed of Abraham, of the tribe of Benjamin.* (Rom 11:1)

Obviously, Paul is speaking here of his physical heritage and lineage. But is the question asking, *Has God cast away the NATION of Israel from being His chosen people?* Or is it asking something else? Let's look at the context:

> *But they [physical Israel] have not all obeyed the gospel. For Isaiah says, "LORD, who has believed our report?" So then faith comes by hearing, and hearing by the word of God. But I say, have they not heard? Yes indeed:*
>
> > *"Their sound has gone out to all the earth,*
> > *And their words to the ends of the world."*
>
> *But I say, did Israel not know? First Moses says:*
>
> > *"I will provoke you to jealousy by those*
> > *who are not a nation, I will move you to*
> > *anger by a foolish nation."*
>
> *But Isaiah is very bold and says:*
>
> > *"I was found by those who did not seek Me;*
> > *I was made manifest to those who did not*
> > *ask for Me."*

But to Israel he says:

> *"All day long I have stretched out My hands*
> *To a disobedient and contrary people*
> *[physical Israel]."*

I say then, has God cast away His people? Certainly not! For I also am an Israelite, of the seed of Abraham, of the tribe of Benjamin. God has not cast away His people whom He foreknew. Or do you not know what the Scripture says of Elijah, how he pleads with God against Israel, saying, "LORD, they have killed Your prophets and torn down Your altars, and I alone am left, and they seek my life"? But what does the divine response say to him? "I have reserved for Myself seven thousand men who have not bowed the knee to Baal." Even so then, at this present time there is a remnant according to the election of grace. And if by grace, then it is no longer of works; otherwise grace is no longer grace. But if it is of works, it is no longer grace; otherwise work is no longer work. What then? [Physical] Israel has not obtained what it seeks; but the elect [spiritual Israel] have obtained it, and the rest were blinded. (Rom 10:16-11:7)

Consider the following option. Paul has just described national Israel as not being obedient to the gospel. He says that God, through the gospel, was found by those who did not seek Him, while Israel is called *a disobedient and contrary people*. The implication is that physical Israel did not find God, while the Gentiles did. Therefore, Paul asks the question *"has God cast away His people"* from the chance of finding Him, from the possibility of obtaining salvation? *"Certainly not! For I also am an Israelite, of the seed of Abraham, of the tribe of Benjamin,"* and I am saved by the gospel of grace—I have not been cast away! *"God has not cast away His people whom He foreknew."* Whom did He foreknow? The remnant! *"Or do you not know what the Scripture says of Elijah, how he pleads with God against Israel, saying, 'LORD, they have killed Your prophets and torn down Your altars, and I alone am left, and they seek my life?' But what does the divine response say to him? 'I have reserved for Myself seven thousand men who have not bowed the knee to Baal.'"* Elijah, like Paul, realized that his nation had rejected God, and that they were truly a *"disobedient and contrary people,"* yet God had reserved a remnant for Himself. *"Even so then, at this present time there is a remnant according to the election of grace"*—the gospel. *"And if by grace, then it is no longer of works"*—physical lineage; *"otherwise grace is no longer grace. But if it is of works"* — carte blanche acceptance based upon national heritage, *"it is no longer grace"* — individual acceptance based upon faith; *"otherwise work is no longer work."*

Although God did choose Israel and set His love on them (Deut 7:7) in what we might term a "national basis," He still dealt with individuals. Thus, it was possible for a physical Israelite to be cut off from His people (Gen 17:14; Exod 12:15). Such a person would not cease being a physical Israelite, for they would still have Hebrew blood flowing through their veins. They would, however, be cut off covenantally from the people of God. Likewise, it was possible for foreigners to be considered part of the covenant nation, as evidenced by Rahab and Ruth being in the genealogy of Christ (Matt 1:5). Rahab and Ruth did not become physical Jews, but they did become part of God's covenant people. We believe Paul was saying that, just as belonging to fleshly, national Israel did not automatically guarantee one's position in the kingdom, neither did it *preclude* one from entering the kingdom. Paul was living evidence!

> *What then? [Physical] Israel has not obtained what it seeks; but the elect [spiritual Israel] have obtained it, and the rest [of physical Israel] were blinded . . . blindness in part has happened to [physical] Israel until the fullness of the Gentiles has come in. And so [by the Gentiles coming in] all [spiritual] Israel [the elect] will be saved.* (Rom 11:7, 25-26)

Therefore, we would postulate that the "fullness" of the Gentiles is not a numeric value, but rather the entrance of the Gentiles into the fullness of New Covenant salvation. Thus, by the Gentiles coming into the fullness of Old Testament Israel's promised salvation along with believing Jews, all spiritual Israel (in which there is neither Jew nor Greek) is saved. Note that Paul claims all Israel will be saved *as it is written*, after which he quotes Isaiah 59:20-21:

> *And so all Israel will be saved, as it is written:*
>
> *"The Deliverer will come out of Zion,*
> *And He will turn away ungodliness from Jacob;*
> *For this is My covenant with them,*
> *When I take away their sins."* (Rom 11:26-27)

Paul's teaching regarding Israel's salvation was not some new revelation, but was grounded in Old Testament Scripture. However, we have seen previously how many Old Testament passages which seemed to address the physical nation of Israel actually pertained to the Church. The full text of Isaiah 59:20-21, from which Paul quotes, reads:

"The Redeemer will come to Zion,
And to those who turn from transgression in Jacob,"
Says the LORD.
"As for Me," says the LORD, *"this is My covenant with them: My*
Spirit who is upon you, and My words which I have put in your
mouth, shall not depart from your mouth, nor from the mouth
of your descendants, nor from the mouth of your descendants'
descendants," says the LORD, *"from this time and forevermore."*
(Isa 59:20-21)

Is this not reminiscent of the New Covenant of which Jeremiah spoke (Jer 31:31ff)? And yet the author of Hebrews ascribes this covenant to the gospel (Heb 8:8ff), not some future age. Indeed, does not Isaiah's *from this time and forevermore* sound like Hebrews' *everlasting covenant* (Heb 13:20)? If Isaiah and Jeremiah were not speaking of the same covenant, are we to believe that there are *two* everlasting covenants—one which fits the New Testament timeframe and another in which all physical/national Israel is saved? Surely the covenant of which Isaiah spoke, and which Paul associated with the turning away of *ungodliness from Jacob*, is the everlasting covenant of the gospel. Although Barnes believed that all the physical Jews would someday be saved, he nonetheless saw the connection of Isaiah's prophecy with the gospel:

[**As it is written**] Isa 59:20. The quotation is not literally made, but the sense of the passage is preserved. The Hebrew is, "There shall come to Zion a Redeemer, and for those who turn from ungodliness in Jacob." There can be no doubt that Isaiah refers here to the times of the gospel. (*Barnes' Notes*, Romans 11:26)

The question may be rightly asked, "does not Jacob represent physical Israel?" There is no doubt that he did in many contexts. However, within the context of Romans 9-11, note that Paul used Jacob to help illustrate that *they are not all Israel who are of Israel*:

But it is not that the word of God has taken no effect. For they are
not all Israel who are of Israel, nor are they all children because
they are the seed of Abraham; but, "In Isaac your seed shall be
called." That is, those who are the children of the flesh, these
are not the children of God; but the children of the promise are
counted as the seed. For this is the word of promise: "At this time

I will come and Sarah shall have a son." And not only this, but when Rebecca also had conceived by one man, even by our father Isaac (for the children not yet being born, nor having done any good or evil, that the purpose of God according to election might stand, not of works but of Him who calls), it was said to her, "The older shall serve the younger." As it is written, "Jacob I have loved, but Esau I have hated." (Rom 9:6-13)

We propose that, just as Abraham had two sons who represented his spiritual and fleshly seeds, Isaac also had two sons, Jacob and Esau, who represented spiritual and fleshly seeds (Rom 9:10ff). Ungodliness was turned away from Jacob, not Esau. Jacob's name was changed to "Israel," and thus when ungodliness was turned away from Jacob (representing the spiritual seed) "all Israel" was saved.

Furthermore, if fleshly Israel was the Israel Paul had in view in Romans 11:26, why were his fellow countrymen persecuting him and claiming he was teaching contrary to the Law (Acts 18:13)? Did not the Jews hope for the regathering of all fleshly Israel? Is that not how they understood *the hope of Israel* and the turning away of *ungodliness from Jacob*? If this was indeed what Paul was teaching, would not the Jews have heralded his praises? Yet, even though Paul did nothing against the Jews or the customs of the fathers, he was in chains for that very *hope of Israel*. Surely, if Paul was advocating the salvation of national Israel, the Jews would not have sought to kill him.

Added to the evidence already presented is the timeframe for the *fullness of the Gentiles* and the *deliverer coming out of Zion to take away their sins*. In this very epistle, Paul wrote to his readers that,

. . . for now our salvation is nearer than when we first believed. The night is far spent, the day is at hand. (Rom 13:11-12)

And the God of peace will crush Satan under your feet shortly. (Rom 16:20)

Surely the approaching salvation and crushing of Satan were part and parcel with the events of AD 70. We have noted previously that all Old Testament prophecy pointed toward the New Testament generation, and that the New Testament generation expected all things to be fulfilled within their lifetimes. There are no grounds for placing either the fullness of the Gentiles or the salvation of all Israel outside of this timeframe. Therefore, we are constrained to interpret "all Israel" as spiritual Israel, because fleshly Israel was not saved—it was destroyed! In this context, we can begin to catch a glimpse of Paul's anguish for his fellow countrymen. Daniel also, at the end of the seventy-year captivity, anguished over his fellow countrymen:

> *Yes, all Israel has transgressed Your law, and has departed so as not to obey Your voice; therefore the curse and the oath written in the Law of Moses the servant of God have been poured out on us, because we have sinned against Him.*
>
> *As it is written in the Law of Moses, all this disaster has come upon us; yet we have not made our prayer before the LORD our God, that we might turn from our iniquities and understand Your truth.* (Dan 9:11, 13)

Like Paul, Daniel also interceded for his fellow countrymen, asking that God would turn His fury away from them and their city (Dan 9:16ff). Although God did allow them to return from their captivity, He also revealed to Daniel the ultimate fate of the nation of Israel: the power of the holy people would be *completely shattered* (12:7). We have shown previously how this was fulfilled in AD 70, and note that Daniel did not prophesy a subsequent regathering or ultimate "saving" of national Israel.

Jesus likewise wept over Jerusalem (Luke 19:41ff), knowing her impending doom; but He never spoke of her being rebuilt. In light of this, are we to believe that Paul had a special revelation that all physical Israel would be saved? On the contrary, does not his *great sorrow and continual grief* indicate that Paul saw the very same fate for physical Israel as did Daniel and Jesus? In fact, is this not what Paul taught the Galatians—that the bondwoman and her son, who represented the Jerusalem and Old Covenant system of Paul's day, must be cast out?

> *For these are the two covenants: the one from Mount Sinai which gives birth to bondage, which is Hagar—for this Hagar is Mount Sinai in Arabia, and corresponds to Jerusalem which now is, and is in bondage with her children—but the Jerusalem above is free, which is the mother of us all. . . . Now we, brethren, as Isaac was, are children of promise. But, as he who was born according to the flesh then persecuted him who was born according to the Spirit, even so it is now. Nevertheless what does the Scripture say? "Cast out the bondwoman and her son, for the son of the bondwoman shall not be heir with the son of the freewoman." So then, brethren, we are not children of the bondwoman but of the free.* (Gal 4:24-26, 28-31)

We believe that this view is strengthened when we make a proper distinction between the olive tree and the branches of Paul's allegory in the passage preceding Romans 11:26:

And if some of the branches were broken off, and you, being a wild olive tree, were grafted in among them, and with them became a partaker of the root and fatness of the olive tree, do not boast against the branches. But if you do boast, remember that you do not support the root, but the root supports you. You will say then, "Branches were broken off that I might be grafted in." Well said. Because of unbelief they were broken off, and you stand by faith. Do not be haughty, but fear. For if God did not spare the natural branches, He may not spare you either. Therefore consider the goodness and severity of God: on those who fell, severity; but toward you, goodness, if you continue in His goodness. Otherwise you also will be cut off. And they also, if they do not continue in unbelief, will be grafted in, for God is able to graft them in again. For if you were cut out of the olive tree which is wild by nature, and were grafted contrary to nature into a cultivated olive tree, how much more will these, who are natural branches, be grafted into their own olive tree? (Rom 11:17-24)

Clearly, the branches that were broken off were unbelieving Jews, while the branches that were grafted in were Gentile believers. The branches do not represent nations, but individuals. God did not graft the Gentiles in on a *national* basis, but on an *individual* basis. So when Paul writes that the natural branches, which were previously broken off, can be grafted in again, we believe that he is referring to Jews coming to a saving knowledge of Christ on an individual basis. Thus, Paul desired to provoke them to jealousy in the hope of saving *some* (Rom 11:14). Paul was a living example of a branch which had been broken off—as evidenced by his initial rejection of the gospel—and then grafted in again. His grafting in again was not the result of national Israel being saved, but because he did not *continue in unbelief* (Rom 11:23).

Because the Gentiles are depicted as a "wild olive tree," and the Jews are depicted as "natural branches, the "natural" olive tree is sometimes understood as being the nation of Israel. If this is so, then why were Jews "broken off"? Did they stop being Israelites? And why were Gentile believers grafted in? Did they become Israelites? No, the "natural" olive tree represents God's *elect*, His remnant. During the days of the Old Covenant, the nation of Israel was the recipient and administrator of that stage of

God's redemptive plan; therefore, it is sometimes difficult to distinguish the nation of Israel from the elect. Recall Paul's Old Testament quotation in which God told Elijah that although most of Israel had gone after Baal, He still had a remnant. That the olive tree represents specifically the elect, and not national Israel, is demonstrated by Arthur Custance in his study *Three Trees: And Israel's History* (from volume 6 of *The Doorway Papers—Time and Eternity*). In his study, he defines the three aspects of a nation's, or individual's, existence: secular, spiritual, and religious. The difference between the spiritual and religious aspect is exemplified by the Pharisees and Sadducees, who, despite being very religious, were, spiritually speaking, whitewashed tombs, full of dead men's bones (Matt 23:27). Custance associates three different trees in Scripture with these three aspects of Israel's existence: The vine, representing national Israel; the fig tree, representing religious Israel; and the olive tree, representing spiritual Israel, the remnant. Custance introduces the association between the olive tree and spiritual Israel, the remnant, as follows:

> In contrast with the vine which has a horizontal growth, the olive grows vertically toward heaven. That the olive tree is associated symbolically with the spiritual history of Israel is stated with equal explicitness in Scripture. The choice of such a tree is most appropriate, for it is from its fruit that olive oil is obtained, and this is the oil of anointing which symbolizes the anointing of the Holy Spirit.
>
> The very first mention of the tree is, not unexpectedly, in connection with the restoration of the earth after the Flood. Noah sends out a dove, and the dove returns with an olive leaf (Gen 8:10, 11). Both the dove and the leaf reinforce the spiritual implications, the emergence of new life. Because God has always left Himself with some witness in Israel in times of direst judgment, the prophets in foretelling what would happen to the nation because of their disobedience speak of the cutting down of the vine and the fig tree and their destruction in the land; but never is it stated that the olive tree will suffer such total uprooting. Thus Jeremiah, the prophet of doom, added the warning (in Jeremiah 11:16) that although the green olive would suffer in this coming judgment, he does not speak of its total destruction, but warns only that the branches of it will be broken. This seems to be the basis of the simile used by Paul in Romans 11:17-27. (*Three Trees: And Israel's History*, p. 4)

As Custance notes, both the fig and the vine are foretold as being destroyed in the land, but not so with the olive tree. This agrees with Paul's analogy of the two sons of Abraham and the two covenants. Hagar and Ishmael, representing physical Jerusalem of Paul's day, were to be cast out (Gal 4:21ff). Nothing could be more diametrically opposed to the notion that all physical/national Israel would be saved. And though the olive tree (the sons of promise of the New Covenant) was persecuted and suffered in the judgment, it was not destroyed.

The typology of the trees is also supported by the fact that Jesus cursed the fig tree because it had no fruit—the outward religion of man cannot produce spiritual life—and in the parable of judgment upon the vine-dressers, also for not presenting fruit to the landowner.

Now in the morning, as they passed by, they saw the fig tree dried up from the roots. (Mark 11:20)

Therefore I say to you, the kingdom of God will be taken from you and given to a nation bearing the fruits of it. (Matt 21: 43)

In the book of Daniel, Nebuchadnezzar had a dream in which his king-ship was also symbolized by a tree. In the following passage, note that when his kingdom was taken away temporarily, the stump and root of the tree remained:

"I saw in the visions of my head while on my bed, and there was a watcher, a holy one, coming down from heaven. He cried aloud and said thus:

'Chop down the tree and cut off its branches,
Strip off its leaves and scatter its fruit.
Let the beasts get out from under it,
And the birds from its branches.
Nevertheless leave the stump and roots in the earth. . . .'
*"And inasmuch as they gave the command to leave the stump and roots of the tree, **your kingdom shall be assured to you**, after you come to know that Heaven rules."* (Dan 4:13-15, 26; emphasis added)

While Nebuchadnezzar's kingdom was assured to him, the fig tree that Christ cursed withered *from the roots*, signifying that it was completely dead—there would be no future bloom. This is reminiscent of the words of Malachi:

"For behold, the day is coming,

Burning like an oven,
And all the proud, yes, all who do wickedly will be stubble.
And the day which is coming shall burn them up,"
Says the LORD *of hosts,*
"That will leave them neither root nor branch." (Mal 4:1)

This also parallels the kingdom of God—as represented by the vineyard—being taken from national Israel and given to the Church, never to return, just as with the Old Testament kingdoms of Saul and David. Hanegraaff provides a noteworthy quote from Colin Chapman's *Whose Holy City?*:

> The fall of Jerusalem is to be an act of divine judgment, compared in a shocking way to the judgment on Babylon described by Isaiah. What seems to be most significant, therefore, is that whereas the Old Testament prophets predicted judgment, exile *and* a return to the land, Jesus predicts destruction and exile, *but says nothing about a return to the land.* Instead of predicting the restoration of Israel, he speaks about the coming of the kingdom of God through the coming of the Son of Man. (*The Apocalypse Code*, p. 194; emphases in original)

Preston writes, "Our point is, that when the Hebrew writer speaks of the inheritance of the Abrahamic promises he never mentions restoration to a physical land or restored city and temple. (*Like Father, Like Son*, p. 191)

Enoch, who lived long before the nation of Israel existed, was one of God's remnant. And we have also seen that Abraham was considered righteous prior to circumcision, that is, before the Mosaic Law. Therefore, we feel that although the three trees center on the nation of Israel, they encompass God's entire redemptive plan throughout history. Just as we see the olive tree pre-dating national Israel (to include Enoch, Abraham, et. al.), so we believe that the olive tree reaches *forward* beyond national Israel, representing God's elect throughout time. Thus the olive tree of Paul's allegory is God's elect, which was in the process of transitioning from the Old Covenant to the New Covenant. Those branches—individual Jews—which did not make the transition, as evidenced by their lack of fruit (cf. John 15:1ff), were broken off. Those Gentiles who were not natural partakers of the Old Covenant yet believed in Christ were grafted into the olive tree of the New Covenant. If the uncultivated branches—Gentiles without the Law, which foreshadowed the New Covenant of which they were fellow-heirs—could be grafted in, how much more can the natural branches—Jews, who were the custodians of that foreshadow—be grafted back in?

In summary, we feel that the following points argue against all physical Israel being saved:

- Paul's many expressions of anguish over his fellow countrymen, hoping to save only *some* of them
- The manner in which all Israel will be saved is by the fullness [salvation] of the Gentiles coming in
- Paul's basis for all Israel being saved is the Old Testament promise of turning ungodliness away from Jacob *forevermore*, which is realized in the *everlasting* covenant of the gospel
- If Paul was indeed teaching that all physical Israel would be saved, his fellow Jews would not have sought to persecute and kill him
- The timeframe for the fulfillment of all Old Testament prophecies, including Israel's salvation, was the New Testament generation
- Neither Jesus nor Daniel foresaw all physical Israel being saved. Rather, Jesus wept over Jerusalem and Daniel was told of the power of the holy people being *completely shattered*
- The "branches" which are broken off or grafted in are not nations, but individuals
- Paul's analogy in Galatians 4 depicts physical Israel (Hagar and Ishmael) being cast out, not saved. It is the spiritual offspring (sons of promise) that are not in bondage, but free (saved)
- Although the olive tree, representing spiritual Israel (the elect), suffered persecution, it was never destroyed. On the other hand, the fig tree, representing the religious system of national Israel, *dried up from the roots*

The fact of "all Israel" being saved during the very time in which Jerusalem is being destroyed and the Old Covenant is passing away may seem paradoxical—even contradictory. Yet we must remember that in God's redemptive plan there are two Israels, two Jerusalems, two covenants, etc., in view. We may use the Exodus and Israel's wandering in the wilderness as an illustration. Did all Israel perish in the wilderness, or was "all Israel" brought into the Promised Land? Both! This is because, in effect, there were two Israels—the rebellious generation which perished, and their children who entered in. Likewise, we feel that a similar principle is to be applied to New Testament Israel. Preston writes:

> The Great Paradox, that Israel would be saved by passing under judgment, has been established. While the concept strikes the modern reader as strange it is Biblical. Israel's shadow form had to pass, but in passing, the body of Christ, the real Israel, was revealed. God had saved the remnant—what constituted all Israel—as promised. (*Like Father, Like Son,* p. 110)

> The Day of the Lord foretold by the Old Covenant prophets, to occur in the last days, when Jehovah would act to save Israel, would entail judgment of Israel. That judgment would remove the outer shell of the Old Covenant world, and reveal the true body, the body of Christ. . . .The understanding of the Great Paradox, the salvation of Israel by means of judgment, helps us to understand, and to answer, what is to the millennialists, a problem. On the one hand, the Bible definitely speaks of the judgment of Jerusalem in the last days, and, on the other hand, speaks of the deliverance of Jerusalem in the last days. The millennialists insist that the preterist over-emphasizes judgment to the neglect of deliverance, and the non-millennialists insist that the millennialist emphasizes deliverance to the neglect of judgment. What is the answer to the seeming conundrum? It is the doctrine of the Two Jerusalems. (Ibid., pp. 169-170)

Some feel that Paul's statement, "*hardening [blindness] has happened in part to Israel until the fullness of the Gentiles has come in,*" indicates a future end to that hardening. Then, when the hardening is removed, all national Israel will recognize Jesus as the Messiah and shall be saved. But again, we are constrained by the time passages of the New Testament to find a fulfillment within that generation. No other New Testament passage speaks of a future gathering of Israel. We feel that the "end" of the hardening can be explained by two post-AD 70 facts: (1) there was no longer any nation to harden, and (2) the veil of types and shadows, which had been over their eyes, no longer existed.

Once again, the above interpretation is not in line with popular views concerning the future of the present day nation of Israel. However, it restores the harmony of the two covenants that we have seen throughout our study. Drawing from the chapter "If You Are Willing to Receive It," we have to ask ourselves in this case, *Are we willing to receive it?* Or will we allow the traditions of man to make the Word of God of no effect? (Mark 7:13)

What about the Creeds and the Early Church?

—ɯ—

Regardless of the importance one places on church creeds or the early church fathers, this question usually arises in one form or another. Naturally, people want to know how Preterism lines up with the teachings of Christianity through the ages and whether the Church ever subscribed to some measure of fulfilled eschatology. While many Preterists have addressed these issues in depth, we can only touch upon them briefly here. We would commend to the reader Samuel M. Frost's scholarly work on these topics, *Misplaced Hope*, as well as the introduction to Ed Stevens' *Questions about the Afterlife* and his online article "What if the Creeds are Wrong?" (www.preterist.org).

First we would note that, while the title "early church fathers" is certainly appropriate in many aspects, others have observed that in at least some respects the early fathers were "church babes." Although these fathers did much to combat the various errant teachings and heresies that arose, the fact that these errant teachings flourished, along with the fact that the early fathers often disagreed amongst themselves, indicates that there was often no consensus of doctrine among them. Even if there had been a consensus, the scant writings that we have are not necessarily representative of the early church as a whole, as Frost notes:

> We do not have what could even be called a representative majority of believers in the early and apostolic church. Charles Hodge wrote, "Ten or twenty writers scattered over such a period cannot reasonably be assumed to speak the mind of the whole church." (*Misplaced Hope*, p. 38)

In short, we do not have the entire testimony of that church at that time. (Ibid., p. 159)

Frost also quotes William Goode:

> It must be added, without any wish to depreciate the value of those remains of antiquity we possess, that it is more than probable, that there were hundreds of bishops in the Primitive Church far better

431

able to give us a correct view of the faith of the Church, than some of those whose writings happen to have come down to us. (Ibid., p. 170)

Frost, Stevens, et al. have noted that while the early church did not profess a Full Preterist view, they viewed many prophecies from a Preterist paradigm. Even though several of them taught the past fulfillment of many prophecies, their misunderstanding of the spiritual nature of the kingdom and its prophecies caused them to look for a future physical coming of Christ. As time progressed, and "this generation" had been stretched to its breaking point (when the last of those died who had been taught by those who had learned from the apostles), the doctrine of "Parousia delay" began to develop. Jeffrey S. Siker, contributing a chapter to John T. Carroll's *The Return of Jesus in Early Christianity*, writes:

> . . . Justin Martyr joins the *Shepherd of Hermas* in the notion of a planned divine pause before the parousia, and hence a slackening of imminent expectations regarding the End . . . . (p. 157)

Over the centuries many of the prophecies which had previously been taught as having been fulfilled in AD 70 were removed from that time-frame and placed in the timeframe of a delayed future Parousia.

We offer Athanasius (ca. 295-373) as an example of Preterist teaching in the early church:

> 39. 3. Perhaps with regard to the other (prophecies) they [The Jews] may be able even to find excuses and to put off what is written to a future time. But what can they say to this [Daniel's prophecy of the seventy weeks], or can they face it at all? Where not only is the Christ referred to, but He that is to be anointed is declared to be not man simply, but Holy of Holies; and Jerusalem is to stand **till His coming**, and thenceforth, prophet and vision cease in Israel. So the Jews are trifling, and **the time in question**, which they refer to the future, **is actually come**. For when did prophet and vision cease from Israel, save **when Christ came**, the Holy of Holies? **For it is a sign, and an important proof, of the coming of the Word of God, that Jerusalem no longer stands**, nor is any prophet raised up nor vision revealed to them,—and that very naturally.

> 40. 2. For when He that was signified **was come**, what need was there any longer of any to signify Him? When the truth was there, what need any more of the shadow? For this was the reason of their

prophesying at all,—namely, till the true Righteousness should come, and He that was to ransom the sins of all. And this was why Jerusalem stood till then—namely, that there they might be exercised in the types as a preparation for the reality. 3. So **when the Holy of Holies was come**, naturally vision and prophecy were sealed and the kingdom of Jerusalem ceased. . . . 6. Their state may be compared to that of one out of his right mind, who sees the earth illumined by the sun, but denies the sun that illumines it. **For what more is there for him whom they expect to do, when he is come? To call the heathen? But they are called already. To make prophecy, and king, and vision to cease? This too has already come to pass. To expose the godlessness of idolatry? It is already exposed and condemned. Or to destroy death? He is already destroyed. 7. What then has not come to pass, that the Christ must do?** What is left unfulfilled, that the Jews should now disbelieve with impunity? For if, I say,—which is just what we actually see,—there is no longer king nor prophet nor Jerusalem nor sacrifice nor vision among them, but even the whole earth is filled with the knowledge of God, and Gentiles, leaving their godlessness, are now taking refuge with the God of Abraham, through the Word, even our Lord Jesus Christ, then it must be plain, even to those who are exceedingly obstinate, that **the Christ is come**, and that He has illumined absolutely all with His light, and given them the true and divine teaching concerning His Father.

. . .

Now, **however, that the devil, that tyrant against the whole world, is slain**, we do not approach a temporal feast, my beloved, but an eternal and heavenly. Not in shadows do we shew it forth, but we come to it in truth. For they [The Jews] being filled with the flesh of a dumb lamb, accomplished the feast, and having anointed their door-posts with the blood, implored aid against the destroyer. But now we, eating of the Word of the Father, and having the lintels of our hearts sealed with the blood of the New Testament, acknowledge the grace given us from the Saviour, who said, 'Behold, I have given unto you to tread upon serpents and scorpions, and over all the power of the enemy.' **For no more does death reign**; but instead of death henceforth is life, since our Lord said, 'I am the life;' so that everything is filled with joy and gladness; as it is written, 'The Lord reigneth, let the earth rejoice.'

For when death reigned, 'sitting down by the rivers of Babylon, we wept,' and mourned, because we felt the bitterness of captivity; but **now that death and the kingdom of the devil is abolished,** everything is entirely filled with joy and gladness. And God is no longer known only in Judæa, but in all the earth, 'their voice hath gone forth, and the knowledge of Him hath filled all the earth.' (*Athanasius: Select Works and Letters*, pp. 57-58, 516, edited by Philip Schaff; online at www.ccel.org. Emphases mine—BLM)

Certainly a few quotes from one early church father do not establish Preterism as the position of the early church. However, it does establish its existence in regards to certain aspects of prophecy. All we are attempting to demonstrate is that the early church fathers cannot be claimed as a unified voice for refuting Preterism. Many eschatological schemes are able to find support in the early church fathers, as Frost notes of Partial Preterist Keith Mathison:

Mathison's reason for using [Justin Martyr's] quote is to show that Justin demonstrates a "lack of consensus on the doctrine of the Millennium" thus justifying a possible support for his [Mathison's] postmillennialism. What is ignored, however, is that there is also a lack of consensus concerning the questions, When will the resurrection occur? How? With what kind of body? When is the timing of the Second Coming? If a lack of consensus on millennialism could imply possible postmillennial "support," then a lack of consensus on these other questions could also lend preterist support. (*Misplaced Hope*, p. 18)

Eusebius, known as the Father of Church History, states that many early church fathers adopted a literal, earthly millennium from the teachings of Papias, which were erroneous because Papias failed to recognize the apocalyptic language of eschatology:

The same writer [Papias] gives also other accounts which he says came to him through unwritten tradition, certain strange parables and teachings of the Savior, and some other more mythical things. To these belong his statement that there will be a period of some thousand years after the resurrection of the dead, and that the kingdom of Christ will be set up in material form on this very earth. I suppose he got these ideas through a misunderstanding of the apostolic accounts, **not perceiving that the things said by them were spoken mystically in figures.** For he appears to have been of very limited understanding, as one can see from his discourses. But it was due to him that so many of the Church Fathers after him adopted a like opinion . . . . (*The Church History of Eusebius*, p. 172, chapter XXXIX, – The Writings of Papias, at www.ccel.org.; emphasis added)

Our goal here is not to establish a "thread" of Preterist thought running throughout the teachings of the early Church, nor to deny that there was a consistent "futuristic" aspect to those teachings. Rather, we wish to make the reader aware of the lack of unity, and variety of views, in the early Church's eschatology. Brian Daley writes:

Eschatological emphases in the early Church varied, apocalyptic hopes died and were revived, and individual or cosmic or ecclesiological or mystical perspectives succeeded one another, not so much in a direct line of development as in response to the social and ecclesial challenges met by Christian communities in each generation, and as an outgrowth of the personal theological interests and allegiances of individual writers. (*The Hope of the Early Church*, p. 3)

Similarly, Carroll states:

In my judgment, it is a mistake to insist that early Christian expectations were consistently one way or another, or that Christianity started out eschatologically charged only to diminish in hope and expectation over time. Instead, both strands have always been present, and both can be seen in second- and third-century Christian writings as well. (*The Return of Jesus in Early Christianity*, p. 151)

At the end of this survey of Patristic eschatological thought, one might justly wonder if it is proper at all to speak in the singular of "the hope of the early Church." The range of images and ideas we have seen among early Christian writers, expressing their expectations for the future of planet and individual, saint and sinner, suggests that one might perhaps better speak of many facets of a rapidly developing, increasingly detailed Christian view of human destiny, of many hopes—and many fears—enveloped within a single, growing, ever more complex tradition of early Christian faith and practice. (Ibid., p. 216)

To return to our starting question: can one legitimately speak of "the hope of the early Church"? If one seeks such a hope in the finished form of conciliar definitions, or of an articulated and widely shared theological system the answer is clearly no; the eschatological consensus we have sketched out here was far less well formed, far less consciously enunciated, in the Patristic centuries, than was the orthodox Christian doctrine of God or of the person of Christ. (Ibid., p. 223)

The point we wish to make is that there was no unified eschatological position of the early church. In addition, there are definite Preterist interpretations of many prophecies associated with the Second Coming, such as death being conquered and the kingdom of the Devil destroyed. Furthermore, Futurist views appear to have developed (or increased in scope) later, as the early church continued on past the New Testament generation to whom the prophecies were given.

When it comes to the creeds of the Church, the importance attached to them is quite varied within Christendom. Do we interpret the Bible in light of the creeds, since they supposedly embody the wisdom of the Church down through the ages? Or do we refine the creeds in light of Scripture? In other words, considering our present topic, if the creeds do not endorse Preterism, must we abandon Preterism; or, alternatively, if Scripture clearly teaches Preterism, we must refine the creeds. In his introduction to *The Creeds of Christianity*, Philip Schaff writes:

In a certain sense it may be said that the Christian Church has never been without a creed (*Ecclesia, sine symbolis nulla*). The baptismal formula and the words of institution of the Lord's Supper are creeds; these and the confession of Peter antedate even the birth of the Christian Church on the day of Pentecost. The Church is, indeed, not founded on symbols, but on Christ; not on any words of man, but on the word of God; yet it is founded on Christ as *confessed* by men, and a creed is man's answer to Christ's question, man's acceptance and interpretation of God's word. . . . In the Protestant system, the authority of symbols, as of all human compositions, is relative and limited. **It is not co-ordinate with, but always subordinate to, the Bible,** as the only infallible rule of the Christian faith and practice. **The value of creeds depends upon the measure of their agreement with the Scriptures.** In the best case a human creed is only an approximate and relatively correct exposition of revealed truth, and **may be improved by the progressive knowledge of the Church,** while the Bible remains perfect and infallible. The Bible is of God; the Confession is man's answer to God's word. . . . Confessions, in due subordination to the Bible, are of great value and use. They are summaries of the doctrines of the Bible, aids to its sound understanding, bonds of union among their professors, public standards and guards against false doctrine and practice. (pp. 5, 7-8 online at www.ccel.org; bold emphasis added)

Frost asserts, "If the Westminster Confession states that the creeds may err, then maybe, just maybe, they did" (*Misplaced Hope*, p. 166). He further observes:

By beginning with history instead of Scripture Hodge contended that, "Man and his authority take the place of God." He affirmed that making history a boundary or interpreter of Scripture leads to the interpretation, not the Scripture, to become "the faith of the people." (Ibid., p. 33)

Note that Schaff stated the creeds may be improved by the progressive knowledge of the Church. Indeed, that is how the creeds developed in order to arrive at their present form. Frost provides additional valuable insight from Berkhof:

The esteemed Louis Berkhof gave two presuppositions for Reformed theology with regard to these matters. The first is that the dogmas of the church are changeable. The very need for a history of dogma supposes this fact, since truth does not have a history. One does not "develop" truth. Truth "is." Scripture cannot be broken, but the interpretation and apprehension of that once and for all faith delivered to the saints in Scripture has undergone change, and even complete transformation, through the centuries.

Here, the creeds of the church are the "fruit of reflection" of the church. However, though the church can be led by the Holy Spirit to affirm her faith in collective affirmations of these statements, the creeds are not infallible. They are highly stable. But, "while characterized by a high degree of stability, [it] is yet subject to change and has in the course of history been enriched with new elements, received more careful formulation, and even undergone certain transformations." (Ibid., pp. 29-30; brackets in original)

Again we see that the dogmas and creeds are changeable. The question which now must be asked is, "Did the early church's progressive knowledge lead them to develop a futuristic understanding of eschatology, or are the creeds overdue for improvement in light of the progressive Preterist understanding of Scripture?" Louis Berkhof provides an interesting observation:

> The doctrine of the last things never stood in the centre of attention, is one of the least developed doctrines, and therefore calls for no elaborate discussion. Its main elements have rather been constant, and these constitute practically the whole dogma of the Church respecting future things. Occasionally deviating views occupied a rather important place in theological discussions, but these were never incorporated into the confessions of the Church. It may be that, as Dr. Orr surmises, we have now reached that point in the history of dogma in which the doctrine of the last things will receive greater attention and be brought to further development. (*History of Christian Doctrines*, p. 259)

Carroll quotes N. T. Wright as saying, "A full reappraisal of the nature and place of eschatology within early Christianity seems called for." (*The Return of Jesus in Early Christianity*, p. 149)

Although the Church throughout history has convened ecumenical councils to define and clarify various doctrines—such as the trinity and deity of Christ—it has yet to convene a council to codify its eschatology. This is precisely what Preterists are advocating—not the abandonment of the creeds or the early church fathers, but calling the Church to develop this final area of theology. Instead of seeing the creeds as "written in stone," Preterists desire to view them as documents which may be improved by the progressive knowledge of the Church. Many Preterists feel that the time has come to "reform" the Church's doctrine of eschatology. Frost continues:

> The Reformation was a time when every aspect of church doctrine was re-questioned. We were now provided with the freedom to do so. We had the sources, and we had the texts of Scriptures unfettered before us for the first time in centuries. . . . I find it highly significant that within a hundred years of the Reformation, and the new directive of scholarship it released, we begin to see partial-preterism come into its own formation. By the nineteenth century preterism made its case. (*Misplaced Hope*, p. 157)

Perhaps now this is the time in which the Spirit has stirred the pot. Perhaps this is the time he is bringing his church to understand what the elect of that first holy generation understood. A reformation of true proportions and whose battle cry is "to the sources!" against an authority of man and creeds with the charge of "heresy," and "schism"! (Ibid., p. 163)

At the 1994 Valley Forge Seminar, Ken Davies concluded a lecture titled "Resurrection in the Creeds" with the following words:

> Have we reached the point in the development of the Church that we can stop reforming? Are we so arrogant as to believe that we have all knowledge and that none can add to our insight? For too long eschatology has been ignored as a subject for debate. Because of the pressing issues and crises of the early centuries of Christianity, such lesser subjects as eschatology were never discussed in detail. Perhaps the time has come to remedy this situation.

Indeed, whether recognized officially or not, the reformation *is* under way. While Preterism may have been considered previously to be a bizarre view held by a small group, its growing numbers and able apologists are bringing the issue steadily to the forefront of Christianity. Unfortunately, the initial stages of any reformation are usually of a more controversial nature than of a "come, let us reason together" nature, as Cunningham notes:

> . . . it holds almost universally in the history of the church, that until a doctrine has been fully discussed in a controversial way by men of talent and learning taking opposite sides, men's opinions regarding it are generally obscure and indefinite, and their language vague and confused, if not contradictory. (as quoted by Frost, *Misplaced Hope*, p. 158)

We cannot help but be reminded of the "vague, confused, and contradictory" language of Futurism, in which "this generation" means "*that* generation"; "near" means "far off"; "soon" means "much later"; and "imminent" could be thousands of years away!

The prophecy reformation is definitely underway, for one can see the "opposite sides" forming. Regrettably, pejorative terms such as "heresy" and "unorthodox" are bandied about much too freely. Many in Christendom simply dismiss this issue because of the naïve view that the early church fathers held a unified futurist view, and/or that the creeds deny Preterism. Hopefully, we have demonstrated that this is not the case. There was no consensus of the early church fathers, especially in the area of eschatology. Furthermore, Preterist views of many prophecies can be found in their writings. The creeds are not inspired dogma, but statements of faith that have been, and can be, changed by the progressive knowledge of the Church. Preterism is not advocating the overthrow of the creeds or Church history, but simply the continuation of the reforming process. Frost claims that judging Preterism by the creeds rather than by Scripture leads to unwarranted judgments of heresy:

> The preterist view does more justice to the credibility of the early church and to the origins of their traditions. They rightly lumped together the Second Coming with the downfall of Jerusalem. This was a signal to them that the end was "near." They had received this message from the apostles. They understood that when the Lord said, "this generation shall not pass until all these things happen" it meant "soon." Their failure was not in finding fulfillment in their own time. (Ibid., p. 208)

> Preterists have an issue with one main point in Christian eschatology: timing. This hardly rises to the level of subverting every other major Christian doctrine. Preterists are not heretics, and those who regard them as such are only hurting themselves in the long run by creating division where division need not be. (Ibid., pp. 48-49)

We do not wish to overstate our arguments, nor give the reader a false perception that Church history through the ages and the creeds are merely a trifling issue. In Keith A. Mathison's *When Shall These Things Be? A Reformed Response to Hyper-Preterism*, Gentry contributes a chapter titled "The Historical Problem with Hyper-Preterism." In this chapter, which deals with the early church fathers and the creeds, he states, "Berkhof has well noted that to urge 'No creed but the Bible' is a 'virtual denial of the guidance of the Holy Spirit in the past history of the Church'" (p. 41). We are not asking the reader to flippantly dismiss the history of the Church through the ages, nor the creeds. Rather, we ask the reader to consider whether, after the Holy Spirit has guided the Church through many doctrinal areas in the past centuries, He is now guiding it in the area of eschatology.

For example, Gentry lists ten of the many early church fathers who all taught some form of resurrection of the "flesh" or "body" in order to "close the door" on Preterism's spiritual resurrection (*When Shall These Things Be?*, pp. 30-31). However, he later summarily dismisses Stevens' (et al.) objection that neither "resurrection of the flesh" nor "resurrection of the body" are terms found in Scripture—the Scripture speaks only of a resurrection *of* or *from* "the dead" (ibid., p. 56ff). Just because a certain number of early church fathers were united on their interpretation of "resurrection of the dead," does that mean that they were correct? It is interesting that of the ten individuals Gentry lists, five of them were united in another area of eschatology—they all believed that they were living in the last days! To those five names—Pseudo Clement, Justin Martyr, Tertullian, Hippolytus and Irenaeus—can be added: Ignatius, *The Didache*, Athanasius, Jerome, Eusebius, Wycliffe, Martin Luther, John Foxe (Foxe's *Book of Martyrs*), William Whiston (translator of Josephus), Sir Isaac Newton, Jonathan Edwards, John Gill, and dozens of others throughout Church history who believed they were living in the last days.

Are we to blithely gloss over the fact that, for centuries, respected names down through Church history have been completely wrong on the *timing* of their eschatology, while at the same time, out of respect for the guidance of the Holy Spirit toward those same people, never give even the hint of a questioning glance at the *nature* of their eschatology?

In response to Gentry's statement that the creeds have been thoroughly "tried and proved," Stevens asks, "No more trials by the tests of time are necessary?" Gentry responds: "Actually, we don't 'assume' that the creeds have been 'tried and proved.' Rather, we point to historical theology and exegetical findings to show their merit" (ibid., p. 41). Thus, if we understand Gentry correctly, historical theology and exegetical findings establish the veracity of the creeds. However, prior to that statement, Gentry spent several pages demonstrating how the creeds define orthodox theology (ibid., pp. 34ff). Thus, Gentry applies circular reasoning by having the creeds define the orthodox theology of the Church through history and having that same historical theology show the merit of the creeds!

One of the quotes Gentry provides is from R. B. Kuiper, who writes, "At different times the illuminated church has formulated the truth in documents known as the creeds" (ibid., p. 38). Is the present-day Church no longer illuminated? How do we determine the illuminated Church from the nonilluminated Church? Our options seem rather limited: (1) we can tenaciously hold to the nature of the Second Coming and resurrection taught by the historical Church, and add our generation to the growing list of those who were sure *they* were living in the last days; (2) we can, like Gentry and other Postmillennial Partial Preterists, believe in a "judgment coming" in AD 70 which *the creeds never mention*, and a future "third" coming which *the Bible never mentions*; (3) or we can be like the Bereans and "examine the Scriptures" to see if the things taught by the historical Church "are so."

Preterists claim that the timing statements of the inspired New Testament and the words of Jesus take precedent over the uninspired creeds and doctrines of the Church. Although Futurist elements can be found in the eschatology of most, if not all, of the early church fathers, we note that this is precisely the area in which so many of them were wrong—they saw the "signs of the times" being fulfilled in *their* day and expected Christ to return in *their* lifetimes. History has proven them wrong, as it has several modern prophecy "experts," now that key dates from the 1980s and Y2K are well behind us. Are we going to add our generation to the growing list of those who have thought that *"this* generation" meant *"my* generation," or are we going to reform eschatology by examining afresh Christ's declaration *"This generation shall not pass"*? R. C. Sproul succinctly sums up the issue:

> Maybe some church fathers made a mistake. Maybe our favorite theologians have made mistakes. Now I can abide with that. I can't abide with Jesus being a false prophet, because I can understand that if Jesus is a false prophet my faith is in vain. (Eschatology Symposium, 1993, Mt. Dora, Florida)

We close this chapter with the conclusion from Dr. Randall Otto's article "Is Preterism Heresy?":

> Orthodox faith and orthodox doctrines are those that honor God rightly, whereas "heresy" refers to the false doctrine of those who "have abandoned the faith" and move others to do the same. If heresy has to do with a denial of the principle that God has provided redemption in Christ, as McGrath says, it is hard to understand how preterism can be viewed as a heresy, for it affirms "the orthodox faith and orthodox doctrines" in all points as expressed in the great creeds and confessions while endeavoring to "honor God rightly" by insisting that the consummation of God's redemptive purpose in Christ's parousia has not been frustrated or postponed, but rather accomplished according to the clear chronology set forth in the New Testament. Preterists believe this evidence is so compelling that they are willing to suffer the accusations and condemnations of others in their efforts to affirm the words of the apostle Paul: "Let God be true, and every man a liar. As it is written: 'So that you may be proved right when you speak and prevail when you judge'" (Rom 3:4). They invite others seriously interested in investigating these matters to do so from within the great tradition for the furtherance of the

reformation, recognizing the need of the church to be "reformed and always reforming according to the Word of God." (*Case Dismissed*, p. 64)

Is This All There Is?

—m—

This is the inevitable, if not the initial, response to the implications of Preterism. Those who have been looking to be "raptured" out of this evil world feel that Preterism robs them of their "blessed hope." Yet by claiming that the *you*, *we* and *us* of the New Testament refer to *our* current generation, we have effectively robbed that same blessed hope from the New Testament saints—the very people to whom it was promised! As someone once said, when we read the New Testament we are reading someone else's mail. This is literally true of the letters to churches and individuals. None of us are members of the church at Galatia, or Ephesus, or Thessalonica, etc., to which that "mail" was addressed. Although the Bible was written *for* us, it was not written *to* us. From our perspective, the Bible is a history book—but it is not a dead history book:

> *For the word of God is living and powerful, and sharper than any two-edged sword, piercing even to the division of soul and spirit, and of joints and marrow, and is a discerner of the thoughts and intents of the heart.* (Heb 4:12)

This means that we must separate the timeless truths and principles of the Bible from its time- and people-specific events and promises. Even the New Testament Church had to do this, as they were encouraged to read each other's letters. Both believers and nonbelievers in the New Testament era were expected to study the Old Testament Scriptures, which were historical to them (with many of the prophecies fulfilled!), and were admonished for not being diligent in this area. Likewise, we are to study the Old and New Testament Scriptures, which are historical to us. Just as the Pharisees of Jesus' day did not read (nor do we) Joshua 6 and interpret it that *they* were (or *we* are) to march around Jericho for seven days, so we cannot take specific instructions and promises to the New Testament generation and apprehend them for ourselves. Similarly, we do not expect that everyone named Timothy believes that Paul is speaking directly to them when he says, "take a little wine for your stomach" (1 Tim 5:23). In the same manner, when Paul replaces Timothy's (or any of the New Testament saints') name with the pronoun "you," or when he refers to himself and Timothy (or others) as "we," we must identify the audience to whom the passage was (or is) relevant.

This does not mean that the spiritual truths conveyed in the Bible are not relevant to us. Thus, even if we are not named Timothy, if we have been foregoing wine for the sake of appearances when it could aid in our digestive process, perhaps we could benefit from Paul's instructions. This discernment between timeless truths and time- and/or people-specific events is not foreign to us. We do this anytime we listen to an audiotape or watch a videotape of a previous church service, be it our own church or another church. If the speaker refers to an event specific to his or her current audience, such as an upcoming church picnic, or a special prayer meeting, we have no trouble realizing that those events do not refer to us as we listen to or watch the service at a later date (perhaps even years later). The speaker may present truths learned from their current building plan or struggles with their City Planners. We do not take this to mean that we are in a building phase ourselves or struggling with our City Planners; but we may be able to apply the truths to a struggle with a particular neighbor. The concept of audience relevance is not something with which we are unacquainted.

As participants in the New Covenant, instead of a priesthood that ministers over us and a Law that dictates how we are to live before our God, we have Christ as our High Priest, the one Mediator between God and man (1 Tim 2:5). The New Covenant is now written on our hearts (Heb 8:10), and our salvation is worked out with fear and trembling as God works in us (Phil 2:12-13). However, we can still sympathize with the reader's feelings of a "hollow" interpretation, for we also raised similar questions upon our introduction to Preterism. We believe that there are two primary reasons for this sense of disillusionment. The first is that the New Covenant and the kingdom of God have been overly literalized in their original presentation to us, and we have been led to expect them in this physical realm. This was our focus of study in "Part I."

The second reason for not appreciating the New Covenant is rooted in our inability to fully comprehend and compare the differences between the "ministry of death" and the gospel of grace. Although we were translated at our conversion from the kingdom of darkness into His kingdom of light, we do not know what it means to be redeemed from the bondage of the law. Those who lived under it were not translated from darkness to light, but only from darkness into the ministry of death, the bondage of the Law. Ultimate salvation was not realized until Christ came to destroy the works of the evil one. Thus, Yom Kippur was more a Day of *Postponement* than a Day of *Atonement*, for the blood of bulls and goats cannot remove sin. On the other hand, Christ is the Lamb that takes away the sins of the world.

Consider the amount of text devoted to the details of the Law in Exodus, Leviticus, and Deuteronomy. These are the "dry" passages that many skip over in their Bible reading, yet this was God's covenant with the Jews. A reading of these books can be quite sobering. We also encourage the reader to take advantage of any of several volumes that describe the sacrificial system, such as Edersheim's *The Temple: Its Ministry and Service* or Brown's *The Tabernacle: Its Priests and Its Services*. Only by putting ourselves "in the shoes" of those who lived under the Law can we even begin to appreciate what it means to be redeemed from it.

In contrast to the burden of the Old Covenant and its complex requirements to maintain one's standing before God, the New Covenant is truly a yoke that is easy and a burden that is light. The 613 laws of the Old Covenant were replaced by the gospel of grace. While it takes several books of the Old Testament to delineate the Law, the gospel can be summed up in any *one* of the following passages:

> *For God so loved the world that He gave His only begotten Son, that whoever believes in Him should not perish but have everlasting life.* (John 3:16)

> *But as many as received Him, to them He gave the right to become children of God, to those who believe in His name: who were born, not of blood, nor of the will of the flesh, nor of the will of man, but of God.* (John 1:12-13)

> *. . . that if you confess with your mouth the Lord Jesus and believe in your heart that God has raised Him from the dead, you will be saved. For with the heart one believes unto righteousness, and with the mouth confession is made unto salvation.* (Rom 10:9-10)

> *For by grace you have been saved through faith, and that not of yourselves; it is the gift of God, not of works, lest anyone should boast.* (Eph 2:8-9)

For readers who live in the "Western" world, and specifically the United States, we can perhaps bring the point closer to home when we consider the events of September 11, 2001. The terrorist activities of that day were a rude awakening for many as to the freedoms that they enjoyed and took for granted. The ensuing conflicts reminded us of the costs of that freedom. Prior to these events, most had never personally experienced a loss of, nor the need to defend, their freedom. In the Vietnam War and Korean War, we "assisted" other countries in their pursuits of freedom; therefore, the latest need to defend our personal freedom as a nation was during World War II, which is practically "ancient" history these days. Thus, most of us have enjoyed a freedom for which we neither had to pay a cost nor fully appreciated. In contrast to this are the people who live in countries where there is no freedom, where events like September 11 are regular occurrences. If we can take the fear and uncertainty that we experienced following September 11 and extrapolate it from an event to a lifestyle, perhaps we can begin to understand what it meant to the Old Testament saints living in bondage of the fear of spiritual death under the Law (Heb 2:15).

The Old Testament saints had to wait outside the temple each year on the Day of Atonement to see if God would accept the sacrifice, thus postponing judgment for their sin; then they had to hope that there would be a future *true* atonement of sin and a resurrection of the dead in which they would take part. Thus, the Old Covenant was a covenant of bondage and death:

> *For these are the two covenants: the one from Mount Sinai which gives birth to bondage, which is Hagar—for this Hagar is Mount Sinai in Arabia, and corresponds to Jerusalem which now is, and is in bondage with her children . . . .* (Gal 4:24-25)

> *. . . for the letter kills, but the Spirit gives life. But if the ministry of death, written and engraved on stones . . . .* (2 Cor 3:6-7)

> *I was alive once without the law, but when the commandment came, sin revived and I died. And the commandment, which was to bring life, I found to bring death. For sin, taking occasion by the commandment, deceived me, and by it killed me.* (Rom 7:9-11)

> *The sting of death is sin, and the strength of sin is the law.* (1 Cor 15:56)

The Old Covenant Law never guaranteed spiritual life; it merely postponed spiritual death and pointed toward the promise of a New Covenant that was not of the letter, which kills, but of the spirit, which gives life. That the Old Covenant merely postponed spiritual death is evidenced by the fact that its sacrifices had to be offered year by year. Christ, on the other hand, died once for all:

Therefore, if perfection were through the Levitical priesthood (for under it the people received the law), what further need was there that another priest should rise according to the order of Melchizedek, and not be called according to the order of Aaron? . . . for the law made nothing perfect; on the other hand, there is the bringing in of a better hope, through which we draw near to God. (Heb 7:11, 19)

For if that first covenant had been faultless, then no place would have been sought for a second. (Heb 8:7)

For the law, having a shadow of the good things to come, and not the very image of the things, can never with these same sacrifices, which they offer continually year by year, make those who approach perfect. (Heb 10:1)

For such a High Priest was fitting for us, who is holy, harmless, undefiled, separate from sinners, and has become higher than the heavens; who does not need daily, as those high priests, to offer up sacrifices, first for His own sins and then for the people's, for this He did once for all when He offered up Himself. (Heb 7:26-27)

We, on the other hand, have the assurance of the written Word that we might believe that Jesus is the Son of God (John 20:31), the testimony of the empty tomb that He has risen with power over death and Hades (Rev 1:18), and the eradication of the temple by God as evidence that the New Covenant has superseded the Old Covenant. As the first fruits of those to be resurrected, Christ is the guarantee of the resurrection of the saints, who are the harvest to follow. Whereas the Old Testament saints could only *hope* in a future resurrection, having only the promise but not having received it, we have *assurance* of our resurrection and standing with God, because Christ's atonement for sin and His resurrection with power over death are historical facts for us:

And all these, having obtained a good testimony through faith, did not receive the promise . . . . (Heb 11:39)

. . . knowing that He who raised up the Lord Jesus will also raise us up with Jesus . . . . (2 Cor 4:14)

Because the sting of death is sin, and the strength of sin is the Law (Old Covenant), Christ's resurrection and the consummation of the New Covenant (as seen in the passing of the Old) guarantee to us the spiritual life for which the previous saints could only hope:

And if Christ is not risen, your faith is futile; you are still in your sins! (1 Cor 15:17)

For this corruptible must put on incorruption, and this mortal must put on immortality. So when this corruptible has put on incorruption, and this mortal has put on immortality, then shall be brought to pass the saying that is written: "Death is swallowed up in victory."
"O Death, where is your sting?
O Hades, where is your victory?"
The sting of death is sin, and the strength of sin is the law. But thanks be to God, who gives us the victory through our Lord Jesus Christ. (1 Cor 15:53-57)

Most assuredly, I say to you, he who hears My word and believes in Him who sent Me has everlasting life, and shall not come into judgment, but has passed from death into life. (John 5:24)

And you He made alive, who were dead in trespasses and sins . . . . (Eph 2:1)

And you, being dead in your trespasses and the uncircumcision of your flesh, He has made alive together with Him, having forgiven you all trespasses, having wiped out the handwriting of requirements that was against us, which was contrary to us. And He has taken it out of the way, having nailed it to the cross. (Col 2:13-14)

The superiority of the New Covenant over the Old cannot be overemphasized. The gospel of grace and the plan of redemption are things into which the very hosts of heaven desired to look in order to understand how a just and holy God would be able to restore fallen man to a relationship with Him:

Of this salvation the prophets have inquired and searched carefully, who prophesied of the grace that would come to you, searching what, or what manner of time, the Spirit of Christ who was in them was indicating when He testified beforehand the sufferings of Christ and the glories that would follow. To them it was revealed that, not to themselves, but to us they were ministering the things which now have been reported to you through those who have preached the gospel to you by the Holy Spirit sent from heaven—things which angels desire to look into. (1 Pet 1:10-12)

Russell comments on the surpassing glory of the New Covenant:

But there was also to be a glorious change in this world. The old made way for the new; the Law was replaced by the Gospel; Moses was superseded by Christ. The narrow and exclusive system, which embraced only a single people, was succeeded by a new and better covenant, which embraced the whole family of man, and knew no difference between Jew and Gentile, circumcised and uncircumcised. The dispensation of symbols and ceremonies, suited to the childhood of humanity, was merged in an order of things in which religion became a spiritual service, every place a temple, every worshipper a priest, and God the universal Father. This was a revolution greater far than any that had ever occurred in the history of mankind. It made a new world; it was the 'world to come,' the *oikoumene mellousa* of Hebrews ii. 5; and the magnitude and importance of the change it is impossible to over-estimate. (*The Parousia*, p. 65)

This is what Paul teaches in Galatians, where he states that the Law did not annul the promise to Abraham and his Seed, but "kept" the saints for the faith that was to be revealed—the fulfillment of the promise. Now all can become sons of God through faith in Christ:

Now to Abraham and his Seed were the promises made. He does not say, "And to seeds," as of many, but as of one, "And to your Seed," who is Christ. And this I say, that the law, which was four hundred and thirty years later, cannot annul the covenant that was confirmed before by God in Christ, that it should make the promise of no effect. For if the inheritance is of the law, it is no longer of promise; but God gave it to Abraham by promise. What purpose then does the law serve? It was added because of transgressions, till the Seed should come to whom the promise was made; and it was appointed through angels by the hand of a mediator. Now a mediator does not mediate for one only, but God is one. Is the law then against the promises of God? Certainly not! For if there had been a law given which could have given life, truly righteousness would have been by the law. But the Scripture has confined all under sin, that the promise by faith in Jesus Christ might be given to those who believe. But before faith came, we were kept under guard by the law, kept for the faith which would afterward be revealed. Therefore the law was our tutor to bring us to Christ, that we might be justified by faith. But after faith has come, we are no longer under a tutor. For you are all sons of God through faith in Christ Jesus. For as many of you as were baptized into Christ have put on Christ. There is neither Jew nor Greek, there is neither slave nor free, there is neither male nor female; for you are all one in Christ Jesus. And if you are Christ's, then you are Abraham's seed, and heirs according to the promise. (Gal 3:16-29)

Having effected the New Covenant, Christ made a public display to the hosts of heaven (Col 2:15) of His triumph over the fallen realm which had brought sin into His perfect creation. Unlike the Old Testament saints who lived in the bondage of the fear of spiritual death, we have been raised from death to life in Christ. All of this was done so that in the ages to come He might show the surpassing riches of His grace toward us:

But God, who is rich in mercy, because of His great love with which He loved us, even when we were dead in trespasses, made us alive together with Christ (by grace you have been saved), and raised us up together, and made us sit together in the heavenly places in Christ Jesus, that in the ages to come He might show the exceeding riches of His grace in His kindness toward us in Christ Jesus. (Eph 2:4-7)

Having always lived in the Church age, in which "*blessed are those who die in the Lord from now on,*" we cannot fathom the bondage of the fear of death under which the Old Covenant saints toiled. We are like those who have never had to go to war to fight for our freedoms, or have never lost loved ones in such a war, but have only known a life of freedom. Hence our lack of appreciation, or at least comprehension, of the glories of the New Covenant and the fact that it is a better covenant:

For on the one hand there is an annulling of the former commandment because of its weakness and unprofitableness, for the law made nothing perfect; on the other hand, there is the bringing in of a better hope, through which we draw near to God . . . by so much more Jesus has become a surety of a better covenant. (Heb 7:18-19, 22)

Just as we can take our personal and national freedoms for granted, we also can take our spiritual freedoms for granted. Instead of asking, "*Is this all there is?*" we need to realize that we have been redeemed "*with the precious blood of Christ*" (1 Pet 1:19); therefore, we should "*walk worthy of God who calls us into His own kingdom and glory*" (1 Thess 2:12).

Paul demonstrates the attitude that we should have in respecting the New Covenant:

For we are the circumcision, who worship God in the Spirit, rejoice in Christ Jesus, and have no confidence in the flesh, though I also might have confidence in the flesh. If anyone else thinks he may have confidence in the flesh, I more so: circumcised the eighth day, of the stock of Israel, of the tribe of Benjamin, a Hebrew of the Hebrews; concerning the law, a Pharisee; concerning zeal, persecuting the church; concerning the righteousness which is in the law, blameless. But what things were gain to me, these I have counted loss for Christ. Yet indeed I also count all things loss for the excellence of the knowledge of Christ Jesus my Lord, for whom I have suffered the loss of all things, and count them as rubbish [Greek = what is thrown to the dogs, i.e., refuse; KJV = dung], that I may gain Christ and be found in Him, not having my own righteousness, which is from the law, but that which is through faith in Christ, the righteousness which is from God by faith; that I may know Him and the power of His resurrection, and the fellowship of His sufferings, being conformed to His death, if, by any means, I may attain to the resurrection from the dead. (Phil 3:3-11)

But what if, instead of offering redemption to fallen man, God had offered it to fallen angels. Then it would be *us* on the "sidelines," without redemption, to which His redemptive plan for the angels was being displayed. Though there are both fallen angels and fallen men, He has chosen not to redeem angels. We, on the other hand, have a plan of redemption available to us, a plan into which the angels desire to look:

For indeed He does not give aid to angels, but He does give aid to the seed of Abraham. (Heb 2:16)

In fact, God's purpose for the Church is that it might display His wisdom, by manifesting His plan of redemption, to beings in the spiritual realm:

. . . and to make all see what is the fellowship of the mystery, which from the beginning of the ages has been hidden in God who created all things through Jesus Christ; to the intent that now the manifold wisdom of God might be made known by the church to the principalities and powers in the heavenly places, according to the eternal purpose which He accomplished in Christ Jesus

our Lord, in whom we have boldness and access with confidence through faith in Him. (Eph 3:9-12)

In the Old Covenant only the high priest could enter the Holy of Holies, and then only once a year. According to the passage above (as well as Hebrews 4:15-16), we can come boldly before the throne of grace—not the physical type, but the heavenly antitype:

> *For we do not have a High Priest who cannot sympathize with our weaknesses, but was in all points tempted as we are, yet without sin. Let us therefore come boldly to the throne of grace, that we may obtain mercy and find grace to help in time of need.* (Heb 4:15-16)

We are inhabitants of the city whose builder and maker is God (Heb 11:10), citizens of the better heavenly country (Heb 11:16), having received the promise toward which all of the Old Testament saints were looking (Heb 11:13, 39). We are participants in the plan of redemption into which angels longed to look (1 Pet 1:12). They sang over the creation of the physical heavens and earth, and now they rejoice over every "new creation" (2 Cor 5:17) that is born again into the new heavens and earth:

> *Where were you when I laid the foundations of the earth?*
> *Tell Me, if you have understanding.*
> *Who determined its measurements?*
> *Surely you know!*
> *Or who stretched the line upon it?*
> *To what were its foundations fastened?*
> *Or who laid its cornerstone,*
> *When the morning stars [angels] sang together,*
> *And all the sons of God shouted for joy?* (Job 38:4-7)

> *Likewise, I say to you, there is joy in the presence of the angels of God over one sinner who repents.* (Luke 15:10)

Yet we have succumbed to an eschatology that looks at this glorious plan of redemption (which causes the angels to rejoice) and makes us ask, "*Is this all there is?*" Though certainly not representative of all who still await the Second Coming of Christ, there are some Futurists who have the attitude, "*Why polish brass on a sinking ship? The world is going to Hell in a hand basket, the days are evil, and the Bible tells us that it will only get worse in these 'last days.' Therefore, why get involved in politics, the arts, our communities, etc.? We can't change what is destined to be.*"

Dispensationalism in particular fosters a defeatist view of Christianity's effect upon the world:

> "We are not winning the battle for world dominion and we never will." (Ed Hindson—*Pre-Trib Perspectives*, Vol. VIII, Number 30, January 2006)

One would think that since the ship has remained afloat for 2,000 years, we might begin to realize that the ship is *not* sinking. If it appears to be listing in the water, it is only because much of the crew has become derelict in their duties. Instead of taking pride in the vessel upon which they sail, seeing it as the answer to the world's problems, they merely see it as a life raft to keep them out of the troubled waters of this world until they are rescued from them.

If we would polish the brass nameplate on the bow, we would see we are not on a sinking ship. Rather we are riding on the HMS *Glorious Gospel of Christ*. Indeed, we would find that the nameplate is not brass, which in the Bible symbolizes judgment, but is gold, the symbol of deity, which speaks of the Heavenly nature of the New Covenant. For the Gospel message is not that this world is about to be judged, but that God in Christ is reconciling the world to Him! In fact, as crewmates on that ship we are ambassadors of Christ with the ministry of reconciliation (2 Cor 5:18-20).

Instead of hoping that we are airlifted off before the ship sinks, we need to pull together as a crew. Then, according to the proper working of each individual member (Eph 4:16), and the building up of one another in our most holy faith (Jude 20), we can take this ship to every port in the world. Thus, *the knowledge of the glory of the Lord shall cover the earth as the waters cover the sea* (Hab 2:14).

Truly, the ingenuity of the Incarnation to provide a sacrifice that would satisfy the requirements of God's holy nature in judging sin, the love of the Father and the Son toward man in instituting that plan, and the fact that there is no plan of redemption for the fallen angels, make the gospel of the New Covenant *The Greatest Story Ever Told.*

Quite obviously, God prefers honest disagreement to dishonest submission.

Phillip Yancey

Conclusion

—∿∿—

W
e have covered a lot of ground in our study, and we commend the reader that has made it this far. Certainly each one of these chapters could easily be the subject of its own book. Yet we hope that our treatments, though brief, have been thorough, accurate, and compelling enough to warrant serious consideration and stimulate further investigation by the reader. Although we acknowledge that there are many issues that we have not addressed, it is hoped that we have covered enough territory to establish the general framework of Preterism, providing the reader a structure upon which to attach subsequent studies of those other issues.

Jesus said, *"When you see Jerusalem surrounded by armies, then know that its desolation is near . . . for these are the days of vengeance, that ALL things which are written may be fulfilled"* (Luke 21:20, 22). If we cannot see in the surrounding and destruction of Jerusalem (with its attending signs in the sky) the fulfillment of the apocalyptic, cloud-coming judgment of the Lord upon *that* generation—which was expected and taught by every New Testament author—then surely we can understand why the Jews are still looking for their Messiah to come.

That the majority of Christianity, including many outstanding scholars and persons of Godly character, do not hold to the views presented herein, we readily admit. We do not deny that a case for Futurism can be built, but we believe that it only remains standing because it is, and must be, supported by a multitude of props, braces, and reinforcements. The everyday student of the Word must rely upon the "higher" education of others to explain to them why, when they read "this generation," it does not mean "this generation." Theologians must enlighten the average reader as to why we cannot take time statements at face value and explain why there are gaps that are indiscernible by a natural understanding of the text. Scholars are needed to explain why breaking the Old Testament precedents of apocalyptic language and cloud comings are justified and not really contrary to Scripture. Elaborate schemes of partial-, double- or typical-fulfillment must be developed to explain to us why apparent fulfillments of prophecy are not the actual fulfillments. Yet we ask, where is there one Scripture that says that the apocalyptic language of the New Testament is to be understood literally? Where is there one verse that indicates that Christ was NOT to be expected within the New Testament generation? Show us from the Scriptures how the "*we, you, us,*" etc., are NOT the audience of the New Testament generation.

Having no formal education in theology, some may suggest that we are unqualified to speak on these matters. However, if the common student of the Word is unable to reach conclusions based upon scriptural precedents and a plain understanding of the text, where does that leave the laity? We affirm that those with higher educations in biblical matters are gifts of God to the Church, for the purpose of edifying the Body (Eph 4:11-12); but there is an exponential difference between having theologians as one of our sources of insight in our studies and requiring them to "rightly divide the Word of Truth" for us. If Scripture—or at the minimum, eschatology—can only be understood when it is explained for us, then why are the following admonitions recorded in Scripture about and to the laity of the day?

> *These were more fair-minded than those in Thessalonica, in that they received the word with all readiness, and searched the Scriptures daily to find out whether these things were so.* (Acts 17:11)

> *For though by this time you ought to be teachers, you need someone to teach you again the first principles of the oracles of God; and you have come to need milk and not solid food. For everyone who partakes only of milk is unskilled in the word of righteousness, for he is a babe. But solid food belongs to those who are of full age, that is, those who by reason of use have their senses exercised to discern both good and evil.* (Heb 5:12-14)

> *Be diligent to present yourself approved to God, a worker who does not need to be ashamed, rightly dividing the word of truth.* (2 Tim 2:15)

> *All Scripture is given by inspiration of God, and is profitable for doctrine, for reproof, for correction, for instruction in righteousness, that the man of God may be complete, thoroughly equipped for every good work.* (2 Tim 3:16-17)

> *I pray also that the eyes of your heart may be enlightened in order that you may know the hope to which he has called you, the riches of his glorious inheritance in the saints . . . .* (Eph 1:18 NIV)

And we have the word of the prophets made more certain, and you will do well to pay attention to it, as to a light shining in a dark place, until the day dawns and the morning star rises in your hearts. Above all, you must understand that no prophecy of Scripture came about by the prophet's own interpretation. For prophecy never had its origin in the will of man, but men spoke from God as they were carried along by the Holy Spirit. (2 Pet 1:19-21 NIV)

Clearly, the Apostles expected and admonished the New Testament saints to study the Word for themselves, reproving those who did not, commending those who did, and praying that the eyes of their hearts would be enlightened. Then is it not incumbent upon us to search the Scriptures to find out whether these things are so, be it Preterism or Futurism? To be sure, theologians are an invaluable help in this process; but when particular doctrines are "out of reach" of the everyday student due to their lack of seminary courses in *Systematic Theology* and *Biblical Languages*, should not a red flag be raised? Rather, our prayer is that we may echo the words of Paul:

Not that we are sufficient of ourselves to think of anything as being from ourselves, but our sufficiency is from God, who also made us sufficient as ministers of the new covenant, not of the letter but of the Spirit; for the letter kills, but the Spirit gives life. (2 Cor 3:5-6)

In contrast to the structure of Futurism, whose foundation and framework need constant support and repair due to significant dates coming and going without the expected fulfillment of prophecy, the Preterist structure stands on its own. Granted, it may be unfamiliar at first sight, but we cannot deny its soundness. To those who would argue that Preterists use the props and braces of "spiritualizing" everything to make interpretations fit their framework, we would reply that it is not Preterists doing so, but the inspired authors of the New Testament. They are the ones truly qualified to take us behind the veil of Moses. The choice is not whether the reader agrees or disagrees with the author—that is inconsequential. The choice is whether one agrees or disagrees with the inspired authors of the New Testament. To say that there is an age yet to come after this everlasting age of the gospel; that Christ has yet to set up a physical kingdom on earth; that apocalyptic language is to be taken literally; etc., is not merely disagreeing with the author of this book—it is disagreeing with the inspired authors of the Holy Scripture.

Although Futurism is overwhelmingly the popular viewpoint of eschatology today, many might be surprised to learn that its popularity is quite recent. Frederic W. Farrar, D.D., F.R.S., was the chaplain to Queen Victoria from 1871-1876, as well as Headmaster of Marlborough College, Canon of Westminster Abbey, Rector of St. Margaret's, Archdeacon of Westminster, and Dean of Canterbury. In *The Early Days of Christianity* (1882), he wrote the following concerning the different views of Revelation:

> There have been three great schools of Apocalyptic interpretation:
> 1. The Præterists, who regard the book as having been mainly fulfilled. 2. The Futurists, who refer it to events which are still wholly future. 3. The Continuous-Historical Interpreters, who see in it an outline of Christian history from the days of St. John down to the End of all things. The second of these schools—the Futurists—has always been numerically small, and at present may be said to be non-existent.

Futurism was said to be as good as nonexistent in 1882! Not only that, but it *has always been numerically small*! Perhaps this helps explain why its current existence depends so much upon external support and braces to keep it standing—because it has never had strong support from the Scripture.

Even staunch Dispensationalist Thomas Ice admits that many are returning to the Preterism of pre-Darby Dispensationalism. John Bray records Ice's personal correspondence with him:

> Thomas Ice, in a letter to me dated September 20, 1989, said: "Many are moving toward a preterist interpretation of the Olivet Discourse and Revelation in our day. It is coming full cycle since the days of Darby. I have a very large collection of literature advocating that view, which was a very prominent view among both liberals and evangelicals 100-150 years ago." And then he added in a letter of November 30, 1989, "I do think that dispensationalism will continue to grow increasingly unpopular as we head into the 1990's." (These statements do not mean that Dr. Ice himself is changing from a dispensationalist—far from it; but they simply indicate that he recognizes the reality of what is going on today among those who are studying eschatology.) (*Matthew 24 Fulfilled*, p. 148; parenthesis in original)

We close our study with a final quote from King, and we ask that God richly bless you as you search the Scriptures to find out whether these things are so.

Any interpretation, therefore, that removes the coming of Christ as taught in the gospels, the epistles, and Revelation from the time and events of that generation, **unwittingly denies the inspiration of God's word**, and builds a false concept of God's eternal purpose with respect to the end-time. (*The Spirit of Prophecy*, p. 262; emphasis added)

He that never changes his opinions, never corrects his mistakes and will never be wiser on the morrow than he is today.

Tryon Edwards (19th century theologian)

Appendix

—⚬—

101 Preterist Time-Indicators for the Second Coming of Christ
(Compiled by David A. Green)

1. "The Kingdom of Heaven is at hand." (Matt 3:2)
2. "Who warned you to flee from the wrath about to come?" (Matt 3:7)
3. "The axe is already laid at the root of the trees." (Matt 3:10)
4. "His winnowing fork is in His hand." (Matt 3:12)
5. "The kingdom of heaven is at hand." (Matt 4:17)
6. "The kingdom of heaven is at hand." (Matt 10:7)
7. "You shall not finish going through the cities of Israel, until the Son of Man comes." (Matt 10:23)
8. ". . . the age [Gk. = about] to come." (Matt 12:32)
9. "The Son of Man is [Gk. = about] to come in the glory of His Father with His angels; and will then recompense every man according to his deeds." (Matt 16:27)
10. "There are some of those who are standing here who shall not taste death until they see the Son of Man coming in His kingdom." (Matt 16:28; cf. Mark 9:1; Luke 9:27)
11. "When the owner of the vineyard comes, what will he do to those vine-growers?" . . . "He will bring those wretches to a wretched end, and will rent out the vineyard to other vine-growers, who will pay him the proceeds at the proper seasons." . . . "Therefore I say to you, the kingdom of God will be taken away from you, and be given to a nation producing the fruit of it." . . . When the chief priests and the Pharisees heard His parables, they understood that He was speaking about them. (Matt 21:40-41, 43, 45)
12. "This generation will not pass away until all these things take place." (Matt 24:34)
13. "From now on, you [Caiaphas, the chief priests, the scribes, the elders, the whole Sanhedrin] shall be seeing the Son of Man sitting at the right hand of Power, and coming on the clouds of heaven." (Matt 26:64; Mark 14:62; Luke 22:69)
14. "The kingdom of God is at hand." (Mark 1:15)
15. "What will the owner of the vineyard do? He will come and destroy the vine-growers, and will give the vineyard to others. . . . They [the chief

463

priests, scribes and elders] understood that He spoke the parable against them." (Mark 12:9, 12)

16. "This generation will not pass away until all these things take place." (Mark 13:30)

17. "Who warned you to flee from the wrath [Gk. = about] to come?" (Luke 3:7)

18. "The axe is already laid at the root of the trees." (Luke 3:9)

19. "His winnowing fork is in His hand . . . ." (Luke 3:17)

20. "The kingdom of God has come near to you." (Luke 10:9)

21. "The kingdom of God has come near." (Luke 10:11)

22. "What, therefore, will the owner of the vineyard do to them? He will come and destroy these vine-growers and will give the vineyard to others." . . . The scribes and the chief priests . . . understood that He spoke this parable against them. (Luke 20:15-16, 19)

23. "These are days of vengeance, in order that all things which are written may be fulfilled." (Luke 21:22)

24. "This generation will not pass away until all things take place." (Luke 21:32)

25. "Daughters of Jerusalem, stop weeping for Me, but weep for yourselves and for your children. For behold, the days are coming when they will say, 'Blessed are the barren, and the wombs that never bore, and the breasts that never nursed.' Then they will begin to say to the mountains, 'Fall on us,' and to the hills, 'Cover us.'" (Luke 23:28-30; cf. Rev 6:14-17)

26. "We were hoping that He was the One who is [Gk. = about] to redeem Israel." (Luke 24:21)

27. ". . . I will come to you. . . . In that Day you shall know that I am in My Father, and you in Me, and I in you. . . . 'Lord, what then has happened that You are about to disclose Yourself to us, and not to the world?'" (John 14:18, 20, 22)

28. "If I want him to remain until I come, what is that to you?" (John 21:22)

29. "This is what was spoken of through the prophet Joel: 'And it shall be in the last days . . . .'" (Acts 2:16-17)

30. "He has fixed a day in which He is [Gk. = about] to judge the world in righteousness . . . ." (Acts 17:31)

31. "There is [Gk. = about] to be a resurrection of both the righteous and the wicked." (Acts 24:15)

32. "As he was discussing righteousness, self-control and the judgment [Gk. = about] to come . . . ." (Acts 24:25)

33. "Not for [Abraham's] sake only was it written, that [faith] was reckoned to him [as righteousness], but for our sake also, to whom it is [Gk. = about] to be reckoned." (Rom 4:23-24)

34. "If you are living according to the flesh, you are [Gk. = about] to die." (Rom 8:13)

35. "I consider that the sufferings of this present time are not worthy to be compared with the glory that is [Gk. = about] to be revealed to us." (Rom 8:18)

36. "It is already the hour for you to awaken from sleep; for now salvation is nearer to us than when we believed. The night is almost gone, and the day is at hand." (Rom 13:11-12)

37. "The God of peace will soon crush Satan under your feet." (Rom 16:20)

38. "The time has been shortened." (1 Cor 7:29)

39. "The form of this world is passing away." (1 Cor 7:31)

40. "Now these things . . . were written for our instruction, upon whom the ends of the ages have come." (1 Cor 10:11)

41. "We shall not all fall sleep, but we shall all be changed, in a moment, in the twinkling of an eye, at the last trumpet; for the trumpet will sound, and the dead will be raised imperishable, and we shall be changed." (1 Cor 15:51-52)

42. "Maranatha!" [The Lord comes!] (1 Cor 16:22)

43. ". . . not only in this age, but also in the one [Gk. = about] to come." (Eph 1:21)

44. "The Lord is near." (Phil 4:5)

45. "The gospel . . . was proclaimed in all creation under heaven." (Col 1:23; cf. Matt 24:14; Rom 10:18; 16:26; Col 1:5-6; 2 Tim 4:17; Rev 14:6-7; 1 Clement 5, 7)

46. ". . . things which are a shadow of what is [Gk. = about] to come." (Col 2:16-17)

47. ". . . we who are alive, and remain until the coming of the Lord . . . We who are alive and remain shall be caught up together with them in the clouds. . . . You, brethren, are not in darkness, that the Day should overtake you like a thief." (1 Thess 4:15, 17; 5:4)

48. "May your spirit and soul and body be preserved complete, without blame at the coming of our Lord Jesus Christ." (1 Thess 5:23)

49. "It is only just for God to repay with affliction those who afflict you, and to give relief to you who are afflicted and to us as well when the Lord Jesus shall be revealed from heaven with His mighty angels in flaming fire." (2 Thess 1:6-7)

50. "Godliness . . . holds promise for the present life and that which is [Gk. = about] to come." (1 Tim 4:8)

51. "I charge you . . . that you keep the commandment without stain or reproach until the appearing of our Lord Jesus Christ." (1 Tim 6:14)

52. ". . . storing up for themselves the treasure of a good foundation for that which is [Gk. = about] to come, so that they may take hold of that which is life indeed." (1 Tim 6:19)

53. "In the last days difficult times will come. For men will be lovers of self . . . . Avoid these men. For of these are those who enter into households and captivate weak women. . . . These also oppose the truth . . . . But they will not make further progress; for their folly will be obvious to all . . . . " (2 Tim 3:1-2, 5-6, 8-9)

54. "I solemnly charge you in the presence of God and of Christ Jesus, who is [Gk. = about] to judge the living and the dead . . . . " (2 Tim 4:1)

55. "God, after He spoke long ago to the fathers in the prophets in many portions and in many ways, in these last days has spoken to us in His Son." (Heb 1:1-2)

56. "Are they not all ministering spirits, sent out to render service for the sake of those who are [Gk. = about] to inherit salvation?" (Heb 1:14)

57. "He did not subject to angels the world [Gk. = about] to come." (Heb 2:5)

58. ". . . and have tasted . . . the powers of the age [Gk. = about] to come." (Heb 6:5)

59. "For ground that drinks the rain which often falls upon it and brings forth vegetation useful to those for whose sake it is also tilled, receives a blessing from God; but if it yields thorns and thistles, it is worthless and near a curse, and its end is for burning." (Heb 6:7-8)

60. "When He said, 'A new covenant,' He has made the first obsolete. But whatever is becoming obsolete and growing old is ready to disappear." (Heb 8:13)

61. "The Holy Spirit is signifying this, that the way of the [heavenly] Holy Places has not yet been revealed, while the outer tabernacle is still standing, which is a symbol for the present time. Accordingly both gifts and sacrifices are offered which cannot make the worshiper perfect in conscience, since they relate only to food and drink and various washings, regulations for the body imposed until a time of reformation." (Heb 9:8-10; cf. Gal 4:19; Eph 2:21-22; 3:17; 4:13)

62. "But when Christ appeared as a high priest of the good things [Gk. = about] to come . . . . " (Heb 9:11)

63. "Now once at the consummation of the ages He has been manifested to put away sin." (Heb 9:26)

64. "For the Law, since it has only a shadow of the good things [Gk. = about] to come . . . . " (Heb 10:1)

65. ". . . as you see the Day drawing near." (Heb 10:25)

66. ". . . the fury of a fire which is about to consume the adversaries." (Heb 10:27)

67. "For yet in a very little while, He who is coming will come, and will not delay." (Heb 10:37)

68. "For here we do not have a lasting city, but we are seeking the one that is [Gk. = about] to come." (Heb 13:14)

69. "Speak and so act, as those who are [Gk. = about] to be judged by the law of liberty." (Jas 2:12)

70. "Come now, you rich, weep and howl for your miseries which are coming upon you. . . . It is in the last days that you have stored up your treasure!" (Jas 5:1,3)

71. "Be patient, therefore, brethren, until the coming of the Lord." (Jas 5:7)

72. "You too be patient; strengthen your hearts, for the coming of the Lord is at hand." (Jas 5:8)

73. ". . . salvation ready to be revealed in the last time." (1 Pet 1:6)

74. "He . . . has appeared in these last times for the sake of you." (1 Pet 1:20)

75. "They shall give account to Him who is ready to judge the living and the dead." (1 Pet 4:5)

76. "The end of all things is at hand; therefore, be of sound judgment and sober spirit for the purpose of prayer." (1 Pet 4:7)

77. "For it is time for judgment to begin with the household of God." (1 Pet 4:17)

78. ". . . as your fellow elder and witness of the sufferings of Christ, and a partaker also of the glory that is about to be revealed." (1 Pet 5:1)

79. "We have the prophetic word . . . which you do well to pay attention as to a lamp shining in a dark place, until the Day dawns and the morning star arises in your hearts." (2 Pet 1:19)

80. "Their judgment from long ago is not idle, and their destruction is not asleep." (2 Pet 2:3)

81. "In the last days mockers will come . . . . For this they willingly are ignorant of . . . . " (2 Pet 3:3, 5)

82. "But the day of the Lord will come like a thief, in which the heavens will pass away with a roar and the elements will be destroyed with intense heat, and the earth and its works will be burned up. Since all these things are to be destroyed in this way, what sort of people ought you to be in holy

conduct and godliness, looking for and hastening the coming of the day of God." (2 Pet 3:10-12)

83. "The darkness is passing away, and the true light is already shining." (1 John 2:8)

84. "The world is passing away, and its desires." (1 John 2:17)

85. "It is the last hour." (1 John 2:18)

86. "Even now many antichrists have arisen; from this we know that it is the last hour." (1 John 2:18; cf. Matt 24:23-34)

87. "This is that of the antichrist, of which you have heard that it is coming, and now it is already in the world." (1 John 4:3; cf. 2 Thess 2:7)

88. "For certain persons have crept in unnoticed, those who were long beforehand marked out for this condemnation . . . . About these also Enoch . . . prophesied, saying, 'Behold, the Lord came with many thousands of His holy ones, to execute judgment upon all, and to convict all the ungodly . . . .'" (Jude 1:4, 14-15)

89. "But you, beloved, ought to remember the words that were spoken beforehand by the apostles of our Lord Jesus Christ, that they were saying to you, 'In the last time there shall be mockers, following after their own ungodly lusts.' These are the ones who cause divisions . . . ." (Jude 1:17-19)

90. ". . . to show to His bond-servants, the things which must shortly take place." (Rev 1:1)

91. "The time is near." (Rev 1:3)

92. "Nevertheless what you have, hold fast until I come." (Rev 2:25)

93. "I also will keep you from the hour of testing which is [Gk. = about] to come upon the whole world." (Rev 3:10)

94. "I am coming quickly." (Rev 3:11)

95. "And she gave birth to a son, a male child, who is [Gk. = about] to rule all the nations with a rod of iron." (Rev 12:5)

96. "And in her [the Great City Babylon] was found the blood of prophets and of saints and of all who have been slain on the earth." (Rev 18:24; cf. Matt 23:35-36; Luke 11:50-51)

97. ". . . to show to His bond-servants the things which must shortly take place." (Rev 22:6)

98. "Behold, I am coming quickly." (Rev 22:7)

99. "Do not seal up the words of the prophecy of this book, for the time is near." (Rev 22:10; cf. Dan 8:26)

100. "Behold, I am coming quickly." (Rev 22:12)

101. "Yes, I am coming quickly." (Rev 22:20)

Bibliography

—ɯ—

Barnes' Notes, Electronic Database. Copyright (c) 1997 by Biblesoft.

Berkhof, Louis—*History of Christian Doctrines*, Reprinted 2002 Banner of Truth Trust.

Berman, Joshua—*The Temple: Its Symbolism and Meaning Then and Now*—Jason Aronson, Inc.

Bray, John—*Matthew 24 Fulfilled*—Published by John L. Bray, © 1996

Carroll, John T.—*The Return of Jesus in Early Christianity*—© 2000 Hendrickson Publishers, Inc.

Clarke, Adam—*Commentary*, Electronic Database. Copyright (c) 1996 by Biblesoft.

Coffman, James Burton—*Commentary*—Abiline Christian University Press, Abilene, Texas.

Custance, Arthur—*Three Trees: And Israel's History*— The Doorway Papers, volume 6—*Time And Eternity*. 1977 published by Zondervan Publishing Co. Copyright © 1988 Evelyn White. All rights reserved.

Daly, Brian—*The Hope of the Early Church: A Handbook of Patristic Eschatology*—1991, Cambridge University Press.

Easton's Bible Dictionary, PC Study Bible formatted electronic database Copyright © 2003 Biblesoft, Inc. All rights reserved.

Edersheim, Alfred—*The Temple: Its Ministry and Services*—Books for the Ages, AGES Software • Albany, OR—USA Version 1.0 © 1997

Eusebius, Pamphilius—*The Church History of Eusebius*—online at www. cccl.org.

Fairbairn, Patrick—*The Typology of Scripture: Two Volumes in One, Complete and Unabridged*—Fourth printing, 1965, Zondervan Publishing House

Farrar, Frederic W.—*The Early Day of Christianity*—1882, A. L. Burt Publishers, New York.

Frost, Samuel M.—*Misplaced Hope*, Bimillennial Press, © 2002 Samuel M. Frost.

Gentry, Dr. Kenneth L. Jr.—*Before Jerusalem Fell*, Revised Edition—American Vision Press, P.O. Box 724088. Atlanta, GA 31139.

——*Christ's Resurrection and Ours*—article available at www.kenneth-gentry.com.

Gill, John—*The New John Gill's Exposition of the Entire Bible* Modernised and adapted for the computer by Larry Pierce of Online Bible. All Rightes Reserved, Larry Pierce, Winterbourne, Ontario.

Gregg, Steve, ed.—*Revelation: Four Views*—1997 Thomas Nelson, Inc. Nashville, TN.

Gumerlock, Francis X.—*The Day and the Hour*—© 2000 American Vision, Atlanta, GA.

Harden, Daniel E.—*Overcoming Sproul's Resurrection Issues*, 1999 Kingdom Publications. © Daniel E. Harden.

Hanegraaff, Hank—*The Apocalypse Code*—Thomas Nelson, Inc. © 2007 Hank Hanegraaff

Harding, Ian D.—*Taken to Heaven in AD 70*, 2005 International Preterist Association. © Ian D. Harding.

Harris, Murray—*From Grave to Glory*, 1990 Academie Books, Zondervan Publishing House, Grand Rapids, MI. © Murray J. Harris.

Hicks, Olan—*A Closer Look at the "AD 70 Theory" of Last Things*— Available online at www.revelationflowchart.home.comcast. net/~revelationflowchart/ad70.pdf

Henry, Matthew—*Commentary on the Whole Bible: New Modern Edition*, Electronic Database. Copyright (c) 1991 by Hendrickson Publishers, Inc.

Horton, Michael—*Putting Amazing Back Into Grace*—Published by Baker Books, second printing, January 2003. © 1991, 1994, 2002 by Michael Scott Horton

Ice, Thomas—*Literal Sacrifices in the Millennium*—http://www.pre-trib. org/article-view.php?id=39

——*Is Modern Israel Fulfilling Prophecy?*—http://www.pre-trib.org

Jamieson, Fausset, and Brown *Commentary*, Electronic Database. Copyright (c) 1997 by Biblesoft.

Josephus, Flavius—*Wars of the Jews*, PC Study Bible formatted electronic database Copyright © 2003 by Biblesoft, Inc. All rights reserved.

——*Antiquities of the Jews*, PC Study Bible formatted electronic database Copyright © 2003 by Biblesoft, Inc. All rights reserved.

King, Max R.—*The Spirit of Prophecy*, 2nd Printing 1983—Warren Printing Incorporated, Warren, Ohio.

——*The Cross and The Parousia of Christ*, 1987 Parkman Road Church of Christ.

LaHaye, Tim and Thomas Ice, co-editors—*The End Times Controversy*— Copyright © 2003 by Pre-Trib Research Center, Published by Harvest House Publishers, Eugene, OR .

Maimonides, Moses—*Guide for the Perplexed*—Translated by M. Friedlander. Published by George Routledge & Sons, Limited.

Martin, Timothy P. & Jeffrey L. Vaughn, PhD.—*Beyond Creation Science*—Apocalyptic Vision Press, Third edition © 2007 Timothy P. Martin & Jeffrey L. Vaughn.

Mauro, Philip—*The Hope of Israel: What Is It?*—Malloy Lithographing, Inc. Ann Arbor, Michigan.

——*The Seventy Weeks and the Great Tribulation*—1923 Hamilton Bros. Scripture Truth Depot, Boston, Mass.

McRay, Ron—*The Last Days?*—© 1990 by Kingdom Press

Otto, Randall E.—*Case Dismissed: Rebutting Common Charges Against Preterism*—International Preterist Association, Inc. © 2000 by Reverend Randall E. Otto, PhD.

Preston, Don K.—*Like Father, Like Son, on Clouds of Glory*—JaDon Production, LLC. © 2006 Don K. Preston.

——*Objection: Overruled!* article in Fulfilled! Magazine, Spring 2008, Vol.3 Issue 1.

——*Seal Up Vision & Prophecy*—Printed by Shawnee Printing Co. © 1991 by Don K. Preston.

Price, Dr. J. Randall—*The Coming Last Days Temple*—Copyright © 1999 by World of the Bible Ministries, Published by Harvest House Publishers, Eugene, OR.

Robertson's Word Pictures—*The Robertson's Word Pictures of the New Testament.* Copyright © Broadman Press 1932,33, Renewal 1960. All rights reserved.

Robinson, John A. T.—*Redating the New Testament*—Wipf and Stock Publishers, © 1976 SCM Press.

Russell, J. Stuart—*The Parousia*, 1999 Edition—Baker Books.

Schaff, Philip, ed.—*Athanasius: Select Works and Letters*—online at www.ccel.org.

——*The Creeds of Christianity*,—online at www.ccel.org.

Seraiah, Jonathin C.—*The End of All Things: A Defense of the Future*—Canon Press. © 1999 by Jonathin Seraiah.

Simmons, Kurt—*The Consummation of the Ages*—Bimillennial Preterist Association. © 2003 by Kurt M. Simmons.

——*The Sword & The Plow*—Electronic newsletter, www.preteristcentral.com.

Sproul, R. C.—*Knowing Scripture*—1977, InterVarsity Press.

——*The Last Days According To Jesus*—1998 Published by Baker Books, Grand Rapids, MI.

Spurgeon, Charles H.—*God Rejoicing in the New Creation*—Metropolitan Tabernacle Pulpit, vol. 37

Stevens, Edward E.—*Expectations Demand A First Century Rapture*—2003 Published by International Preterist Association, Bradford, Penn.

——*What Happened In 70 AD?*—1988 Published by Edward E. Stevens, Bradford, Penn.

Strong, James—*New Exhaustive Strong's Numbers and Concordance with Expanded Greek-Hebrew Dictionary.* Copyright (c) 1994, Biblesoft and International Bible Translators, Inc.

Terry, Milton S.—*Biblical Hermeneutics*—Reprinted by Academie Books, Zondervan Publishing House, Grand Rapids, MI.

Thayer's Greek Lexicon, Electronic Database. Copyright (c) 2000 by Biblesoft

Walvoord, John F.—*Major Bible Prophecies*—1991 Published by Zondervan Publishing House, Grand Rapids, MI.

Wesley, John—*John Wesley's Explanatory Notes on the Whole Bible, The New Testament* 1754.

Wycliffe, John—*The Wycliffe Bible* Commentary, Electronic Database. Copyright (c) 1962 by Moody Press.

Wilmington, Harold—*Wilmington's Bible Handbook*— Biblesoft electronic database. Copyright © 1997 by Harold L. Willmington. Produced with permission of Tyndale House Publishers, Inc. All rights reserved.

Quotes

—⚏—

A mind once stretched by a new idea never regains its original dimension.
Oliver Wendell Holmes, Jr.

All of us need to be constantly asking ourselves what it is which we
want to believe to be true, and whether our desires so to believe are
stronger than our desires to know the truth, however uncongenial
to us that truth may be.
Antony Flew (renowned former atheist)

Is it faith to understand nothing, and merely submit your
convictions implicitly to the Church?
John Calvin

We must follow wherever the argument leads.
Socrates

When you have eliminated the impossible, whatever remains,
however improbable, must be the truth.
Sherlock Holmes

Quite obviously, God prefers honest disagreement to
dishonest submission.
Phillip Yancey

He that never changes his opinions, never corrects his mistakes and
will never be wiser on the morrow than he is today.
Tryon Edwards (19th century theologian)

CPSIA information can be obtained
at www.ICGtesting.com
Printed in the USA
BVOW03s2327161116
468008BV00002B/136/P